REAL WORLD
BANKING
AND
FINANCE

READINGS IN ECONOMICS, BUSINESS, AND SOCIAL POLICY FROM

DOLLARS&SENSE

EDITED BY DOUG ORR, CHRIS STURR, MARTY WOLFSON,

AND THE *DOLLARS & SENSE* COLLECTIVE

D09968084

REAL WORLD BANKING AND FINANCE

ISBN: 978-1-878585-77-6

Published by:
Economic Affairs Bureau, Inc. d/b/a *Dollars & Sense*
29 Winter Street, Boston, MA 02108
617-447-2177; dollars@dollarsandsense.org.
For order information, contact Economic Affairs Bureau or visit: www.dollarsandsense.org.

Real World Banking and Finance is edited by the *Dollars & Sense* Collective, which also publishes *Dollars & Sense* magazine and the classroom books *Real World Macro, Real World Micro, Current Economic Issues, Real World Globalization, Real World Latin America, Real World Labor, The Economic Crisis Reader, The Wealth Inequality Reader, The Environment in Crisis, Introduction to Political Economy, Unlevel Playing Fields: Understanding Wage Inequality and Discrimination, Striking a Balance: Work, Family, Life*, and *Grassroots Journalism*.

The 2010 *Dollars & Sense* Collective:
Arpita Banerjee, Ben Collins, Katharine Davies, Amy Gluckman, Ben Greenberg, Mary Jirmanus, Vera Kelsey-Watts, James McBride, John Miller, Larry Peterson, Linda Pinkow, Paul Piwko, Smriti Rao, Alejandro Reuss, Dave Ryan, Bryan Snyder, Chris Sturr, Ramaa Vasudevan, and Jeanne Winner.

Co-editors of this volume: Doug Orr, Chris Sturr, and Marty Wolfson
Editorial assistance: Katharine Davies, Amy Gluckman, and Lauren Price

Cover design: Chris Sturr, based on a design by David Garrett, dgcommunications.com.

Cover photos: Lettering and columns above the entrance to the Federal Reserve Bank of San Francisco (Wikimedia Commons; photo by Brokensphere, Creative Commons Attribution-Share Alike 3.0 license,); the "Eye of Providence" on reverse side of the Great Seal of the United States, as seen on U.S. dollar bill (Wikimedia Commons; photo is in the public domain); statue of an eagle located on the Marriner S. Eccles Federal Reserve Board Building, Washington, D.C. (Wikimedia Commons; photo by AgnosticPreacherKid, Creative Commons Attribution-Share Alike 3.0 license).

Production: Chris Sturr and Katharine Davies.

Printed in U.S.A.

CONTENTS

Chapter 1

MONEY, THE FEDERAL RESERVE, AND THE ECONOMY

Article 1.1

THE MONEY SUPPLY

BY ELLEN FRANK
September/October 2005

> Dear Dr. Dollar:
>
> *Of all the mysteries of economics, the one I find the most obscure is the money sup-ply. I know that commercial banks increase the money supply by lending more money than they actually have on hand, but I also hear people worry that the government will cover its deficits by "printing money." Can the government actu-ally do that? When, if ever, is the money supply increased because the government simply prints more of the stuff?*
>
> — Stuart Baker, Tallahassee, Fla.

Money is whatever a society uses to carry out economic transactions. In the United States, this means cash as well as balances in bank accounts which can be accessed with checks or debit cards (called "demand deposits" because the cash is available to the depositor on demand). Whenever a bank books a loan or pays a vendor for a credit card purchase, it creates a demand deposit and so expands the supply of money. However, in all modern capitalist economies, the money-creating activities of private financial firms are overseen by a government or quasi-govern-ment institution called a central bank.

It is this central bank—the Federal Reserve in the United States—that actu-ally prints paper money. (Coins are minted by the U.S. Treasury Department.) However, very little of the Fed's activity involves the actual printing of paper cur-rency; the Fed creates money mostly through so-called open market purchases. Here's how this works:

All federally-chartered banks are required to hold a certain percentage of their deposits in *reserve*—i.e., not to lend them out. When the economy grows, households and businesses spend more and borrow more. People withdraw cash from their accounts, leaving banks with fewer reserves. At the same time, banks are making new loans and creating new deposits—and thus need additional cash to hold in reserve in order to maintain the required reserve ratio.

To ensure that banks have adequate reserves to keep the economy running, the Fed will go into the open market and buy Treasury securities that are currently held by financial institutions or by wealthy individuals. (These securities represent the public debt: funds that the U.S. government had borrowed by selling bonds and notes to the public.) To pay for its purchases, the Fed credits the seller with new cash and the seller's bank with new cash reserves.

Open-market purchases can thus be thought of as liquidating the national government's debt. What was once a non-liquid (meaning it couldn't be used to purchase goods) interest-bearing debt of the Treasury is converted to reserves in the banking system. So the government does routinely increase the money supply by "printing more of the stuff," if not literally. And the way the money gets into the hands of the public is by transforming the government's debt (issued to finance deficits) into cash.

Conservatives in the business press indeed agonize constantly over governments irresponsibly "printing money" to cover their debts. If this is what governments do all the time anyway, why the worry? The answer lies in our definition of government. In the United States, there are two public institutions involved in monetary matters: the Treasury department—part of the executive branch, run by political appointees of an elected president and subject to Congress' power of the purse; and the Federal Reserve, which is a network of quasi-private regional banks overseen by a board of governors, few of whom are beholden to sitting politicians since their terms run for 14 years.

In this set-up, the branch of government responsible for deciding when or whether to increase the money supply (the central bank) is separate from and not directly accountable to the branches of government that decide how much to spend and borrow (the president and legislature). Macroeconomic policymaking is thus split between two institutions, one elected and (at least somewhat) accountable to the public, and one unelected and accountable mostly to large financial institutions.

The United States is hardly alone in this bifurcation of economic policy. The European Central Bank, for example, is probably even less accountable to the public than the Fed; the same is true of the central banks of many of the larger developing countries.

The consequences can be best seen in government responses to unemployment and recession. Elected officials may want to borrow to finance public works and social services so as to alleviate poverty and unemployment—without curbing private spending by raising tax collections. If they do not "print money" to cover the resulting deficits, the increased economic activity could use up bank reserves and push up interest rates, stifling further growth.

An accountable central bank would probably be under pressure to liquidate the debt and keep interest rates low. An unaccountable central bank, however, can thwart the government's social spending by refusing to print money, conducting its own countervailing economic policy. While it is true that runaway inflation can result from excessive printing of money—a concern responsible governments must balance against the need to meet compelling social needs—independent central banks, overly obedient to the financial interests of the wealthy, tend to tap the breaks long before that point.

When conservative financial interests decry "printing money" to pay for government spending, they are really troubled by the possibility that the levers of economic policy will be controlled by those who are accountable to the general public rather than those who are accountable to them. ❏

Article 1.2

WHAT IS MONEY?

BY DOUG ORR
November/December 1993; updated October 2010

We all use money every day. Yet many people do not know what money actually is. There are many myths about money, including the idea that the government "prints" all of it and that it has some intrinsic value. But actually, money is less a matter of value, and more a matter of faith.

Money is sometimes called the universal commodity, because it can be traded for all other commodities. But for this to happen, everyone in society must believe that money will be accepted. If people stop believing that it will be accepted, the existing money ceases to be money. In the early 1990s in Poland, people stopped accepting the zloty, and used vodka as money instead.

In addition to facilitating exchanges, money allows us to "store" value from one point in time to another. If you sell your car today for $4,000, you probably won't buy that amount of other products today. Rather, you store the value as money, probably in a bank, until you want to use it.

The "things" that get used as money have changed over time, and "modern" people often chuckle when they hear about some of them. The Romans used salt (from which we get the word "salary"), South Sea Islanders used shark's teeth, and several societies actually used cows. The "Three Wise Men" brought gold, frankincense and myrrh, each of which was money in different regions at the time.

If money does not exist, or is in short supply, it will be created. In POW camps, where guards specifically outlaw its existence, prisoners use cigarettes instead. In the American colonies, the British attempted to limit the supply of British pounds, because they knew that by limiting the supply of money, they could hamper the development of independent markets in the colonies. Today, the United States uses a similar policy, through the International Monetary Fund, in dealing with Latin America.

To overcome this problem, the colonists began to use tobacco leaves as money. This helped the colonies to develop, but it also allowed the holders of large plots of land to grow their own money! When the colonies gained independence, the new government decreed gold to be money, rather than tobacco, much to the dismay of Southern plantation owners. Now, rather than growing money, farmers had to find or buy it.

To aid the use of gold as money, banks would test its purity, put it in storage, and give the depositor paper certificates of ownership. These certificates, "paper money," could then be used in place of the gold itself. Since any bank could store gold and issue certificates, by the beginning of the Civil War, over 7,000 different types of "paper money" were in circulation in the United States, none of it printed by the government.

Only the bankers knew how much gold was in their vaults. If a customer wanted a loan, rather than give them gold, the bank would just print more paper money. Over time it became obvious that bankers were printing excessive amounts of money. In 1864, the government outlawed the printing of money by private banks, but this attempt to control the amount of money was unsuccessful.

While paper money is easier to use than gold, it is still risky to carry around large amounts of cash. It is safer to store the paper in a bank and simply sign over its ownership to make a purchase. We sign over the ownership of our money by writing a check. When the government outlawed printing money, checking account money became a new form of money and banks make loans by creating new checking accounts.

How Banks Create Money

Banks are central to understanding money, because in addition to storing it, they help to create it. Bankers realize that not everyone will withdraw their money at the same time, so they loan out much of the money that has been deposited. It is from the interest on these loans that banks get their profits, and through these loans the banking system creates new money.

If you deposit $100 cash in your checking account at Chase Manhattan Bank, you still have $100 in money to use, because checks are also accepted as money. Chase must set aside some of this cash as "reserves," in case you or other depositors decide to withdraw money as cash. Current regulations issued by the Federal Reserve Bank (the Fed) require banks to set aside an average of three cents out of each dollar. So Chase can make a loan of $97, based on your deposit. Chase does not make loans by handing out cash but instead by putting $97 in the checking account of the person, say Emily, taking out the loan. So from your initial deposit of $100 in cash, the economy now has $197 in checking account money.

The borrower, Emily, pays $97 for some product or service by check, and the seller, say Ace Computers, deposits the money in its checking account. The total amount of checking account money is still $197, but its location and ownership have changed. If Ace Computer's account is at Citibank, $97 in cash is transferred from Chase to Citibank. This leaves just $3 in cash reserves at Chase to cover your original deposit. However, Citibank now has $97 in "new" cash on hand, so it sets aside three cents on the dollar ($2.91) and loans out the rest, $94.09, as new checking account money. Through this process, every dollar of "reserves" yields many dollars in total money.

If you think this is just a shell game and there is only $100 in "real" money, you still don't understand money. Anything that is accepted as payment for a transaction is "real" money. Cash is no more real than checking account money. In fact, most car rental companies will not accept cash as payment for a car, so for them, cash is not money!

As of June 2010, there was $883 billion of U.S. currency, i.e. "paper money," in existence. However, somewhere between 50% and 70% of it is held outside the United States by foreign banks and individuals. U.S. $100 bills are the preferred currency of choice used to facilitate illegal international transactions, such as the drug trade. The vast majority of all money actually in use in the United States is not cash, but rather checking account money. This type of money, $1,590 billion, was created by private banks, and was not "printed" by anyone. In fact, this money exists only as electronic "bits" in banks' computers. (The less "modern" South Sea Islanders could have quite a chuckle about that!)

The amount of money that banks can create is limited by the total amount of reserves, and by the fraction of each deposit that must be held as reserves. Prior to 1914, bankers themselves decided what fraction of deposits to hold as reserves. Since then, this fraction has been set by the main banking regulator, the Fed.

Until 1934, gold was held as reserves, but the supply of gold was unstable, growing rapidly during the California and Alaska "gold rushes," and very slowly at other times. As a result, at times more money was created than the economy needed, and at other times not enough money could be created. Starting in 1934, the U.S. government decided that gold would no longer be used as reserves. Cash, now printed by the Fed, could no longer be redeemed for gold, and cash itself became the reserve asset.

Banks, fearing robberies, do not hold all of their cash reserves in their own vaults. Rather, they store it in an account at a regional Fed bank. These accounts count as reserves. What banks do hold in their vaults is their other assets, such as Treasury bonds and corporate bonds.

The Fed and Bank Reserves

The only role of the government in creating money is indirectly through the Fed. While the governors and chairman of the Fed are appointed and approved by the government, once approved , they are not directly controlled by either the Congress or the eExecutive branch. If the Fed wants to expand the money supply, it must increase bank reserves. To do this, the Fed buys Treasury bonds from a bank, and pays with a check drawn on the Fed itself. By depositing the check in its reserve account at the Fed, the bank now has more reserves, so the bank can now make more loans and create new checking account money.

By controlling the amount of reserves, the Fed attempts to control the size of the money supply. But as recent history has shown, this control is limited. During the late 1970s, the Fed tried to limit the amount of money banks could create by reducing reserves, but banks simply created new forms of money, just like the POW camp prisoners and colonial farmers. In 1979, there was only one form of checking account money. Today, there are many, with odd names such as NOWs, ATSs, repos, and money market deposit accounts. If there is a profit to be made creating money, banks will find a way.

In 2010, we have the opposite problem. The Fed is trying to expand the money supply, but banks are refusing to create new money. In good times, banks hold as few reserves as possible, so they can profit from making loans. In times of crisis, banks fear that we will lose faith in the commercial banking system and all try to take out our "money" as cash. Since there is far more electronic money than cash, this is impossible. But if the bank cannot give us our money in the form we want it, the bank fails. Most failed banks either close completely or are purchased by other banks. Since the start of 2007, over 300 banks, with assets totaling more than $637 billion, have failed.

Since all banks fear they will be next, they want as many reserves as possible. Excess reserves are any reserves above those required by the Fed. During the 1990s, these averaged about $1 billion for the entire banking system. During the crisis of 2001, they spiked to the then unheard of level of $19 billion. As of June 2010, excess reserves in the banking system were $1,035 billion! This is the classic case of trying to push on a string (see Article 1.7Gerald Freidman "Pushing on Strings," by Gerald Friedman, in this chapter). The Fed can create reserves, but only banks can create money, and they are not yet willing to make any new loans. This is even more truetruer given that the Fed, for the first time, is now paying interest on assets held as reserves, which lowers the incentives to make loans.

These amorphous forms of money function only because we believe they will function, which is why the continued stability of the banking system is so critical. While it is true that the bailout ofcrisis in the banking system was not handled very wellas well as it could have been, and that many people who created the crisis are still profiting from it, preventing the banks from failing abruptly and disrupting the payments system was necessary. In a modern market economy, banks create the money, and no market economy can function without its money. Money only exists if we believe in it, so we have to maintain the faith. To maintain the faith we need more democratic control over money creation. This can only come if regulation of the financial system is greatly expanded. ❏

Sources: Money supply, Federal Reserve Board, http://www.federalreserve.gov/releases/h6/ current/; Excess reserves, St. Louis Federal Reserve Bank, http://research.stlouisfed.org/fred2/ series/EXCRESNS; Bank Failures, Federal Deposit Insurance Corporation (FDIC) http://www. fdic.gov/bank/individual/failed/banklist.html.

Article 1.3

THE DISCOUNT RATE

BY ELLEN FRANK
March/April 2002

Dear Dr. Dollar:
The Federal Reserve keeps fussing with the "discount rate" and everybody thinks it's important. This is, if I understand it right, the rate banks charge each other for overnight loans. Now presumably someone makes money on the interest that's charged and someone loses money (or makes less) when the rate is lowered. But no one screams. Why not? If it's because the charges among banks just cancel one another out, then why does the rate even matter? Or is it that the Federal Reserve itself charges this interest, in which case the taxpayers lose when the rate is lowered?

—Peter Marcuse, New York

To answer your question, we should first understand how the U.S. Federal Reserve system works. The quasi-public Federal Reserve has two parts, neither of which is actually part of the federal government. First, there are the district banks—12 Federal Reserve Banks scattered across the country, charged with regulating and overseeing the commercial banks in their region and each wholly owned by those banks. Then there is the Board of Governors, a seven-member board with a vast research staff, based in Washington, D.C., and chaired by Alan Greenspan.

Every six weeks, the board and the presidents of the regional banks meet together as the so-called *Federal Open Market Committee* (FOMC), where they set targets for the *fed funds rate*—a rate that commercial banks charge one another for overnight loans. After the fed funds target is announced, the district banks will generally raise or lower the *discount rate*—the rate that commercial banks pay when they borrow from their local Fed—so that the two rates stay roughly equal.

In order to reduce the fed funds rate, the FOMC directs traders at the New York Federal Reserve Bank to buy U.S. Treasury bills on the financial markets. The Fed creates new money—quite literally, since paper printed by the Fed *is* money—to pay for these bills. When this new money enters the economy, it tends to be deposited in banks that, suddenly awash in cash, must find borrowers for it if they are to earn a profit. (To raise interest rates the FOMC does the opposite, selling U.S. Treasury bills and taking cash out of circulation.)

Since the district banks are owned not by the federal government but by the commercial banks, reductions in the discount rate do not affect the public treasury. And since commercial banks are both borrowers and the lenders in the fed funds market, gains and losses for the banks do tend, as you suspect, to cancel out. The point of reducing the fed funds rate, though, is to drive down other interest rates. If the financial markets are swimming in cheap cash, then competition for borrowers ought to push down rates on auto loans, business loans, mortgages, rates on bonds, and so forth.

Financial firms earn money by charging interest. In general, they prefer high interest rates to low. But they prefer low interest rates to watching their business dry up and their clients default on loans. Banks recognize that in a recession, lower interest rates may be necessary to spur growth and prevent bankruptcies. They accept the Fed's authority to reduce rates and print new money when circumstances warrant it. And they also know that the Fed, traditionally, has been their advocate—if not their mouthpiece—in Washington.

The district banks are owned outright by the finance industry and appointees to the Board of Governors nearly always have close industry ties. Greenspan himself has a well-established record as an "inflation hawk" who tends to err on the side of high interest rates. Moreover, in his nearly 12 years as Fed chair, Greenspan has presided over the slow erosion of the Fed's policy authority, so that a lower fed funds rate often does not translate into lower interest rates for businesses and consumers. Over the past year, for example, the FOMC cut its target fed funds rate from 6.0% to 1.75%, yet rates on home mortgages have fallen by only one percentage point. If the Fed really wanted to bring down long-term interest rates (like mortgage rates), it could buy not only short-term Treasury bills but also long-term bonds. The Fed could use a variety of other means to lower interest rates set in other markets (like the bond market), but such policies could eat into the finance industry's earnings. Instead, the Fed's recent interest rate reductions have meant that banks pay lower rates on deposits, while earning fairly high rates on loans to consumers and businesses.

If the recession persists and competition for credit-worthy customers intensifies, however, lending rates will fall and banks will feel the pinch of the Fed's cheap credit policy. But don't expect to see Citigroup lambasting the Fed on the *New York Times* editorial page or lobbying Congress to oust Greenspan. The banks have a more direct avenue for airing their complaints. Every six weeks, on the day before the FOMC meets to set interest rate policy, the Board meets with the Federal Advisory Council—a group of private bankers from each of the 12 Fed districts—to hear their advice on how high interest rates should be.

Economist Edwin Dickens from Drew University, who has done extensive archival research on the Fed, notes that banks often "are adamant that they can't take the hit in income" if the Fed cuts rates. Records show that they have often thwarted rate cuts, even in recessions. So if lowered rates begin to squeeze financial earnings, the finance industry won't scream. Who needs to scream when you can whisper? ❑

Article 1.4

FOCUS ON THE FED
The "bond market" versus the rest of us

BY DOUG ORR AND ELLEN FRANK
October 1999; revised October 2010

Why should anyone involved in environmental issues, education reform efforts, efforts to house the homeless, or anyone else care about monetary policy? After all, it only affects the financial markets, right? *Wrong.* Monetary policy is holding all other social policy hostage, and is part of the cause of the rapid increase in income inequality in the United States. Whenever any policy change is proposed, be it in health care, housing, or transportation, the first question politicians ask is, "What will the 'bond market' think about this?"

"The bond market" is a euphemism for the financial sector of the U.S. economy and the Federal Reserve Bank (the Fed), which regulates that sector. The Fed is the central bank of the United States. It controls monetary policy, and uses its power to help the banking industry and the holders of financial assets, while thwarting government attempts to deal with pressing social problems.

Since 1979, the Fed has had an unprecedented degree of independence from government control. This independence has put it in a position to veto any progressive fiscal policy that Congress might propose. To understand how this situation developed, we must understand the function of banks, the structure of the Fed, and the role of monetary policy.

Banks and Instability

Government regulates the banking industry because private sector, profit-driven banking is inherently unstable. Banks do more than just store money—they help create it. If you deposit a dollar in the bank, you still have that dollar. Commercial banks will set aside three cents as "reserves" to "cover" your deposit, and the remaining 97 cents is loaned out to someone else who now has "new money." By making loans, banks create new money and generate profit. The drive to maximize profits often leads banks to become overextended: making too many loans and holding too few reserves. This drive for profits can undermine a bank's stability.

If depositors think the bank is holding too few reserves, or is making overly speculative loans, they might try to withdraw their money as cash. Large numbers of depositors withdrawing cash from a bank at the same time is called a "run on the bank." Since banks only hold 3% of their deposit liabilities as cash, even a moderate-sized "run" would be enough to drain the bank of its cash reserves. If a bank has no reserves, it is insolvent and is forced to close. At that point, all remaining deposits in the bank cease to exist, and depositors lose their money.

The failure of a bank affects more than just that bank's depositors. One bank's excesses tend to shake people's faith in other banks. If the run spreads, "bank panics" can occur. During the 1800s, such panics erupted every five to ten years, bankrupting between 10% and 25% of the banks in the United States and creating a major recession each time.

The Creation of the Fed

The panic of 1907 bankrupted some of the largest banks and led to demands by the public for bank reforms that would stabilize the system. Reform proposals ranged from doing almost nothing to nationalizing the entire banking industry. As a compromise, the Federal Reserve was created in 1913. The U.S. government saw the Fed as a way for bankers to regulate themselves, and structured the Federal Reserve System so that it could be responsive to its main constituents: banks and other financial-sector businesses that are now called, euphemistically, "the bond market." While ideally it should serve the interests of the general public when it conducts monetary policy, in reality the Fed balances two, conflicting goals: maintaining the stability of "the bond market" and maximizing financial-sector profits. Over time, Congress and the President have varied the degree of independence that they have given to the Fed to choose between these goals.

Initially, the Fed enjoyed a high degree of independence. During the 1920s, the Fed allowed member banks to engage in highly speculative activities, including using depositor's money to play the stock market. While many banks were very profitable, speculative excesses caused almost 20% of the banks in existence in 1920 to fail during the following decade. With the onset of the Great Depression, between 1929 and 1933, more than 9,000 banks, 38% of the total, failed. Since the Fed had not achieved its first goal, in 1935 Congress responded with laws that put many new regulations on banks, and reduced the Fed's independence.

Fed Independence Lost

Under the new regulations, "investment banks" were not allowed to take deposits, but were allowed to play the markets, while "commercial banks" were restricted to taking deposits and making commercial loans. Deposits were now insured by the FDIC. Thus, the only opportunity for making a profit was to maintain a "spread" between the interest rate paid on deposits and that charged on loans. Loans are made for relatively long terms, and deposits are not. If the short-term interest rate on deposits varies widely, the spread will grow and shrink, which makes bank profits unstable. In order to stabilize bank profits, during the 30 years after 1935, the Treasury mandated that the Fed keep the short-term rate approximately constant.

Under this arrangement, Congress indirectly controlled monetary policy. If Congress wanted to stimulate the economy it could increase government spending or cut taxes. Both led to an increase in spending and an increase in the demand for money. To keep interest rates, which are the price of money, from rising, the Fed had to increase the supply of money. Thus, the Fed "accommodated" fiscal policy decisions made by Congress and the President.

During most of this period, growth was moderate and prices were stable. The Fed went along because this arrangement did not threaten bank profits. Starting in the mid-1960s, however, stimulative fiscal policy started to push up the inflation rate, which did threaten bank profits. A confrontation over Fed independence ensued and grew in intensity throughout the 1970s.

Inflation's Impact

Contrary to the view commonly propagated by the media, inflation does not affect everyone equally. In fact, there are very clear winners and losers. Inflation is an increase in the average level of prices, but some prices rise faster than average and some rise slower. If the price of the thing you are selling is rising faster than average, you win. Otherwise, you lose. Inflation redistributes income, but in an arbitrary manner. This uncertainty makes inflation unpopular, even to the winners. However, one industry always loses from unexpected inflation, and that industry is finance.

Banks make loans today that will be repaid, with interest, in the future. If inflation reduces the value of those future payments, the banks' profits will be reduced. So bankers are interested in the "real interest rate," that is, the actual (nominal) interest rate on the loan minus the rate of inflation. If the interest rate on commercial bank loans is 7% and the rate of inflation is 3%, the real rate of interest is 4%. In the early postwar period, real interest rates were relatively stable at about 2%.

From 1965 on, unexpected increases in inflation reduced the real interest rate. This cheap credit was a boon to home buyers, farmers, and manufacturers, but it greatly reduced bank profits. Banks wanted inflation cut. The Keynesian view of monetary policy offered a simple but unpopular solution: raise interest rates enough to cause a recession. High unemployment and falling incomes would take the steam out of inflation.

But, putting people out of work to help bankers would be a hard sell. The Fed needed a different story to justify shifting its policy from stabilizing interest rates to fighting inflation. That story was "monetarism," a theory that claims that changes in the money supply affect prices, but nothing else in the economy.

The Monetarist Experiment

On October 6, 1979, Fed Chair Paul Volcker, using monetarist theory as a justification, announced that the Fed would no longer try to keep interest rates at targeted levels. He argued that Fed policy should concentrate on controlling inflation, and to do so he would now focus on limiting the money supply growth rate. Since neither Congress nor the President attempted to overrule Volcker, this change ushered in an era of unprecedented independence for Fed monetary policy.

During the next three years, the Fed reduced the rate of growth in the money supply, but this experiment did not yield the results predicted by the monetarists. Instead of a swift reduction in the rate of inflation, the most immediate outcome was a rapid rise in the real interest rate and the start of the worst recession since the Great Depression.

As the Keynesian view predicted, the recession occurred because high interest rates slowed economic growth and increased unemployment. In 1979, the unemployment rate was 5.8%. By 1982 it had reached 10.7%, the first double-digit rate since the Depression. With fewer people working and buying products, the inflation rate, which had been 8.7% in 1979, finally started to slow in 1981 and was approaching 4% by the end of 1982. Tight money policies by the Fed kept nominal interest rates from falling as fast as inflation. This raised real interest rates on commercial loans from 0.5% in 1979 to 10% in 1982.

The Fed's fight against inflation had a severe impact on the entire economy. All businesses, especially farming and manufacturing, run on credit. The rise in interest rates, combined with lower prices, squeezed the profits of farmers and manufacturers.

Both of these industries rely heavily on exports, and so were also hurt by the negative effect of high interest rates on the competitiveness of U.S. exports. Real interest rates in the United States were the highest in the world, thereby attracting financial investment from abroad. In order for foreigners to buy financial assets in the United States, they first had to buy dollars. This demand for dollars drove up their value in international markets. While a "strong" dollar means imports are relatively cheap, it also means that U.S. exports are expensive. Foreign countries could not afford to buy our "costly" agricultural and manufactured exports. As a result, during this period, bankruptcy rates in these two industries were massive, higher than during the 1930s.

Despite its high cost to the rest of the economy, the monetarist experiment did not benefit many banks. Initially, the high real interest rates appeared to help bank profits. Regulations capped the interest rates banks could pay on deposits, but rates charged on loans were not regulated. This increased the profit on loans. Many investors, however, started moving their deposits to less regulated financial intermediaries, such as mutual funds and new forms of "shadow banks" that could pay higher rates on deposits. In addition, the recession forced many borrowers to declare bankruptcy and default on their loans. Both of these factors pushed banks toward insolvency.

Reversing Course

It was bank losses, not the pain in the rest of the economy, that led Volcker to announce in September 1982 that he was abandoning monetarism. His new policy aimed to provide enough reserves to keep most banks solvent and to allow a *slow* recovery from the recession. Unemployment remained high for the next five years, so inflation continued to slow. Real interest rates stayed near 8% through 1986, so interest-sensitive industries, such as farming and manufacturing, did not take part in the recovery.

Volcker made his allegiance to the banking industry very clear during a meeting, in February 1985, with a delegation of state legislators, laborers, and farmers who were demanding easier money and lower interest rates. He told them, "Look, your constituents are unhappy, mine aren't."

Yet by 1985, the crisis in the savings and loan industry was spreading into commercial banking. To provide cash ("liquidity") to the banks, Volcker allowed the money supply to grow by 12% during 1985 and by 17% in 1986. Monetarists raised the specter of a return to double-digit inflation. Instead, the rate of inflation continued to slow, demonstrating that a simple link between the money supply and inflation hypothesized by monetarist theory does not exist.

The Veto

Despite the failure and subsequent abandonment of monetarist policies, the Fed still uses monetarist *theory* to justify its continued focus on "fighting inflation." The myth that monetary policy only affects inflation provides a convenient "cover" that allows the Fed to serve its narrow constituency: "the bond market." From the end of World War II to 1979, real interest rates averaged 2.1%. Since 1980, they have averaged 5.7%. Real interest rates remain high because "the bond market" worries about any possible increase in future inflation, but high rates continue to hollow out the manufacturing sector.

Fighting inflation benefits the bond market. However, despite the near-depression that monetarism caused in the 1980s and the extremely slow rate of economic growth that has occurred since, the Fed continues to claim that fighting inflation serves the interests of the entire country. The public's widespread belief in this myth denies progressives in Congress the support they need to force the Fed back into accommodating fiscal policy. It also provides support for those in Congress that want to block any expansion of social programs.

If Congress decides to spend more for environmental clean-up, housing the homeless, or education, "the bond market" will raise the specter of renewed inflation. The Fed will then raise interest rates, as it did in June 1999 as a "preemptive strike" to prevent inflation, and sent the economy into a recession. The increase in interest rates slowed the economy, increased unemployment, reduced government revenues, and returned the federal budget to a deficit. Since Congress knows it will be incorrectly blamed for this outcome, it won't pass any legislation "the bond market" doesn't like. This is how the bond market holds Congress hostage. As long as Congress and the President allow the Fed to follow an inflation-fighting policy, the Fed can maintain a veto threat over the elected government.

The Fed has not vetoed Obama's fiscal policy stimulus because Fed Chairman Ben Bernanke realizes that the second premise of monetarist theory, that the Fed can always increase the money supply, is also wrong. The Fed has pumped more than $1 trillion in reserves into the banking system, and almost all of them sit as excess reserves. This is a classic example of what Keynes called a "liquidity trap." In this case, monetary policy is powerless to stimulate the economy. Only fiscal policy can bring us out of the "Great Recession." Unfortunately, the veto power of the Fed has been replaced by the veto power of the Republican "Party of No," which has filibustered every attempt to revive the economy. Apparently, making Obama look ineffective is more important to them than the well-being of the American people.

While the Fed has not vetoed Obama's fiscal policy, it has again demonstrated that its banking constituents are more important than the general public and the overall economy. If a commercial bank finds itself short on reserves, it has the option of borrowing reserves from the Fed through what is called the "discount window." It has this name because a member bank would bring assets to an actual Fed bank and trade those assets for reserves "at a discount." The value of assets the Fed received was more than the value of the reserves lent. Historically, the Fed only lent to commercial banks that were members of the Federal Reserve System.

During the current crisis, the Fed has greatly expanded its role. While investment banks and hedge funds cannot borrow at the discount window, the Fed still found a way to help them. The Fed agreed to trade Treasury bonds, which are completely safe from default, for "equal amounts" of mortgage backed securities that have a high probability for default. In this case, the value of assets received by the Fed were far less than the assets they lent to the investment banks and hedge funds because of the higher risk of default.

In both cases, the Fed had the power to impose restrictions on these loans. These restrictions could have included the requirement that banks attempt to renegotiate any mortgage loan, including a reduction in principle owed, before starting the process of foreclosure. This would have helped millions of American families avoid losing their homes. It would have also helped the recovery of the economy from the current Great Recession. But since this requirement would have reduced the profits of member banks, the Fed chose not to do this. Only now that these member banks have been exposed for fraudulently foreclosing on millions of loans has the Fed finally started to "investigate" the problem.

The Fed has also played a large role in the rapid increase in income and wealth inequality that started in the 1980s and has accelerated ever since. The two decades following World War II are often called the "golden age" of the U.S. economy. On average, Gross Domestic Product (GDP) grew 4.3% each year, and unemployment averaged 4.6%. Average real wages, that is, wages adjusted for inflation, grew at an annual rate of 2.1%, rising from $10.86 an hour in 1950 to $18.21 in 1973 (both measured in 2005 dollars). This period saw the creation of a true middle class in the United States.

In the three decades since 1980, GDP growth has averaged 2.7% each year, unemployment has averaged 6.2% (2.3% and 6.7% if we exclude the higher-growth Clinton years). Average real wages *declined* every year from 1980 to 1996. In fact, the real wage in 2009 was $16.40 an hour, exactly the same as in 1966. If wages had continued to grow at 2.1%, the average wage today would be $38.50. Without the slow growth policies of the Fed and the anti-labor policies started under Reagan, the average income of the majority of the people in the United States would be more than twice as large. Instead, we've seen a hollowing out of the middle class, and a rapid transfer of wealth and income to those already wealthy.

Where Do Interest Payments Go?

By focusing on inflation rather than interest rates, the media deflect attention from a critical social issue—how high interest rates transfer income from the indebted middle class to the very rich. If ownership of financial assets was evenly distributed among households, the growth in interest income would not be of much importance. But ownership of financial assets is heavily concentrated. As of 2007, the top 5% of households, those with incomes more than $183,000, controlled 60.5% of all wealth in the U.S. The top 10% controlled 71.6%. Yet these numbers understate the concentration of financial wealth. Almost 80% of families in the United States have almost no assets, outside the equity in their homes and vehicles. Despite the media hype about the "democratization" of the stock market, between 1989 and 1995 the concentration of stock ownership increased. Detailed studies of wealth data collected by the Fed report that in 2007 the wealthiest 5% of households owned 93.6% of all directly owned bonds and 82.4% of all directly owned stocks. The top 10% if households owned 98.4% of all bonds and 90.4% of all stocks.

The "poorest" nine-tenths of the U.S. population—that is, most of us—have virtually no financial assets. Such families gain little from rising interest rates. But the higher mortgage, credit card, and auto payments that result take a real toll on living standards. Each uptick in the real interest rate entails a transfer of income from the lowest 90% of the population to the highest 10%. And most of that income goes to the very, very wealthy, who are yet another part of "the bond market" served by the Fed.

Economist James Galbraith has called today's high interest rates a form of taxation without representation. The term is apt. Tax increases are passed by Congress, which has at least some public oversight. Interest rate hikes are decided by the Fed, an institution over which the President, Congress, and the public have virtually no control.

Like taxes, rising interest rates are a drain on the resources and income of the vast majority of U.S. households. But unlike tax revenues that can be used to provide education, environmental clean-up, homeless shelters, roads, airports, and other infrastructure, interest payments flow into the pockets of the very rich, who become ever so much richer. ❏

Resources: Arthur B. Kennickell, , "Ponds and Streams: Wealth and Income in the U.S,, 1989 to 2007," *Federal Reserve Working Paper 2009-13* (Jan. 2009); Lawrence Mishel, Jared Bernstein, and Heidi Shierholz, *The State of Working America 2008/2009.*

Article 1.5

TRANSFORMING THE FED

BY ROBERT POLLIN
November 1992

The U.S. financial system faces deep structural problems. Households, businesses, and the federal government are burdened by excessive debts. The economy favors short-term speculation over long-term investment. An unrepresentative and unresponsive elite has extensive control over the financial system. Moreover, the federal government is incapable of reversing these patterns through its existing tools, including fiscal, monetary, and financial regulatory policies.

I propose a dramatically different approach: transforming the Federal Reserve System (the "Fed") into a public investment bank. Such a bank would have substantial power to channel credit in ways that counter financial instability and support productive investment by private businesses. The Fed would use its powers to influence how and for what purposes banks, insurance companies, brokers, and other lenders loan money.

The U.S. government has used credit allocation policies, such as low-cost loans, loan guarantees, and home mortgage interest deductions, extensively and with success. Its primary accomplishment has been to create a home mortgage market that, for much of the period since World War II, provided non-wealthy households with unprecedented access to home ownership.

I propose increasing democratic control over the Federal Reserve's activities by decentralizing power to the 12 district Fed banks and instituting popular election of their boards of directors. This would create a mechanism for extending democracy throughout the financial system.

My proposal also offers a vehicle for progressives to address two separate but equally serious questions facing the U.S. economy:

- how to convert our industrial base out of military production and toward the development and adoption of environmentally benign production techniques; and

- how to increase opportunities for high wage, high productivity jobs in the United States. The U.S. needs such jobs to counteract the squeeze on wages from increasingly globalized labor and financial markets.

Transforming the Federal Reserve system into a public investment bank will help define an economic path toward democratic socialism in the United States.

My proposal has several strengths as a transitional program. It offers a mechanism for establishing democratic control over finance and investment—the area where capital's near-dictatorial power is most decisive. The program will also work within the United States' existing legal and institutional framework. We could implement parts of it immediately using existing federal agencies and with minimal demands on the federal budget.

At the same time, if an ascendant progressive movement put most of the program in place, this would represent a dramatic step toward creating a new economic system. Such a system would still give space to market interactions and the pursuit of greed, but would nevertheless strongly promote general well-being over business profits.

How the Fed Fails

At present the Federal Reserve focuses its efforts on managing short-term fluctuations of the economy, primarily by influencing interest rates. When it reduces rates, it seeks to increase borrowing and spending, and thereby stimulate economic growth and job opportunities. When the Fed perceives that wages and prices are rising too fast (a view not necessarily shared by working people), it tries to slow down borrowing and spending by raising interest rates.

This approach has clearly failed to address the structural problems plaguing the financial system. The Fed did nothing, for example, to prevent the collapse of the savings and loan industry. It stood by while highly speculative mergers, buyouts, and takeovers overwhelmed financial markets in the 1980s. It has failed to address the unprecedented levels of indebtedness and credit defaults of private corporations and households.

New Roles for the Fed

Under my proposal, the Federal Reserve would shift its focus from the short to the long term. It would provide more and cheaper credit to banks and other financiers who loan money to create productive assets and infrastructure—which promote high-wage, high-productivity jobs. The Fed would make credit more expensive for lenders that finance speculative activities such as the mergers, buyouts, and takeovers that dominated the 1980s.

The Fed would also give favorable credit terms to banks that finance decent affordable housing rather than luxury housing and speculative office buildings. It would make low-cost credit available for environmental research and development so the economy can begin the overdue transition to environmentally benign production. Cuts in military spending have idled many workers and productive resources, both of which could be put to work in such transformed industries.

Finally, the Fed would give preferential treatment to loans that finance investment in the United States rather than in foreign countries. This would help counter the trend of U.S. corporations to abandon the domestic economy in search of lower wages and taxes.

The first step in developing the Fed's new role would be for the public to determine which sectors of the economy should get preferential access to credit. One example, suggested above, is industrial conversion from military production to investment in renewable energy and conservation.

Once the public establishes its investment goals, the Fed will have to develop new policy tools and use its existing tools in new ways to accomplish them. I propose that a transformed Federal Reserve use two major methods:

- set variable cash ("asset reserve") requirements for all lenders, based on the social value of the activities the lenders are financing; and

- increase discretionary lending activity by the 12 district Federal Reserve banks.

Varying Banks' Cash Requirements

The Fed currently requires that banks and other financial institutions keep a certain amount of their assets available in cash reserves. Banks, for example, must carry three cents in cash for every dollar they hold in checking accounts. A bank cannot make interest-bearing loans on such "reserves." I propose that the Fed make this percent significantly lower for loans that finance preferred activities than for less desirable investment areas. Let's say the public decides that banks should allocate 10% of all credit to research and development of new environmental technologies, such as non-polluting autos and organic farming. Then financial institutions that have made 10% of their loans in environmental technologies would not have to hold any cash reserves against these loans. But if a bank made no loans in the environmental area, then it would have to hold 10% of its total assets in reserve. The profit motive would force banks to support environmental technologies without any direct expenditure from the federal budget.

All profit-driven firms will naturally want to avoid this reserve requirement. The Fed must therefore apply it uniformly to all businesses that profit through accepting deposits and making loans. These include banks, savings and loans, insurance companies, and investment brokerage houses. If the rules applied only to banks, for example, then banks could circumvent the rules by redefining themselves as another type of lending institution.

Loans to Banks That Do the Right Thing

The Federal Reserve has the authority now to favor some banks over others by making loans to them when they are short on cash. For the most part, however, the Fed has chosen not to exercise such discretionary power. Instead it aids all banks equally, through a complex mechanism known as open market operations, which increases total cash reserves in the banking system. The Fed could increase its discretionary lending to favored banks by changing its operating procedures without the federal government creating any new laws or institutions. Such discretionary lending would have several benefits.

First, to a much greater extent than at present, financial institutions would obtain reserves when they are lending for specific purposes. If a bank's priorities should move away from the established social priorities, the Fed could then either refuse to make more cash available to it, or charge a penalty interest rate, thereby discouraging the bank from making additional loans. The Fed, for example, could impose such obstacles on lenders that are financing mergers, takeovers, and buyouts.

In addition, the Fed could use this procedure to more effectively monitor and regulate financial institutions. Banks, in applying for loans, would have to submit to the Fed's scrutiny on a regular basis. The Fed could more closely link its regulation to banks' choices of which investments to finance.

Implementing this procedure will also increase the authority of the 12 district banks within the Federal Reserve system, since these banks approve the Fed's loans. Each district bank will have more authority to set lending rates and monitor bank compliance with regulations.

The district banks could then more effectively enforce measures such as the Community Reinvestment Act, which currently mandates that banks lend in their home communities. Banks that are committed to their communities and regions, such as the South Shore Bank in Chicago, could gain substantial support under this proposed procedure.

Other Credit Allocation Tools

The Fed can use other tools to shift credit to preferred industries, such as loan guarantees, interest rate subsidies, and government loans. In the past the U.S. government has used these techniques with substantial success. They now primarily support credit for housing, agriculture, and education. Indeed, as of 1991, these programs subsidized roughly one-third of all loans in the United States.

Jesse Jackson's 1988 Presidential platform suggested an innovative way of extending such policies. He proposed that public pension funds channel a portion of their money into a loan guarantee program, with the funds used to finance investments in low cost housing, education, and infrastructure.

There are disadvantages, however, to the government using loan guarantee programs and similar approaches rather than the Fed's employing asset reserve requirements and discretionary lending. Most important is that the former are more expensive and more difficult to administer. Both loan guarantees and direct government loans require the government to pay off the loans when borrowers default. Direct loans also mean substantial administrative costs. Interest subsidies on loans are direct costs to government even when the loans are paid back.

In contrast, with variable asset reserve requirements and discretionary lending policies, the Fed lowers the cost of favored activities, and raises the cost of unfavored ones, without imposing any burden on the government's budget.

Increasing Public Control

The Federal Reserve acts in relative isolation from the political process at present. The U.S. president appoints seven members of the Fed's Board of Governors for 14-year terms, and they are almost always closely tied to banking and big business. The boards of directors of the 12 district banks appoint their presidents, and these boards are also composed of influential bankers and business people within each of the districts.

The changes I propose will mean a major increase in the central bank's role as an economic planning agency for the nation. Unless we dramatically improve democratic control by the public over the Fed, voters will correctly interpret such efforts as an illegitimate grasp for more power by business interests.

Democratization should proceed through redistributing power downward to the 12 district banks. When the Federal Reserve System was formed in 1913, the principle behind creating district banks along with the headquarters in Washington was to disperse the central bank's authority. This remains a valuable idea, but the U.S. government has never seriously attempted it. Right now the district banks are highly undemocratic and have virtually no power.

One way to increase the district banks' power is to create additional seats for them on the Open Market Committee, which influences short-term interest rates by expanding or contracting the money supply.

A second method is to shift authority from the Washington headquarters to the districts. The Board of Governors would then be responsible for setting general guidelines, while the district banks would implement discretionary lending and enforcement of laws such as the Community Reinvestment Act.

The most direct way of democratizing the district banks would be to choose their boards in regular elections along with other local, regional, and state-wide officials. The boards would then choose the top levels of the banks' professional staffs and oversee the banks' activities.

Historical Precedents

Since World War II other capitalist countries have extensively employed the types of credit allocation policies proposed here. Japan, France, and South Korea are the outstanding success stories, though since the early 1980s globalization and deregulation of financial markets have weakened each of their credit policies. When operating at full strength, the Japanese and South Korean programs primarily supported large-scale export industries, such as steel, automobiles, and consumer electronics. France targeted its policies more broadly to coordinate Marshall Plan aid for the development of modern industrial corporations.

We can learn useful lessons from these experiences, not least that credit allocation policies do work when they are implemented well. But substantial differences exist between experiences elsewhere and the need for a public investment bank in the United States.

In these countries a range of other institutions besides the central bank were involved in credit allocation policies. These included their treasury departments and explicit planning agencies, such as the powerful Ministry of International Trade and Industry (MITI) in Japan. In contrast, I propose to centralize the planning effort at the Federal Reserve.

We could create a new planning institution to complement the work of the central bank. But transforming the existing central banking system rather than creating a new institution minimizes both start-up problems and the growth of bureaucracies.

A second and more fundamental difference between my proposal and the experiences in Japan, France, and South Korea is that their public investment institutions were accountable only to a business-oriented elite. This essentially dictatorial approach is antithetical to the goal of increasing democratic control of the financial system.

The challenge, then, is for the United States to implement effective credit allocation policies while broadening, not narrowing, democracy. Our success ultimately will depend on a vigorous political movement that can fuse two equally urgent, but potentially conflicting goals: economic democracy, and equitable and sustainable growth. If we can meet this challenge, it will represent a historic victory toward the construction of a democratic socialist future. ❏

Resources: Robert Pollin, "Transforming the Federal Reserve into a Public Investment Bank: Why it is Necessary; How it Should Be Done," in G. Epstein, G. Dymski and R. Pollin, eds., *Transforming the U.S. Financial System,* M.E. Sharpe, 1993.

Article 1.6

BIG LIES ABOUT CENTRAL BANKING

BY JOSEPH STIGLITZ
June 2003

An independent central bank focused exclusively on price stability has become a central part of the mantra of "economic reform." Like so many other policy maxims, it has been repeated often enough that it has come to be believed. But bold assertions, even from central bankers, are no substitute for research and analysis.

Research suggests that if central banks focus on inflation, they do a better job at controlling inflation. But controlling inflation is not an end in itself: it is merely a means of achieving faster, more stable growth, with lower unemployment.

These are the real variables that matter, and there is little evidence that independent central banks focusing exclusively on price stability do better in these crucial respects. George Akerlof, who shared the Nobel Prize with me in 2001, and his colleagues have argued forcefully that there is an optimal rate of inflation, greater than zero. So ruthless pursuit of price stability actually harms economic growth and well being. Recent research even questions whether targeting price stability reduces the tradeoff between inflation and unemployment.

A focus on inflation may make sense for countries with long histories of inflation, but not for others, like Japan. America's central bank, the Federal Reserve, is mandated not only to ensure price stability, but also to promote growth and full employment. There is broad consensus in the US against a narrow mandate, such as that of the European Central Bank. Today, Europe's growth languishes, because the ECB is constrained by its single-minded focus on inflation from promoting economic recovery.

Technocrats and financial market players who benefit from this institutional arrangement have done an impressive job of convincing many countries of its virtues, and of the need to treat monetary policy as a technical matter that should be put above politics. That might be the case if all that central bankers did was, say, choose computer software for clearing payments.

But central banks make decisions that affect every aspect of society, including rates of economic growth and unemployment. Because there are tradeoffs, these decisions can only be made as part of a political process.

Some argue that in the long run there are no tradeoffs. But, as Keynes said, in the long run, we are all dead. Even if it were impossible to lower unemployment below some critical level without fuelling inflation, there is uncertainty about what that critical level is. Accordingly, risk is unavoidable: monetary policy that is too loose risks inflation; if it is too tight, it can cause unnecessary unemployment, with all the suffering that follows.

During America's growth boom in the 1990s, the Clinton Administration believed that it was worth risking pushing the unemployment rate lower, especially when the social gains—declining welfare rolls, reduced violence—were added to the direct economic benefits. By contrast, the IMF urged tighter monetary policy, because it put far less weight on the cost of unemployment, seemingly no weight on the ancillary social benefits of reducing it, and much greater weight on the costs of potential inflation.

The economic analysis of Clinton's Council of Economic Advisers turned out to be right; the models of the IMF (and the Fed) were wrong. America secured a much lower rate of unemployment without inflation—eventually unemployment fell to below 4%.

But that is not the point: the point is that no one could be sure. A calculated risk is always unavoidable. Who bears it varies with different policies, and that is a decision that cannot—or at least should not—be left to central bank technocrats. While there is a legitimate debate about the degree of independence accorded to central banks and other decision-making bodies, within a democracy, the perspectives of those whose well-being is affected by the decisions taken should be represented in the process.

Workers, for instance, who have much to lose if the central bank pursues an excessively tight policy, do not have a seat at the table. But financial markets—which do not have much to lose from unemployment, but are affected by inflation—are typically well represented. And yet financial markets hardly have a monopoly on technical competency.

Indeed, many in the financial community have little understanding of the intricate workings of the macroeconomic system—as evidenced by their frequent mistakes in managing it. For example, most US recessions since 1945 were caused by the Fed stepping on the brakes too hard. Similarly, central banks adopted monetarism with a fervor in the late 1970's and early 1980's, just as empirical evidence discrediting the underlying theories was mounting.

Whatever the merits of a common currency, those in Europe deliberating about adopting the Euro should consider whether to tie their fortunes to an institutional arrangement whose flaws are increasingly apparent. Likewise, developing countries need to consider not only the central bank's independence, but also its mandate and representativeness. They need to balance concerns about economic efficiency with those of democratic accountability.

In many new democracies, citizens are bewildered. The virtues of the new regime are first praised, but then they are told that the macroeconomic policy decisions about which they care most are too important to be left to democratic processes. Citizens are warned against the risks of populism (meaning the will of the people?).

There are no easy answers. But in too many countries, nor is there democratic debate about the alternatives. ❏

Article 1.7

PUSHING ON STRINGS

The explosion of U.S. banks' excess reserves since last fall
illustrates the dramatic failure of monetary policy.

BY GERALD FRIEDMAN
May/June 2009

Monetary policy is not working. Since the economic crisis began in July 2007, the Federal Reserve has dramatically cut interest rates and pumped out over a trillion dollars, increasing the money supply by over 15% in less than two years. These vast sums have failed to revive the economy because the banks have been hoarding liquidity rather than investing it.

The Federal Reserve requires that banks hold money on reserve to back-up deposits and other bank liabilities. Beyond these required reserves, in the past banks would hold very small amounts of excess reserves, holdings that they minimized because they earn very little or no interest. Between the 1950s and September 2008, all the banks in the United States held more than $5 billion in excess reserves only once, after the September 11 attacks. This changed with the collapse of Lehman Brothers. Beginning with less than $2 billion in August 2008, excess reserves soared to $60 billion in September and then to $559 billion in November before rising to $798 b. in January 2009. They hovered around that level for nearly a year until jumping again in the winter of 2009-10.

This explosion of excess reserves represents a signal change in bank policy that threatens the effectiveness of monetary policy in the current economic crisis. Aware of their own financial vulnerability, even insolvency, frightened bank managers responded to the collapse of major investment houses like Lehman Brothers by grabbing and hoarding cash. (The spike in excess reserves also coincides with a

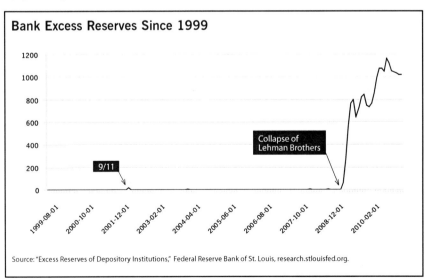

Bank Excess Reserves Since 1999

Source: "Excess Reserves of Depository Institutions," Federal Reserve Bank of St. Louis, research.stlouisfed.org.

change in Federal Reserve policy to begin paying interest on required and excess reserves. The rate paid, however—about 0.25%—is so low that it would not deter banks from making real investments and loans. On the other hand, the payment of interest amounts to a subsidy to banks by the Federal Reserve, and, ultimately, the United States Treasury, worth tens of billions of dollars.) At the same time, a general loss of confidence and spreading economic collapse persuaded banks that in any case there are few to whom they could lend with good confidence that they will be repaid. Clearly, our banks have decided that they need, or at least want, the money more than do consumers and productive businesses.

Banks could have been investing this money by lending to businesses needing liquidity to buy inventory or pay workers. Had they done so then monetarist economists would be shouting from the rooftops, at least in the university halls, about how monetary policy prevented another Great Depression. Instead, even the *Wall Street Journal* is proclaiming that "We're All Keynesians Again" because monetary policy has failed. Monetary authorities, the *Journal* explains, can create money but they cannot force banks to lend or to invest it in productive activities. The Federal Reserve confronts a reality shown in the graph above: it can't push on a string.

If the banks won't lend, then we need more than monetary policy to get out of the current crisis. The Obama stimulus was an appropriate response to the failure of string-pushing. But to solve a crisis this large will need much more government stimulus, and we will need programs to move liquidity from bank vaults to businesses and consumers. It may be time to stop waiting on the banks, and to start telling them what to do with our money. ❑

Article 1.8

IS THE FED A CONSPIRACY?

BY ARTHUR MacEWAN
March/April 2007

> Dear Dr. Dollar:
> *Some of my friends believe that the Federal Reserve and international bankers (Rothschilds, Rockefellers, etc.) run the world. They think the Federal Reserve was formed in secret and is pretty much a conspiracy. This is all hooked up with other conspiracy theories and right-wing views that make me uncomfortable. What do you think? Isn't the banking system part of the whole capitalist system? How does the Federal Reserve work; does it really have so much power?*
> —Carol Brown, New York, N.Y.

The Federal Reserve is a very powerful institution, and the people who run the world's large banks are a very powerful group of people. No one would claim otherwise. Also, the bankers have common interests, and, like any other group of people with common interests, they do what they can to bring about government policies that favor those interests.

Because the Federal Reserve (the "Fed"), as the central bank of the United States, implements policies that most directly affect the bankers, they of course are quite concerned with what the Fed does, how it is structured, and who runs it. And, like other elite groups, bankers certainly meet in private—in "secret," if one prefers—to figure out how best to get what they want.

With all that said, however, the idea that a small cabal of bankers runs the world through the operations of the Fed is wrong on several counts.

First of all, financial operatives are not the only powerful economic group. There are, for example, the people who run the large oil companies, the Silicon Valley operations, and the pharmaceutical firms, to name a few of the currently important capitalist clusters. These other groups have some common interests with the bankers, and they often all work together, both in private and in public, to achieve their common ends; they do not call in the press every time a few of them meet. (A recent example: when Vice President Cheney held a meeting to formulate the Bush administration's energy policy, the list of attendees—widely assumed to be top energy sector executives—was kept secret.) But to boil down this large class of people to a few bankers both distorts reality and obscures the conflicts that sometimes exist among them.

Second, not only are there often differences among these groups, but there are often contradictions between different things that they want. For example, they want a well-trained work force, but they do not want the high taxes that would be needed to pay for that training; they want freedom from government regulations, but they want the economic stability that often depends on government regulation; they want free access to international markets, but they want special preferences (as compared to foreign companies) within the United States; they want to pay low wages, but they want a populace with enough income to buy their products.

Third, while this set of people is undoubtedly very powerful in affecting the operation of our economic lives and in shaping history, they do not shape history just as they please. They simply can't control everything—as the problem that the Fed has with long-term interest rates illustrates (see below). They cannot control the economy just as they would like and they cannot control the rest of us just as they would like. Formal democracy, however limited, is a useful device. The power that the rest of us have can be a substantial constraint on the actions of big business—bankers, energy executives, and all the others.

But let's return to the Fed. What does it do, and how? The Fed has a variety of functions involving regulation of the banking system, including influencing the amount of money in circulation and interest rates (the price people pay to use other people's money). Of special importance, the Fed can influence the amount of loans that banks issue. When a bank issues a loan, this creates more spending power. This spending power (usually in the form of increasing the amount in the borrower's checking account) is the same thing as more money in circulation. So by influencing banks' loan actions, the Fed influences the money supply.

Right-wingers who view the Fed and the banks as an evil cabal tend to claim that by allowing banks to increase the money supply, the Fed is debasing our currency. The increased money supply lowers the value of money in relation to other goods, and the money prices of other goods rise—i.e., inflation. Moreover, they view this as a way of allowing the government to engage in excessive spending: the government can borrow from the public, but then, because of inflation, can repay in dollars that have less worth.

This fascination of some right-wingers with inflation and the debasement of the currency is ironic because, in fact, the Fed often (although not always) acts in exactly the opposite manner—*limiting* the growth of the money supply and *restricting* inflation. Banks, and businesses generally, like stable prices and stable interest rates. One reason is that a low-inflation policy keeps unemployment rates higher than they otherwise would be, weakening the bargaining power of workers and shifting the distribution of income in favor of capitalists.

A further irony: the Fed is not as powerful as either its proponents or its critics think. The Fed really has control only over short-term interest rates. Long-term interest rates, however, are more important (as they affect major investment decisions) and are influenced by many forces beyond the Fed's control. The expectations of business about future ups and downs of the economy—and about the myriad events that affect those fluctuations—are the central factors determining long-term interest rates. Neither capitalists' behavior nor capitalist economies are so easily controlled. If they were, then there would never be any stock market crashes, burst financial bubbles, or other serious disruptions.

By the way, the Fed was not formed in secret. The Fed was created by legislative action, formally and publicly. But there were certainly private (secret) meetings that laid the groundwork for it. Of course, the same is true of legislative actions affecting the pharmaceutical industry, Silicon Valley, insurance firms, and the list goes on. Nothing that special about the creation of the Fed.

Finally, while I am sure that there are many decent people who see the Fed and the bankers as the source of the world's problems, this view is often part of a larger anti-Semitism. The focus on "Jewish financiers" (the Rothschilds, for example) as the source of our economic and other problems is as old as it is wrong and offensive. ❑

Article 1.9

BERNANKE'S BAD TEACHERS

BY GERALD FRIEDMAN
July/August 2009

Addressing a conference honoring Milton Friedman on his 90th birthday in 2002, the future chairman of the Federal Reserve Board, Ben Bernanke, praised Friedman's 1963 book, written with Anna J. Schwartz, *A Monetary History of the United States*. Before Friedman and Schwartz, most economists saw the Great Depression of the 1930s as proof that capitalist economies do not tend towards full-employment equilibrium. But Friedman and Schwartz restored the prior orthodoxy by blaming the Great Depression on bad monetary policy by the Federal Reserve while exonerating American capitalism. The Great Depression was "the product of the nation's monetary mechanism gone wrong."

It is significant that Friedman and Schwartz never use the phrase "the Great Depression"; instead, they speak of "the Great Contraction" of the 1930s, addressing the reduction in the money supply while treating the fall in employment and output as a secondary matter, the consequence of bad government policy that caused "the Great Contraction." By flattering the prejudices of economists who want to believe in the natural stability of free markets, Friedman and Schwartz's story has become the accepted explanation of America's worst economic disaster.

Bernanke, for one, confesses that he was inspired by their work; "hooked" in graduate school, "I have been a student of monetary economics and economic history ever since." Pushing on an open door, Friedman and Schwartz persuaded most orthodox economists, and that part of the political elite that listens to economists, that the economic collapse that began in 1929 was an accident that would have been avoided by reliance on free markets and competent Federal Reserve monetary policy.

Bernanke closed his 2002 remarks with a promise. "Let me end my talk," he said, "by abusing slightly my status as an official representative of the Federal Reserve. I would like to say to Milton and Anna: Regarding the Great Depression. You're right, we did it. We're very sorry. But thanks to you, we won't do it again."

Bernanke had five years to ponder this promise before he faced a worthy challenge; and then he acted with the vigor of a Friedman/Schwartz acolyte. When this decade's housing bubble began to deflate in early 2007, major financial firms like New Century Financial and Bear Stearns reported major losses, and confidence in the U.S. financial system began to collapse as swiftly as in 1929–33. In early August, the rising tide reached tsunami dimensions when the International Monetary Fund warned of a trillion dollars in bank losses from bad mortgages. This was Bernanke's moment. Channeling Friedman and Schwartz, careful to avoid the mistakes of 1929–33, the Federal Reserve moved quickly in early August 2007 to provide liquidity to financial markets. It acted again on August 17 by cutting mortgage rates. More cuts came on September 18, on October 31, and on December 11. Then, on December 12, the Fed announced the creation of a new facility formed with the Europeans (Term Auction Facility, or TAF) to provide $24 billion in additional liquidity to financial markets. After still more interest-rate cuts in January 2008, a new special lending facility, with $100 billion, was established on March 2, along with another $75 billion for the TAF. Then, on March 11, another new facility was created, the Term Securities Lending Facility, with $200 billion. And all this was long before the bailouts of Fannie Mae, Freddie Mac, AIG, or the federal government's trillion-dollar Troubled Asset Relief Program (TARP).

If insanity consists of doing the same thing over and over again and expecting different results, then the Federal Reserve went insane after the summer of 2007. Never before has it acted this aggressively in trying to get ahead of a financial market meltdown. Under Bernanke, the Fed has increased the money supply by over 16% in less than two years, nearly mirroring the 18% drop in the money supply in the same period after the stock market collapse of 1929. Had he lived, Milton Friedman would have been proud.

The one thing that has not changed between the crisis of 1929 and the crisis of 2007 has been the behavior of the real economy. Bernanke has avoided his predecessors' monetary policy mistakes, but he has not prevented a sharp economic downturn. Since 2007, the economy has lost nearly 6 million jobs, including over half a million in the last month. At 8.9%, the April 2009 unemployment rate unnervingly equals the 1930 figure. We have a long way to go before we hit Great Depression level unemployment; but we are only in the second year of this collapse. And monetary policy is not helping.

Here, then, we see the legacy of Friedman and Schwartz. Confident that capitalist free markets naturally move towards a full-employment equilibrium, Bernanke and his allies saw the need for only one type of government action: providing liquidity to the banks in order to strengthen confidence in the financial markets. Guided by Friedman and Schwartz, Bernanke has provided nearly unlimited aid to the Wall Street bankers and financiers responsible for our current economic collapse. And he has starved the real economy—businesses, workers, and homeowners—to avoid interfering in free markets.

Bernanke has conducted an economic policy as cruel as it has been ineffective. But the blame here goes beyond Milton Friedman and Anna Schwartz. It lies squarely on the economics profession. ❏

Chapter 2

THE BANKING AND FINANCE INDUSTRY

Article 2.1

FINANCIALIZATION: A PRIMER

BY RAMAA VASUDEVAN
November/December 2008

You don't have to be an investor dabbling in the stock market to feel the power of finance. Finance pervades the lives of ordinary people in many ways, from student loans and credit card debt to mortgages and pension plans.

And its size and impact are only getting bigger. Consider a few measures:

• U.S. credit market debt—all debt of private households, businesses, and government combined—rose from about 1.6 times the nation's GDP in 1973 to over 3.5 times GDP by 2007.

• The profits of the financial sector represented 14% of total corporate profits in 1981; by 2001-02 this figure had risen to nearly 50%.

These are only a few of the indicators of what many commentators have labeled the "financialization" of the economy—a process University of Massachusetts economist Gerald Epstein succinctly defines as "the increasing importance of financial markets, financial motives, financial institutions, and financial elites in the operation of the economy and its governing institutions."

In recent years, this phenomenon has drawn increasing attention. In his latest book, pundit Kevin Phillips writes about the growing divergence between the real (productive) and financial economies, describing how the explosion of trading in myriad new financial instruments played a role in polarizing the U.S. economy. On the left, political economists Harry Magdoff and Paul Sweezy had over many years pointed to the growing role of finance in the operations of capitalism; they viewed the trend as a reflection of the rising economic and political power of "rentiers"—those whose earnings come from financial activities and from forms of income arising from ownership claims (such as interest, rent, dividends, or capital gains) rather than from actual production.

From Finance to Financialization

The financial system is supposed to serve a range of functions in the broader economy. Banks and other financial institutions mop up savings, then allocate that capital, according to mainstream theory, to where it can most productively be used. For households and corporations, the credit markets facilitate greatly increased borrowing, which should foster investment in capital goods like buildings and machinery, in turn leading to expanded production. Finance, in other words, is supposed to facilitate the growth of the "real" economy—the part that produces useful goods (like bicycles) and services (like medical care).

In recent decades, finance has undergone massive changes in both size and shape. The basic mechanism of financialization is the transformation of future streams of income (from profits, dividends, or interest payments) into a tradable asset like a stock or a bond. For example, the future earnings of corporations are transmuted into equity stocks that are bought and sold in the capital market. Likewise, a loan, which involves certain fixed interest payments over its duration, gets a new life when it is converted into marketable bonds. And multiple loans, bundled together then "sliced and diced" into novel kinds of bonds ("collateralized debt obligations"), take on a new existence as investment vehicles that bear an extremely complex and opaque relationship to the original loans.

The process of financialization has not made finance more effective at fulfilling what conventional economic theory views as its core function. Corporations are not turning to the stock market as a source of finance for their investments, and their borrowing in the bond markets is often not for the purpose of productive investment either. Since the 1980s, corporations have actually spent more money buying back their own stock than they have taken in by selling newly issued stock. The granting of stock options to top executives gives them a direct incentive to have the corporation buy back its own shares—often using borrowed money to do so—in order to hike up the share price and allow them to turn a profit on the sale of their personal shares. More broadly, instead of fostering investment, financialization reorients managerial incentives toward chasing short-term returns through financial trading and speculation so as to generate ballooning earnings, lest their companies face falling stock prices and the threat of hostile takeover.

What is more, the workings of these markets tend to act like an upper during booms, when euphoric investors chase the promise of quick bucks. During downturns these same mechanisms work like downers, turning euphoria into panic as investors flee. Financial innovations like collateralized debt obligations were supposed to "lubricate" the economy by spreading risk, but instead they tend to heighten volatility, leading to amplified cycles of boom and bust. In the current crisis, the innovation of mortgage-backed securities fueled the housing bubble and encouraged enormous risk-taking, creating the conditions for the chain reaction of bank (and other financial institution) failures that may be far from over.

Financialization and Power

The arena of finance can at times appear to be merely a casino—albeit a huge one—where everyone gets to place her bets and ride her luck. But the financial system carries a far deeper significance for people's lives. Financial assets and liabilities represent claims on ownership and property; they embody the social relations of an economy at a particular time in history. In this sense, the recent process of financialization implies the increasing political and economic power of a particular segment of the capitalist class: rentiers. Accelerating financial transactions and the profusion of financial techniques have fuelled an extraordinary enrichment of this elite.

This enrichment arises in different ways. Financial transactions facilitate the reallocation of capital to high-return ventures. In the ensuing shake-up, some sectors of capital profit at the expense of other sectors. More important, the capitalist class as a whole is able to force a persistent redistribution in its favor, deploying its newly expanded wealth to bring about changes in the political-economy that channel even more wealth its way.

The structural changes that paved the way for financialization involved the squashing of working-class aspirations during the Reagan-Thatcher years; the defeats of the miners' strike in England and of the air traffic controllers' (PATCO) strike in the United States were perhaps the most symbolic instances of this process. At the same time, these and other governments increasingly embraced the twin policy mantras of fighting inflation and deregulating markets in place of creating full employment and raising wages. Corporations pushed through legislation to dismantle the financial regulations that inhibited their profitmaking strategies.

Financialization has gathered momentum amid greater inequality. In the United States, the top 1% of the population received 14.0% of the national after-tax income in 2004, nearly double its 7.5% share in 1979. In the same period the share of the bottom fifth fell from 6.8% to 4.9%.

And yet U.S. consumption demand has been sustained despite rising inequality and a squeeze on real wages for the majority of households. Here is the other side of the financialization coin: a massive expansion of consumer credit has played an important role in easing the constraints on consumer spending by filling the gap created by stagnant or declining real wages. The credit card debt of the average U.S. family increased by 53% through the 1990s. About 67% of low-income families with incomes less than $10,000 faced credit card debt, and the debt of this group saw the largest increase—a 184% rise, compared to a 28% increase for families with incomes above $100,000. Offered more and more credit as a privatized means of addressing wage stagnation, then, eventually, burdened by debt and on the edge of insolvency, the working poor and the middle class are less likely to organize as a political force to challenge the dominance of finance. In this sense, financialization becomes a means of social coercion that erodes working-class solidarity.

As the structures created by financial engineering unravel, the current economic crisis is revealing the cracks in this edifice. But even as a growing number of U.S. families are losing their homes and jobs in the wake of the subprime meltdown, the financial companies at the heart of the crisis have been handed massive bailouts and their top executives have pocketed huge pay-outs despite their role in abetting the meltdown—a stark sign of the power structures and interests at stake in this era of financialization. ❑

Sources: Robin Blackburn, "Finance and the Fourth Dimension," *New Left Review* 39 May-June 2006; Robert Brenner, "New Boom or Bubble," *New Left Review* 25 Jan-Feb 2004; Tamara Draut and Javier Silva, "Borrowing to make ends meet," *Demos*, Sept 2003; Gerald Epstein, "Introduction" in G. Epstein, ed., *Financialization and the World* Economy, 2006; John Bellamy Foster, "The Financialization of Capitalism," *Monthly Review*, April 2007; Gretta Krippner, "The financialization of the US economy," *Socio-Economic Review* 3, Feb. 2005; Thomas Palley, "Financialization : What it is and why it matters," Political Economy Research Institute Working Paper #153, November 2007; A. Sherman and Arin Dine, "New CBO data shows inequality continues to widen," Center for Budget Priorities, Jan. 23, 2007; Kevin Phillips, *Bad Money: Reckless Finance, Failed Politics, and the Global Crisis of American Capitalism*, 2008.

Article 2.2

(MIS)UNDERSTANDING A BANKING INDUSTRY IN TRANSITION

Under deregulation the industry became dysfunctional—but economists still won't revise their anti-regulation script.

BY WILLIAM K. BLACK
November/December 2007

The U.S. financial system is, once again, in crisis. Or, more precisely, twin crises—first, huge numbers of defaults among subprime mortgage borrowers, and second, massive losses for the holders of new-fangled investments comprised of bundles of loans of varying risk, including many of those subprime mortgages.

These crises should shock the nation. Our largest, most sophisticated financial institutions have followed business practices that were certain to produce massive losses—practices so imprudent, in precisely the business task (risk management) that is supposed to be their greatest expertise, that they have created a worldwide financial crisis.

Why? Because their CEOs, acting on the perverse incentives created by today's outrageous compensation systems, engaged in practices that vastly increased their corporations' risk in order to drive up reported corporate income and thereby secure enormous increases in their own individual incomes. And those perverse incentives follow them out the door: CEOs Charles Prince, at Citicorp, and Stanley O'Neal, at Merrill Lynch, had dismal track records of similar failures prior to the latest disasters, but they collected massive bonuses for their earlier failures and will receive obscene termination packages now. Pay and productivity (and integrity) have become unhinged at U.S. financial institutions.

As this goes to print, Treasury Department officials are working with large financial institutions to cover up the scale of the growing losses. This is the same U.S. Treasury that regularly prates abroad about the vital need for transparency. And a former Treasury Secretary, Robert Rubin, who failed utterly in his fiduciary duty as lead board member at Citicorp to prevent the series of recent abuses, will become Citicorp's new CEO.

To even begin to understand events in the U.S. and global banking industries, you have to look back at the seismic shifts in the industry over the past 30 to 40 years, and at the interplay between those shifts and government policy. The story that continues to unfold is one of progressively worse policies that make financial crises more common and more severe.

These policies have their boosters, though. Chief among them are neoclassical banking and finance economists, whose ideology and methodologies lead them into blatant misreadings of the realities of the industry and the causes of its failures. When the history of this crisis-ridden era in global finance is written, the economists will no doubt be given a significant share of the blame.

A New Era of Crisis

The changes in the U.S. banking industry in recent decades have been so great that a visitor from the 1950s would hardly recognize the industry. Over two decades of intense merger and acquisition activity has left a far smaller number of banks, with assets far more concentrated in the largest ones. Between 1984 and 2004, the number of banks on the FDIC's rolls fell from 14,392 to 7,511; the share of the U.S. banking industry's assets held by the ten largest banks rose from 21% in 1960 to nearly 60% in 2005. At the same time, nonbank businesses that lend, save, and invest money have proliferated, as have the products they sell: a vast array of new kinds of loans and exotic savings and investment vehicles. And the lines have blurred between all of the different players in the industry—between banks and thrifts (e.g., savings and loans), between commercial banks and investment banks.

These changes were made possible by the deregulation of the industry. Bit by bit, beginning in the 1970s, the banking regulations put into place in the wake of the Great Depression were repealed, culminating in the Gramm-Leach-Bliley Act in 1999, which removed the remaining legal barriers to combining commercial banking, investment banking, and insurance under one corporate roof. The

Deposit Insurance Spreads Despite Economists' Protests

Banking economists now overwhelmingly criticize deposit insurance. This represents a major change. The prior consensus, shared by Milton Friedman and John Kenneth Galbraith alike, praised deposit insurance for ending the periodic runs on uninsured banks that helped cause the Great Depression. Today, however, the conventional economic wisdom is that deposit insurance may stop runs, but at the expense of encouraging banks to make imprudent loans and take excessive risks. (Neoclassical economists widely view insurance as inherently creating an incentive for insured parties to act in unduly risky ways because of the safety net that insurance provides—a phenomenon termed "moral hazard.")

This claim is dubious: economists do not offer a credible mechanism whereby deposit insurance could lead to the ills they claim it causes. Deposit insurance does not protect the shareholders or the CEO—the two groups (the first, in theory; the second, in practice) that control a bank. It is the depositors who are insured. Thus, they must be the ones who are subject to moral hazard—in other words, the argument against deposit insurance must be based on the claim that it reduces the incentive of depositors to exercise "private market discipline" by pulling their money out of a bank they believe is being poorly run or looted. But there is no credible evidence that depositors are capable of either discerning frauds or avoiding runs on healthy banks based on false rumors. Indeed, studies have shown that even private-sector financial experts who specialize in evaluating the health of banks cannot do so effectively.

Proponents of the view that deposit insurance causes banking failures display an unrecognized logical inconsistency. Their proposed reform is to rely on private market discipline to prevent management from looting the bank or lending imprudently in a bubble. But, if we assume hypothetically that private market discipline is effective against CEOs who would be so inclined, then it should normally be effective despite the presence of deposit insurance. Deposit insurance does not remove private market discipline where the bank is owned by shareholders (unless the CEO owns all the stock) or where the bank issues uninsured subordinated debt. Yet during the S&L crisis, control fraud (the looting of an institution by its own managers or owners) was most common in S&Ls owned in stock form, with the largest losses overwhelmingly among stock S&Ls. In these cases deposit insurance did not new world of combined financial services is exemplified by the deal, inked (but ostensibly illegal) before the 1999 law was passed, that merged the insurance and investment-banking giant Travelers with Citibank, at the time the nation's number-one commercial bank.

These transformational changes in domestic banking, along with the related effects of economic globalization both in the United States and abroad, have produced recurrent crises in the financial sector. Indeed, the current era has seen over 100 major banking crises, in countries around the globe. Thomas Hoenig, head of the Kansas City Federal Reserve Bank, emphasized the remarkable and disturbing facts in a meeting with fellow heads of supervision:

> A 1996 survey by the IMF [International Monetary Fund] … found that 73 percent [133 of 181] of their member countries had experienced significant banking problems during the preceding 15 years. Many of these problems led to substantial declines in GDP [and] serious disruptions in credit and capital markets. …

To date none of these crises has led to a global Great Depression. Only a few were larger in absolute terms than the 1980s S&L debacle in the United States. Yet

preclude private market discipline; market discipline was simply inadequate to prevent control fraud. Some opponents of deposit insurance proclaim the S&L debacle to be their primary example—a flat misreading of the facts.

The empirical evidence economists use to support their critique of deposit insurance is inconsistent. Moreover, even where the adoption of deposit insurance is correlated with a rise in bank failures, the causal relationship may be just the opposite of what economists claim. Nations with early signs of an impending banking crisis may adopt deposit insurance to reduce the risks of runs. Developing nations tend to adopt deposit insurance in conjunction with privatization—which itself often prompts a banking crisis. More broadly, in part because of the fall of the Soviet Union and the rise of the neoliberal "Washington Consensus," the number of nations adopting deposit insurance increased sharply in the last two decades. Banking crises have indeed been far more common over this same period—precisely because these radical transitions have been occurring in nations with weak institutions, too few regulators with too little experience, patterns of bank ownership that maximize conflicts of interest, and substantial corruption.

In addition, empirical studies rely on subjective coding of different countries' deposit insurance policies, often done by economists who oppose deposit insurance. In countries with no formal deposit insurance, implicit government guarantees for banks are common. There are good theoretical and historical reasons to argue that such implicit guarantees—common in crony capitalism and kleptocracies—create greater moral hazard than explicit deposit insurance does because they can be structured to bail out a bank's shareholders and CEO as well as its creditors (as was done in Chile). But there is no way to code accurately for whether there was an implicit guarantee (or whether bank CEOs believed there was an implicit guarantee) in a particular country at a particular time.

Despite these weaknesses in both evidence and analysis, World Bank economists draw firm conclusions, opposing the adoption of deposit insurance in any nation and clearly hoping for its elimination. But the world has rejected their advice. By 2006, 95 countries had deposit insurance, over four times the number in 1983. Moreover, economists' suggestions on how to "improve" deposit insurance (require banks to issue subordinated debt, charge variable rates for deposit insurance, or require private insurance of accounts) are rarely adopted and have proven unsuccessful in practice.

many imposed a much greater relative cost, measured as a percentage of the country's GDP. Some caused severe, depression-like economic problems in the affected nation. Some produced contagion effects that caused severe crises in other nations. And acute banking crises can cause long-term harm. Japan is a rich nation and can afford a 15-year banking crisis—but the world economy cannot. The crisis cut Japan's economic growth to near-zero for a decade, in turn creating contagion effects in the many countries for whom Japan was a major trading partner or a significant source of capital investment. Tens of millions of people remain in poverty in Asia and Africa as a result.

The recurrent banking crises have come as a shock to the United States, given the dearth of bank failures over the first three decades after World War II. The first severe postwar U.S. banking crisis was stemmed from the large loans that top U.S. banks made to sovereign borrowers (i.e., nations), largely in Latin America. The banks had claimed that sovereign loans offered high returns with minimal default risk because the nation could always repay the loan by printing more money. Citibank head Walter Wriston notoriously implied that countries could not go broke. The claim was absurd. However, banking regulators took no effective action to restrain this lending.

The 1982 Mexican default led to contagion and fears of an international meltdown, but the Federal Reserve and the Bank for International Settlements (BIS) took effective action. Brazil experienced a long economic slowdown that contributed to an imminent default on its loans from major U.S. banks. A Brazilian default could have rendered several of our largest banks insolvent. The banks were rescued by a combination of bailouts to Brazil through the IMF and the World Bank and flawed (albeit permissible under so-called Generally Accepted Accounting Principles, or GAAP) "troubled-debt restructuring" to cover up the losses. Brazil used the bailouts to pay minimal interest on the U.S. bank loans and ultimately recovered; while several U.S. banks took serious losses, none failed.

On the heels of this crisis came the savings and loan crisis, an unprecedented debacle which saw the collapse of some 1,000 S&Ls and which cost U.S. taxpayers about $125 billion dollars—primarily the cost of repaying to depositors money that criminal S&L heads had literally stolen from their institutions.

The causes of these crises are varied. They typically occur, however, when large banks are in essence looted by their owners and managers (a phenomenon known as "control fraud") or when there are financial bubbles in which assets become massively overvalued.

Economists who conduct case studies of banking crises commonly report the existence of substantial control fraud. Looting played a prominent role in the S&L debacle. Here is the conclusion of the National Commission on Financial Institution Reform, Recovery and Enforcement (NCFIRRE):

The typical large failure was a stockholder-owned, state-chartered institution in Texas or California where regulation and supervision were most lax. ... The failed institution typically had experienced a change of control and was tightly held, dominated by an individual with substantial conflicts of interest. ... In the typical large failure, every accounting trick available was used to make the institution look profitable, safe, and solvent. Evidence of fraud was invariably present as was the ability of the operators to "milk" the organization through high dividends and salaries, bonuses, perks and other means. In short, the typical large failure was one in which management exploited virtually all the perverse incentives created by government policy.

Looting has played a significant role in banking crises around the world. It became so prevalent in the states of the former Soviet Union that it inspired a new term of art, "tunneling," to describe the process of the CEO and owners converting a company's funds to their private benefit.

In addition to the national banking crises, fraud has caused spectacular failures of large banks. The Bank for Credit and Commerce International (BCCI—known informally as the "Bank for Crooks and Criminals International"), Barings Bank, and Continental Bank all stunned the public when they failed. BCCI was the largest bank in the developing world, Barings was England's oldest bank, and Continental was America's third largest bank. Each one collapsed with minimal public warning.

And, of course, more recently control fraud played a role in a number of spectacular business failures outside of the banking industry including Enron, WorldCom, and Tyco. This fact makes it obvious that the conventional economic wisdom, which blames this era's wave of bank failures and banking crises on regulation and deposit insurance (which are specific to the banking industry) is just wrong. Despite this, mainstream economists persist in their diagnosis, rarely scrutinizing the deregulation and privatization that many observers believe in fact triggered these crises.

...They First Make Proud

Economists have dominated the creation of public policies to prevent banking crises. Their track record has been abysmal. They designed and implemented the disastrous deregulation that produced the U.S. S&L debacle, they praised Japan's and East Asia's banking structures just before they collapsed, and they designed the IMF's crisis intervention strategy that intensified losses and human misery. They also designed and praised privatization programs in many transition economies that led to banking crises; they planned (and in some cases profited from) the catastrophic failure of "shock therapy" in Russia. The irony is that when financial experts were most confident in their consensus, they erred the most grievously. As Mark Twain

Offshore Banks

One particularly dark side of globalization is the rise of new offshore banks. While Switzerland now has reasonably workable procedures for tracking the funds of kleptocrats and drug traffickers, several small nations have adopted extreme forms of bank secrecy designed to cater to the needs of criminals and tax evaders. Corporations often incorporate in a tax haven because of the extremely low tax rates. In the late 1990s, the Organisation for Economic Co-operation and Development, an organization of the world's industrialized countries, created an initiative to try to curtail these abuses. Conservative think tanks sought to kill the OECD plan and convinced President Bush to block its implementation as one of his earliest actions. The administration reduced its opposition to the OECD initiative after the 9/11 attacks, when it became clear that terrorists used the offshore banks as their preferred means to move funds.

remarked: "It's not the things you *don't* know that cause disasters; it's the things you *do* know, *but aren't true.*"

This record of failure is disappointing and has caused great human suffering. Remarkably, the economists' hubris is unaffected by it. They are now engaged in a war against deposit insurance and regulation. At this juncture, they are losing that war, but they are persevering in their effort to reclaim their domination over banking policy.

Neoclassical banking economists are failing in this arena for three reasons. First, they neither study nor understand fraud mechanisms and the institutions that are essential to limit fraud and corruption. Second, they are shackled by an ideology that *presumes* that unfettered markets always produce the best outcomes and that government intervention is always bad. For instance, in their writings many of the World Bank's banking economists display a passionate contempt for democratic government and banking regulators. Third, they are mono-disciplinary. They rarely cite (and no doubt rarely examine) the literature in other relevant fields such as political science, sociology, and white-collar criminology.

Indeed, although it should be central to their study of crisis prevention, they rarely even cite the work of economist and 2001 Nobel Prize winner George Akerlof. Based on their study of the S&L crisis, which found that looting was a major cause of total S&L losses, Akerlof and Paul Romer developed an economic model of the looting control fraud.

Looters use accounting fraud to make a company *appear* extraordinarily profitable. Consider the S&L crisis. The worst S&L control frauds were the ones reporting the highest profitability. Moreover, the control frauds were routinely able to get a

---

They Just Never Learn

Today's financial crisis offers a superb example of how their methods lead mainstream economists to endorse both private practices and public policies that are perverse. The current crisis exemplifies a variant of accounting control frauds—one in which the CEO and top managers "skim" rather than loot the company—and demonstrates the unrecognized economic costs of obscenely high CEO pay. The incentives created by typical CEO compensation packages in the financial services industry produce bad investment decisions, decisions that increase the CEO's ability to skim, but that expose the financial institution to losses and the nation and world to recurrent financial crises.

Consider the plight of the honest chief financial officer (CFO) in the modern financial world. His counterparts at rival firms are earning record returns by investing in subprime mortgages. Economists trumpet studies showing that banks' income is boosted by practices he questions, including:

- Making more subprime mortgages
- Making more of the worst mortgages such as "Ninja" loans (no verification of income, job or assets), also known as "liars' loans"
- Making subprime loans at particularly high interest rates—which draws in the riskiest borrowers because only the worst credit risks and frauds will apply
- Making loans as quickly as possible
- Growing as quickly as possible
- Reducing internal controls against fraud
- Making loans in cities known to be "hot spots" for mortgage fraud
- Qualifying borrowers by offering "teaser" interest rates that will soon increase substantially

Big 8 audit firm to give them "clean" GAAP (or Generally Accepted Accounting Principles, the official standard of review in the U.S. accounting industry) opinions for false financial statements.

Economists, in turn, relied on *reported* accounting profits and share prices (which rose along with reported profits) to determine whether a given S&L was well run. But relying on reported accounting earnings or stock prices *must* lead to perverse results when a wave of looting control frauds is expanding. Thanks to their fraudulent accounting, whatever strategies control frauds follow will look profitable, and hence praiseworthy. In the S&Ls, this led economists to praise (1) domination by an owner/CEO; (2) extremely rapid growth; (3) changes of control; and (4) large investments in acquisition, development, and contruction (ADC) loans and direct investments. Lo and behold, these factors turned out to characterize the worst failures. In other words, standard econometrics techniques led economists to praise that which was fraudulent and fatal. The error was so great that they identified the worst S&L in the nation as the best.

Worse, economists persist in the same error. During the recent expansion of the even larger wave of looting control frauds such as Enron, economists touted (1) conflicts of interest at the top audit firms (which they euphemistically restyled as "synergies"); (2) using a top-tier auditor; (3) rapid growth; and (4) granting the CEO greater stock options as positive factors that were leading to increased profits and higher share prices. It was only after the looters began to collapse that variables like these reversed their sign (from a positive to a negative correlation) and displayed their true relationship to business failure. Economists are doomed to repeat these mistakes until they adopt statistical techniques that cannot be gamed by accounting fraud.

> - Making loans in areas with rapidly inflating housing bubbles
> - Purchasing and holding in portfolio high-yield CDOs (collateralized debt obligations, the investment instruments backed by bundles of mortgages and other loans, often of high risk)
> - Keeping minimal reserves against losses
>
> When a housing bubble is expanding, these practices dramatically increase fees and other noninterest income, minimize expenses, and produce relatively few losses. (Losses remain low as long as house prices are rising because borrowers who get in trouble can sell their house for more than they owe or else refinance based on its market value.) Note that this pretty income picture requires accounting and securities fraud, though: reserving properly for the future losses inherent in subjecting the financial institution to this vastly increased default risk would remove the fictional accounting gain.
>
> The combination of dramatically increased revenue, moderately reduced expenses, and minimal loss means that financial institutions that invest heavily in subprime mortgages and CDOs must report record profits while the bubble is hyperinflating.
>
> So what is our honest CFO to do? If she does not follow the pack, her company will report substantially lower income. Its stock price will fall relative to its rivals. The CEO's and CFO's compensation and wealth will fall sharply as raises disappear, bonuses decline, and the value of their shares and stock options falls. The CFO may be fired.
>
> The upshot is that modern compensation systems and the short-term perspective of investors and senior managers all result in perverse incentives to make grossly imprudent investments in those assets experiencing the worst bubbles. This creates a destructive cycle in which large numbers of financial institutions follow the same dysfunctional strategy, which in turn extends and inflates the bubble and produces even more accounting control frauds.

The Economists' War against Banking Regulation

In keeping with their skewed analysis of the recent wave of bank failures and banking crises, banking economists, including those at the World Bank and the IMF, have been waging a war against banking regulation. It is a curious assault that rests on implicit and false dichotomies between market and regulation and between types of regulation.

The World Bank economists recognize that regulation is vital to mandate accurate disclosure of corporate financial information and aid private market enforcement, but appear to believe that regulatory strength is unnecessary to induce banks to provide accurate information. That view is illogical and incorrect. Obtaining accurate information about banks is the heart of banking examination. Regulators use their powers primarily to pry out accurate information from the fraudulent; control frauds do not cooperate voluntarily.

Economists' rationale for opposing strong banking regulators typically rests on public choice theory, which holds that the actors in political systems act to maximize their own self-interest. This analysis paints politicians as corrupt and regulators as "captured" by the industries they are supposed to be regulating. World Bank economist Thorsten Beck and his colleagues summed up this view in 2003 and 2006 working papers:

> Politicians may induce banks to divert the flow of credit to politically connected firms, or powerful banks may "capture" politicians and induce official supervisors to act in the best interest of banks … .

> Government solutions to overcome market failures … have been proven wrong in Bangladesh as across the developed and developing world. … Indeed, powerful regulators are worse than futile—they are corrupt and harmful.

Again, this analysis is nonsensical. If banks can dominate politicians and strong regulators, they can certainly dominate the design of the disclosure standards they face. In that case, pursuant to the economists' own logic, the banks will submit, and politicians beholden to them will permit, deceptive financial reports that grossly overstate banks' value. (This has, in fact, been done in many cases.) Accounting fraud, in turn, renders markets deeply inefficient and causes private market discipline to become perverse. The looters report record profits. Credit is supposed to flow to the most profitable banks. So private markets *aid* the CEOs looting their banks by providing them with the funds to expand rapidly. Again, the failure to understand bank accounting fraud mechanisms, which have been well explained by Akerlof and Romer, leads to a deeply flawed analysis. (In lieu of Akerlof and Romer, the anti-regulation economists frequently cite work sponsored by Michael Milken's institute. Milken was the notorious junk-bond king and looter who caused large losses during the S&L crisis by recruiting and funding several of the worst control frauds, such as Charles Keating. Today, Milken's institute blames the S&L debacle on regulation and seeks to rehabilitate his reputation.)

This overarching logical error, their hostility to democracy, and their view of public officials as inevitably rapacious leads economists to a claim that only *private* parties should exert discipline against banks. The view has a number of problems. First, it is overstated. Regulators in some nations do resist political pressure. In the S&L crisis, many regulators did their job despite intense political pressure and saved over a trillion dollars in the process. On the other hand: if, over time, people are taught to believe that it is normal and rational for public officials to be rapacious, this can become a self-fulfilling prophecy as those who aim to enrich themselves sign on to become officials.

Moreover, the argument proves too much. If the banks (or politicians) are powerful enough to act illegitimately *through* regulators, they are powerful enough to act illegitimately *without* regulators to achieve the same result. The argument is also based on a fundamental misunderstanding of control frauds. It is not the "powerful banks" Beck and his coauthors refer to that put pressure on regulators or politicians—it is the CEOs or their agents who do. They do not coerce regulators "to act in the best interest of banks." They coerce them in an attempt to act to help the CEO loot the bank.

In fact, the evidence shows that private parties are *more* subject to capture than public officials. Looting control frauds are routinely able to get top-tier audit firms to give their blessing to massive accounting fraud. The ratings agencies do no better against control fraud. Our most prestigious law firms have helped CEOs loot and destroy their clients. Private deposit insurance funds for thrifts used to exist in many states. None do now. The Maryland, Ohio, and Utah funds were each destroyed by the very first thrift that collapsed in their state thanks to control fraud. No private insurer made more than a feeble effort to exercise discipline. Instead, they acted as boosters for the CEOs who looted and destroyed their own thrifts and brought down the insurance funds with them.

Finally, the empirical studies on banking regulation rely on coding of data by economists who typically oppose regulation, rendering the results unreliable. The risks of subjective bias are acute. There is no objective measure of "strong" regulation, or capture, or "rent seeking behavior." We know that economists have claimed that the Bank Board under Chairman Edwin Gray was captured during the S&L crisis. Not so. In fact, *private* experts were routinely captured by the S&L control frauds. Plus, the studies focus on formal supervisory power, yet informal banking supervision is widespread and often a regulator's most effective tool.

Overall, empirical studies find that better quality regulation (again, to be fair, a subjective concept) reduces banking losses.

International Convergence

Despite the flawed logic and lack of empirical support for their views, conventional banking economists, including those at the World Bank, continue to voice opposition to the creation of strong supervisory agencies. For now, however, their call has been rejected.

In the 1980s, the U.S. government reacted to Japan's emergence as the new (apparent) dominant financial power by claiming that Japan gained an unfair advantage because its banks were permitted to operate with lower capital reserves. If all other factors are held constant, a bank held to a lower capital reserve requirement can grow more quickly, lend more cheaply, and finance greater economic growth. Complaining that the playing field was not level, the United States insisted on an international agreement to set minimum bank capital standards. The U.S. effort succeeded in 1988, when the largest industrial nations adopted the Basel Accord. More recently, the accord was revised and expanded ("Basel II") to include more closely calibrated minimum capital requirements as well as a supervisory strategy of "prompt corrective action" against banks that fail to meet the capital requirements and a strategy to make private market discipline more effective by requiring banks to disclose more information.

The Basel Accord was a major step towards greater international uniformity of banking regulation ("convergence") among developed nations. The expansion of the European Union is another major force for convergence, as candidate nations must adopt modern banking laws and regulatory structures meeting the EU's minimum standards.

Banks are also subject to an increasing number of international treaties designed to restrict money laundering and bribery. There are, however, very few enforcement actions or prosecutions, so enforcement does not appear to be effective at this time. In addition, offshore banks remain an enormous loophole limiting the effectiveness of convergence.

New banking crises have diminished substantially in nations complying with the Basel accords. Of course, it is too early to judge whether the Basel process is responsible for this success. However, we do have cross-country evidence showing that weak regulation leads to recurrent waves of control fraud. Tests of Basel's effectiveness by one of the World Bank economists find positive relationships between stronger regulation and bank health. (These tests employed a methodology that posed less risk of subjective bias by the economists conducting the studies, but they remain inherently subjective.)

The economists' frustration, however, is understandable. They are skilled research scientists for whom econometric studies are the epitome of proof. Contrary case studies are mere "anecdotal evidence" that are fully encompassed within their data and, therefore, require no refutation. Moreover, their worldview is shaped by public choice theory. They view banking regulators as corrupt, "rent seeking" parasites who merely pretend to virtue. Alternatively, in their "capture" model, regulators are cowards who roll over to aid the control frauds. They have not been banking regulators, so they are uncontaminated and can see the truth as the empirical data reveal it to them.

Regulators, however, dominate much of the Basel process. They view the economists' disdain as an inaccurate and insulting caricature that indicates their ignorance of the real-world banking business. Regulators tend to believe in their experiences, which overwhelmingly teach that control frauds exploit regulatory weaknesses and that normally honest, sober bankers act like frat boys on spring break during financial bubbles. Imprudent lending is the norm in bubbles. Regulators have seen many econometric "proofs" of propositions they know to be false from experience. Some of them have a reasonably sophisticated understanding of the illusion of precision in empirical work and the many opportunities for subjective coding to lead even the best scholars into error. To date, the regulators have staved off the economists' war against banking regulation, and even the World Bank's economists have had to concede that the *initial* results of the Basel process are extremely positive.

Basel II does have a worrying component. It encourages the large banks to value their assets (which implicitly means evaluating their risk) using their own proprietary models. It is easy for these models to be designed so as to dramatically overstate asset values. The problem is compounded by the nature of proprietary models: they are secret, complex, and (perhaps) subject to frequent adjustment. That makes them a nightmare to try to regulate. And in what is essentially a form of control fraud, modern compensation systems, especially in the United States, create powerful incentives for top managers to overstate banks' asset values in order to puff up their own pay packages. Such abuse is so common that instead of "mark to market," the usual term for bringing the valuation of an asset into line with its market price, the process is often known to insiders as "mark to myth."

In the United States, the word "deregulation" still has a positive ring for many despite the disastrous results of this country's experiment in loosening the reins on the banking industry. So perhaps it is ironic that it was the United States that instigated an international effort to develop convergent banking regulations worldwide. International convergence is moving forward, and for now the pace of new financial crises has slowed. The Basel process is indeed leveling the playing field among financial services companies around the world. But what kind of field will emerge? Does the Basel process offer any hope of reshaping the new world of banking into one that better meets consumer needs and better serves the broader public interest? If the banking economists, with their ideological commitment to oppose any regulation, are kept at bay, then at least we may find out. ❑

Sources: C.E.V Borio and R. Filosa, "The Changing Borders of Banking: Trends and Implications," *BIS Working Paper* 23, 10/94; Center for International Private Enterprise, "Financial Reform: Paving the Way for Growth and Democracy," *Economic Reform Today*, 1995; J. Bisignano, "Precarious Credit Equilibria: Reflections on the Asian Financial Crisis," *BIS Working Papers*, 3/99; W. K. Black, The Best Way to Rob a Bank is to Own One, 2005; L.J. White, T*he S&L Debacle: Public Policy Lessons for Bank and Thrift Regulation*, 1991; Federal Home Loan Bank Board, "Agenda for Reform: A Report on Deposit Insurance," 1983; K. Calavita et al., *Big Money Crime: Fraud and Politics in the Savings and Loan Industry*, 1997; W. K. Black et al., "The Savings and Loan Debacle of the 1980's: White-Collar Crime or Risky Business?" *Law & Policy* 17; G. Akerlof and P. M. Romer, "Looting: The Economic Underworld of Bankruptcy for Profit," *Brookings Papers on Econ Activity*, 1993; M. Mayer, *The Greatest-Ever Bank Robbery*, 1990; T. Curry and L. Shibut, "The Cost of the Savings and Loan Crisis: Truth and Consequences," *FDIC Banking Review*, Fall 2000; W. K. Black, "Reexamining the Law-and-Economics Theory of Corporate Governance," *Challenge*, 1993; C-J Lindgren et al., "Bank Soundness and Macroeconomic Policy," IMF, 1996; T. M. Hoenig, "Exploring the Macro-Prudential Aspects of Financial Sector Supervision," speech to the Meeting for Heads of Supervision, BIS, Basel, Switzerland, 4/27/04; V. A. Atanasov et al., "The Anatomy of Financial Tunneling in an Emerging Market," McCombs School of Business, Research Paper Fin-04-06; N. Passas, "The Genesis of the BCCI Scandal," *J Law and Soc*, 3/66; P. L. Zweig, *Belly Up: The Collapse of the Penn Square Bank*, 1986; R. J. Herring, "BCCI & Barings: Bank Resolutions Complicated by Fraud and Global Corporate Structure"; H.R. Davia et al., *Accountant's Guide to Fraud Detection and Control* (2nd ed.), 2000;

P. Blustein, "The Chastening: Inside the Crisis that Rocked the Global Financial System and Humbled the IMF," *Public Aff,* 2001; W. K. Black, "A Tale of Two Crises," Kravis Leadership Inst Rvw, Fall 2002; Federal Reserve Bank of San Francisco, *Economic Letter,* 3/06; B. H. Soral et al., "Fraud, banking crisis, and regulatory enforcement: Evidence from micro-level transactions data," *European Journal of Law and Econ,* 4/06; J. L. Pierce, *The Future of Banking,* 1991; E. J. Kane, *The Gathering Crisis in Federal Deposit Insurance,* MIT Univ Press, 1985; A. Demirguc-Kunt and E. Detragiache, "Does Deposit Insurance Increase Banking System Stability? An Empirical Investigation," *J Monetary Econ,* 10/02; D. Pyle, review of "The Gathering Crisis in Federal Deposit Insurance" in *J Econ Lit,* 9/86; J. Santos, "Bank Capital Regulation in Contemporary Banking Theory: A review of the literature," in *Financial Markets, Institutions & Instruments,* 2001; A.B. Ashcraft, "Does the Market Discipline Banks? New Evidence from Regulatory Capital Mix," 10/2/06; T. Beck et al., "Bank Supervision and Corporate Finance," *World Bank Policy Research Working Paper,* 5/03; D. R. Brumbaugh, Jr, *Thrifts Under Siege: Restoring Order to American Banking,* 1988; T. Beck et al., "Bank Supervision and Corruption in Lending," 9/3/05; A. Demirguc-Kunt et al., "Banking on the Principles: Compliance with Basel Core Principles and Bank Soundness," *IMF Working Paper* 10/06; R. La Porta et al., "Related Lending," *Quarterly J Econ,* 2003; S. Johnson et al., "Tunnelling," Am Econ Assoc Papers & Proceedings, 2000; R. Haselmann et al., "How Law Affects Lending," *Columbia Law and Economics Working Paper,* 9/06; J. D. Edwards and J. H. Godwin, "Why Sound Accounting Standards Count," *Econ Reform Today,* 1995; J. R. Barth, *The Great Savings and Loan Debacle,* 1991.

Article 2.3

THE SAD FUTURE OF BANKING
Reforms fail to address the "control fraud" that caused the financial crisis.

BY WILLIAM K. BLACK
October 2010

A truly amazing thing has happened in banking. After the worst financial crisis in 75 years sparked the "Great Recession," we have

- Failed to identify the real causes of the crisis;
- Failed to fix the defects that caused the crisis;
- Failed to hold the CEOs, professionals, and anti-regulators who caused the crisis accountable—even when they committed fraud;
- Bailed out the largest and worst financial firms with massive public funds;
- Covered up banking losses and failures—impairing any economic recovery;
- Degraded our integrity and made the banking system even more encouraging of fraud;
- Refused to follow policies that have proved extremely successful in past crises;
- Made the systemically dangerous institutions (SDIs) even more dangerous;
- Made our financial system even more parasitic, harming the real economy;

And pronounced this travesty a brilliant success.

The Bush and Obama administrations have made an already critically flawed financial system even worse. The result is that the banking industry's future is bad for banking, terrible for the real economy, horrific for the public—and wonderful for the top executives at the largest banks. This is significantly insane. It appears that we will need to suffer another great depression before we are willing to put aside the crippling dogmas that have so degraded the financial system, the real economy, democracy, and the ethical standards of private and public elites.

The Economics Blindfold

Why did most of the experts neither foresee nor understand the forces in the U.S. banking industry that caused this meltdown? The short answer is: their dogmatic belief in neoclassical economic theory that is impervious to the facts, or what I like to call theoclassical economics.

Neoclassical economics is premised on the asserted effectiveness of private market discipline. This (oxymoronic) discipline is the basis for the "efficient markets" and "efficient contracts" hypotheses that are the pillars of faith supporting modern finance theory and much of neoclassical microeconomics. Collectively, these hypotheses lead to absolute faith that markets exclude fraud. "A rule against fraud is not an essential or even necessarily an important ingredient of securities markets," wrote eminent corporate law scholars Frank Easterbrook and Daniel Fischel in their 1991 The Economic Structure of Corporate Law, in a typical statement of that faith.

How are markets supposed to exclude fraud? Easterbrook and Fischel offer two reasons. The first, a circular argument, lies in theoclassical economists' core belief that markets are by nature efficient. Markets that allow frauds cannot be efficient. Therefore, markets must exclude fraud.

The other argument rests on "signaling" theory. The logical premise is that honest firms have a financial incentive to signal to investors and creditors that they are honest. The false premise is that honest firms have the unique ability to signal that they are honest. Easterbrook and Fischel claim that there are three signals of honesty that only honest firms can transmit: hiring a top-tier audit firm, having the CEO own substantial stock in the firm, and operating with extreme leverage, i.e., a high ratio of debt to capital. The reality, which Fischel knew before he co-authored the treatise, was that firms engaging in so-called control fraud can mimic each of these signals. Control fraud occurs when the executives at a seemingly legitimate firm use their control to loot the firm and its shareholders and creditors. In banking, accounting is the weapon of choice for looting. Accounting control frauds have shown the consistent ability to get "clean" accounting opinions from top tier audit firms; their CEOs use their stock ownership to loot the firm; and they love to borrow extensively, as that allows them to loot the firm's creditors.

In fact, the claim that markets inherently exclude fraud runs contrary to all of our experience with securities markets. The role of epidemics of accounting control frauds in driving recent financial crises is well documented. The national commission that investigated the causes of the savings and loan debacle found that at the "typical large failure," "fraud was invariably present." Similarly, the Enron and WorldCom scandals were shown to be accounting control frauds. Savings and loan regulators used their hard-won understanding of accounting control fraud to stop a developing pattern of fraud in California in 1990-1991, involving S&Ls making so-called liar's loans. We recognized that making mortgage loans without adequate underwriting creates intense "adverse selection," i.e., it means more lending to borrowers who are not creditworthy, and that such lending was guaranteed to result in high reported (albeit fictional) income and high real losses. Theoclassical economists, however, refused to acknowledge these frauds because recognizing the existence of control fraud would challenge the assumptions underlying their faith-based economic theories.

This economic dogma was so dominant that it drove regulatory policy in the United States, Europe, and Japan during the last three decades. Regulations ignored control fraud and assumed that paper profits produced by fraud were real. The result, from the mid-1990s on, was regulatory complacency endorsed by economists who actually praised the worst of the emerging control frauds because of their high reported profits. So it is no surprise that the recent U.S. banking crisis was driven by an epidemic of lending fraud, primarily mortgage lenders making millions of "liar's loans" annually. According to Credit Suisse, for instance, 49% of all mortgage originations in 2006 were stated-income loans, meaning loans based on applicants' self-reported incomes with no verification. MARI, the Mortgage Bankers Association experts on fraud, warned in 2006 that these loans caused endemic fraud:

> Stated income and reduced documentation loans … are open invitations to fraudsters. It appears that many members of the industry have little historical appreciation for the havoc created by low-doc/no-doc products that were the rage in the early 1990s. Those loans produced hundreds of millions of dollars in losses for their users.
>
> One of MARI's customers recently reviewed a sample of 100 stated income loans upon which they had IRS Forms 4506. When the stated incomes were compared to the IRS figures, the resulting differences were dramatic. Ninety percent of the stated incomes were exaggerated by 5% or more. More disturbingly, almost 60% of the stated amounts were exaggerated by more than 50%. These results suggest that the stated income loan deserves the nickname used by many in the industry, the "liar's loan."

Why would scores of lenders specialize in making liar's loans after being warned by their own exports and even by the FBI that such loans led to endemic fraud? (Not that they needed any warnings. Bankers have known for centuries that underwriting is essential to survival in mortgage lending. Even the label "liar's loan," widely used in the industry, shows that bankers knew such loans were commonly fraudulent.) How could these fraudulent loans be sold to purportedly the most sophisticated underwriters in the history of the world at grossly inflated values blessed by the world's top audit firms? How could hundreds of thousands of fraudulent loans be pooled into securities, the now-infamous collateralized debt obligations (CDOs), and receive "AAA" ratings from the top rating agencies? How could markets that are supposed to exclude all fraud instead accommodate millions of fraudulent loans that hyper-inflated the largest financial bubble in history and triggered the Great Recession?

The answer is that making bad loans allows lenders to grow extremely rapidly and charge premium yields. This maximizes reported accounting income, which in turn boosts executive compensation and optimizes looting. The financial system is riddled with incentives so perverse that it is criminogenic—it creates fraud epidemics instead of preventing fraud. When compensation levels for banking executives and professionals are very large and based substantially on reported short-term income, financial firms become superb vehicles for control fraud. Add in deregulation and desupervision, and the result is an environment ripe for a fraud epidemic.

Accounting is the weapon of choice for financial sector control frauds. The recipe for a lender to maximize (fictional) reported accounting income has four ingredients:

1. Extremely rapid growth
2. Lending regardless of borrower creditworthiness, at premium yields
3. Extreme leverage
4. Minimal loss reserves

The first two ingredients are related. A U.S. housing lender operates in a mature, reasonably competitive industry. A mortgage lender cannot grow extremely rapidly by making high quality mortgages. If it tried to do so, it would have to cut its yield substantially in order to gain market share. Its competitors would respond by cutting their yields and the result would be modest growth and a serious loss of yield, reducing reported profits. Any lender, however, can guarantee extremely rapid growth and charge borrowers a premium yield simply by making loans to borrowers who most likely cannot repay them. Worse, hundreds of lenders can follow this same recipe because there are tens of millions of potential homebuyers in the United States who would not able to repay their loans. Indeed, when hundreds of firms follow the same recipe, they hyper-inflate the resultant financial bubble, which in turn allows borrowers to refinance their loans and thereby delay their defaults for years.

Economists George Akerlof and Paul Romer explained in 1993 that accounting fraud is a "sure thing" and explained why it caused bubbles to hyper-inflate, then burst. Note that the same recipe that produces record fictional income in the short-term eventually produces catastrophic real losses. The lender will fail (unless it is bailed out or able to sell to the "greater fool"), but with their compensation largely based on reported income, the senior officers can walk away wealthy. This paradox—the CEO prospers by causing the firm's collapse—explains Akerlof and Romer's title, Looting: The Economic Underworld of Bankruptcy for Profit.

Senior executives can also use their ability to hire, promote, compensate, and fire to suborn employees, officers, and outside professionals. As Franklin Raines, chairman and CEO of Fannie Mae, explained to Businessweek in 2003:

> Investment banking is a business that's so denominated in dollars that the temptations are great, so you have to have very strong rules. My experience is where there is a one-to-one relation between if I do X, money will hit my pocket, you tend to see people doing X a lot. You've got to be very careful about that. Don't just say: "If you hit this revenue number, your bonus is going to be this." It sets up an incentive that's overwhelming. You wave enough money in front of people, and good people will do bad things.

Raines knew what he was talking about: he installed a compensation system at Fannie Mae that produced precisely these perverse incentives among his staff and made him wealthy by taking actions that harmed Fannie Mae.

In an earlier work, Akerlof had explained how firms that gained a competitive advantage through fraud could cause a "Gresham's" dynamic in which bad ethics drove good ethics from the marketplace. The national commission that investigated the savings and loan debacle documented this criminogenic dynamic: "[A]busive operators of S&L[s] sought out compliant and cooperative accountants. The result was a sort of "Gresham's Law" in which the bad professionals forced out the good." The same dynamic was documented by N.Y. Attorney General Andrew Cuomo's 2007 investigation of appraisal fraud, which found that Washington Mutual blacklisted appraisers who refused to inflate appraisals. An honest secured lender would never inflate, or permit the inflation of, appraisals.

Failure to Respond

The U.S. government's response to the meltdown has been not merely inadequate, but actually perverse. The Bush and Obama administrations' banking regulators have left frauds in charge of failed banks and covered up the banks' losses, allowed the behemoths of the industry to become even larger and more dangerous, and passed a "reform" law that fails to mandate the most critical reforms.

In March 2009, Congress, with the explicit encouragement of Federal Reserve Board Chairman Bernanke and the implicit acceptance of the Obama administration, successfully extorted the Financial Accounting Standards Board on behalf of the banking industry to force it to change the banking rules so that banks did not have to recognize losses on their bad assets until they sold them. Normal accounting rules sensibly require banks to recognize losses on bad loans when the problems with the loans are not "temporary." The losses at issue in the recent crisis were caused by system-wide fraud and the collapse of the largest financial bubble in world history. They were not temporary—moreover, they were (and are) massive. If banks had recognized these losses as they were required to do under pre-existing accounting rules, many of them would have had to report that they were unprofitable, badly undercapitalized, or even insolvent.

Gimmicking the accounting rules so bankers could lie about their asset values has caused the usual severe problems. First, it allows CEOs to pretend that unprofitable banks are profitable and so continue to pay themselves massive bonuses. This is not only unfair; it contributes to a broadly criminogenic environment. Second, it leads banks to hold onto bad home loans and other assets at grossly inflated prices, preventing markets from clearing and prolonging the recession. This is the Japanese scenario that led to the country's "lost decade" (now extended). Third, it makes it harder for regulators to supervise vigorously, should they try to do so, because many regulatory powers are triggered only when losses occur with the resulting failure to meet capital requirements. Indeed, the assault on honest accounting was launched with the express purpose of evading the Prompt Corrective Action law, passed in 1991 on the basis of bitter experience: when savings-and-loan CEOs who had looted "their" institutions were allowed to remain in control of them by using fraudulent accounting, the losses and the fallout of the S&L crisis kept growing. Fourth, it embraces dishonesty as an official policy. Indeed, it implies that the solution to the accounting fraud that massively inflated asset valuations is to change the accounting rules to encourage the massive inflation of those same asset values. Effective regulation is impossible without regulatory integrity; lying about asset values destroys integrity.

Even in the case of the roughly 20 massive U.S. financial institutions considered "too big to fail," the public policy response has been perverse. (The Bush and Obama administrations and their economists have claimed that if any of these giant banks were to fail, it would cause a systemic global crisis, hence the "too big to fail" moniker. I am dubious that a systemic crisis would inevitably result, but I agree that these banks are so large that they pose a systemic danger to the global economy.) The terminology itself demonstrates how economists err in their analysis—and how much they identify with the CEOs who helped cause the Great Recession. They refer to the largest banks as "systemically important institutions," as if these banks deserved gold stars. By the prevailing logic, however, the massive banks are the opposite. They are ticking time bombs that can take down the global financial system if they fail. So "systemically dangerous institutions," or SDIs, would be more apt.

It should be a top public policy priority to end the ability of any single bank to pose a global systemic risk. That means that the SDIs should be forbidden to grow, required to shrink over a five-year period to a size at which they no longer pose a systemic risk, and intensively supervised until they shrink to that size. In particular, regulation of the SDIs must end the existing perverse incentives that are so criminogenic—executive compensation systems tied to short-term reported income, the accounting cover-up which has gutted the Prompt Corrective Action law, the use of compensation and hiring and firing powers to create a "Gresham's" dynamic among the SDIs' personnel and outside professionals, and the use of political contributions to impair effective regulation. These reforms are vital for all banks but particularly urgent for the SDIs, with their potential to cause massive damage.

Instead, the opposite has been done. Both administrations have responded to the financial crisis by allowing (indeed, encouraging) SDIs, even insolvent ones, to acquire other failed financial firms and become even larger and more systemically dangerous to the global economy. The SDIs' already perverse incentives were made worse by giving them a bailout plus the accounting cover-up of their losses on terms that made the U.S. Treasury and the Federal Reserve the "fools" in the market.

With small- and medium-size banks likely to continue to fail in high numbers due to residential and commercial real estate losses, the financial crisis has increased the long-term trend toward extreme concentration in the financial industry. The SDIs will pursue diverse business strategies. Some will continue their current strategy of borrowing short-term at extremely low interest rates and reinvesting the proceeds primarily in government bonds. They will earn material, not exceptional, profits but will do little to help the real economy recover. Others will invest in whatever asset category offers the best (often fictional) accounting income. They will drive the next U.S.-based crisis.

What about the long-awaited bank reform law, which Congress finally delivered in July 2010 in the form of the Dodd-Frank Act? The law does not address the fundamental factors that have caused recurrent, intensifying financial crises: fraud, accounting, executive and professional compensation, and regulatory failure. Instead, it deals primarily with the excuses Treasury Secretary Paulson and Federal Reserve Chairman Bernanke offered for their failures. The new law gives regulators (weak) authority to place a failing SDI in receivership. Paulson and Bernanke claimed they had no legal authority to place Lehman in receivership, but they did not place insolvent megabanks over which they had clear legal authority in receivership either. The Bush administration's problem was always a lack of regulatory will, not a lack of authority. The Dodd-Frank Act also creates a regulatory council that is supposed to identify systemic risks. The council, however, will be dominated by economists of the same theoclassical stripe who not only failed to identify the systemic risks that produced the modern financial crises that this essay discusses, but actually praised the criminogenic incentives that caused those crises. The most hopeful part of the Dodd-Frank Act is the creation of a bureau with the mission of protecting financial consumers. No one can predict at this juncture whether it will accomplish its mission.

The chief international reform, the Basel III accord, shares the fundamental deficiency of the Dodd-Frank Act. Dominated as they were by theoclassical economists, the Basel negotiations not surprisingly produced an agreement that ignores the underlying causes of the crisis. Instead, it focuses on one symptom of the crisis—extreme leverage, the third ingredient of the recipe for optimizing accounting control fraud. The remedy was to restore capital requirements to roughly the levels required under Basel I (Basel II eviscerated European banks' capital requirements). Fortunately, the U.S. did not fully implement the Basel II capital reserve reductions, which means that the leverage of non-fraudulent U.S. banks has been significantly lower than their European counterparts.

However, capital requirements only have meaning under honest accounting. Once one takes into account the fictional "capital" produced by the accounting fraud that first massively inflated asset values and now hides the losses—along with the revised accounting rules that will be exploited to create fictional income in the future—the irrelevance of the proposed Basel III capital requirements becomes clear.

If the Dodd-Frank Act of 2010 and the Basel III proposals are the limits of our response to the crisis, then the most probable outcome in the near- and medium-term is the Japanese scenario—a weak, delayed, and transitory recovery followed by periodic recessions. Banks will remain weak and a poor provider of capital for economic expansion.

With private market "discipline" having become criminogenic, the only hope for preventing the current crisis was vigorous regulation and supervision. Unfortunately, the dogmatic belief that markets automatically prevent fraud led to complacency and the appointment of anti-regulators chosen for their willingness to praise and serve their banking "customers." (The "reinventing government" initiative championed by former Vice President Al Gore and by George W. Bush when he was Texas' governor indeed instructed banking regulators to refer to bankers as their "customers.") President Obama has generally left in office, reappointed, or promoted the heads (or their "acting" successors) of the Office of the Comptroller of the Currency, the Office of Thrift Supervision, the Federal Reserve, the Federal Reserve Bank of New York, and the Federal Housing Finance Agency. Several of these leaders did not simply fail as federal regulators; they actually made things worse by aggressively preempting state regulatory efforts against fraudulent and predatory mortgage lenders.

None of the reforms to date addresses the fundamental criminogenic incentive structures that have produced recurrent, intensifying financial crises. True, liar's loans have been largely eliminated, and in 2008 the Federal Reserve finally used its regulatory authority under the Home Ownership and Equity Protection Act of 1994 to regulate mortgage bankers (after most of the worst ones had failed), but none of this came soon enough to contain the current crisis and none of it will prevent the next one. The accounting control frauds merely need to switch to a different asset category for a time. ❑

Sources: George A. Akerlof, "The Market for 'Lemons': Quality Uncertainty and the Market Mechanism," Quarterly Journal of Economics 84(3):488–500 (1970); George A. Akerlof and Paul G. Romer, "Looting: The Economic Underworld of Bankruptcy for Profit," in W. Brainard and G. Perry, eds., Brookings Papers on Economic Activity 2:1-73 (1993); William K. Black, "Reexamining the Law-and-Economics Theory of Corporate Governance," Challenge 46(2):22-40 (2003); William K. Black, The Best Way to Rob a Bank Is to Own One: How Corporate Executives and Politicians Looted the S&L Industry, Austin: University of Texas Press (2005); Frank Easterbrook and Daniel Fischel, The Economic Structure of Corporate Law, Cambridge, Mass.: Harvard University Press (1991); National Commission on Financial Institution Reform, Recovery and Enforcement (NCFIRRE), Origins and Causes of the S&L Debacle: A Blueprint for Reform, Washington, D.C.:Government Printing Office (1993).

Article 2.4

NOT TOO BIG ENOUGH
Where the big banks come from.

BY ROB LARSON
July/August 2010

The government bailout of America's biggest banks set off a tornado of public anger and confusion. When the House of Representatives initially rejected the bailout bill, the *Wall Street Journal* attributed it to "populist fury," and since then the public has remained stubbornly resentful over the bailout of those banks considered "too big to fail." Now, the heads of economic policy are trying to gracefully distance themselves from bailouts, claiming that future large-scale bank failures will be avoided by stronger regulation and higher insurance premiums.

Dealing with the collapse of these "systemically important banks" is a difficult policy issue, but the less-discussed issue is how the banking industry came to this point. If the collapse of just one of our $100 billion megabanks, Lehman Brothers, was enough to touch off an intense contraction in the supply of essential credit, we must know how some banks became "too big to fail" in the first place. The answer lies in incentives for bank growth. After the loosening of crucial industry regulations, these incentives have driven the enormous waves of bank mergers in the last thirty years.

Geographical Growth

Prior to the 1980s, American commercial banking was a small-scale affair. State-chartered banks were prohibited by state laws from running branches outside their home state, or sometimes even outside their home county. Nationally chartered banks were likewise limited, and federal law allowed interstate acquisitions only if a state legislature specifically decided to permit out-of-state banks to purchase local branches. No states allowed such acquisition until 1975, when Maine and other states began passing legislation allowing at least some interstate banking. The trend was capped in 1994 by the Riegle-Neal Act, which removed the remaining restrictions on interstate branching and allowed direct cross-state banking mergers.

This geographic deregulation allowed commercial banks to make extensive acquisitions, in state and out. When Wells Fargo acquired another large California bank, Crocker National, in 1986 it was the largest bank merger in U.S. history. Since "the regulatory light was green," a single banking company could now operate across the uniquely large U.S. market, opening up enormous new opportunities for economies of scale in the banking industry.

Economies of scale are savings that companies enjoy when they grow larger and produce more output. The situation is similar to a cook preparing a batch of cookies for a Christmas party, and then preparing a batch for New Year's while all the ingredients and materials are already out. Producing more output (cookies) in one afternoon is more efficient than taking everything out again later to make the New Year's batch separately. In enterprise, this corresponds to spreading the large costs of startup investment over more and more output, and is often thought of as lower per-unit costs as the level of production increases. In other words, there's less effort per cookie if you make them all at once. Economies of scale, when present in an industry, create a strong incentive for firms to grow larger, since profitability will improve. But they also give larger, established firms a valuable cost advantage over new competitors, which can put the brakes on competition.

Once unleashed by the policy changes, these economies of scale played a major role in the industry's seemingly endless merger activity. "In order to compete, you need scale," said a VP for Chemical Bank when buying a smaller bank in 1994. Of course, in 1996 Chemical would itself merge with Chase Manhattan Bank.

Economies of Scale in Banking and Finance

Economies of scale are savings that companies benefit from as they grow larger and produce more output. While common in many industries, in banking and finance, these economies drove bank growth after industry deregulation in the 1980s and 90s. Some of the major scale economies in banking are:

- **Spreading investment over more output.** With the growth in importance of large-scale computing power and sophisticated systems management, the costs of setting up a modern banking system are very large. However, as a firm grows it can "spread out" the cost of that initial investment over more product, so that its cost per unit decreases as more output is produced.

- **Consolidation of functions.** The modern workforce is no stranger to the mass firings of "redundant" staff after mergers and acquisitions. If one firm's payroll staff and computer systems can handle twice the employees with little additional expense, an acquired bank may see its payroll department harvest pink slips while the firm's profitability improves. When Citicorp merged with the insurance giant Travelers Group in 1998, the resulting corporation laid off over 10,000 workers—representing 6% of the combined company's total workforce and over $500 million in reduced costs for Citigroup. This practice can be especially lucrative in a country like the United States, with a fairly unregulated labor market where firms are quite free to fire. Despite the economic peril inflicted on workers and their families, this consolidation is key to increasing company efficiency post-merger. Beyond back-office functions, core profit operations may also benefit from consolidation. When Bank of America combined its managed mutual funds into a single fund, it experienced lower total costs, thanks to trimming overhead from audit and prospectus mailing expenses. Consolidating office departments in this fashion can yield savings of 40% of the cost base of the acquired bank.

- **Funding mix.** The "funding mix" used by banks refers to where banks get the capital they then package into loans. Smaller institutions, having only limited deposits from savers, must "purchase funds" by borrowing from other institutions. This increases the funding cost of loans for banks, but larger banks will naturally have access to larger pools of deposits from which to arrange loans. This funding cost advantage for larger banks relative to smaller ones represents another economy of scale.

- **Advertising.** The nature of advertising requires a certain scale of operation to be viable. Advertising can reach large numbers of potential customers, but if a firm is small or local, many of those customers will be too far afield to act on the marketing. Large firm size, and especially geographic reach, can make the returns on ad time worth the investment.

Spreading big investment costs over more output is the main source of generic economies of scale, and in banking, the large initial investments are in sophisticated computer systems. The cost of investing in new computer hardware and systems development is now recognized as a major investment obstacle for new banks, although once installed by banks large enough to afford them, they are highly profitable. The *Financial Times* describes how "the development of bulk computer processing and of electronic data transmission…has allowed banks to move their back office operations away from individual branches to large remote centers. This had helped to bring real economies of scale to banking, an industry which traditionally has seen diseconomies set in at a very modest scale."

Economies of scale are common in manufacturing, and in the wake of deregulation the banking industry was also able to exploit a number of them. Besides spreading out the cost of computer systems, economies of scale may be present in office consolidation, in the funding mix used by banks, and in advertising. (See sidebar.)

Industry-to-Industry Growth

BusinessWeek's analysis is that the banking industry "has produced large competitors that can take advantage of economies of scale…as regulatory barriers to interstate banking fell," although not until the banks could "digest their purchases." The 1990s saw hundreds of bank purchases annually and hundreds of billions in acquired assets.

But an additional major turn for the industry came with the Gramm-Leach-Bliley Act of 1999 (GLB), which further loosened restrictions on bank growth, this time not geographically but industry-to-industry. After earlier moves in this direction by the Federal Reserve, GLB allowed for the free combination of commercial banking, insurance, and the riskier field of investment banking. These had been separated by law for decades, on the grounds that the availability of commercial credit was too important to the overall economy to be tied to the volatile world of investment banking.

GLB allowed firms to grow further, through banks merging with insurers or investment banks. The world of commercial credit was widened, and financial mergers this time exploited economies of scope—where production of multiple products jointly is cheaper than producing them individually. As commercial banks, investment banks, and insurers have expanded into each others' fields in the wake of GLB, their different lines of business can benefit from single expenses—for example, banks perform research on loan recipients that can also be used to underwrite bond issues. Scope economies such as these allow the larger banks to both run a greater profit on a per-service basis and attract more business. Thanks to the convenience of "one stop shopping," Citigroup now does more business with big corporations, like IT giant Unisys, than its component firms did pre-merger.

Exploiting economies of scope to diversify product lines in this fashion can also help a firm by reducing its dependence on any one line of business. Bank of America weathered the stock market downturn of 2001 in part because its corporate debt underwriting business was booming. Smaller, more specialized banks can become "one-trick ponies" as the *Wall Street Journal* put it—outdone by larger competitors with low-cost diversification thanks to scope economies.

These economies of scope are parallel to the scale economies, since both required deregulatory policy changes to be unleashed. Traditionally, banking wasn't seen as an industry with the strong economies of scale seen in, say, manufacturing. But the deregulation and computerization of the industry have allowed these firms to realize returns to greater scale and wider scope, and this has been a main driver of the endless acquisitions in the industry in recent decades.

Market Power

The enormous proportions that the banking institutions have taken on following deregulation have meant serious consequences for market performance. A number of banks have reached sufficient size to exercise market power—the ability of firms to influence prices and to engage in anticompetitive behavior. The market power of our enormous banks allows them to take positions as price leaders in local markets, where large firms use their dominance to elevate prices (i.e., increase fees and rates on loans, and decrease interest rates on deposits). Large firms can do this because smaller firms may perceive that lowering their prices to take market share could be met by very drastic reductions in prices from the larger firm in retaliation. Large firms, having deeper pockets, may be able to withstand longer periods of operating at a loss than the smaller firms.

Small banks are likely to perceive that the colossal size and resources of the megabanks make them unprofitable to cross—better to follow along and charge roughly what the dominant, price-leading firm does. Empirical research by Federal Reserve Board senior economist Steven Pilloff supported this analysis, finding that the arrival of very large banks in local markets tended to increase bank profitability for reasons of price leadership, due to the larger banks' economies of scale and scope, financial muscle, and diversification.

Examples of the use of banking industry market power are easy to find. Several bills now circulating in Congress deal with the fees retail businesses pay to the banks and the credit card companies. When consumers make purchases with their Visas or MasterCards, an average of two cents of each dollar goes not to the retailer but to the credit card companies that run the payment network and the banks that supply the credit. These "interchange fees" bring in over $35 billion in profit in the United States alone, and they reflect the strong market power of the banks and credit card companies over the various big and small retailers. The 2% charge comes to about $31,000 for a typical convenience store, just below the average per-store yearly profit of $36,000, and this has driven a coalition of retailers to press for congressional action.

Visa has about 50% of the credit card market (including debit cards), and MasterCard has 25%, which grants them profound market power and strong bargaining positions. Federal Reserve Bank of Kansas City economists found the United States "maintains the highest interchange fees in the world, yet its costs should be among the lowest, given economies of scale and declining cost trends." The *Wall Street Journal*'s description was that "these fees…have also been paradoxically tending upward in recent years when the industry's costs due to technology and economies of scale have been falling." Of course, there's only a paradox if market power is omitted from the picture. The dominant size and scale economies of the banks and the credit card oligopoly allow for high prices to be sustained—bank muscle in action against a less powerful sector of the economy. The political action favored by the retailers includes proposals for committees to enact price ceilings or (interestingly) collective bargaining by the retailers. As is often the case, the political process is the reflection of the different levels and positions of power of various corporate institutions, and the maneuvering of their organizations.

Market power brings with it a number of other advantages. A powerful company is likely to have a widespread presence, make frequent use of advertising, and be able to raise its profile by contributing to community organizations like sports leagues. This allows the larger banks to benefit from stronger brand identity—their scale and resources make customers more likely to trust their services. This grants a further advantage in the form of customer tolerance of higher prices due to brand loyalty.

Political Clout

Crucially, large firms with market power are free to participate meaningfully in politics—using their deep pockets to invest in electoral campaigns and congressional lobbying. The financial sector is among the highest-contributing industries in the United States, with total 2008 campaign contributions approaching half a billion dollars, according to the Center For Public Integrity. So it's unsurprising that they receive so many favors from the government, since they fund the careers of the decision-making government personnel. This underlying reality is why influential Senator Dick Durbin said of Congress, "The banks own the place."

Finally, banks may grow so large by exploiting scale economies and market power that they become "systemically important" to the nation's financial system. In other words, the scale and interconnectedness of the largest banks is considered to have reached a point where an abrupt failure of one or more of them may have "systemic" effects—meaning the broader economic system will be seriously impaired. These "too big to fail" banks are the ones that were bailed out by act of Congress in the fall 2008. Once a firm becomes so enormous that the government must prevent its collapse for the good of the economy, it has the ultimate advantage of being free to take far greater risks. Riskier investments come with higher returns and profits, but the greater risk of collapse that accompanies them will be less intimidating to huge banks that have an implied government insurance policy.

Some analysts have expressed doubt that such firms truly are too large to let fail, and that the banks have pulled a fast one. It might be pointed out in this connection that in the past the banks themselves have put their money where their mouths are—they have paid out of pocket to rescue financial institutions they saw as too large and connected to fail. An especially impressive episode took place in 1998, when several of Wall Street's biggest banks and financiers agreed to billions in emergency loans to rescue Long Term Capital Management. LTCM was a high-profile hedge fund that borrowed enormous sums of capital to make billion-dollar gambles on financial markets.

America's biggest banks aren't in the habit of forking over $3.5 billion of good earnings, but they had loaned heavily to LTCM and feared losing their money if the fund went under. The Federal Reserve brought the bankers together, and in the end, they paid up to bail out their colleagues, and the *Wall Street Journal* reported that it was the Fed's "clout, together with the self-interest of several big firms that already had lent billions of dollars to Long-Term Capital, that helped fashion the rescue." Interestingly, the banks insisted on real equity in the firm they were pulling out of the fire, and they gained a 90% stake in the hedge fund. Comparing this to the less-valuable "preferred stock" the government settled for in its 2008 bailout package of the large banks is instructive. The banks also got a share of control in the firm they rescued, again in stark contrast to the public bailout of some of the same banks.

Even Bigger?

In fact, the financial crisis and bailout led only to further concentration of the industry. The crisis gave stronger firms an opportunity to pick up sicker ones in another "wave of consolidation," as *BusinessWeek* put it. And a large part of the government intervention itself involved arranging hasty purchases of failing giants by other giants, orchestrated by the Federal Reserve. For example, the Fed helped organize the purchase of Bear Stearns by Chase in March 2008 and the purchase of Wachovia by Wells Fargo in December 2008. Even the bailout's "capital infusions" were used for further mergers and acquisitions by several recipients. The Treasury Department was "using the bailout bill to turn the banking system into the oligopoly of giant national institutions," as the *New York Times* reported.

The monumental growth of the largest banks owes a lot to the industry's economies of scale and scope, once regulations were relaxed so firms could exploit them. While certainly not unique to finance, these dynamics have brought the banks to such enormous size that their bad bets can put the entire economy in peril. Banking therefore offers an especially powerful case for the importance of these economies and the role of market power, since it's left the megabanks holding all the cards.

In fact, many arguments between defenders of the market economy and its critics center on the issue of competition vs. power—market boosters reliably insist that markets mean efficient competition, where giants have no inherent advantage over small, scrappy firms. However, the record in banking clearly shows that banks have enjoyed a variety of real benefits from growth. The existence of companies of great size and power is a quite natural development in many industries, due to the appeal of returns to scale and power. This is why firms end up with enough power to influence government policy, or such absurd size that they can blackmail us for life support.

And leave us crying all the way to the bank. ❑

Sources: Judith Samuelson and Lynn Stout, "Are Executives Paid Too Much?" *Wall Street Journal,* February 26, 2009; Tom Braithwaite, "Geithner Presses Congress for Action on Reform," *Financial Times,* September 23, 2009; Phillip Zweig, "Intrastate Mergers Between Banking Giants Might Not Be Out of the Question Anymore," *Wall Street Journal,* March 25, 1986; Bruce Knecht, "Chemical Banking plans acquisition of Margaretten," *Wall Street Journal,* May 13, 1994;

Eric Weiner, "Banks Will Post Good Quarterly Results," *Wall Street Journal*, January 10, 1997; Gabriella Stern, "Four Big Regionals To Consolidate Bank Operations," *Wall Street Journal*, July 22, 1992; "Pressure for change grows," *Financial Times*, September 27, 1996; Tracy Corrigan and John Authers, "Citigroup To Take $900 million charge: Cost-cutting Program to Result in Loss of 10,400 Jobs," *Financial Times*, December 16, 1998; Eleanor Laise, "Mutual-Fund Mergers Jump Sharply," *Wall Street Journal*, March 9, 2006; Steven Pilloff, "Banking, commerce and competition under the Gramm-Leach-Bliley Act," *The Antitrust Bulletin*, Spring 2002; David Humphrey, "Why Do Estimates of Bank Scale Economies Differ?" *Economic Review* of Federal Reserve Bank of Richmond, September/October 1990, note four; Michael Mandel and Rich Miller, "Productivity: The Real Story," *BusinessWeek*, November 5, 2001; John Yang, "Fed Votes to Give 7 Bank Holding Firms Additional Power in Securities Sector," *Wall Street Journal*, July 16, 1987; "Banking Behemoths—What Happens Next: Many companies Like to Shop Around For Their Providers of Financial Services," *Wall Street Journal*, September 14, 2000; Carrick Mollenkamp and Paul Beckett, "Diverse Business Portfolios Boost Banks' Bottom Lines," *Wall Street Journal*, July 17, 2001; *Journal of Financial Services Research*, "Does the Presence of Big Banks Influence Competition in Local Markets?" May 1999; "Credit-Card Wars," *Wall Street Journal*, March 29, 2008; *Economic Review* of the Federal Reserve Bank of Kansas City, "Interchange Fees in Credit and Debit Card Markets: What Role for Public Authorities," January-March 2006; "Credit Where It's Due," *Wall Street Journal*, January 12, 2006; Keith Bradsher, "In One Pocket, Out the Other," *New York Times*, November 25, 2009; Center For Public Integrity, Finance/Insurance/Real Estate: Long-Term Contribution Trends, opensecrests.org; Dean Baker, "Banks own the U.S. government," *Guardian*, June 30, 2009; Anita Raghavan and Mitchell Pacelle, "To the Rescue? A Hedge Fun Falters, So the Fed Persuades Big Banks to Ante Up," *Wall Street Journal*, September 24, 1998; Theo Francis, "Will Bank Rescues Mean Fewer Banks?" *BusinessWeek*, November 25, 2008; Joe Nocera, "So When Will Banks Give Loans?" *New York Times*, October 25, 2008.

Article 2.5

BONANZAS AS USUAL
The megabanks' denial about bad loans unleashes profit and pay.

BY ROB LARSON
November/December 2010

Since the catastrophic bank collapses of 2008 and the government rescue of the finance industry, Wall Street has staged a dramatic comeback. Since the bailout, profits are up, capital reserves are up, stock prices are up, government direct aid has been paid back, and executive compensation is exploding. But a closer look shows bank stability is just skin-deep, and dense accounting rules hide a powder keg of bad debt and mounting funding issues. While the recent paper-thin re-regulation of finance was a major political victory, the banks' core business is headed downhill and even worse trouble seems to lie ahead.

All of the big four U.S. megabanks—Bank of America, Citigroup, Chase, and Wells Fargo—reported either decreases or very modest increases in their massive profitability during 2010. But this surprisingly weak performance would have been even more disappointing without a pair of accounting maneuvers. One was a bookkeeping measure allowing banks to book projected profit from buying back their debt when their bonds become cheaper. But the banks rarely buy back their debt, so this is essentially a paper gain. The other penstroke that boosted profit was consumption of money set aside to protect against losses on loans—as banks have grown more outwardly confident about the economic recovery, they have lowered their stated expectations of bad loans and designated some of their capital cushions as profit.

But these shallow techniques for elevating profit weren't enough to compensate for the decline in banks' core business—interest income, the money collected from loans minus that paid out to depositors. That income has consistently dropped this year, mainly due to falling loan volume. Banks are making fewer loans to consumers and businesses, citing a "lack of demand," which obscures the quite favorable credit rating now required to get a loan. The lower supply of qualified applicants as job losses persist, combined with locking out applicants with spottier credit history and a general consumer preference to reduce total debt, have all caused bank loan books to continue to shrink in the feeble recovery.

The market has not rewarded the banks for the elaborate camouflage of this core weakness, and their stock prices have lately sagged as a result. But executive compensation is another story, and traders' pay is also rebounding into the $200,000-to-$500,000 range, while tens of millions of Americans struggle to keep food on the table. Meanwhile Obama's much-hailed "pay czar" in charge of monitoring finance executive compensation, Kenneth Feinberg, has reported that within three months of receiving their bailouts, the megabanks had paid out $1.6 billion in bonuses—up to a quarter of their TARP rescue totals. However, the "czar" has no formal power to rescind exorbitant pay now that the majors have repaid their government capital infusions, and compensation will now be monitored by a rather unintimidating consortium of regulators. With the CEOs of the bank majors making about a million a year each in straight salary, no upward limit is in sight for financier compensation. But the banking institutions themselves may have some bumpy days ahead.

Extend and Pretend and Descend

While the banking majors were relieved of much of their bad home mortgage-based investments by government purchases in the course of the financial crisis and aftermath, large loans related to commercial real estate remained on their books. Many of these loans were to growing businesses and overoptimistic developers, and have frequently failed to perform, as the recession has rendered projects unprofitable, reducing borrowers' ability to repay.

But the loans are often for sobering amounts, upwards of tens of millions of dollars, and rather than foreclose on such large credit lines, banks large and small are engaging in what has come to be called "extend and pretend." The practice involves not taking legal measures on underperforming commercial real-estate loans, but rather "restructuring" loans with new, more favorable terms for the borrowers, like below-market interest rates or extended timelines for repayment. The goal of the practice is to prevent foreclosure on large loans, with the hope that extending maturities will give borrowers enough time to recover their business and repay.

There are several problems with this practice. First, it conceals the real condition of the commercial real-estate market. Second, the restructured loans are usually still foreclosed upon in the end—in first quarter of fiscal year 2010, 44% of restructured loans were still a month or more delinquent, a fact related to the startling two-thirds of commercial real-estate loans maturing by 2014 that are underwater—meaning that the property is worth less than the bank loan itself. Finally, the bad loans take up space on bank balance sheets that could go to real lending. This suggests that the banks' current predicament may lead to a miniature version of 1990s Japan, where refusal to accept real-estate loan losses led to a decade of slow growth, in part due to banks' inability to make fresh loans when demand recovered.

However, the "extend and pretend" policy presents one major benefit to the big banks: restructuring these loans allows banks to count them as "performing" rather than delinquent or worse, which means banks may reduce their capital reserves against losses. This enables banks to claim their capital cushions as profit; banks remain in denial about their bad loans, and this itself allows the recent profit increases. And when banks are one day obliged to confront these serious losses, they may find they no longer have the capital cushion to absorb the damage.

This ominous hidden liability is on top of the better-publicized problem of banks' under-performing residential mortgage holdings. The mortgage delinquency rate is now hovering around 10% nationwide, and including those behind on payments and those on the verge of eviction, fully one U.S. mortgage in seven is in some kind of trouble. Importantly, the bad mortgage debt on banks' books has ceased to be a primarily "subprime" phenomenon of low-income loan recipients; over a third of new foreclosures early this year were prime fixed-rate loans, as the layoff-intensive recovery pulls the rug out from under mortgage recipients.

One Hand Regulates the Other

July's Wall Street Reform and Consumer Protection Act was expected to be a return to at least moderate finance regulation, even if a far cry from the more sweeping controls of the 1930s. But the slap-on-the-wrist nature of the bill became clear when stock prices of the megabanks *rose* 3% on its passage. The bill delegates dozens of important decisions, from what constitutes a systemically important bank to credit ratings disclosure, to the regulatory agencies themselves. Crucially, bank regulators are expecting what the press calls a "lobbying blitz," as former employees of the regulators are bankrolled by Wall Street to lobby for industry discretion and relaxed standards on every rule. Highlights include:

- While now stuck with limits on overdraft fees and the "interchange fees" charged to merchants for debit card processing, banks are phasing out free checking accounts and elevating fees elsewhere, since they have the market power to do so. Many depositors are unable to afford checking account fees, of course, but the *New York Times* expects the banks to "jettison unprofitable customers."

- The Volcker Rule would limit banks' "proprietary trading," investments made with a bank's own money rather than clients' funds. The practice was damaging during the financial crisis, but banks have already found a work-around for the new rule. Banks are moving star proprietary traders to client desks, where they will primarily conduct derivatives trade for clients, but will also be able to engage in the barred practice on the side, further blurring the client/proprietary distinction.

- Derivatives will now be listed on established indexes and will require collateral as a cushion against losses, having previously been traded ad-hoc by individual banks. This removes significant risk from the banks themselves, reducing them to competing on service rather than generating large securitization fees. Importantly, businesses that use derivatives for legitimate purposes, such as farmers buying futures contracts to secure favorable grain prices, are exempted from the bill's indexing and collateralizing requirements.

- The bill includes a resolution authority that gives regulators a procedure to "unwind" a bank—overseeing its bankruptcy in an orderly fashion and at its creditors' expense. Additionally, the Kanjorski amendment to the bill gives regulators the authority to break up any financial institution considered to be a systemic threat to the financial system. But it seems unlikely that regulators, typically close to the firms they regulate, would let a titan go down regardless of their resolution authority.

- The new Consumer Financial Protection Bureau requires more information transparency from banks in their communications with customers. However, despite apocalyptic predictions from bank spokespeople, it is notable that banks with under $10 billion in assets are exempt from its rules. This excludes the small and medium-sized lenders that make up 98% of U.S. banks, but does include the large proportion of the industry run by the majors.

Sources: Congressional Oversight Panel, Small Banks In the Capital Purchase Program, July 14, 2010; Eric Dash and Nelson Schwartz, "Banks Seek to Keep Profits as New Oversight Rules Loom," *New York Times*, July 15, 2010; Aaron Lucchetti and Jenny Strasburg, "What's a 'Prop' Trader Now?—Banks Move Those Who Wager With Firms' Money to Client-Focused Jobs," *Wall Street Journal*, July 6, 2010; Randall Smith and Aaron Luchetti, "The Financial-Regulation Overhaul," *Wall Street Journal*, June 26, 2010; Damian Paletta, "Late Change Sparks Outcry Over Finance-Overhaul Bill," *Wall Street Journal*, July 2, 2010; Michael Phillips, "Finance Overhaul Casts Long Shadow on the Plains," *Wall Street Journal*, July 14, 2010; "Killing Them Softly," *The Economist*, August 26, 2010; "Not All On the Same Page," *The Economist*, July 1, 2010; Eric Lichtblau, "Ex-Regulators Get Set to Lobby on New Financial Rules," *New York Times*, July 27, 2010.

Notably, the home mortgages still held by the banks are listed on bank balance sheets at inflated values since they are for homes bought at the housing bubble peak, and government has not forced the banks to account them at any reasonable value. And beside this additional hidden weakness and the space taken up on bank balance sheets by this bad mortgage debt, the banking majors are vulnerable to moves by insurers and other investors to force the banks to repurchase securitized home loans sold to them at wildly inflated prices. So far, losses on affected and expected repurchases have cost the biggest four U.S. banks nearly $10 billion, with further losses anticipated.

Meanwhile, the banks have allowed extremely few mortgage borrowers to modify their mortgages or reduce their principal—the National Bureau of Economic Research has found that just 8% of delinquent borrowers received any modification, while a pitiful 3% have received reductions in their total owed principal. However, about half of all seriously delinquent borrowers have had foreclosure proceedings brought by their bank. Of course, banks ultimately benefit more from a renegotiated loan that is paid off than from a foreclosure, but the long timeline required in the foreclosure process allows the banks to once again push back acknowledgement of the loss.

The banks' rush to foreclose is reflected in the recent suspension of the practice by several megabanks, after discovery that foreclosure standards were not being followed, with single employees overseeing upwards of 400 foreclosures daily, far more than can be properly reviewed according to legal standards. The state attorneys general investigation, adds to the legal swamp that may slow down the flood of foreclosures, but also testifies to the large banks' preference for foreclosure over loan modification.

Lending on Borrowed Time

Banks face other market difficulties in the near future. One involves the increased reliance of the large banks on short-term borrowing to fund their loan portfolios. While banks have issued bonds to raise loan capital for years, in recent years they have grown increasingly dependent on short-term borrowing—the average maturity of recent bank bond issues is under five years, the shortest in decades. This is in fact why the seizing up of the credit markets in 2008 was such a big deal—banks were in immediate trouble if they couldn't borrow. Of course, the government bailout included guarantees for short-term bonds, leading the banks to become even more reliant upon them.

This means banks must "turn over" their debt more frequently—they must issue fresh bonds to raise capital to pay off the maturing older bonds—and U.S. banks must refinance over a trillion dollars through 2012. The problem is that the banks will be competing with huge bond rollovers from state and federal government, which are heavily indebted because of upper-class tax cuts, as well as expensive wars and recent rounds of stimulus at the federal level. Even the powerful megabanks may struggle in this environment—as the *New York Times* puts it, "The cost of borrowing is likely to rise faster than banks can pass it on to customers." The total demand for institutional credit may significantly spike in coming years, meaning perhaps higher interest rates as states and finance houses compete for the bond market's favor, or a further decline in lending by banks due to pro-hibitive funding costs.

Meanwhile, smaller banks have experienced a different post-crisis environment. Despite some TARP bailout crumbs, they have gone under in record numbers—140 failed in 2009, with 2010 on track for a yet larger figure. Most of these smaller fry succumb to losses or suffocate under bad loans following the real estate bubble of the last decade. This sector of the industry is ironically on track to cause more taxpayer losses from non-repayment of bailout funds than the majors, which have attracted the most scorn for taking TARP funds.

Compounding these stabilized but still shaky banking positions, the industry is now subject to a significantly reshaped regulatory environment. In addition to the major finance reform bill enacted in July, banks face new international capital standards in the Basel Rules and new regulatory scope for the Federal Reserve as

---

Basel Faulty

The Basel III bank guidelines are meant to be the G-20's coordinated global response to the crisis of 2008, establishing consistent rules limiting banking risk. But like the American bill, the lightweight standards were greeted by stock jumps for the bank majors, since the process was heavily influenced by massive financial industry lobbying and other, national-ist factors.

Perhaps most notably, the biggest banks' minimum leverage ratio—how much hard capital banks must hold to cushion against sudden losses—has been set at a modest 7% of assets. However, banks need not meet this requirement until 2019, with only a 2.5% re-quirement by 2015. Further, the Basel Committee has caved to industry demands to count assets like deferred-tax funds, mortgage-service rights, and investments in other firms as capital. These are now allowed to make up 15% of a bank's capital cushion, despite being il-liquid and thus not very helpful in a crisis. Notably, some U.S. megabanks had reserve levels close to these on the eve of the finance crisis, and of course found them to be insufficient.

A related issue is how much long-term funding (vs. short-term bonds) the banks issue, making them less-vulnerable to sudden credit market lockups as in 2008. The committee failed to reach agreement on this issue, and the rule has been postponed until 2015, along with many others, including "calibration," the specific required reserve level banks must maintain based on their importance to the overall finance system.

One obstacle to progress is the distinctly nationalist approach taken by the regulators, who aim to minimize the weight of regulations that will affect the banks based in their home countries. The United States has pushed aggressively for broader definitions of capital, since U.S. banks still hold large volumes of mortgage securitization rights. Germany wants "flex-ible" enforcement of the reserve requirements for its undercapitalized banks; France wants allowances for its banks to continue to own insurers, and so on. The result is banking regu-lators fighting tooth and nail against regulating their own banks.

In this way, the standards meant to prevent banks from reverting to their old systemi-cally risky ways have been heavily diluted, diminishing Basel to a fig leaf. As the *Wall Street Journal* accurately predicted, "significant moves by the Basel Committee to back away from its initial proposals...[are] likely to provoke criticism that regulators are caving to industry pressure and missing a chance to impose restraints that could reduce the risk of future costly crises."

Sources: Damian Paletta and David Enrich, "Banks Gain in Rules Debate," *Wall Street Journal*, July 15, 2010; Damian Paletta and David Enrich, "Risks Rulebooks Is Nearly Done—Key Aspects of Banks' New Restraints Are Agreed Upon," *Wall Street Journal*, July 27, 2010; Damien Paletta, "Banks Get New Restraints," *Wall Street Journal*, September 13, 2010.

well. But all these reforms have been limited by massive lobbying spending by Wall Street, coming to over $700 million in the last 18 months alone, as estimated by the Center For Responsive Politics. (See boxes.)

A crucial part of the picture is the uncertainty caused by the notorious secrecy of the financial world. Large parts of the modern finance system do not accept deposits as commercial banks do, and therefore face far less regulation, allowing them to disclose much less information about their investments and leverage. Additionally, even the commercial banks are not obliged to report changes to the terms of their commercial real-estate holdings, obscuring the full extent of "extend-and-pretend" practices. And the Federal Reserve, for its part, has fought to preserve its own institutional secrecy. The Wall Street reform bill does include provisions for limited audits of the Fed's open-market operations and discount window, the basic monetary policy tools used to manipulate interest rates and to modulate economic activity. But this casts little light on the Fed's expansive holdings in mortgage securities and other paper bought from the banks in the course of the 2008-9 bailout. From the banks to the regulators, secrecy—and thus uncertainty—colors the picture.

In the end, moderately higher capital requirements and the public listing and indexing of derivatives may take the financial system back to short-term stability, but banks remain stuck with significant bad loans limiting core interest income, and continue to rely on market bubbles and on their outsized political power. They also face a difficult short-term bond market in the near future in addition to some higher regulatory costs, and crucially, their core business is further limited by weak credit demand in the low-expectations recovery. Unsurprisingly, compensation has rocketed back into seven figures in spite of these circumstances.

So while ordinary Americans limp along in a jobless recovery, the banks have their execs instead of Hell to pay. ❑

Sources: Eric Dash, "JPMorgan Chase Profit Rises as Loans Provisions Fall," *New York Times*, October 13, 2010; Eric Dash, "Citigroup Reports $2.2 Billion Profit in Third Quarter," *New York Times*, October 18, 2010; Bradley Keoun, "Bank Profits Are Worse Than They Look," *Bloomberg Businessweek*, July 22, 2010; Matthias Rieker and Marshall Eckblad, "Banks Generate Profits, but Struggle to Lend," *Wall Street Journal*, July 22, 2010; Eric Dash, "Federal Report Faults Banks on Huge Bonuses," *New York Times*, July 22, 2010; "Bankers' Pay," *New York Times*, July 27, 2010; Carrick Mollenkamp and Lingling Wei, "To Fix Sour Property Deals, Lenders 'Extend and Pretend,'" *Wall Street Journal*, July 7, 2010; David Streitfeld, "Mortage Data Leaves Bankers Uncertain of Trend," *New York Times*, May 19, 2010; Floyd Norris, "Banks Stuck With Bill for Bad Loans," *New York Times*, August 19, 2010; Manuel Adelino et al, "Why Don't Lenders Renegotiate More Home Mortgages? Redefaults, Self-Curse and Securitization," NBER, July 2009; Jack Ewing, "Crisis Awaits World's Banks as Trillions Come Due," *New York Times*, July 11, 2010; AP, FDIC Closes 6 Banks, Including 3 in Florida," *New York Times*, July 16, 2010; Randall Smith and Robin Sidel, "Banks Keep Failing, No End in Sight," *Wall Street Journal*, September 27, 2010; Binyamin Appelbaum, "Mortgage Securities It Holds Pose Sticky Problem for Fed," *New York Times*, July 22, 2010; Peter Goodman, "Policy Options Dwindle as Economic Fears Grow," *New York Times*, August 28, 2010; Center For Responsive Politics, Lobbying Spending Database, FIRE 2010, opensecrets.org.

Article 2.6

PRIVATE EQUITY EXPOSED

An insider gives a peek at a notoriously secretive industry.

BY ORLANDO SEGURA, JR.
July/August 2008

Today, private equity seems to be everywhere. Enter a Dunkin' Donuts, and you experience private equity. Scan your radio dial, and you're likely to encounter private equity. Purchase gifts for your children at Toys "R" Us, and you engage with private equity. The private equity industry, like other alternative investment industries that have risen to prominence over the last two decades, exerts tremendous economic and political influence in the United States and globally. It is important, then, to understand how this industry works and thrives. For the past three years, I have had the opportunity to see firsthand the inner workings of the industry—first as a consultant to large buyout firms, and then as a financial analyst for one of the firms themselves. Drawing on these experiences, I will try to shed some light on this notoriously secretive industry and answer three important questions: How do private equity firms make money? How do private equity firms affect the distribution of financial risk in society as a whole? And how does the regulatory landscape in the United States give private equity firms an advantage in the market?

How Do Private Equity Firms Make Money?

Specialized transactions called leveraged buyouts are central to what private equity firms do, and it is important to be familiar with the mechanics of these transactions in order to understand how these firms generate profit. Private equity firms are private partnerships that raise money from large investors—pension funds, other investment funds, and wealthy individuals (often the same people who are running the private equity firms)—and use that money to purchase other companies. This is the "buyout" part.

The "leveraged" part is the more important one, however. Private equity firms do not simply employ the money they raise on their own to buy companies. They borrow money from investment banks to complete the transactions. In most instances, this borrowed money constitutes the majority of the funding needed to pay for the company. At one point in the industry's infancy, firms were able to borrow 90% or more of the purchase price of the "target" companies. Today, as credit markets have tightened, that number is lower, but on average it still exceeds 50% of purchase price. When the buyout transaction is completed, the payback for this debt becomes the responsibility of the acquired company and is placed on its balance sheet as a liability. Most private equity firms retain ownership of the businesses they buy for three to five years and then sell them for a profit, often to other private equity firms.

The ability to use such leverage vastly increases the potential returns on private equity firms' investments. A simple analogy helps show how this works. Imagine you decide to buy a house that costs $100,000 in a neighborhood where property values are appreciating. You put a very small $1,000 down payment on the house and borrow the other $99,000 from the bank. In three years' time, the house has doubled in value and you are now able to sell it for $200,000. After you repay the loan, you have $100,000 in profit—a return of 100 times your original $1,000 investment. Now, imagine if you had only been able to borrow $1,000 from the bank; you would have had to make a $99,000 down payment. The house still appreciates to a value of $200,000, but in this scenario you have turned your original $99,000 investment into a $100,000 profit, generating only a return roughly equal to your original investment. In the first scenario, you put much less of your own equity at risk, yet you generate the same absolute profit as in the second scenario. This simple example illustrates the power of leverage, and why private equity firms would want to maximize the share of borrowed money they invest.

Why have investment banks been willing to lend private equity firms so much money? Part of the reason is that they are able to pass the debt along by selling, or "syndicating," it. Banks package the debt into securities called collateralized debt obligations, or CDOs, which they sell on the open market. CDOs have existed since 1987, but did not achieve prominence in the markets until 2001, when banks began devising sophisticated models that allowed them to rapidly price and sell these securities.

The benefit banks derive from their ability to segment and distribute the risks associated with the debt they underwrite for private equity firms cannot be overstated. They lower their downside risk associated with default on these loans because they only hold onto a small portion of the entire loan package, or "facility." So banks can underwrite more debt than they would be able to if they held onto the loans in full. And they can take in more lucrative fees, too. The banks get most of their revenues from fees for originating the loans, generally 2% to 3% of the amount of the loan.

All told, such large amounts of capital being used to purchase companies creates hefty profits for the investment banks and the private equity firms, not to mention the ancillary professional service industries required to complete the deals, including accountants, lawyers, and consultants.

This is simply the tip of the profit iceberg for private equity firms, however. The real money comes in what is called "carry"—the share of profits that the funds' managers are entitled to when they sell a business. Remember, the more these firms borrow for a transaction—the more they "leverage"—the more any increase in value translates into equity profit. The industry norm is for private equity partnerships to keep 20% of the profit that they make when they sell a company.

And apart from the über-profits they "earn" from selling the highly leveraged businesses they own, private equity firms charge hefty management fees to *both* the investors in the fund and to the companies they buy. The "market" management fee that private equity firms charge their investors ranges between 2% and 2.5% of the total fund size. The companies they purchase must likewise pay a quarterly "management fee," usually around 2% of the purchase price of the company. Effectively, private equity firms earn money in return for being given money *and* for spending money. As the value of many of the companies that private equity firms buy can soar into the hundreds of millions, or even billions, of dollars, this represents a low-risk, assured stream of income. On a fund of $10 billion, these fees alone can translate into hundreds of millions of dollars in revenue a year.

How do private equity firms affect the distribution of financial risk in society?

The profits that financial players like private equity firms and investment banks enjoy come at a price. Today, there are hundreds of billions of dollars in CDOs that are spread throughout the economy, most owned by individual investors. Of course, it is the businesses private equity firms own that are carrying the underlying loans that were bundled to create the CDOs. These businesses risk default if they are not able to make the payments on these debts. And the more the private equity firm was able to borrow to purchase the company, the greater the risk the business faces because it will have to manage larger debt payments on an ongoing basis. An ordinary business downturn that the business might have been able to weather may now thrust it into default if it cannot manage the high debt payments resulting from the leveraged buy-out. And if enough of these businesses get into trouble, the holders of the CDOs will see the value of their investments tumble. We are seeing this happen now with the sub-prime crisis, which was fueled by devaluation in mortgage-backed securities.

The ability of banks and private equity firms to siphon the benefits while distributing the risks of leverage is rooted in the legal frameworks that "incentivize" such behavior (to use the industry jargon). Private equity firms are shielded from the extreme downside financial risks because of their peculiar form of corporate governance. Private equity firms set up each company they buy as a separate corporation with limited liability. This means that if one of the highly leveraged businesses experiences a downturn and is unable to pay its loans, the only equity that is at stake is what was used to purchase that business. Thus, a private equity fund can still post healthy returns even if some businesses in its portfolio go bankrupt.

As we've seen, private equity firms have an incentive to leverage their business buyouts as much as possible. But this increases the risk of default for the individual businesses they own because they are forced to pay such large principal and interest payments to support the debt that has been placed on their shoulders. Thus, not only do private equity firms increase the systemic risk across the economy by issuing publicly traded CDOs that provide their leverage, they also increase the more immediate risk for those who work for the businesses they own by saddling them with heavy debt obligations.

The "loosening" of the credit markets, fueled partly through the ascendance of CDOs, predictably led private equity firms to execute ever-larger transactions. In 2007, the Blackstone Group purchased Equity Office Properties for $39 billion and in one fell swoop became one of the largest holders of real estate in the world. Currently, Bain Capital is in the process of completing the purchase of Clear Channel Communications, the largest owner of radio stations in the United States. These are but two of many multi-billion dollar transactions by private equity firms that have occurred over the past decade, and which until now have largely gone unnoticed by the general public. These colossal companies, like all businesses bought up by private equity firms, are now at an increased risk should their profit margins weaken or interest rates rise in a cyclical downturn of the economy. To ensure that their requisite loan payments are made, the new managers of these companies, appointed by and acting on behalf of the private equity firm owner, may cut costs by simply laying off workers and offshoring certain functions. The market implications of contractions in the economy are thus amplified by the actions of private equity firms.

How does the regulatory landscape give private equity firms a market advantage?

With the profits that can be earned in private equity, it is no surprise that the industry has grown as much as it has recently, and it is no surprise that private equity firms are able to attract some of the brightest business minds in the market. Predictably, self-interested individuals are drawn to these firms, aiming to maximize the amount of money they can earn. But that is not the whole story. The regulatory landscape in the United States has given private equity firms a number of advantages in the market—limited transparency into the business dealings of the firms and the businesses they own, capital-gains tax advantages, a lack of consumer protection in the credit markets, lax antitrust law enforcement, among others. In effect, the legal landscape is ripe for private equity firms to thrive.

Since private equity firms have at their disposal all these levers for generating profit so seamlessly, one would imagine that the government would tax their earnings at an effectively higher tax rate than normal business earnings. This could not be further from the truth. Owners of corporations in the United States are afforded numerous tax breaks and incentives from writing off "losses" or deducting "business expenses" from taxable earnings. On this front, private equity firms have cleverly found ways to go above and beyond the call of duty. Virtually all private equity firms are structured as limited liability partnerships, or LLPs. This confers two explicit benefits to the partners. First, they are protected from any downside in their equity investments, meaning that if one of their investments goes bust, they will only lose the equity that they put into that specific business. Second, they are protected under a tax shelter that allows the majority of their profits to be taxed at a very low rate. Because they are partnerships that technically earn "capital gains" on the profitable sale of a business, they are taxed at a flat 15% rate, as opposed to the 28% to 33% income tax rate that ordinary individuals pay. Thanks to this loophole, private equity managers are taxed at lower rates than their secretaries and administrative assistants who make as much money in a year as their bosses make in a day.

Many European countries have recently instituted laws in recognition of the legal and regulatory advantages that private equity owners have enjoyed since the industry's inception. In the UK this past year, for example, Parliament passed a law that took away private equity firms' tax advantages, which incidentally were very similar to what currently exists in the United States. Here, House Democrats recently introduced a bill to do away with the capital gains tax structure for private equity firms and tax them at ordinary income tax rates. This would have raised private equity firms' tax rates on their carry from a flat 15% to a flat 35%. But Charles Schumer (D-N.Y.), head of the Senate Finance Committee, came out against the bill, killing it for now.

It is no coincidence that, as a senator from New York, Schumer receives tens of thousands of dollars from private equity bosses and relies on their support for an ever-increasing portion of his campaign funding. Of course, he is not alone. The private equity industry created its own PAC in 2007, the Private Equity Council, to lobby against efforts to increase taxes on the industry. To date, they have succeeded; there is every reason to believe they will continue to succeed. Schumer's fellow senator from New York, Hillary Clinton, is a loyal recipient of private equity money and joined him in opposing the bill. On the Republican side, former New York City mayor Rudy Giuliani has taken a predictable pro-private-equity stance, as did his competitor in the Republican presidential primaries, Mitt Romney, who made hundreds of millions of dollars as a partner of Bain Capital, one of the leading private equity firms in the world. The political muscle of the industry is as strong as its economic success.

The legal framework that actively encourages this industry to thrive has spawned a new breed of capitalism, one in which businesses are treated as assets to be bought and sold rather than as social institutions that are sources of people's livelihood. Perhaps we should ask: What value do these firms confer upon the economy, and through it, on society? Private equity firms do not foster innovation in the economy, they do not create jobs, and for the most part they do not actively manage the businesses they own. Rather, they redirect the benefits of equity ownership to a small and insular group of people instead of creating social value for everyone. It is time to learn more about how and why these institutions exert their power and, at the very least, to demand more transparency, thoughtful regulation, and fairer taxation in return for the privilege of being able to operate in our economy. ❑

Sources: Tomas Krüger Andersen, "Legal Structure of Private Equity and Hedge Funds," 2007 (available at isis.ku.dk/kurser/blob.aspx?feltid= 155330); Martin Arnold, "Doubt Cast on Buy-Out Firms' Huge Profits," *Financial Times*, November 23, 2007; Neil Hodge, "Private Equity: A Debt to Society?" *Financial Management*, September 2007.

Article 2.7

HEDGE FUNDS

BY ARTHUR MacEWAN
July/August 2008

> Dear Dr. Dollar:
> *When one hedge fund makes $3 billion, who has lost $3 billion? Where does the money come from that hedge funds capture? Who produced the value?*
> — Peter Marcuse, Waterbury, Conn.

As with any "winnings" in the financial markets, the money obtained by hedge funds comes directly from some losers who are also operating in the financial markets. On the surface, the situation might appear like a poker game: when one player wins the pot, some other players lose. Those of us not sitting at the table neither win nor lose.

However, while financial markets do involve a lot of gambling, the analogy to a poker game is limited. Those of us who are not sitting in on "the game" do suffer some substantial losses from the operations of hedge funds. Hedge fund operators, along with other operators in the financial system, have taken an active role in increasing the size of their "pot"—that is, in shifting the income distribution upward, moving money from lower-income workers to business owners and high-salaried professionals. So value created by the rest of us becomes the hedge funds' billions.

Contrary to their popular image, however, hedge funds are not making billions and billions of dollars for their investors. In fact, the performance of hedge funds is not significantly better than the performance of other types of investment funds. Nonetheless, although the investors in hedge funds are not doing especially well, the *managers* of the hedge funds are making off with billions.

The key to the incomes of hedge fund managers lies more in the nature of what the funds are than in how well they do. After all, aside from some notable exceptions, hedge funds as a group have not done especially well.

So what are hedge funds? Hedge funds are a category of mutual funds. In all mutual funds, the money of multiple investors is pooled and invested according to the decisions of the funds' managers. Regular mutual funds are subject to various government regulations, as are some other financial institutions, for example, commercial banks. The rationale for these regulations is that they protect the individual investors.

Hedge funds, however, avoid most regulations by limiting participation to a small number of "qualified" individuals and institutions (e.g., pension funds or college endowment funds) with large sums of money. To be "qualified," an investor must have a net worth of at least $5 million, excluding his or her home. Because they have large sums of money, these wealthy investors supposedly do not need the protection that regulation is assumed to provide.

Largely unregulated, hedge funds can undertake highly risky types of investments that would be off limits to regular mutual funds. With these more risky investments, they are *sometimes* able to obtain very high returns. They can also operate with a good deal of secrecy, exempt from the reporting requirements of regular mutual funds.

Like other investment funds, hedge funds charge a fee to the individuals and institutions that provide them with money. But hedge funds have been able to charge relatively high fees, including performance fees on top of the basic management fees. The basic fees run 1.5% to 2% of the total investment, and the performance fees typically run 20% of positive returns—sometimes higher. In some cases, management fees run to 5% combined with performance fees of over 40%. Furthermore, while hedge fund managers get their hefty performance fees when their funds achieve positive returns, they do not lose anything when their funds have negative returns. In effect, they are saying to their investors: If I perform well, we both win; if I perform poorly, you lose. So it is not difficult to see why the managers of hedge funds do so well.

It is difficult, however, to see why so many investors put their money into hedge funds. Part of the explanation lies in the fact that rich individuals are often not smart investors, and they are drawn in by the popular image, the billions made by some funds, and the aura of success surrounding the stories of hedge fund managers who take home billions. And the institutional investors in hedge funds—local pension funds or college endowment funds, for example—are not especially "smart" either. Perhaps it is also the case that investors with large sums of money are willing to put at least some of their money into hedge funds, looking for the higher returns that the funds do sometimes obtain.

But whatever returns are obtained "sometimes," overall hedge funds do not do significantly better than other types of investment funds. While the secrecy of hedge funds makes it difficult to determine their overall returns, one 2006 study concludes: "...overall performance of hedge funds … is about the same as that of U.S. equities [as measured by the Standard and Poor's Index of 500 equities] …[H]edge funds underperformed the stock market … during the six year, 'bull market' run-up to 1999, while on average they outperformed the stock market during the six year 'bear market' (or lull period) through 2005."

And recently the story has been quite poor: in the period from January 2007 up to May of 2008, hedge funds returned on average 3.1% and were out-performed by rich-world corporate bonds. (These figures are only for hedge funds that are open to new investors and thus, presumably, report how they have been doing. Hedge funds that are not accepting new investors are more opaque.) One might conclude that hedge funds are an undistinguished group of investments.

There are, however, some things that distinguish hedge funds—most particularly the huge payments that are often obtained by the people who run the funds. The most outstanding recent example is John Paulson, who in 2007 took in $3.7 billion running his Paulson & Co. hedge funds. Several others did pretty well also: George Soros was number two last year, at $2.9 billion, and James Simons was third at $2.8 billion

The top 25 hedge fund managers got themselves $22.3 billion in 2007, up substantially from a meager $14 billion in 2006. It is, we may assume, the stories of these individuals that generates the aura of success surrounding hedge funds.

How did hedge fund managers do so well when the economy was moving into bad times? In Paulson's case, according to Bloomberg.com, "Paulson & Co., which oversees about $28 billion, made money betting on the collapse of subprime mortgages in 2007. The Paulson Credit Opportunities Fund soared almost sixfold, helped by bets on slumping housing and subprime mortgage prices, according to investor letters obtained by Bloomberg." More generally, the hedge fund managers rely on their fee structure, as described above, to assure that, regardless of bad times, they come out well.

If rich individuals and institutional investors were the only ones to take the hit when the John Paulsons take home their astronomical fees, perhaps the rest of us could shrug it off. If they want to pay excessive fees to take part in the glitter—and possible large returns—of high stakes finance, that's their problem.

But the rest of us do pay a price. First of all, there is the ridiculously favorable tax treatment that hedge fund managers have been able to garner. Most important, they are allowed to classify their payments as capital gains rather than as salaries, and thereby they pay a low tax rate on their incomes—typically only 15%, compared to the top tax rate of 35%.

There is simply no good reason for this favorable treatment of hedge fund managers' incomes—other than the apparent power they are able to wield. The result is that the rest of us either pay more in taxes or get by with fewer public services.

Also important, hedge fund managers are not passive investors. They do not accept as a given the current profit levels of the companies they invest in, and simply try to claim a larger share of those profits. Instead, at least at times (but their secrecy makes it difficult to determine how often and to what extent), they take an active role in attempting to push up their profits. Along with private equity funds, with which the hedge funds are closely associated and sometimes overlap, they can push firms to downsize and reorganize, lay off workers, outsource, or alter their overall investment strategies.

For instance, according to a May 15, 2008 report in the "Silicon Alley Insider," John Paulson, who through his funds owns 4% of Yahoo stock, has joined corporate raider Carl Icahn in a proxy fight, an attempt to force Yahoo to accept a Microsoft buy-out offer.

There is no reason to think that any general social interest is served when hedge fund managers attempt to affect the operation of the firms in which they have holdings. In the Yahoo example, the impact on the rest of us may be obscure, but when it comes to layoffs, downsizing, outsourcing, and the like, it is clear that many people outside of the financial markets—people who have no seat at the gambling tables— pay a large price for the gains of hedge funds, and especially of fund managers.

Stagnant wages of workers in recent decades and the increased share of total national income going to corporate profits are the consequence of large, long-run economic forces—the decline of unions, globalization, conservative government policies, and technological shifts to name a few. But the hedge funds are one of the instruments by which these forces have their impact on the rest of us, shifting the value that we create into the financial markets and then taking as large a share as they can. ❏

Sources: Andy Baker, "Better than beta? Managers' superior skills are becoming harder to prove," *The Economist*, February 28, 2008; Arindam Bandopadhyaya and James L. Grant, *A Survey of Demographics and Performance In the Hedge Fund Industry*, Working Paper 1011, Financial Services Forum, College of Management, University of Massachusetts Boston, July, 2006; "Hedge-Fund Performance," *The Economist*, May 15, 2008; Tom Cahill and Poppy Trowbridge, "Paulson's $3.7 Billion Top Hedge Fund Pay, Alpha Says," Bloomberg.com, April 16, 2008; Henry Blodget, "Hedge-Fund Mogul Paulson Joins Icahn in Yahoo Siege; 30% of Proxy Vote in Bag," Silicon Alley Insider, May 15, 2008.

Article 2.8

WHAT WERE THE BANKERS THINKING?

BY ARTHUR MacEWAN
March/April 2010

Dear Dr. Dollar,

As I understand it, the main cause of the current economic mess was that banks made a lot of bad housing loans. When the people who took out those loans couldn't make their payments, the banks got in trouble and then the whole economy got in trouble. So why did the bankers make all those bad loans? What were they thinking!?

—Sara Boyle, Manchester, Conn.

They were thinking they could make a lot of money. To a large extent, they were right. Sure, they finally started losing. But you won't see many bankers in soup kitchen lines.

Here's how it worked. The actual makers of the mortgage loans were willing to make high-risk loans because they quickly put these loans into bundles (electronic bundles) and sold the bundles to investors. So the makers of the mortgages—mortgage companies, commercial banks, savings and loans, and credit unions—were not harmed when someone stopped payment on a mortgage. These bundles are called mortgage-backed securities, a form of Collateralized Debt Obli-gations (CDOs). CDOs are a type of derivative—a financial instrument (i.e., a vehicle for financial investment) the value of which is derived from some other financial instrument, in this case the set of mortgages in the bundle.

The underwriters—the financial firms handling the marketing of these CDOs, usually large investment banks—then had to get them rated by one of the rating agencies. Moody's, Standard & Poor's, and Fitch are the three big firms, controlling 85% of the market, that evaluate the risk involved in financial instruments. The rating agencies, however, are paid by the underwriters, so they have a conflict of interest that gave them an incentive to rate the CDOs too high, indicating less risk than was really involved. Also, the underwriters could shop among the rating agencies to get the best rating. In general, the rationale for good ratings was that the mortgage-based CDOs were relatively safe because they included many mortgages, creating at least an aura of diversity. Diversity is always taken as implying low risk. (Except, of course, when there is a general failure.)

Also, buyers of the CDOs could buy insurance on these investments, just in case something did go wrong. The insurance policies on the CDOs are called "credit default swaps"—another set of derivatives, the value of which is derived from the value of the CDOs. The credit default swaps, like the CDOs themselves, were then treated in the financial market as another type of financial instrument.

Many investment banks made a lot of money holding these derivatives as well as in buying and selling them. The banks got high returns on the derivatives they held and they got fees for buying and selling derivatives. Bear Stearns and Lehman

Brothers, the two investment banks that went under in 2008, had made lots of money on these activities between 2002 and 2006.

To understand the actions of the banks, it is important to recognize that the salaries and, especially, the large bonuses that the bankers obtained in these operations were based on the immediate, short-run profits that they generated. If in one year (say in 2005) they made lots of money through the fees on buying and selling the derivatives and through the returns on holding the derivatives, then it didn't matter that things fell apart soon after (in 2007). None of the bankers had to give back their salaries or bonuses. (These operations were facilitated by the general lack of regulation of derivative trading.)

Of course when things did fall apart, no one would buy the CDOs or the credit default swaps. These were the "toxic assets" that were held by many large banks and other investors and which "poisoned" the financial system. Some of the people who had made lots of money in salaries and bonuses also held stock in, for example, Bear Stearns or Lehman Brothers, and they lost money on those stocks.

There was, however, still a problem. Lots of financial institutions had taken out loans for which these CDOs and credit default swaps were collateral. With the value of these derivatives collapsing, it looked as though the creditors might lose their money. This was when people started talking about a collapse of the financial system.

Not to worry. The government stepped in and made sure that the creditors got their money.

So, it turns out that a whole set of arrangements—from the initial making of the mortgage to the salary-bonus system to the government bail- out—protected the bankers and other actors from the risks of their actions. The arrangements encouraged excessively risky behavior that ultimately placed a huge cost on the rest of us.

But the bankers? They pretty much came out OK. No, you won't see many bankers in soup kitchen lines. ❏

Article 2.9

NO EXPENSE TOO GREAT
A History of the Savings and Loan Bailout

BY DORENE ISENBERG AND VINCE VALVANO
May 1989; revised June 1993

The savings and loan (S&L) crisis has led to new regulations and regulators, and to dramatic changes in the S&L industry. But the $200 billion taxpayer-financed bailout is not a response to our needs for low-interest mortgage loans and stable community lenders. Many of those who produced and profited from the crisis have crafted the bailout, and so it bears all the limitations of its creators.

The explicit costs of the bailout are captured in the $200 billion figure, but there are many other costs that can't be calculated. The restructuring and decline of S&Ls has caused massive losses in jobs, economic growth, and well-being. The bailout bears partial responsibility for the stagnant economy of the early 1990s.

Though the S&L crisis emerged early in the 1980s, it took until 1989 for the government to plan and finance a bailout. In the intervening years several attempts were made to address the evolving problem, but it was a politically unpopular topic. The Bush and Reagan administrations preferred to let the regulators and insurers grapple with it.

Even after the bailout legislation was passed, most politicians knew that too little money had been allocated to save the industry. With government deficits taking center stage, federal spending of tens of billions of dollars to salvage risk-hungry S&Ls was not the type of program that voters would be wild about supporting. To hide their dilemma, Congress and succeeding presidents based bailout funding on unrealistically hopeful predictions. Since these predictions have not come to pass, each president has returned to Congress almost annually with requests for additional tens of billions of dollars. The crisis has peaked but the bailout's costs continue to escalate.

Financial Stability

The financial disruptions of the Great Depression led to greater regulation of the financial sector. One of the key elements designed to promote stability was deposit insurance. In 1933, Congress created the Federal Savings and Loan Insurance Corporation (FSLIC), a private corporation that is government sponsored. Federally chartered S&Ls (thrifts) bought insurance which covered their deposits. The size of the deposit covered has increased over time, with accounts of up to $100,000 covered since 1980.

The purpose of deposit insurance was to stem the fear of a "run." Should a thrift go belly up due to bad loans or investments, FSLIC guaranteed that the institution's losses would not wipe out any insured deposits. Were the federal government, through the FSLIC, to delay, let alone refuse, to pay off depositors at bankrupt S&Ls, it would risk creating a massive run on thrifts and, possibly, commercial banks—leading to a full-scale financial panic.

In return for deposit insurance protection, S&Ls accepted close supervision by federal regulators and pledged to limit their activities to a safe and socially useful business: making long-term home mortgage loans at relatively low interest rates. In contrast to the Wall Street side of the financial sector, the S&L side shunned risk and the search for big profits.

Deregulation

This low-risk policy succeeded—until the 1980s, S&L failures averaged less than ten per year. The system, however, began to unravel in the late 1970s and early 1980s. Many thrifts were hurt when high inflation pushed up interest rates and thus the cost of their funds (deposits), while earnings remained tied to long-term, low-interest mortgages.

During the same period, new types of financial instruments evolved, such as money market mutual funds, that offered individual depositors much higher interest rates than were available from traditional savings accounts. This forced thrifts to compete more vigorously for funds in the financial markets. The new competition caused an outflow of deposits from the S&Ls in the early 1980s, weakening the industry's financial health.

In response, the S&Ls pressed Washington to relax its regulatory hold over the industry. Congress and Reaganite bank regulators willingly obliged. They allowed the thrifts to offer higher interest rates to attract deposits, leading in turn to the demise of affordable home mortgages. Thrifts were also permitted to invest in a wider range of assets: commercial real estate, financial futures contracts, and junk bonds, among other high-risk projects. Conflict-of-interest rules governing lending were also eased, providing incentives for developers and other entrepreneurs to buy thrifts and use them to finance their own deals.

The federal government deemed such deregulation necessary because the S&Ls were no longer assured a steady supply of low-cost deposits. Now they needed the leeway to make loans and investments that would produce higher returns than standard home mortgages. By definition, however, such projects were considerably riskier than the home mortgage business. And S&L loan officers didn't have much collective experience in evaluating these more complex projects.

With the end of restrictions on the interest rates that S&Ls could pay on deposits, it became extremely easy for any thrift, no matter how obscure, to attract funds. As long as it was willing to offer a premium interest rate, a thrift could attract large sums of Wall Street money. These so-called "brokered deposits" would be broken into $100,000 chunks to qualify for government deposit insurance. Of course, if a thrift was paying a premium for its deposits, it naturally had to invest the money in riskier projects in order to turn a profit. Moreover, brokered deposits were inherently unstable—they could disappear just as quickly as they arrived, lured by higher interest rates elsewhere.

Despite the increasing financial shakiness of the industry, deposits poured into the newly liberated thrift sector. Between 1980 and 1989, they grew from less than 1% of total deposits to 7%. Thrifts that were already in bad shape tended to be the ones that relied most on brokered deposits. The autopsies on many failed thrifts showed 50% of their deposits to have been brokered. The ballooning of S&L deposits after deregulation dramatically increased the potential liabilities facing the FSLIC insurance fund.

Meanwhile, Reagan administration deregulators repeatedly denied requests by the Federal Home Loan Bank Board (FHLBB)—the regulator of federally chartered thrifts—for funding for more thrift examiners. In the face of a rapidly growing and increasingly complex industry, the FHLBB was unable to monitor the financial condition of many thrifts. The Bank Board reacted to this situation by relaxing its supervision of the industry and loosening capital requirements, making it easier for impaired thrifts to continue operating.

A transformation was taking place in the financial sector. Deregulation, coupled with inflation, recession, financial innovations, and increased competition among all the banks and thrifts produced hundreds of sick and dying S&Ls. These impaired S&Ls created a new set of problems. Neither the regulators nor the industry were ready or able to cope with these changes.

The Dead and Brain Dead

By definition, a thrift dies (it becomes bankrupt or insolvent) when its liabilities (customer deposits) exceed the value of its assets (loans and various investments). Unlike other businesses, however, when a thrift becomes insolvent it is not forced by its creditors to shut down, thanks to the miracle of deposit insurance. A broke thrift can continue indefinitely to generate from depositors the cash it needs to stay in business—so, functionally, it's only brain dead.

Most of those involved with S&Ls don't have much of an incentive to demand that a bankrupt thrift close down. Depositors, who need not worry about losing their money (as long as their account at any one thrift doesn't exceed $100,000), don't pay close attention to the financial condition of any particular thrift. Equity owners know that by the time an S&L has gone over the edge, its stock has lost most of its value, so they can't lose much more if the thrift keeps operating at a loss. Managers often have an ownership stake in the thrift, so they have a more pronounced interest in its continued operation. They can continue to collect often hefty salaries and perks, and hope for a turnaround.

In this environment, the decision to close a failing thrift rests largely in the hands of federal regulators. Once a thrift becomes insolvent, the way to minimize taxpayer costs is for regulators to close it down, pay off the depositors from FSLIC's coffers, and sell the thrift's assets to recoup as much of the deposit liability as possible. The problem with this process (besides the disruption it causes to the local community), known as liquidation, is that it requires FSLIC to lay out cash up front to pay depositors.

For example, say the Longhorn Savings and Loan of Houston (fictitious) becomes insolvent. To liquidate the thrift, the FSLIC would have to pay its depositors $500 million right away. Longhorn's assets at that point are worth, at most, only $300 million and many of those assets aren't easily converted into cash. It would take a lot of time and effort by the FSLIC to sell assets such as commercial or residential property in order to partially recoup its payments to depositors.

In the early 1980s, FSLIC was faced with hundreds of Longhorn S&Ls, but instead of shutting them down, it allowed them to stay in business. The number of "brain dead" thrifts quickly outpaced the ability of regulators to liquidate them. The insurance fund was simply not large enough for the job. In 1980, the number of operating insolvents was 17; by 1986, it had soared to 468. This increase, the result of FSLIC's own insolvency, is mirrored by the decline in thrift shutdowns. They peaked in 1982, at 252, while in 1986 only 83 thrifts were closed.

The Southwest Plan

In the fall of 1988, as thrift losses climbed ever higher, the FHLBB embarked on a more aggressive strategy, dubbed the "Southwest Plan," to tackle S&L insolvencies. Strapped for cash and unable to liquidate S&Ls on its own, FHLBB negotiated the sales of 220 bankrupt thrifts, primarily in the Southwest, to private investors. In return for putting up small amounts of capital, these investors received big tax breaks and a guaranteed rate of return on their assets.

Congress and many others criticized these sales for continuing the tradition of putting S&Ls into the hands of financial speculators, while providing generous government guarantees. For example, one group of thrifts was sold to a corporate raider who put $300 million of capital, only $65 million of which was his own, into the deal and walked away with $900 million in tax breaks. The FHLBB argued that this was the best it could do, given its lack of cash in hand to liquidate insolvent thrifts.

Aside from the complaints of overly generous terms for investors, critics also charged that the Bank Board was underestimating the cost to insurers (soon to be taxpayers) of these sales. The Bank Board members believed that in the long run the revenue from the sales would exceed the cost of liquidation. But, instead, by 1989 $40 billion was needed to pay off the FSLIC notes issued to finance the Southwest Plan. These expenses added significantly to the overall cost of the S&L crisis.

The Bailout

Finally, the government acknowledged the bankruptcy of FSLIC and the hundreds of "brain dead" S&Ls by passing the Financial Institutions Reform, Recovery and Enforcement Act of 1989 (FIRREA). This legislation signed FSLIC's death certificate along with that of hundreds of S&Ls. It created an institution for liquidating "brain dead" S&Ls, procured money to liquidate them, and reconfigured the thrifts' industrial and regulatory structure.

The Resolution Trust Corporation (RTC) was set up to sell, merge, or liquidate the "brain dead" thrifts. Like the Southwest Plan before it, the purchasers received big tax breaks and, in many cases, a guaranteed rate of return on their assets. Initially, Congress gave the RTC $50 billion, with which it took over 267 of the failed thrifts. Many more insolvents, however, continued to operate because the funds and staffing were insufficient to completely resolve the problem. While the $50 billion was in addition to the $40 billion required to settle the Southwest Plan's outstanding balance, both were a drop in the bucket compared to what was needed.

In addition to the RTC, Congress also created a new insurance corporation, the Savings Association Insurance Fund (SAIF). SAIF, in contrast to the FSLIC, is a part of the Federal Deposit Insurance Corporation (FDIC), the insurer of commercial banks.

In the early 1980s, deregulation attempted to homogenize the depository institutions. Instead of allowing each institution to maintain and further define its special area of expertise, the government pushed to erase the differences between the thrifts and banks. By merging the insurance funds into one corporation, the loan specializations that used to differentiate the S&Ls from commercial banks—an emphasis on home mortgage loans versus commercial lending—were being eradicated.

Further evidence of this move is the RTC policy, and prior to it the FSLIC policy, that promotes commercial bank acquisitions of failing S&Ls. As of July, 1992, of the 651 resolutions, 383 S&Ls were acquired by banks and only 180 were acquired by other S&Ls. These 383 S&Ls represented 58% of the total assets resolved by the RTC.

The Continuing Crisis

With FIRREA's passage the financial crisis in the savings and loan industry was addressed, but not solved. The RTC has closed 651 thrifts and taken 60 more under conservatorship. These thrifts had $111 billion in assets most of which were low quality, and thus less marketable. The higher quality assets were usually sold off before the RTC takeover. The annual number of failing S&Ls has slowed, but in 1992 the Congressional Budget Office (CBO), a non-partisan government organization, estimated that as many as 700 more institutions may fail by 1997.

Even as the rate of failures is declining, the cost of the bailout is climbing. Congress' initial $50 billion funding in 1989 was followed by $30 billion in 1991 and $25 billion in 1993. According to the FIRREA action plan, the RTC should have all of the "brain deads" resolved by September 1993. The CBO's estimate of more insolvent thrifts on the horizon, however, coupled with the RTC's generous asset return policy (in many cases if an acquired asset fails to perform as expected, the RTC must buy it back) portends a longer life for the RTC and a need for more taxpayer money.

The total current cost of the S&L bailout is estimated at $205 billion. This will become about $500 billion over time if we include 30 years of interest payments on the U.S. Treasury bonds sold to finance the cost. The current cost averages out to an $800 payment by every living American.

These are the explicit costs. The alterations that the financial sector continues to undergo are producing numerous costs that are not as easily quantified. The thrifts that remain after the shakeout are larger, but fewer in number, so they serve fewer communities. Their offerings of financial services have grown, but their old specialty, the home mortgage loan, is now only one of their many services and is harder to obtain.

The cheap home mortgage loan that U.S. financial policy made available in earlier decades has been eliminated by the various Congressional acts that have deregulated and then reregulated the S&L industry. While the low market interest rates of the early 1990s have made home mortgages relatively affordable for the moment, the regulations which ensured that S&Ls would provide low cost loans have been wiped off the books. S&Ls still make home loans, but less of them, and mortgage rates are now tied to general market interest rates—so they can rise again at any time. Partial responsibility for the decreased affordability of housing lies here. Additionally, home mortgage lending pumped deposits from thrifts back into their local communities. With fewer S&Ls, and with home mortgages being a smaller percentage of their assets, local institutions have reduced their investment in communities.

Financial or Economic Stability?

The post-Great Depression S&L regulatory structure aided in producing stable financial institutions and inexpensive funds for mortgage lending. The current restructuring has kept the savings and loan crisis from blossoming into a full-scale depression, but has greatly contributed to the economy's sustained recession since 1990.

The restructuring has also shifted the cost of the crisis. Instead of the S&L industry, its stockholders, and the depositors paying for the bailout, a larger group, taxpayers, is paying for the thrift crisis. This expands the size of the group sharing the bailout's cost, and extends the period over which it will be born to 20-30 years. As a result, the impact on each individual will be smaller than in previous financial crises such as the Great Depression.

Shifting this burden produces two problems, however. The greater tax burden could depress household spending, which may foster a period of extended stagnation. Also, like the earlier Chrysler and Continental Illinois bailouts, the government's policy uses public money without giving people a voice in how the money is used. Taxpayers were never asked whether they supported the S&L bailout or how it should proceed. The blame for the thrift mess is easy to spread around. Congress, the Reagan and Bush administrations, the S&L industry, regulators, and a variety of fast-buck entrepreneurs who bought up S&Ls for use as personal money machines all contributed to the crisis. Unfortunately, this same group of interested parties has produced the new industrial and regulatory structure. Will the new structure provide a financial environment that helps to stabilize the economy, or is it merely a boondoggle in which taxpayers shoulder the burden?

The Clinton administration's proposal for a system of community development banks and credit unions is an acknowledgment of the disastrous mess this financial crisis has made in our communities. While such a system would be a good first step, the need for loans to homebuyers and community businesses far outdistances the paltry $354 million in funding over 1993-97 that Clinton proposed in his original economic plan. This level of spending can't begin to remedy the financial and productive disruptions we have experienced throughout the past 15 years. What remains to be seen is whether the whole fiasco will spark renewed grassroots pressure for public accountability, social responsibility, and a democratic voice in the financial sector. ❑

Resources: M. Mayer, *The Greatest-Ever Bank Robbery* (Charles Scribner's, 1992); "Staff Report of the Committee on Banking, Finance, and Urban Affairs," U.S. House of Representatives, December 1992; "Taking the Measure of the Resolution Trust Corporation," RTC Review, August 1992; "Thrift Industry Crisis: Causes and Solutions," R. Brumbaugh, Jr. and A. Carron, Brookings Papers on Economic Activity, 2:1987.

Chapter 3

MORTGAGES, CONSUMER CREDIT, AND PREDATORY LENDING

Article 3.1

AMERICA'S GROWING FRINGE ECONOMY

BY HOWARD KARGER

November/December 2006

Financial services for the poor and credit-challenged are big business.

Ron Cook is a department manager at a Wal-Mart store in Atlanta. Maria Guzman is an undocumented worker from Mexico; she lives in Houston with her three children and cleans office buildings at night. Marty Lawson works for a large Minneapolis corporation. What do these three people have in common? They are all regular fringe economy customers.

The term "fringe economy" refers to a range of businesses that engage in financially predatory relationships with low-income or heavily indebted consumers by charging excessive interest rates, superhigh fees, or exorbitant prices for goods or services. Some examples of fringe economy businesses include payday lenders, pawnshops, check-cashers, tax refund lenders, rent-to-own stores, and "buy-here/pay-here" used car lots. The fringe economy also includes credit card companies that charge excessive late payment or over-the-credit-limit penalties; cell phone providers that force less creditworthy customers into expensive prepaid plans; and subprime mortgage lenders that gouge prospective homeowners.

The fringe economy is hardly new. Pawnshops and informal high-interest lenders have been around forever. What we see today, however, is a fringe-economy sector that is growing fast, taking advantage of the ever-larger part of the U.S. population whose economic lives are becoming less secure. Moreover, in an important sense the sector is no longer "fringe" at all: more and more, large mainstream financial corporations are behind the high-rate loans that anxious customers in run-down storefronts sign for on the dotted line.

The Payday Lending Trap

Ron and Deanna Cook have two children and a combined family income of $48,000—more than twice the federal poverty line but still $10,000 below Georgia's median income. They are the working poor.

To make ends meet, the Cooks borrow from payday lenders. When Ron and Deanna borrow $300 for 14 days they pay $60 in interest—an annual interest rate of 520%! If they can't pay the full $360, they pay just the $60 interest fee and roll over the loan for another two weeks. The original $300 loan now costs $120 in interest for 30 days. If they roll over the loan for another two-week cycle, they pay $180 in interest on a $300 loan for 45 days. If the payday lender permits only four rollovers, the Cooks sometimes take out a payday loan from another lender to repay the original loan. This costly cycle can be devastating. The Center for Responsible Lending tells the tale of one borrower who entered into 35 back-to-back payday loans over 17 months, paying $1,254 in fees on a $300 loan.

The Cooks take out about ten payday loans a year, which is close to the national average for payday loan customers. Although the industry claims payday loans are intended only for emergencies, a 2003 study of Pima County, Ariz., by the Southwest Center for Economic Integrity found that 67% of borrowers used their loans for general non-emergency bills. The Center for Responsible Lending found that 66% of borrowers initiate five or more loans a year, and 31% take out twelve or more loans yearly. Over 90% of payday loans go to borrowers with five or more loans a year. Customers who take out 13 or more loans a year account for over half of payday lenders' total revenues.

The Unbanked

Maria Guzman and her family are part of the 10% of U.S. households—more than 12 million—that have no relationship with a bank, savings institution, credit union, or other mainstream financial service provider. Being "unbanked," the Guzmans turn to the fringe economy for check cashing, bill payment, short-term pawn or payday loans, furniture and appliance rentals, and a host of other financial services. In each case, they face high user fees and exorbitant interest rates.

Without credit, the Guzmans must buy a car either for cash or through a "buy-here/pay-here" (BHPH) used car lot. At a BHPH lot they are saddled with a 28% annual percentage rate (APR) on a high-mileage and grossly overpriced vehicle. They also pay weekly, and one missed payment means a repossession. Since the Guzmans have no checking account, they use a check-casher who charges 2.7% for cashing their monthly $1,500 in payroll checks, which costs them $40.50 a month or $486 a year.

Like many immigrants, the Guzmans send money to relatives in their home country. (Money transfers from the United States to Latin America are expected to reach $25 billion by 2010.) If they sent $500 to Mexico on June 26, 2006, using Western Union's "Money in Minutes," they would have paid a $32 transfer fee. Moreover, Western Union's exchange rate for the transaction was 11.12 pesos for the U.S. dollar, while the official exchange rate that day was 11.44. The difference on $500 was almost $14, which raised the real costs of the transaction to $46, or almost 10% of the transfer amount.

Without a checking account, the Guzmans turn to money orders or direct bill pay, both of which add to their financial expenses. For example, ACE Cash Express charges 79 cents per money order and $1 or more for each direct bill payment. If the Guzmans use money orders to pay six bills a month, the fees total nearly $57 a year; using direct bill pay, they would pay a minimum of $72 in fees per year.

All told, the Guzmans spend more than 10% of their income on alternative financial services, which is average for unbanked households. To paraphrase James Baldwin, it is expensive to be poor and unbanked in America.

The Cooks and the Guzmans, along with people like Marty Lawson caught in a cycle of credit card debt (see sidebar on next page), may not fully appreciate the economic entity they are dealing with. Far from a mom-and-pop industry, America's fringe economy is largely dominated by a handful of large, well-financed multinational corporations with strong ties to mainstream financial institutions. It is a comprehensive and fully formed parallel economy that addresses the financial needs of the poor and credit-challenged in the same way as the mainstream economy meets the needs of the middle class. The main difference is the exorbitant interest rates, high fees, and onerous loan terms that mark fringe economy transactions.

Credit Cards, College Students, and the Fringe Economy

Marty Lawson is one of the growing legions of the credit poor. Although he earns $65,000 a year, his $50,000 credit card debt means that he can buy little more than the essentials. This cycle of debt began when Marty received his first credit card in college.

Credit cards are the norm for today's college students. A 2005 Nellie Mae report found that 55% of college students get their first credit card during their freshman year; by senior year, 91% have a credit card and 56% carry four or more cards.

College students are highly prized credit card customers because of their high future earnings and lifetime credit potential. To ensnare them, credit card companies actively solicit on campus through young recruiters who staff tables outside university bookstores and student centers. Students are baited with free t-shirts, frisbees, candy, music downloads, and other come-ons. Credit card solicitations are stuffed into new textbooks and sent to dormitories, electronic mailboxes, and bulletin boards. According to Junior Achievement, the typical college freshman gets about eight credit card offers in the first week of the fall semester. The aggressiveness of credit card recruiters has led several hundred colleges to ban them from campus.

Excited by his newfound financial independence, Marty overlooked the fine print explaining that cash advances carried a 20% or more APR. He also didn't realize how easily he could reach the credit limit, and the stiff penalties incurred for late payments and over-the-credit-limit transactions. About one-third of credit card company profits come from these and other penalties.

Marty applied for a second credit card after maxing out his first one. The credit line on his second card was exhausted in only eight months. Facing $4,000 in high-interest credit card bills, Marty left college to pay off his debts. He never returned. Dropping out to repay credit card debt is all too common, and according to former Indiana University administrator John Simpson, "We lose more students to credit card debt than academic failure." Not coincidentally, by graduation the average credit card debt for college seniors is almost $3,000. Credit card debt worsens the longer a student stays in school. A 2004 Nellie Mae survey found the average credit card debt for graduate students was a whopping $7,831, a 59% increase over 1998. Fifteen percent of graduate students carry credit card balances of $15,000 or more.

The Scope of the Fringe Economy

The unassuming and often shoddy storefronts of the fringe economy mask the true scope of this economic sector. Check-cashers, payday lenders, pawnshops, and rent-to-own stores alone engaged in at least 280 million transactions in 2001, according to Fannie Mae Foundation estimates, generating about $78 billion in gross revenues. By comparison, in 2003 combined state and federal spending on the core U.S. social welfare programs—Temporary Aid to Needy Families (AFDC's replacement), Supplemental Security Income, Food Stamps, the Women, Infants and Children (WIC) food program, school lunch programs, and the U.S. Department of Housing and Urban Development's (HUD) low-income housing programs—totaled less than $125 billion. Revenues in the combined sectors of the fringe economy—including subprime home mortgages and refinancing, and used car sales—would inflate the $78 billion several times over and eclipse federal and state spending on the poor.

There can be no doubt that the scope of the fringe economy is enormous. The Community Financial Services Association of America claims that 15,000 payday lenders extend more than $25 billion in short-term loans to millions of households each year. According to Financial Service Centers of America, 10,000 check-cashing stores process 180 million checks with a face value of $55 billion.

The sheer number of fringe economy storefronts is mind-boggling. For example, ACE Cash Express—only one of many such corporations—has 68 locations within 10 miles of my Houston zip code. Nationwide there are more than 33,000 check-cashing and payday loan stores, just two parts of the fringe economy. That's more than the all the McDonald's and Burger King restaurants and all the Target, J.C. Penney, and Wal-Mart retail stores in the United States combined.

ACE Cash Express is the nation's largest check-casher and exemplifies the growth and profitability of the fringe economy. In 1991 ACE had 181 stores; by 2005 it had 1,371 stores with 2,700 employees in 37 states and the District of Columbia. ACE's revenues totaled $141 million in 2000 and by 2005 rose to $268.6 million. In 2005 ACE:

- cashed 13.3 million checks worth approximately $5.3 billion (check cashing fees totaled $131.6 million);
- served more than 40 million customers (3.4 million a month or 11,000 an hour) and processed $10.3 billion in transactions;
- processed over 2 million loan transactions (worth $640 million) and generated interest income and fees of $91.8 million;
- added a total of 142 new locations (in 2006 the company anticipates adding 150 more);
- processed over $410 million in money transfers and 7.6 million money orders with a face value of $1.3 billion;
- processed over 7.8 million bill payment and debit card transactions, and sold approximately 172,000 prepaid debit cards.

Advance America is the nation's leading payday lender, with 2,640 stores in 36 states, more than 5,500 employees, and $630 million this year in revenues. Dollar Financial Corporation operates 1,106 stores in 17 states, Canada, and the United Kingdom. Their 2005 revenues were $321 million. Check-into-Cash has more than 700 stores; Check N' Go has 900 locations in 29 states. Almost all of these are publicly traded NASDAQ corporations.

There were 4,500 pawnshops in the United States in 1985; now there are almost 12,000, including outlets owned by five publicly traded chains. In 2005 the three big chains—Cash America International (a.k.a Cash America Pawn and SuperPawn), EZ Pawn, and First Cash—had combined annual revenues of nearly $1 billion. Cash America is the largest pawnshop chain, with 750 locations; the company also makes payday loans through its Cash America Payday Advance, Cashland, and Mr. Payroll stores. In 2005, Cash America's revenues totaled $594.3 million.

The Association of Progressive Rental Organizations claims that the $6.6 billion a year rent-to-own (RTO) industry serves 2.7 million households through 8,300 stores in 50 states. Many RTOs rent everything from furniture, electronics, major appliances, and computers to jewelry. Rent-A-Center is the largest RTO corporation in the world. In 2005 it employed 15,000 people; owned or operated 3,052 stores in the United States and Canada; and had revenues of $2.4 billion. Other leading RTO chains include Aaron Rents (with 1,255 stores across the United States and Canada and gross revenues of $1.1 billion in 2005) and RentWay (with 788 stores in 34 states and revenues of almost $516 million in 2005).

These corporations represent the tip of the iceberg. Low-income consumers spent $1.75 billion for tax refund loans in 2002. Many lost as much as 16% of their tax refunds because of expensive tax preparation fees and/or interest incurred in tax refund anticipation loans. The interest and fees on such loans can translate into triple-digit annualized interest rates, according to the Consumer Federation of America, which has also reported that 11 million tax filers received refund anticipation loans in 2000, almost half through H&R Block. According to a Brookings Institution report, the nation's largest tax preparers earned about $357 million from fringe economy "fast cash" products in 2001, more than double their earnings in 1998. All for essentially lending people their own money!

The fringe economy plays a big role in the housing market, where subprime home mortgages rose from 35,000 in 1994 to 332,000 in 2003, a 25% a year growth rate and a tenfold increase in just nine years. (A subprime loan is a loan extended to less creditworthy customers at a rate that is higher than the prime rate.) According to Edward Gramlich, former member of the Board of Governors of the Federal Reserve System, subprime mortgages accounted for almost $300 billion or 9% of all mortgages in 2003.

While the fringe economy squeezes its customers, it is generous to its CEOs. According to Forbes, salaries in many fringe economy corporations rival those in much larger companies. In 2004 Sterling Brinkley, chairman of EZ Corp, earned $1.26 million; ACE's CEO Jay Shipowitz received $2.1 million on top of $2.38 million in stocks; Jeffrey Weiss, Dollar Financial Group's CEO, earned $1.83 million; Mark Speese, Rent-A-Center's CEO, made $820,000 with total stock options of $10 million; and Cash America's CEO Daniel Feehan was paid almost $2.2 million in 2003 plus the $9 million he had in stock options.

Fringe-economy corporations argue that the high interest rates and fees they charge reflect the heightened risks of doing business with an economically unstable population. While fringe businesses have never made their pricing criteria public, some risks are clearly overstated. For example, ACE assesses the risk of each check-cashing transaction and reports losses of less than 1%. Since tax preparers file a borrower's taxes, they are reasonably assured that refund anticipation loans will not exceed refunds. To further guarantee repayment, they often establish an escrow account into which the IRS directly deposits the tax refund check. Pawnshops lend only about 50% of a pawned item's value, which leaves them a large buffer if the pawn goes unclaimed (industry trade groups claim that 70% of customers do

---

A Glossary of the Fringe Economy

- **Payday loans** are small, short-term loans, usually of no more than $1,500, to cover expenses until the borrower's next payday. These loans come with extremely high interests rates, commonly equivalent to 300% APR. The Center for Responsible Lending conservatively estimates that predatory payday lending practices cost American families $3.4 billion annually.
- **Refund anticipation loans (RALs)**, provided by outlets of such firms as H&R Block, Western Union, and Liberty Tax Service, are short-term loans, often with high interest rates or fees, secured by an expected tax refund. Interest rates can reach over 700% APR-equivalent.
- **Check cashing stores** (ACE Cash Express is the biggest chain) provide services for people who don't have checking accounts. These stores are most often located in low-income neighborhoods and cash checks for a fee, which can vary greatly but is typically far higher than commercial banks charge for the same service. Check cashing fees have steadily increased over the past ten years.
- **Money Transfer companies** (outlets of such companies as Western Union, Moneygram, and Xoom) allow people to make direct bill payments and send money either to a person or bank account for a fee, typically 10% of the amount being sent, not including the exchange rate loss for money sent internationally. the total cost can reach up to 25% of the amount sent.
- **Pawnshops** give loans while holding objects of value as collateral. The pawnbroker returns the object when the loan is repaid, usually at a high interest rates. If the borrower doesn't repay the loan within a specified period, the pawnbroker sells the item. For example, the interest charge on a 30-day loan of $10 could be $2.20, equivalent to a 264% APR. Most pawnshops are individually owned but regional chains are now appearing.
- **Rent-to-own (RTO) stores**—two leading chains are Rent-A-Center and Aaron Rents—rent furniture, electronics, and other consumer goods short-term or long-term. The consumer can eventually own the item after paying many times the standard retail price through weekly rental payments with an extremely high interest rate, commonly around 300% APR. If the consumer misses a payment, the item is repossessed.
- **Buy here/pay here (BHPH) car lots** offer car loans on used cars on-site, with interest rates much higher than auto loans issued by commercial banks. Customers are often saddled with high-interest loans for high-mileage, overpriced vehicles. If a customer misses one payment, the car is repossessed. The largest BHPH company is the J.D. Byrider franchise, with 124 dealerships throughout the country.

redeem their goods). The rent-to-own furniture and appliance industry charges well above the "street price" for furniture and appliances, which is more than enough to offset any losses. Payday lenders require a post-dated check or electronic debit to assure repayment. Payday loan losses are about 6% or less, according to the Center for Responsible Lending.

Much of the profit in the fringe economy comes from financing rather than the sale of a product. For example, if a used car lot buys a vehicle for $3,000 and sells it for $5,000 cash, their profit is $2,000. But if they finance that vehicle for two years at a 25% APR, the profit jumps to $3,242. This dynamic is true for virtually every sector of the fringe economy. A customer who pays off a loan or purchases a good or service outright is much less profitable for fringe economy businesses than customers who maintain an ongoing financial relationship with the business. In that sense, profit in the fringe economy lies with keeping customers continually enmeshed in an expensive web of debt.

Funding and Exporting America's Fringe Economy

Fringe economy corporations require large amounts of capital to fund their phenomenal growth, and mainstream financial institutions have stepped up to the plate. ACE Cash Express has a relationship with a group of banks including Wells Fargo, JP Morgan Chase Bank, and JP Morgan Securities to provide capital for acquisitions and other activities. Advance America has relationships with Morgan Stanley, Banc of America Securities LLC, Wachovia Capital Markets, and Wells Fargo Securities, to name a few. Similar banking relationships exist throughout the fringe economy.

The fringe economy is no longer solely a U.S. phenomenon. In 2003 the HSBC Group purchased Household International (and its subsidiary Beneficial Finance) for $13 billion. Headquartered in London, HSBC is the world's second largest bank and serves more than 90 million customers in 80 countries. Household International is a U.S.-based consumer finance company with 53 million customers and more than 1,300 branches in 45 states. It is also a predatory lender. In 2002, a $484 million settlement was reached between Household and all 50 states and the District of Columbia. In effect, Household acknowledged it had duped tens of thousands of low-income home buyers into loans with unnecessary hidden costs. In 2003, another $100 million settlement was reached based on Household's abusive mortgage lending practices.

HSBC plans to export Household's operations to Poland, China, Mexico, Britain, France, India, and Brazil, for starters. One shudders to think how the fringe economy will develop in nations with even fewer regulatory safeguards than the United States. Presumably, HSBC also believes that predatory lending will not tarnish the reputation of the seven British lords and one baroness who sit on its 20-member board of directors.

What Can be Done?

The fringe economy is one of the few venues that credit-challenged or low-income families can turn to for financial help. This is especially true for those facing a penurious welfare system with a lifetime benefit cap and few mechanisms for emergency assistance. In that sense, enforcing strident usury and banking laws to curb the fringe economy while providing no legal and accessible alternatives would hurt the very people such laws are intended to help by driving these transactions into a criminal underground. Instead of ending up in court, non-paying debtors would wind up in the hospital. Simply outlawing a demand-driven industry is rarely successful.

One strategy to limit the growth of the fringe economy is to develop more community-based lending institutions modeled on the Grameen Bank or on local cooperatives. Although community banks might charge a higher interest rate than commercial banks charge prime rate customers, the rates would still be significantly lower than in the existing fringe sector.

Another policy option is to make work pay, or at least make it pay better. In other words, we need to increase the minimum wage and the salaries of the lower middle class and working poor. One reason for the rapid growth of the fringe economy is the growing gap between low and stagnant wages and higher prices, especially for necessities like housing, health care, pharmaceuticals, and energy.

Stricter usury laws, better enforcement of existing banking regulations, and a more active federal regulatory system to protect low-income consumers can all play a role in taming the fringe economy. Concurrently, federal and state governments can promote the growth of non-predatory community banking institutions. In addition, commercial banks can provide low-income communities with accessible and inexpensive banking services. As the "DrillDown" studies conducted in recent years by the Washington, D.C., non-profit Social Compact suggest, low-income communities contain more income and resources than one might think. If fringe businesses can make billions in low-income neighborhoods, less predatory economic institutions should be able to profit there too. Lastly, low and stagnant wages make it difficult, if not impossible, for the working poor to make ends meet without resorting to debt. A significant increase in wages would likely result in a significant decline in the fringe economy. In the end, several concerted strategies will be required to restrain this growing and out-of-control economic beast. ❏

Sources: "2003 Credit Card Usage Analysis" (2004) and "Undergraduate Students and Credit Cards in 2004" (2005) (Nellie Mae); Alan Berube, Anne Kim, Benjamin Forman, and Megan Burns, "The Price of Paying Taxes: How Tax Preparation and Refund Loan Fees Erode the Benefits of the EITC" (Brookings Institution and Progressive Policy Institute, May 2002); James H. Carr and Jenny Shuetz, "Financial Services in Distressed Communities: Framing the Issue, Finding Solutions," Financial Services in Distressed Communities: Issues and Answers (2001, Fannie Mae Foundation); "Making the Case for Financial Literacy: A Collection of Current Statistics Regarding Youth and Money" (Junior Achievement); Amanda Sapir and Karen Uhlich, "Pay Day Lending in Pima County Arizona" (Southwest Center for Economic Integrity, 2003); Keith Urnst, John Farris, and Uriah King, "Quantifying the Economic Cost of Predatory Payday Lending" (Center for Responsible Lending, 2004).

Article 3.2

THREE MILLION AMERICANS ARE DEBT POOR

BY STEVEN PRESSMAN AND ROBERT SCOTT

July/August 2007

Signs of the debt crisis facing a growing number of U.S. households are not hard to find. The subprime lending debacle, with its mushrooming rates of mortgage default and foreclosure, has been front-page news for months—perhaps because it has made victims of Wall Street firms as well as Main Street homeowners. Although less of a focus in the media, consumer debt—that is, household debt excluding mortgages and home-equity loans—is rising as well. Consumer indebtedness has reached record levels in the United States, currently averaging more than $21,000 per household, according to Federal Reserve data.

Rising consumer indebtedness can put families from across the income spectrum into precarious financial straits. However, it is poor and low- to middle-income families for whom the combination of stagnating incomes and rising debt creates the greatest risks. Yet the standard approach to calculating a poverty level of income and estimating the number of Americans who are poor fails to account for rising debt and the interest payments on that debt. If it did, about three million more Americans, including over half a million children, would be recognized as living below the poverty line.

Weighing Debt, Measuring Poverty

Consumer debt comes in many shapes and sizes (see sidebar). To measure the burden of household debt, economists generally look at the consumer debt-to-income ratio. Households with high incomes generally have lower debt-to-income ratios (see "Household Debt-to-Income Ratios"). Poor and near-poor households, on the other hand, are heavily in debt. The average amount of consumer debt per poor household is over $7,300, with debt-to-income ratios exceeding 60%.

Such high levels of consumer debt are new. For the median U.S. household, consumer debt has increased nearly tenfold in real terms (i.e., adjusted for inflation) since the early 1960s and is now growing at over 5% a year. Debt levels and debt-to-income ratios for low-income households have risen even faster than for more prosperous households. And predictably, interest payments (relative to income) have now reached their highest level ever. In 2005, the average household spent over 4% of its income servicing consumer debt, compared to just 0.8% in 1959 (see "Servicing Consumer Debt").

Rising debt and interest payments distort much economic data; most noteworthy is how they affect estimates of poverty. In 2005 (the most recent year for which data are available), 12.6% of Americans were poor according to the official U.S. Census Bureau tabulation. The poverty rate stood at 11.7% in 2001, when the Bush administration took office; it rose each year, hitting 12.6% in 2004 and again in 2005. But even these disheartening figures are too optimistic. Policymakers assume that when income (adjusted for inflation) goes up, households' living standards rise as well. But this assumption ignores the problem of rising debt. When more income must go to pay down debt or even just to cover interest charges, households have less money to meet day-to-day expenses and their living standards stagnate or fall.

The U.S. government's official definition of poverty was developed in the early 1960s by economist Mollie Orshansky of the Social Security Administration. In Orshansky's model, still used by the federal government today, the poverty-level income is equal to a basic food budget for a family of a given size multiplied by three. The model assumes, in other words, that food represents about one-third of a family's budget. Every year, the poverty threshold is adjusted based on the annual rise in consumer prices.

For a single person under age 65, the poverty threshold was $10,488 in 2006; for a single mother with two children, it was $16,242. For a family of four, the 2006 figure was $20,444—equal in real dollars, i.e., in purchasing power, to the 1962 poverty line of $3,100 for a family of four.

The current poverty thresholds are widely seen as unrealistic at best. So how to measure poverty has become a contentious issue, and Orshansky's methodology has for some time been criticized on a number of grounds by academics and policy-makers. Some have pointed out that the food budgets Orshansky used were meant for emergency purposes only and could not sustain people for an extended period of time. Indeed, the food budgets she used were set at 80% of a permanent nutrition-ally adequate diet. Others have complained that her estimates fail to account for taxes paid by the poor and the near-poor, who may pay little or no income tax but are still subject to payroll taxes. Still others criticize the model for overlooking gov-ernment benefits that low-income families receive, such as Food Stamps, Medicaid,

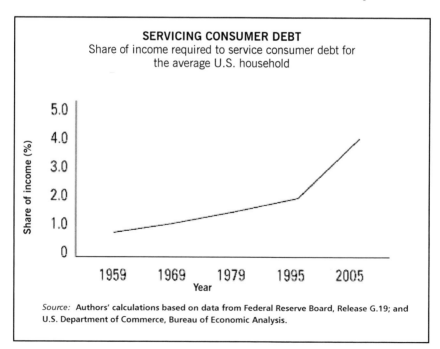

SERVICING CONSUMER DEBT
Share of income required to service consumer debt for the average U.S. household

Source: Authors' calculations based on data from Federal Reserve Board, Release G.19; and U.S. Department of Commerce, Bureau of Economic Analysis.

Types of Consumer Debt

Families take on consumer debt for many reasons and in many ways. Here are the most significant forms of consumer debt:

Installment debt— The largest category of consumer debt for the average household, amounting to more than $8,000 per household (2004). These loans are used for large purchases (computers, televisions, furniture, home appliances) and typically have long repayment periods and low interest rates.

Vehicle debt— Averaging more than $5,000 per household, the second largest category of consumer debt. With increasing sprawl, people rely on their cars more and more to get to work and school; U.S. households now have on average 1.9 vehicles—for 1.8 drivers. But vehicles are expensive; few people can afford to buy one (let alone two or three) outright. Those with strong credit histories may qualify for optimal terms on car loans, including very low interest rates, but others can borrow only in the subprime market, at far higher rates.

Education debt— A relatively new phenomenon, but one that has been rising rapidly. College tuitions have risen far faster than inflation over the past two decades, in part because the government has reduced aid to colleges and universities. At the same time, financial aid for students has increasingly come in the form of loans rather than grants. These factors, in combination, account for the fact four-year college students today graduate with a median debt of about $16,000.

Revolving credit card debt— Different from installment debt in that monthly payments and interest rates can both vary over time. Unless a credit card bill is paid in full each month, interest charges are applied to the remaining balance. Interest rates on credit card debt range from 0% to over 30%, with a national average of 14%; the average U.S. household owes about $3,000 in credit card debt.

and housing vouchers, arguing that the value of these benefits should be added to household income.

In all these debates, Americans' rising indebtedness has gone unnoticed. Many Americans have incomes above the poverty line, but because they must use a portion of their income to service their debt, they cannot buy the goods and services needed to escape poverty. These people are debt poor, and they should be recognized as poor by the government.

Using the Federal Reserve's *Survey of Consumer Finances*, we calculated that indebtedness of households with incomes up to 50% above the poverty line increased from $150 (the equivalent of around $1,000 today) in the early 1960s to over $4,000 in 2005. At the going interest rate, a typical low-income household in 2005 spent more than $400 servicing its past debt, compared to interest payments of just $10 to $20 (around $100 today) in the early 1960s. In the late 1950s, when poverty was first measured, both consumer debt and interest were negligible for poor households—mostly because the poor had limited access to formal credit markets.

Taking account of higher interest payments by American households, we calculate that the poverty rate for 2005 should have been around 13.6%, nearly 8% higher than the official rate. Put into concrete terms, this means that three million additional Americans should be counted as poor due to their high consumer debt and interest payments.

HOUSEHOLD DEBT-TO-INCOME RATIOS, BY INCOME (2004)

Income Range	$35,000 to $40,000	$40,000 to $45,000	$45,000 to $50,000	$50,000 to $55,000	$55,000 and more
D-I Ratio	61%	44%	48%	39%	29%

Source : Federal Reserve Board, Survey of Consumer Finances, 2004.

The effect of consumer debt on child poverty rates is particularly worrisome. Ayana Douglas-Hall and Heather Koball of the National Center for Children in Poverty already refer to children as the United States' "new poor" because 18% of children (13.4 million, in 2005) live in households with incomes below the poverty level. This marks an increase of 12% over the past five years. But again, this figure is too low. When interest on consumer debt is factored in, child poverty rises to 19%. Over half a million children in the United States are debt poor today, none of whom are included in official government poverty estimates.

Lifting the Burden

There are several reasons for the growing phenomenon of debt poverty. The federal minimum wage has been set at $5.15 an hour since 1997 and, until the increase Congress enacted this year takes effect, is at its lowest level in real terms (i.e., in purchasing power) in the past 50 years. At the same time, globalization, the skill requirements of a global economy, and an administration hostile to U.S. workers have all been forces restraining real income gains for low- and middle-income households.

A number of policy changes would help to remedy the problem. In addition to the minimum-wage increase, Congress should raise the child care tax credit and enact limits on credit-card interest rates. We also need to educate low-— and middle-income people about the potential dangers of consumer credit. Finally, the government must provide more money to colleges and universities, especially those that cater to middle- and low-income students, so that they can keep their tuition and fee increases under the rate of inflation. Doing so would both reduce families' debt and increase college attendance and future earnings.

Unless the problem of fast-rising consumer indebtedness is recognized and addressed in short order with steps such as these, George W. Bush is likely to become one of the very few presidents since the Great Depression to preside over rising poverty rates. And if we take rising consumer debt into account, he is likely to preside over the largest increase in poverty since the government began to measure it. ❏

Resources: Jeffrey J. Williams, "Debt Education: Bad for America, Bad for the Young," *Dissent*, Summer 2006; Leslie Miller, "Cars, Trucks Now Outnumber People," *Salon*, Aug. 29, 2003; Federal Reserve Board, *Survey of Consumer Finances*, 2004.

Article 3.3

THE HOMEOWNERSHIP MYTH

BY HOWARD KARGER
Spring 2007

Anyone who has given the headlines even a passing glance recently knows the subprime mortgage industry is in deep trouble. Since 2006 more than 20 subprime lenders have quit the business or gone bankrupt. Many more are in serious trouble, including the nation's number two subprime lender, New Century Financial. The subprime crisis is also hitting Wall Street brokerages that invested in these loans, with reverberations from Tokyo to London. And the worst may be yet to come. At least $300 billion in subprime adjustable-rate mortgages will reset this year to higher interest rates. CNN reports that one in five subprime mortgages issued in 2005-2006 will end up in foreclosure. If these dire predictions come true, it will be the equivalent of a nuclear meltdown in the mortgage and housing industries.

What's conspicuously absent from the news reports is the effect of the subprime lending debacle on poor and working-class families who bought into the dream of homeownership, regardless of the price. Sold a false bill of goods, many of these families now face foreclosure and the loss of the small savings they invested in their homes. It's critical to examine the housing crisis not only from the perspective of the banks and the stock market, but also from the perspective of the families whose homes are on the line. It is also critical to uncover the systemic reasons for the recent burst of housing-market insanity that saw thousands upon thousands of families getting signed up for mortgage loans that were highly likely to end in failure and foreclosure.

Like most Americans, I grew up believing that buying a home represents a rite of passage in U.S. society. Americans widely view homeownership as the best choice for everyone, everywhere and at all times. The more people who own their own homes, the common wisdom goes, the more robust the economy, the stronger the community, and the greater the collective and individual benefits. Homeownership is the ticket to the middle class through asset accumulation, stability, and civic participation.

For the most part, this is an accurate picture. Homeowners get a foothold in a housing market with an almost infinite price ceiling. They enjoy important tax benefits. Owning a home is often cheaper than renting. Most important, homeownership builds equity and accrues assets for the next generation, in part by promoting forced savings. These savings are reflected in the data showing that, according to the National Housing Institute's Winton Picoff, the median wealth of low-income homeowners is 12 times higher than that of renters with similar incomes. Plus, owning a home is a status symbol: homeowners are seen as winners compared to renters.

Homeownership may have positive effects on family life. Ohio University's Robert Dietz found that owning a home contributes to household stability, social involvement, environmental awareness, local political participation and activism, good health, low crime, and beneficial community characteristics. Homeowners are better citizens, are healthier both physically and mentally, and have children who achieve more and are better behaved than those of renters.

Johns Hopkins University researchers Joe Harkness and Sandra Newman looked at whether homeownership benefits kids even in distressed neighborhoods. Their study concluded that "[h]omeownership in almost any neighborhood is found to benefit children. ... Children of most low-income renters would be better served by programs that help their families become homeowners in their current neighborhoods instead of helping them move to better neighborhoods while remaining renters." (Harkness and Newman also found, however, that the positive effects of homeownership on children are weaker in unstable low-income neighborhoods. Moreover, the study cannot distinguish whether homeownership leads to positive behaviors or whether owners were already predisposed to these behaviors.)

Faith in the benefits of homeownership—along with low interest rates and a range of governmental incentives—have produced a surge in the number of low-income homeowners. In 1994 Bill Clinton set—and ultimately surpassed—a goal to raise the nation's overall homeownership rate to 67.5% by 2000. There are now 71 million U.S. homeowners, representing close to 68% of all households. By 2003, 48% of black households owned their own homes, up from 34.5% in 1950. Much of this gain has been among low-income families.

Government efforts to increase homeownership for low-income families include both demand-side (e.g., homeowner tax credits, housing cost assistance programs) and supply-side (e.g., developer incentives) strategies. Federal housing programs insure more than a million loans a year to help low-income homebuyers. Fannie Mae and Freddie Mac—the large, federally chartered but privately held corporations that buy mortgages from lenders, guarantee the notes, and then resell them to investors—have increasingly turned their attention to low-income home-buyers as the upper-income housing market becomes more saturated. Banking industry regulations such as the Community Reinvestment Act and the Home Mortgage Disclosure Act encourage homeownership by reducing lending discrimination in underserved markets.

The Housing and Urban Development department (HUD) has adapted some of its programs originally designed to help renters to focus on homeownership. For instance, cities and towns can now use the federal dollars they receive through HOME (the Home Investment Partnerships Act) and Community Development Block Grants to provide housing grants, down payment loans, and closing cost assistance. The American Dream Downpayment Initiative, passed by Congress in 2003, authorized up to $200 million a year for down payment assistance to low-income families. Private foundations have followed suit. The Ford Foundation is currently focusing its housing-related grants on homeownership rather than rental housing; the foundation views homeownership as an important form of asset-building and the best option for low-income people.

While homeownership has undeniable benefits, that doesn't mean it is the best option for everyone. For many low-income families, buying a home imposes burdens that end up outweighing the benefits. It is time to re-assess the policy emphasis on homeownership, which has been driven by an honest belief in the advantages of homeownership, but also by a wide range of business interests who stand to gain when a new cohort of buyers is brought into the housing market.

The Downsides of Homeownership

Low-income families can run into a range of pitfalls when they buy homes. These pitfalls may stem from the kinds of houses they can afford to buy (often in poor condition, with high maintenance costs); the neighborhoods they can afford to buy in (often economically distressed); the financing they can get (often carrying high interest rates, high fees, and risky gimmicks); and the jobs they work at (often unstable). Taken together, these factors can make buying a home a far riskier proposition for low-income families than it is for middle- and upper-income households.

Most low-income families only have the financial resources to buy rundown houses in distressed neighborhoods marked by few jobs, high crime rates, a dearth of services, and poor schools. Few middle-class homebuyers would hitch themselves to 30-year mortgages in these kinds of communities; poor families, too, have an interest in making the home-buying commitment in safe neighborhoods with good schools.

Homeownership is no automatic hedge against rising housing costs. On the contrary: lower-end affordable housing stock is typically old, in need of repair, and expensive to maintain. Low-income families often end up paying inflated prices for homes that are beset with major structural or mechanical problems masked by cosmetic repairs. A University of North Carolina study sponsored by the national nonprofit organization NeighborWorks found that almost half of low-income homebuyers experienced major unexpected costs due to the age and condition of their homes. If you rent, you can call the landlord; but a homeowner can't take herself to court because the roof leaks, the plumbing is bad, or the furnace or hot water heater quits working.

Besides maintenance and repairs, the expenses of homeownership also include property taxes and homeowners insurance, both of which have skyrocketed in cost in the last decade. Between 1997 and 2002 property tax rates rose nationally by more than 19%. Ten states (including giants Texas and California) saw their property tax rates rise by 30% or more during that period. In the suburbs of New York City, property tax rates grew two to three times faster than personal income from 2000 to 2004.

Nationally, the average homeowner's annual insurance premiums rose a whopping 62% from 1995 to 2005—twice as fast as inflation. Low-income homeowners in distressed neighborhoods are hit especially hard by high insurance costs. According to a Conning and Co. study, 92% of large insurance companies run credit checks on potential customers. These credit checks translate into insurance scores that are used to determine whether the carrier will insure an applicant at all, and if so, what they will cover and how much they will charge. Those with poor or no credit are denied coverage, while those with limited credit pay high premiums. Needless to say, many low-income homeowners do not have stellar credit scores. Credit scoring may also partly explain why, according to HUD, "Recent studies have shown that, compared to homeowners in predominantly white-occupied neighborhoods, homeowners in minority neighborhoods are less likely to have private home insurance, more likely to have policies that provide less coverage in case of a loss, and are likely to pay more for similar policies."

With few cash reserves, low-income families are a heartbeat away from financial disaster if their wages decline, property taxes or insurance rates rise, or expensive repairs are needed. With most—or all—of their savings in their homes, these families often have no cushion for emergencies. HUD data show that between 1999 and 2001, the only group whose housing conditions worsened—meaning, by HUD's definition, the only group in which a larger share of households spent over 30% of gross household income on housing in 2001 than in 1999—were low- and moderate-income homeowners. The National Housing Conference reports that 51% of working families with critical housing needs (i.e., those spending more than 50% of gross household income on housing) are homeowners.

Most people who buy a home imagine they will live there for a long time, benefiting from a secure and stable housing situation. For many low-income families, this is not what happens. Nationwide data from 1976 to 1993 reveal that 36% of low-income homeowners gave up or lost their homes within two years and 53% exited within five years, according to a 2005 study by Carolina Katz Reid of

---

THE NEW WORLD OF HOME LOANS

The new home loan products, marketed widely in recent years but especially to low- and moderate-income families, are generally adjustable-rate mortgages (ARMs) with some kind of twist. Here are a few of these "creative" (read: confusing and risky) mortgage options.

Option ARM: With this loan, borrowers choose each month which of three or four different—and fluctuating—payments to make:

- full (principal+interest) payment based on a 30-year or 15-year repayment schedule.
- interest-only payment—does not reduce the loan principal or build homeowner equity. Borrowers who pay only interest for a period of time then face a big jump in the size of monthly payments or else are forced to refinance.
- minimum payment—may be lower than one month's interest; if so, the shortfall is added to the loan balance. The result is "negative amortization": over time, the principal goes up, not down. Eventually the borrower may have an "upside down" mortgage where the debt is greater than the market value of the home.

According to the credit rating firm Fitch Ratings, up to 80% of all option ARM borrowers choose the minimum monthly payment option. So it's no surprise that in 2005, 20% of option ARMs were "upside down." When a negative amortization limit is reached, the minimum payment jumps up to fully amortize the loan for the remaining loan term. In other words, borrowers suddenly have to start paying the real bill.

Even borrowers who pay more than the monthly minimums can face payment shocks. Option ARMs often start with a temporary super-low teaser interest rate (and correspondingly low monthly payments) that allows borrowers to qualify for "more house." The catch? Since the low initial monthly payment, based on interest rates as low as 1.25%, is not enough to cover the real interest rate, the borrower eventually faces a sudden increase in monthly payments.

the University of Washington. Reid found that very few low-income families ever bought another house after returning to renting. A 2004 HUD research study by Donald Haurin and Stuart Rosenthal reached similar conclusions. Following a national sample of African Americans from youth (ages 14 to 21) in 1979 to middle age in 2000, the researchers found that 63% of the sample owned a home at some point, but only 34% still did in 2000.

Low-income homeowners, often employed in unstable jobs with stagnant incomes, few health care benefits, limited or no sick days, and little vacation time, may find it almost impossible to keep their homes if they experience a temporary job loss or a change in family circumstances, such as the loss of a wage earner. Homeownership can also limit financial opportunities. A 1999 study by econo-mists Richard Green (University of Wisconsin) and Patric Hendershott (Ohio

Balloon Loan: This loan is written for a short 5- to 7-year term during which the borrower pays either interest and principal each month or, in a more predatory form, interest only. At the end of the loan term, the borrower must pay off the entire loan in a lump sum—the "balloon payment." At that point, buyers must either refinance or lose their homes. Balloon loans are known to real estate pros as "bullet loans," since if the loan comes due—forcing the owner to refinance—during a period of high interest rates, it's like getting a bullet in the heart. According to the national organizing and advocacy group ACORN, about 10% of all subprime loans are balloons.

Balloon loans are sometimes structured with monthly payments that fail to cover the interest, much less pay down the principal. Although the borrower makes regular payments, her loan balance increases each month: negative amortization. Many borrowers are unaware that they have a negative amortization loan until they have to refinance.

Shared Appreciation Mortgage (SAM): These are fixed-rate loans for up to 30 years that have easier credit qualifications and lower monthly payments than conventional mortgages. In exchange for a lower interest rate, the borrower relinquishes part of the future value of the home to the lender. Interest rate reductions are based on how much appreciation the borrower is willing to give up. SAMs discourage "sweat equity" since the homeowner receives only some fraction of the appreciation resulting from any improvements. Not surprisingly, these loans have been likened to sharecropping.

Stated-Income Loan: Aimed at borrowers who do not draw regular wages from an employer but live on tips, casual jobs that pay under the table, commissions, or investments, this loan does not require W-2 forms or other standard wage documentation. The trade-off: higher interest rates.

No-Ratio Loan: The debt-income ratio (the borrower's monthly payments on debt, including the planned mortgage, divided by her monthly income) is a standard benchmark that lenders use to determine how large a mortgage they will write. In return for a higher interest rate, the no-ratio loan abandons this benchmark; it is aimed at borrowers with complex financial lives or those who are experiencing divorce, the death of a spouse, or a career change. —*Amy Gluckman*

State University) found that states with the highest homeownership rates also had the highest unemployment rates. Their report concluded that homeownership may constrain labor mobility since the high costs of selling a house make unemployed homeowners reluctant to relocate to find work.

Special tax breaks have been a key selling point of homeownership. If mortgage interest and other qualifying expenses come to less than the standard deduction ($10,300 for joint filers in 2006), however, there is zero tax advantage to owning. That is one reason why only 34% of taxpayers itemize their mortgage interest, local property taxes, and other deductions. Even for families who do itemize, the effective tax saving is usually only 10 to 35 cents for every dollar paid in mortgage interest. In other words, the mortgage deduction benefits primarily those in high income brackets who have a need to shelter their income; it means little to low-income homeowners.

Finally, homeownership promises growing wealth as home prices rise. But the homes of low-income, especially minority, homeowners generally do not appreciate as much as middle-class housing. Low-income households typically purchase homes in distressed neighborhoods where significant appreciation is unlikely. Among other reasons, if financially-stressed property owners on the block can't afford to maintain their homes, nearby property values fall. For instance, Reid's longitudinal study surveyed low-income minority homeowners from 1976 to 1994 and found that they realized a 30% increase in the value of their homes after owning for 10 years, while middle- and upper-income white homeowners enjoyed a 60% jump.

"Funny Money" Mortgages And Other Travesties

Buying a home and taking on a mortgage are scary, and people often leave the closing in a stupor, unsure of what they signed or why. My partner and I bought a house a few years ago; like many buyers, we didn't retain an attorney. The title company had set aside one hour for the closing. During that time more than 125 single-spaced pages (much of it in small print) were put in front of us. More than 60 required our signature or initials. It would have been difficult for us to digest these documents in 24 hours, much less one. When we asked to slow down the process, we were met with impatience. After the closing, Anna asked, "What did we sign?" I was clueless.

Yet buying a home is the largest purchase most families will make in their lifetimes, the largest expenditure in a family budget, and the single largest asset for two-thirds of homeowners. It's also the most fraught with danger.

For low-income families in particular, homeownership can turn out to be more a crushing debt than an asset-building opportunity. The primary reason for this is the growing chasm between ever-higher home prices and the stagnant incomes of millions of working-class Americans. The last decade has seen an unprecedented surge in home prices, which have risen 35% nationally. While the housing bubble is largely confined to specific metropolitan areas in the South, the Southwest, and the two coasts (home prices rose 50% in the Pacific states and 60% in New England), there are also bubbles in midwestern cities like Chicago and Minneapolis. And although the housing bubble is most pronounced in high-end properties, the prices of low-end homes have also spiked in many markets.

Current incomes simply do not support these inflated home prices. For example, only 18% of Californians can afford the median house in the state using traditional loan-affordability calculations. Even the fall in mortgage interest rates in the 1990s and early 2000s was largely neutralized by higher property taxes, higher insurance premiums, and rising utility costs.

This disparity might have put a dent in the mortgage finance business. But no: in 2005, Americans owed $5.7 trillion in mortgages, a 50% increase in just four years. Over the past decade the mortgage finance industry has developed creative schemes designed to squeeze potential homebuyers, albeit often temporarily, into houses they cannot afford. It is a sleight of hand that requires imaginative and risky financing for both buyers and financial institutions.

Most of the "creative" new mortgage products fall into the category of subprime mortgages—those offered to people whose problematic credit drops them into a lower lending category. Subprime mortgages carry interest rates ranging from a few points to ten points or more above the prime or market rate, plus onerous loan terms. The subprime mortgage industry is growing: lenders originated $173 billion in subprime loans in 2005, up from only $25 billion in 1993. By 2006 the subprime market was valued at $600 billion, one-fifth of the $3 trillion U.S. mortgage market.

Subprime lending can be risky. In the 37 years since the Mortgage Bankers Association (MBA) began conducting its annual national mortgage delinquency survey, 2006 saw the highest share of home loans entering foreclosure. In early 2007, according to the MBA, 13.5% of sub-prime mortgages were delinquent (compared to 4.95% of prime-rate mortgages) and 4.5% were in foreclosure. By all accounts, this is just the tip of the iceberg. However, before the current collapse the rate of return for subprime lenders was spectacular. *Forbes* claimed that subprime lenders could realize returns up to six times greater than the best-run banks.

In the past there were two main kinds of home mortgages: fixed-rate loans and adjustable-rate loans (ARMs). In a fixed-rate mortgage, the interest rate stays the same throughout the 15- to 30-year loan term. In a typical ARM the interest rate varies over the course of the loan, although there is usually a cap. Both kinds of loans traditionally required borrowers to provide thorough documentation of their finances and a down payment of at least 10% of the purchase price, and often 20%.

Adjustable-rate loans can be complicated, and a Federal Reserve study found that fully 25% of homeowners with ARMs were confused about their loan terms. Nonetheless, ARMs are attractive because in the short run they promise a home with an artificially low interest rate and affordable payments.

Even so, traditional ARMs proved inadequate to the tasks of ushering more low-income families into the housing market and generally keeping home sales up in the face of skyrocketing home prices. So in recent years the mortgage industry created a whole range of "affordability" products with names like "no-ratio loans," "option ARMS," and "balloon loans" that it doled out like candy to people who were never fully apprised of the intricacies of these complicated loans. (See box for a glossary of the new mortgage products.) These new mortgage options have opened the door for almost anyone to secure a mortgage, whether or not their circumstances auger well for repayment. They also raise both the costs and risks of buying a home—sometimes steeply—for the low- and moderate-income families to whom they're largely marketed.

Beyond the higher interest rates (at some point in the loan term if not at the start) that characterize the new "affordability" mortgages, low-income homebuyers face other costs as well. For instance, predatory and subprime lenders often require borrowers to carry credit life insurance, which pays off a mortgage if the homeowner dies. This insurance is frequently sold either by the lender's subsidiary or else by a company that pays the lender a commission. Despite low payouts, lenders frequently charge high premiums for this insurance.

As many as 80% of subprime loans include prepayment penalties if the borrower pays off or refinances the loan early, a scam that costs low-income borrowers about $2.3 billion a year and increases the risk of foreclosure by 20%. Pre-payment penalties lock borrowers into a loan by making it difficult to sell the home or refinance with a different lender. And while some borrowers face penalties for paying off their loans ahead of schedule, others discover that their mortgages have so-called "call provisions" that permit the lender to accelerate the loan term even if payments are current.

And then there are all of the costs outside of the mortgage itself. Newfangled mortgage products are often sold not by banks directly, but by a rapidly growing crew of mortgage brokers who act as finders or "bird dogs" for lenders. There are approximately 53,000 mortgage brokerage companies in the United States employing an estimated 418,700 people, according to the National Association of Mortgage Brokers; *BusinessWeek* notes that brokers now originate up to 80% of all new mortgages.

Largely unregulated, mortgage brokers live off loan fees. Their transactions are primed for conflicts of interest or even downright corruption. For example, borrowers pay brokers a fee to help them secure a loan. Brokers may also receive kickbacks from lenders for referring a borrower, and many brokers steer clients to the lenders that pay them the highest kickbacks rather than those offering the lowest interest rates. Closing documents use arcane language ("yield spread premiums," "service release fees") to hide these kickbacks. And some hungry brokers find less-than-kosher ways to make the sale, including fudging paperwork, arranging for inflated appraisals, or helping buyers find co-signers who have no intention of actually guaranteeing the loan.

Whether or not a broker is involved, lenders can inflate closing costs in a variety of ways: charging outrageous document preparation fees; billing for recording fees in excess of the law; "unbundling," whereby closing costs are padded by duplicating charges already included in other categories.

All in all, housing is highly susceptible to the predations of the fringe economy. Unscrupulous brokers and lenders have considerable latitude to ply their trade, especially with vulnerable low-income borrowers.

Time to Change Course

Despite the hype, homeownership is not a cure-all for low-income families who earn less than a living wage and have poor prospects for future income growth. In fact, for some low-income families homeownership only leads to more debt and financial misery. With mortgage delinquencies and foreclosures at record levels, especially among low-income households, millions of people would be better off today if they had remained renters. Surprisingly, rents are generally more stable than housing prices. From 1995 to 2001 rents rose slightly faster than inflation, but not as rapidly as home prices. Beginning in 2004 rent increases began to slow—even in hot markets like San Francisco and Seattle—and fell below the rate of inflation.

In the mid-1980s, low- and no-downpayment mortgages led to increased foreclosures when the economy tanked. Today, these mortgages are back, along with a concerted effort to drive economically marginal households into homeownership and high levels of unsustainable debt. To achieve this goal, the federal government spends $100 billion a year for homeownership programs (including the $70-plus billion that the mortgage interest deduction costs the Treasury).

Instead of focusing exclusively on homeownership, a more progressive and balanced housing policy would address the diverse needs of communities for both homes and rental units, and would facilitate new forms of ownership such as community land trusts and cooperatives. A balanced policy would certainly aim to expand the stock of affordable rental units. Unfortunately, just the opposite is occurring: rental housing assistance is being starved to feed low-income homeownership programs. From 2004 to 2006, President Bush and the Congress cut federal funding for public housing alone by 11%. Over the same period, more than 150,000 rental housing vouchers were cut.

And, of course, policymakers must act to protect those consumers who do opt to buy homes: for instance, by requiring mortgage lenders to make certain not only that a borrower is eligible for a particular loan product, but that the loan is suitable for the borrower.

The reason the United States lacks a sound housing policy is obvious if we follow the money. Overheated housing markets and rising home prices produce lots of winners. Real estate agents reap bigger commissions. Mortgage brokers, appraisers, real estate attorneys, title companies, lenders, builders, home remodelers, and everyone else with a hand in the housing pie does well. Cities raise more in property taxes, and insurance companies enroll more clients at higher premiums. Although housing accounts for only 5% of GDP, it has been responsible for up to 75% of all U.S. job growth in the last four years, according to the consulting firm Oxford Analytica. Housing has buffered the economy, and herding more low-income families into homes, regardless of the consequences, helps keep the industry ticking in the short run. The only losers? Renters squeezed by higher rents and accelerating conversion of rental units into condos. Young middle-income families trying to buy their first house. And, especially, the thousands of low-income families for whom buying a home turns into a financial nightmare. ❏

Sources: Carolina Katz Reid, *Studies in Demography and Ecology: Achieving the American Dream? A Longitudinal Analysis of the Homeownership Experiences of Low-Income Households,* Univ. of Washington, CSDE Working Paper No. 04-04; Dean Baker, "The Housing Bubble: A Time Bomb in Low-Income Communities?" *Shelterforce Online,* Issue #135, May/June 2004, www.nhi.org/online/issues/135/bubble.html; Howard Karger, *Shortchanged: Life and Debt in the Fringe Economy* (Berrett-Koehler, 2005); National Multi Housing Council (www.nmhc.org).

Article 3.4

HOW TO STOP THE FORECLOSURES
A Review of the Policy Proposals

BY FRED MOSELEY
July/August 2008; updated October 2010

Over one million U.S. homeowners have already lost their homes due to foreclosures since the mortgage crisis began last summer. Another one million homeowners are 90 days past due on their mortgages (foreclosure notices usually go out after 90 days) and two million more are 30 days past due, so three million more households may face foreclosure in the months ahead. If current policies do not change, it is estimated that up to five million homeowners would lose their homes due to foreclosure over the next few years. Five million is roughly 10% of the total number of U.S. homes with mortgages. This is clearly the worst housing crisis since the Great Depression, and will wreak havoc in the lives of millions of families unless something is done. A high foreclosure rate also has a deteriorating effect on surrounding neighborhoods, further depressing housing prices and quality of life.

Many of those facing foreclosure are low- to middle-income homeowners who were enticed into buying houses by fraudulent mortgage companies and low "teaser" interest rates that are adjusted up ("reset") after two to three years. As long as housing prices were increasing, homeowners could always refinance their mortgages and get a new teaser rate for another few years. However, now that house prices are falling, these homeowners can no longer refinance, and many of them cannot afford to pay the higher interest rates when they are reset. Falling prices also mean that many of these homeowners owe more on their mortgage than the current value of their house (i.e., they have "negative equity" in their house). The recession is also resulting in declining employment and income, meaning even more homeowners are struggling to make their monthly mortgage payments. The further housing prices decline, and the worse the recession is, the worse the foreclosures will be, in a vicious cycle.

Clearly, the federal government must take some positive actions to stop the spreading foreclosures, especially for low- and middle-income families, who would suffer the most. But what should those actions be? At a minimum, policies should apply only to owner-occupied homes, and not to "investor" or "speculative" homeowners (those who buy houses in order to sell them later at a higher price). But beyond this, various policies have been proposed, and not all of them would truly help homeowners at risk.

Workouts, Not Bailouts

There are two main types of anti-foreclosure policies: bailouts and workouts. In bailouts, the government gives aid either to lenders (e.g., by purchasing bad mortgages at their full original value) or to homeowners (e.g., by giving them loans so they can repay their lenders). Of course, aid to homeowners indirectly bails out the lenders as well. In workouts, the terms of the original mortgage contract are modified, either by reducing the rate of interest or reducing the principal owed, or both, in order to make the loan more affordable. So far, most of the proposals to deal with the foreclosure crisis have been workouts more than bailouts, although there are elements of bailout in some of them as well. The lenders made fortunes on these risky mortgages during the housing bubble, so if someone has to suffer losses now, it should be the lenders. There should be no bailouts of the lenders in any way.

Lender-Initiated Workouts

There are two types of workouts, depending on whether they are initiated by the lenders or the homeowners. Most of the policies proposed and enacted so far have been initiated by the lenders, i.e., they are voluntary on the part of the lenders. The main policy of the Bush administration is called "Hope Now," in which the lenders voluntarily postpone the resets of interest rates that are scheduled to take place in the months ahead, and leave the principal of the loan unchanged (or sometimes the foregone interest is added to the principal). The Bush administration claims that over 500,000 mortgages have been modified in this way in recent months, and estimates that another 500,000 mortgages will be modified in the months ahead. However, critics argue that these numbers are exaggerated and that many of these modifications have been simply allowing homeowners more time to make the same payments. It is likely that in the months ahead, many of these homeowners still will not be able to make their payments, and many of them will be foreclosed on, which has led some critics to call this the "No Hope" plan. The only lasting solution is to reduce the mortgage principal owed to more affordable levels. The main problem now is not the reset of interest rates, but rather declining housing prices, which has the effect that more and more homeowners now owe more money on their mortgage than their house is worth.

The House and Senate have recently passed two versions of a similar bill that is primarily a workout, but also is potentially part bailout, and is also lender-initiated. The bill would replace existing mortgages with new mortgages that would have a value of 85% of the current market value of the houses, and these refinanced mortgages would be guaranteed by the Federal Housing Administration (how this "current market value" is to be determined is a crucial detail which so far has not been specified). For example, a homeowner with an original mortgage of $300,000 would have the principal reduced to $225,000, and the monthly payments reduced by a similar proportion. This 15% "write-down" of the principal, plus the prior 10% decline of prices, means that the total write-down for lenders will be a maximum of approximately 25% (and less to the extent that the borrower made a down payment or has accumulated equity through monthly payments). The bill would permit FHA to guarantee up to $300 billion in new mortgages, which it estimates could help up to 1.5 million homeowners. President Bush initially threatened a veto, but has since promised to sign the bill. In any case, it remains unclear how many lenders will voluntarily implement this refinancing.

Another problem with this bill is that housing prices in some areas are likely to fall more than an additional 15%. Mortgages on these houses are likely to be the ones that the lenders will voluntarily refinance, and any further losses would be borne by the government (i.e., by the taxpayers). This will be a partial bailout of the lenders.

Homeowner-Initiated Workouts

Another bill has been introduced into the House (H.R. 3609) and Senate (S. 26360) that would provide workouts that would be initiated by the homeowners and would be mandatory for the lenders. These bills would allow bankruptcy judges to modify mortgage contracts (by reducing the principal and/or by reducing the interest rate) in order to make monthly payments more affordable for homeowners. It used to be possible for bankruptcy judges to modify mortgage contracts, but this was explicitly prohibited in a 1993 bankruptcy law. One can see the hand of the mortgage bankers in the writing of that provision. Modifications on other types of loans are allowed: for investment properties, for vacation homes, and even for boats, but no modifications allowed for primary residences! So all that needs to be done is to delete this one phrase in the law which prohibits modifications for primary residences. A significant advantage of this plan is that it would not cost taxpayers anything.

One problem with this bill is that homeowners would have to declare bankruptcy, which is expensive (about $2,000) and would hurt their credit rating in the future. But at least they would still have their home, with an affordable mortgage, and thus would have the chance to restore their credit rating.

This bill is supported by the AFL-CIO, SEIU, NAACP, ACORN, the Center for Responsible Lending, and many other consumer protection groups. It is of course strongly opposed by the Mortgage Bankers Association, and does not seem to have enough support for passage at the present time.

Another homeowner-initiated plan has been proposed by Dean Baker of the Center for Economic and Policy Research. According to this "own-to-rent" plan, homeowners faced with foreclosure would have the option to stay in their houses as tenants, rather than as owners, and would pay the prevailing rental rates, which are generally much lower than mortgage payments. Eligibility for the plan would be capped at the median house price in a metropolitan area and thus would not benefit high-income homeowners. This plan also would not cost taxpayers anything. A bill along these lines was recently introduced in the House (H.R. 6116).

Looking ahead

The presidential candidates have had disappointingly little to say about the foreclosure crisis and anti-foreclosure policies. Senator Barack Obama has expressed support for the FHA guarantee bill, but not yet for the bankruptcy modification bill. In good Republican tradition, McCain advocates "no government intervention." But the foreclosure crisis is likely to worsen in the coming months, and the public may well demand more policies to address this growing problem. The homeowner-initiated policies are preferable because they provide the most protection for homeowners against foreclosure. Both of these options should be available to homeowners facing foreclosure, especially for those with low or moderate incomes.

The guiding principles of government anti-foreclosure policies should be: (1) homeowners should be allowed to stay in their homes; and (2) there should be no bailouts for the lenders. And the long-run objective of government housing policies should be: decent affordable housing for all. ❑

Resources: For more information about H.R. 3609 and S. 26360, visit the website of the Center for Responsible Lending (www.responsiblelending.org). For more information about Dean Baker's "own-to-rent" plan (introduced in the House as H.R. 6116), visit the website of the Center for Economic and Policy Research (www.cepr.net).

Update on the Foreclosure Crisis, October 2010

More than two years after this article was originally published, the foreclosure crisis continues, and threatens to get worse. So far, over 3 million homeowners have lost their homes due to foreclosure since the crisis began. In addition, over 2 million mortgages are now in the process of foreclosure and another 5 million are 30 to 90 days delinquent. Eleven million mortgages are "underwater," i.e. the amount owed is greater than the current value of the house. Estimates of the total number of foreclosures under current policies range from 6 million to 10 million (12% to 20% of all mortgages). If unemployment remains very high for several more years, as seems very likely, foreclosures will be toward the high end of these estimates. It takes a paycheck to make a mortgage payment.

The main policy of the Obama administration to deal with foreclosures—the Home Affordable Modification Program or HAMP, which offers to pay lenders part of the cost of the modifications—has not been very effective. As of July 2010, only about 420,000 homeowners have received permanent modifications of their mortgages (after a three-month period of temporary modifications), and it is likely that a majority of these will probably default in the years ahead because the modification was not significant enough. (Fitch forecasts that the default rate of modified mortgages will be 75%; Barclays forecasts 60%.)

Therefore, the main effect of HAMP so far has been to delay foreclosures, due to temporary modifications, rather than to stop foreclosures. This delay has been somewhat beneficial for homeowners, but it means that "the worst is yet to come," unless government policies change significantly.

The main problem with HAMP, as with the earlier Bush policies, is that it is voluntary on the part of lenders, and lenders have generally not been very willing to "volunteer." Almost half of the modifications so far have been by the Fannie Mae and Freddie Mac, which are owned by the government.

I continue to think, as I argued in my original article, that the best way to avoid this escalating foreclosure crisis is to require that lenders participate in modifications initiated by homeowners or the government, and that these modifications should reduce the principal (the amount owed) of mortgages "underwater" to their current market value, rather than just reduce interest rates or delay payments. Bankruptcy judges should be allowed to modify mortgage contracts. Special judgeships should be created to ajudicate mortgage modifications. As long as participation is voluntary on the part of lenders, participation will be minimal and insufficient. There should also be a general moratorium on foreclosures until appropriate policies can be worked out and implemented.

Finally, the government should not pay the lenders for any of their losses. The lenders made plenty of profit on these mortgages in the good times, and there is no good reason why taxpayers should suffer the losses from the lenders' bad loans.

As this second edition goes to press (October 2010), the foreclosure crisis has taken a significant turn for the worse. It was disclosed recently that major mortgage servicers who carry out the foreclosures (GMAC, JPMorgan Chase, and Bank of America) have skirted the rules for providing documentation to justify foreclosures in an attempt to rush the process as quickly as possible. Their employees have routinely signed thousands of legal affidavits that they have the titles to the houses that are being foreclosed, even though they are not certain that this is true. The term "robo-signer" has entered the lexicon of the financial crisis. The banks mentioned above have halted foreclosures in the 23 states that require court approval of foreclosures, and they face likely opposition in other states as well, including investigations by state attorneys general. It looks like the federal government will probably impose some kind of moratorium on foreclosures in order to review all these procedures. The Obama administration should use this moratorium to institute mandatory mortgage modifications, as outlined above. ❑

Article 3.5

THE COMMUNITY REINVESTMENT ACT: A LAW THAT WORKS

BY JIM CAMPEN

November/December 1997; updated October 2010

A t an American Bankers Association convention in the early 1980s, bank consultant Ken Thomas was surprised to hear howls of laughter emerge from one of the meeting rooms. He stepped in to find the speaker ending his presentation with a flourish, pointing to the initial letters of the words projected behind him. "In conclusion," he shouted above the laughter and applause, "you can have your Community Reinvestment Act Programs, you can have your Community Reinvestment Act Policies, you can have your Community Reinvestment Act Personnel. But—as you can see—it's all just ... CRAP!"

The bankers' laughter may have been justified at the time, as the Reagan administration and its bank regulators ignored the law that a nationwide grassroots movement of community activists had successfully pushed Congress to enact in 1977. But as the Community Reinvestment Act (CRA) marks its twentieth anniversary this year, no one is laughing at it anymore.

In fact, the CRA is one of the most remarkable success stories of the 1990s. Under strong pressure from a second wave of grassroots activism that began ten years ago, many banks have recognized the potential for profitable business in neighborhoods that they had written off without a second thought not so long ago. Mortgage loans to minority and low-income homebuyers have soared. Hundreds of local partnerships among banks, community-based organizations and government agencies have resulted in tens of thousands of new units of affordable housing.

The CRA has acquired broad and deep support, due to the difference that it has made in hundreds of communities throughout the United States. This support paid off in 1996 when the CRA emerged intact from a determined attempt by congressional Republicans, following their 1994 electoral victory, to gut the law .

In spite of this legislative success and its many accomplishments, the future of the CRA remains uncertain. Its opponents may have lost a battle, but they have not given up the war, and the need for vigilant defense of the CRA will remain. Moreover, the dramatic ongoing transformation of the banking industry poses new challenges to successful implementation of the CRA.

A Collection of Laws

In fact, the CRA is the centerpiece of several laws that have worked together to increase flows of credit to borrowers and neighborhoods that banks have traditionally neglected. The CRA itself simply says that banks are obliged to serve the credit needs of all the communities where they are located. It requires regulators to examine each bank's record of doing so and to take this record into account when deciding whether or not to approve applications for new branches or mergers with other banks. (Throughout this article, the term "banks" refers to Savings & Loans and other thrift institutions as well as to commercial banks.)

The movement that won passage of the CRA in 1977 was primarily concerned about "redlining" of inner-city neighborhoods by lenders. The term refers to some bankers' practice of actually drawing red lines on maps to indicate areas off-limits for lending. Banks were using deposits collected in these neighborhoods to make loans in the suburbs. Gale Cincotta, of the Chicago-based National People's Action, was probably the most prominent of the many community leaders throughout the country who demanded that this disinvestment be replaced by reinvestment of the community's own money back into the community.

Two years earlier, in 1975, the community reinvestment movement had won passage of the Home Mortgage Disclosure Act (HMDA), which requires each bank to report annually on the number and dollar amount of mortgage loans made in every neighborhood in every metropolitan area. This disclosure made it possible to monitor where banks were and were not making mortgage loans.

Because the driving concern of the community reinvestment movement was saving neighborhoods, both the CRA and HMDA were focused on geographic communities. A separate set of "fair lending laws" prohibits discrimination against individual borrowers on the basis of race, national origin, sex, age, and other characteristics. The two most important of these laws, both legacies of the civil rights movement, are the Fair Housing Act of 1968, which prohibits discrimination in the home purchase and home rental process (including lending), and the Equal Credit Opportunity Act of 1974, which outlaws discrimination in all types of lending.

The Awakening

Until about ten years ago, the government agencies charged with enforcing these laws all but ignored them. U.S. Senate Banking Committee hearings in 1988, for example, revealed that even after a rebuke from the General Accounting Office for inadequate CRA examinations, bank regulators actually reduced the total hours devoted to CRA exams by 68% between 1981 and 1984. Moreover, only nine out of over 50,000 bank applications submitted since the passage of the CRA had been denied on the grounds of inadequate CRA performance. HMDA data were of notoriously poor quality and were frequently inaccessible to community groups. And the 1980s ended with the bank regulators having acted on only one case of lending discrimination during the entire life of the fair lending laws. As Mildred Brown, president of the national grassroots organization ACORN, told the senators, "Banks are breaking the law and the regulators are their accomplices."

Two initiatives by community activists during the second half of the 1980s turned the CRA into an effective anti-discrimination tool. First, activists recognized that the emergence of interstate banking provided a new leverage point, as bank holding companies sought regulatory approval for their expansion plans. Community groups challenged these proposals on the grounds of weak performance in meeting community credit needs. Confronted with the resulting uncertainty and delay, most banks responded by negotiating "CRA agreements" that committed them to expand their lending programs in return for withdrawal of the challenges.

The second initiative was the use of HMDA data to document dramatic disparities between the amount of mortgage lending in minority and white neighborhoods. Most significantly, "The Color of Money," a May 1988 Atlanta Journal-Constitution series, showed that in 1986 banks made 5.4 times as many mortgage loans per 1,000 homes in Atlanta's white neighborhoods as in comparable black neighborhoods. The Pulitzer Prize-winning series sparked investigations that generated similar findings, and publicity, in several other cities, and led to the Senate hearings later that year that highlighted the bank regulators' indefensible neglect of their responsibilities.

In 1989, the CRA and HMDA were strengthened by important amendments that increased public disclosure and accountability for both banks and regulators. Starting the next year, each bank's CRA performance rating became publicly available, along with a written report by its regulator. Furthermore, starting with 1990 applications, HMDA data were expanded to contain information on each application received, including the applicant's race and income and whether the application was approved or denied.

When they were released in the fall of 1991, the expanded HMDA data showed that the mortgage denial rate for blacks was more than twice that for whites. Bankers argued that the higher denial rate for blacks might simply reflect their weaker credit histories, smaller down payments and other factors not included in HMDA data.

But just one year later the Federal Reserve Bank of Boston announced the results of a study that proved the bankers wrong. Using statistical methods that separated out the effects of all other known factors, the study found that racial discrimination was a major reason why blacks and Hispanics were denied mortgage loans more frequently than whites [see "Lending Insights," in this chapter].

The Fruits of CRA

As publicity and pressure mounted, the laws enacted in the mid-1970s finally began to produce dramatic benefits. Once the spotlight began to shine on mortgage lending patterns, and the Justice Department reached some high-profile settlements in lending discrimination cases, loans to blacks and Hispanics soared. Between 1991 and 1995, while conventional home-purchase loans to whites increased by two-thirds, loans to blacks tripled (from 45,000 to 138,000 a year) and those to Hispanics more than doubled. During the same period, loans in predominantly minority neighborhoods rose by 137%, while loans in areas where the population was almost all white grew by just 37%.

Meanwhile, all of the mega-mergers that have recently transformed the banking industry were vulnerable to CRA challenges. In order to ensure regulatory approval, in each case banks have negotiated agreements with the community to provide more low-income loans. By mid-1997, according to Comptroller of the Currency Eugene Ludwig (the principal regulator of the nation's largest banks), these CRA Agreements had produced total commitments (some extending ten years into the future) for over $215 billion of increased loans and investments in underserved areas.

Fighting to Survive

While some banks recognized that the increased pressures had pushed them to make what turned out to be profitable loans, most resented the growing scrutiny of their performance and called for rollback of the CRA. When the Republicans gained control of Congress after the 1994 elections, bank lobbyists convinced them to make the Community Reinvestment Act a prime target. The prospects for survival of a meaningful CRA looked bleak as the confident Republicans, led by senators Richard Shelby (Alabama) and Connie Mack (Florida) and Florida Representative Bill McCollum, offered a series of innocuous-sounding "reforms."

A "small-bank exemption" for banks of less than $100 million in assets, coupled with a "self-certification" provision that would have allowed banks with up to $250 million to evaluate their own CRA performance, would have eliminated CRA oversight for 88% of all banks. And a "safe harbors" provision would have prohibited challenges to proposed mergers of banks with a CRA rating of "satisfactory" or better—at a time when more than 95% of all banks, including all of the biggest ones, had such ratings. Any difference between amending the CRA in these ways and repealing it outright would have been purely cosmetic.

The banks' Republican allies offered three arguments to support their position, none of which could withstand serious scrutiny. First, they claimed that the CRA imposed a massive regulatory burden on small banks. While grossly exaggerated in any case, this claim was rendered obsolete by an overhaul of CRA regulations in early 1995. The revised regulations replaced an excessive emphasis on process and paperwork with a focus on actual performance, and drastically streamlined the process for banks with less than $250 million in assets.

Second, CRA opponents claimed that it requires risky loans that could undermine a bank's profitability and threaten its survival. Actually, the reverse is closer to the truth. The 1980s were marked by massive speculative lending to wealthy real estate developers and get-rich-quick schemers that resulted in the failure of more than two thousand banks and S&Ls. Yet not a single bank failure has been caused by making too many bad loans to disadvantaged borrowers.

Recently, Federal Reserve Board researchers found "no evidence of lower profitability" at banks that specialize in mortgage lending to lower-income borrowers and neighborhoods and, in a nationwide survey by the Kansas City Fed, 98% of banks reported that their CRA lending was profitable. A recent investigation by the Comptroller of the Currency found that affordable home loans had "the same level of losses" as standard mortgages.

Overall, the look-the-other-way attitude toward CRA enforcement of the 1980s was accompanied by a steady fall in bank profit rates, while the increasingly serious enforcement of the CRA in the 1990s has coincided with five straight years of record bank profits.

The third argument raised against CRA—that it was ineffective and all of the efforts to enforce it in the 1990s had accomplished little—was contradicted not just by statistics but by massive support from cities and towns around the country attesting to how much had, in fact, been accomplished. One open letter to Congress was signed by over 2,000 community-based organizations and more than 200 mayors.

The swell of grassroots support overwhelmed pressure from industry lobbyists and produced unanimous opposition by congressional Democrats to every proposal that would have weakened the CRA. In addition, the Clinton administration never wavered from an early pledge to veto any bill containing such provisions. (Of course, since supporting the CRA required virtually no budgetary resources, it was easier for Clinton to take a strong stance.) When the dust of battle finally cleared at the end of 1996, the CRA emerged intact.

Challenges Ahead

With this important victory behind it, the community reinvestment movement now faces several important challenges and opportunities—in addition to the need for continuing vigilance against future legislative attacks on the CRA:

- Aiding small businesses and rural households. A major increase in lending to small and minority-owned businesses is needed to support the economic development essential to healthy communities. Because HMDA data played such a central role in generating pressure to remedy the glaring disparities in mortgage lending, activists eagerly anticipate analyzing the data on lending to small businesses that will become available in late 1997 (as mandated by the 1995 revisions to the CRA regulations).

Similarly, community groups in rural areas are looking forward to analyzing this year's HMDA data, which will for the first time include data on mortgage lending outside of metropolitan areas. Both rural and urban groups want to maintain access to banking services by halting wholesale branch closures in lower-income areas—such as the 140 mostly rural branches that KeyCorp announced it will close or the hundreds of branches that Wells Fargo abandoned after its 1996 merger with First Interstate.

- Extending CRA-type obligations to other financial institutions. As banks and other kinds of financial firms enter more and more into each other's businesses, it makes little sense to continue exempting these other firms from responsibilities to serve lower-income and minority communities.

Study after study has demonstrated that mortgage companies devote far smaller shares of their total loans to disadvantaged borrowers and neighborhoods than banks do. Mortgage companies, who now make the majority of mortgage loans, benefit enormously from being able to sell their loans to the government-sponsored enterprises Fannie Mae and Freddie Mac. In order to retain this benefit, the companies should be required to provide for community credit needs.

Regulation of insurance companies takes place at the state level, where the companies benefit from taxpayer-supported guarantee funds that make their policies more attractive to customers. In Massachusetts, community organizations won passage of a law in 1996 that requires property insurers to disclose—HMDA-style—the geographic distribution of their homeowner policies. Activists are now campaigning to require that life insurance companies invest part of their assets in ways that benefit the lower-income and minority neighborhoods where many of their policy-holders live.

- Dealing with the growing dominance of mega-banks. With virtually all restrictions on interstate banking phased out by mid-1997, the rapid consolidation among large U.S. banks will accelerate. Giant banking companies such as NationsBank, KeyCorp, BankAmerica, Wells Fargo, and Norwest will continue to expand their geographic scope, homogenize their operations, and centralize their decision-making power.

Although some of the megabanks have excellent overall records of CRA performance, their corporation-wide programs do not match the needs of every city and town. As decision-making authority migrates from local offices to regional or even national headquarters, "it is becoming harder and harder to get the big banks to deal with the specifics of local situations—even though responsiveness to the particular needs of local communities is exactly what CRA is all about," notes Debby Goldberg of the Center for Community Change's Neighborhood Revitalization Project.

- Monitoring discriminatory interest rates on loans. As enforcement of the fair lending laws has increased in the last few years (for example, the Comptroller of the Currency made 23 referrals to HUD and the Department of Justice from 1993 to 1996, compared to just one referral in the preceding quarter-century), most cases have involved racial discrimination either in marketing practices or decisions to deny applications. Recently, however, attention has shifted to the fact that companies charge some borrowers more than others. One exploitative technique—a specialty of the Fleet Financial Group, which has been caught at it more than once—is for a megabank to steer vulnerable loan applicants, who are disproportionately black and Hispanic, to a related finance company where fees and interest rates are higher.

Another method is to use supposedly independent mortgage brokers to negotiate individualized loan terms with vulnerable (often elderly, female and/or minority) borrowers. This arrangement allows the brokers to impose higher interest rates and larger hidden fees of up to 12% of the loan amount into the monthly payments. Such actions cost Long Beach (California) Mortgage Company (formerly Long Beach Bank) a $4 million settlement with the Justice Department when they were caught red-handed. Earlier, Long Beach had received awards for making many loans to minority borrowers—underlining the need to consider loan pricing as well as the number of loans when evaluating a lender's performance.

- Holding the bank regulators accountable. As Rochelle Nawrocki of National People's Action observes, "If our history has taught us anything, it's that only we make CRA work—not bankers, regulators, or Congress." Regulators will enforce the law only when under strong pressure to do so. Currently, CRA activists realize the need to scrutinize how regulators implement the revised

CRA examination procedures for big banks that took effect in mid-1997; to question whether the fact that almost one-third of banks examined last year were rated "outstanding" reflects lowered standards; and to ensure that regulatory changes adopted as part of continuing deregulation of banking don't undermine the CRA.

Unless the bank regulators as well as banks are continually held accountable for their actions, the fact that the CRA remains the law of the land may again make no more difference than it did during the Reagan years. ❑

Resources: NCRC Reinvestment Compendium, National Community Reinvestment Coalition (ncrc.org); CRA Watch, Center for Community Change (communitychange.org); "CRA and Fair Lending Regulations," Douglas Evanoff & Lewis Segal, Economic Perspectives (Federal Reserve Bank of Chicago), Nov./Dec. 1996; Disclosure, National People's Action (http://www.npa-us.org).

Updating the Community Reinvestment Act (October, 2010)

Thirteen years after the preceding article was written, the need to update the Community Reinvestment Act is greater than ever. When Congress passed the "Financial Services Modernization Act" of 1999, capping a decades-long process of deregulating banks and other financial companies, it rejected the compelling arguments by community groups that the CRA needed to be "modernized" as well. The industry-friendly Republicans who controlled the Senate Banking Committee adamantly opposed any strengthening of the CRA.

As a result, the impact of the CRA continued to erode, as an ever-greater share of total mortgage lending fell outside its reach. The CRA was enacted in 1977 because banks were collecting deposits in inner-city neighborhoods but failing to reinvest the funds back into those same areas. For this reason, CRA performance evaluations were focused on "assessment areas" defined in terms of where bank branches were located. At that time, this covered the great majority of all mortgage lending. By 2005, however, according to the Federal Reserve, only one in four home-purchase loans (26%) were made by banks in their CRA assessment areas. The rest of the loans were made by banks in areas where they didn't have branches (Wells Fargo Bank makes loans in all 50 states, although it only has branches in 24), by affiliated companies that didn't have to be included in CRA evaluations (such as CitiBank's sister company, CitiFinancial, that specialized in high-cost loans), and by independent mortgage companies not related to banks (including many, such as Ameriquest and New Century, that focused on high-cost predatory lending).

Within this shrinking area of coverage, the CRA continued to have an important impact, encouraging banks to make responsible home loans that borrowers could afford to repay and discouraging predatory subprime loans. The Federal Reserve found that only 7% of the loans that banks made in 2005 in their assessment areas were high-cost loans, compared to 24% of the loans that they made elsewhere, and 38% of the loans made by mortgage companies. My own research in Massachusetts found that in 2006, at the height of the subprime boom, banks whose local lending was covered by the CRA accounted for only 655 out of 40,173 subprime loans in the state (just 1.6% of the total). Conservative claims that the CRA was responsible for the subprime lending crisis have things exactly backwards. If CRA had been expanded to cover the entire mortgage lending industry as part of the 1999 "financial modernization" law, the subprime lending crisis might never have happened.

In the aftermath of the crisis, it is even more vital to finally update the CRA—both to prevent predatory lending from re-emerging once the current crisis is over, and to ensure that those responsible for the crisis provide the credit and capital that local communities need to recover. Accordingly, community-based organizations have stepped up their campaigns for expanding and modernizing CRA. Last year, National People's Action and the PICO National Network (together representing more than 70 community-based organizations nationwide) got the Federal Reserve to agree to hold a series of day-long meetings with local leaders and hundreds of activists in nine hard-hit cities across the country, from Richmond, Calif., to Brockton, Mass. In Washington, D.C., meanwhile, the National Community Reinvestment Coalition has led a broad collection of local, regional, and national groups in bringing pressure to bear on regulators and elected officials.

The most important proposals for updating and strengthening the CRA include: extending CRA coverage to bank lending in all of the communities where they do business and to all lending by all affiliated companies; extending CRA coverage to independent mortgage companies; extending CRA-like responsibilities to Wall Street firms such as investment banks and hedge funds; increasing emphasis on basic banking services, including convenient branch offices, affordable small-dollar loans, and inexpensive checking and savings accounts for lower-income families; and expanding the attention given to evaluating performance in meeting the credit and banking needs of people and communities of color.

Some of these long-overdue measures to expand the CRA's coverage and operation would require legislation, such as the American Community Investment Reform Act of 2010, introduced in the House of Representatives in September. But many others could be implemented under the current law, by the bank regulators charged with implementing the CRA. The struggle continues, on both fronts. ❏

Resources: Revisiting the CRA: Perspectives on the Future of the Community Reinvestment Act, Federal Reserve Banks of Boston and San Francisco, 2009 (www.bos.frb.org/commdev/cra/Revisiting-the-CRA.htm); the National Community Reinvestment Coalition (www.ncrc.org); National People's Action (www.npa-us.org); PICO National Network (www.piconetwork.org).

Article 3.6

LENDING INSIGHTS: HARD PROOF THAT BANKS DISCRIMINATE

BY JIM CAMPEN
January/February 1994; revised October 1999

> *"These really are horrifying numbers."*
> — Comptroller of the Currency Eugene A. Ludwig on banks' 1992 record
> denying mortgages to minorities, Nov. 4, 1993.

As appalling as it was, the latest annual report on mortgage lending shocked few observers when the Clinton administration's top regulators unveiled it before the Senate Banking Committee in early November. In keeping with past patterns, black mortgage applicants were turned down more than twice as often as whites in 1992. Indeed, the most closely watched single number indicated that things were getting worse rather than better: The ratio of the black denial rate to the white denial rate rose from 2.16 in 1991 to 2.26 in 1992.

What was different this year was the response to the statistics. Instead of denying the obvious as they have in the past, government officials acknowledged that discrimination is "alive and well in America," as Housing Secretary Henry Cisneros put it. Bank regulators, along with Attorney General Janet Reno, testified that they are intensifying efforts to identify and punish lenders who discriminate.

And bankers, rather than disputing charges that they had discriminated, emphasized their efforts to do better. Since researchers found what one Massachusetts banker referred to as a "smoking gun" in October 1992, bankers have recognized that they can no longer offer credible denials. The crucial evidence, from a study by the Federal Reserve Bank of Boston, finally established beyond a reasonable doubt that banks discriminate along racial lines when making mortgage loans.

The banks' quandary is the triumph of a nationwide grassroots "community reinvestment" movement that for over twenty years has been employing innovative strategies to challenge banks' failure to meet the credit needs of low-income and minority neighborhoods and individuals. That banks discriminate has, of course, long been obvious to those receiving the short end of the stick. But community advocates recognized that obtaining proof of discrimination would be the key to combatting it. So, they fought not only for laws that regulate banks, but also for requirements that banks furnish relevant information on their lending practices. They then used this data to publicize banks' abysmal performances, sparking the public outrage necessary to make banks more responsive to the needs of low-income and minority communities.

Their first major legislative victory was the 1975 enactment of the Home Mortgage Disclosure Act (HMDA—pronounced HUMdah), which required each bank to report the number and dollar amount of the mortgage and home improvement loans by census tract (census tracts are areas a few blocks square, containing a few thousand people, for which detailed demographic and socio-economic data are available). Two years after HMDA took effect, Congress adopted the Community Reinvestment Act (CRA). The CRA declares that banks have an "affirmative obligation" to serve the credit needs of local communities, including low and moderate income areas—which are often communities of color. A lesser-known set of fair lending laws, including the Fair Housing Act of 1968 and the Equal Credit Opportunity Act of 1974, explicitly prohibit racial discrimination. Only very recently, however, have bankers and regulators begun to take the CRA and the fair lending laws at all seriously.

The Information Game

In the absence of earnest enforcement efforts by bank regulators, it fell primarily to independent community-oriented researchers to document discriminatory lending practices. Their efforts to build this case, beginning with the struggle to enact HMDA, have followed a recurring pattern.

Typically, community groups made charges only to see them dismissed by the banks as unsupported by solid evidence. The groups then struggled to make more data available, so researchers would be able to produce more definitive results. Consistently, though, the banks and their defenders (including, in many cases, the regulatory agencies) criticized the resulting studies as inconclusive. The limited nature of the data available, they argued, made it impossible to rule out other possible explanations of racial disparities in lending patterns. But with this maneuver, the banks backed themselves into a corner: They were now in no position to deny demands from community advocates for additional data to fill out the picture. So another round would begin, as researchers used the more extensive data supplied by the banks to produce results even more suggestive of racial discrimination.

By the end of the 1980s, this cycle had yielded an impressive array of studies that combined HMDA data with Census Bureau information on the racial composition and income level of census tracts in order to document mortgage lending discrimination. The *Atlanta Journal-Constitution*'s Pulitzer Prize-winning series "The Color of Money" (May 1988) compared stable, middle-income neighborhoods that were at least 80% white to those that were at least 80% nonwhite. It found that between 1984 and 1986, Atlanta banks and savings & loans (S&Ls) made 4.5 times as many loans per 1,000 single-family structures in white neighborhoods as in comparable black neighborhoods.

In city after city, studies documented similarly dramatic racial disparities in mortgage lending. Between 1981 and 1987 in Boston, for instance, banks made 2.9 times as many mortgage loans per 1,000 housing units in low-income white neighborhoods as in minority neighborhoods with similar incomes. In Detroit, the ratio of the mortgage lending rate (loans per 1,000 homes) in middle-income white neighborhoods to that in middle-income black neighborhoods rose every year between 1981 and 1986, reaching 3.14 to 1 in 1986. Similar patterns appeared in Chicago, Los Angeles, Milwaukee, and New York as well as in 14 cities observed by the Center for Community Change. A survey of 23 studies by Professor Anne Shlay of Temple University showed that all 23 found a negative impact of race on conventional mortgage lending.

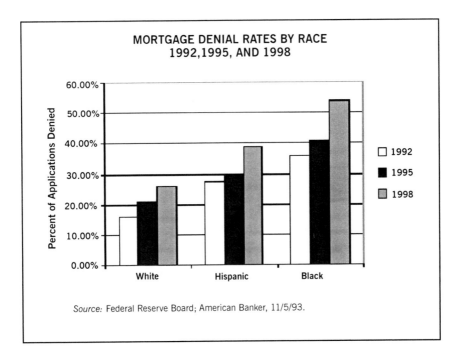

MORTGAGE DENIAL RATES BY RACE
1992, 1995, AND 1998

Source: Federal Reserve Board; American Banker, 11/5/93.

Bankers acknowledged that these results were troubling, but argued that they didn't prove that banks were discriminating. First, the bankers suggested that the low level of lending in minority neighborhoods might reflect a low level of applications rather than a high level of bank denials. They also pointed out that the data referred only to the location of the homes being purchased. Since it provided no direct information about the race or income level of the applicants, they argued that the data failed to prove discrimination against minority individuals.

These defensive arguments by bankers helped make it possible for the community reinvestment movement to finally succeed in broadening the scope of HMDA. As part of the S&L bailout bill adopted in August 1989, HMDA was amended to require banks to report on all mortgage applications received, rather than just on loans made. Beginning January 1, 1990, banks had to record the race, income, and sex of each applicant, the result of the application, and the previously required information on the census tract in which the home was located.

In October 1991, the Federal Reserve reported the results of its analysis of the expanded HMDA data for 1990. It was the most extensive set of mortgage lending data ever assembled—more than six million loan applications reported by over 9,000 mortgage lenders. The most striking single result of their analysis was the difference in denial rates for black and white applicants. Overall, 34% of black applications for conventional home mortgages were rejected, compared to a 14% rejection rate for whites. (Hispanics were rejected at a 21% rate; rejection rates for Asians were slightly lower than for whites.) Large differentials persisted even when comparisons were limited to applicants in the same income categories. In many cities, high-income blacks experienced higher denial rates than low-income whites. As the chart indicates, these disparities in denial rates continued through the 1990s.

Lenders could no longer claim that low levels of lending resulted solely from a lack of demand for loans by minority applicants rather than from their own decisions on which applications to accept. They were, however, quick to adopt a fallback position. In its reponse to the grossly unequal denial rates revealed by the expanded HMDA data, the American Bankers Association (ABA) emphasized that the data didn't include "information critical to judging the creditworthiness of loan applicants." It was entirely possible, the bankers suggested, that differences in applicants' credit histories, wealth, job instability, or other economic characteristics accounted for the more frequent rejection of minority loan applicants. ABA chief lobbyist Ed Yingling maintained that "the HMDA numbers don't show a whole lot; they don't mean a whole lot."

These denials persisted in the face of both statistical and tangible evidence of racial discrimination by banks. Court cases and case studies compiled by community-based organizations supplemented the faceless statistical studies with the stories of real human beings. Banks were closing offices in minority neighborhoods while opening them elsewhere, and new surveys revealed that banks had disproportionately few black executives. It would have been perverse, in light of all this evidence, for anybody to doubt that banks were in fact discriminating.

But that did not deter the banking industry from commissioning social scientists to argue that the case for discrimination was based entirely on "circumstantial evidence." They took the position that, according to the standards of statistical research in the social sciences, the conclusion had not been proven beyond a reasonable doubt.

The "Smoking Gun"

Meanwhile, researchers at the Federal Reserve Bank of Boston—which has been a somewhat liberal outpost in the overwhelmingly conservative Federal Reserve System—were pursuing another path. If conclusions had been limited by missing data, they reasoned, why not collect and analyze all of the data necessary to resolve the issue? Taking advantage of the Fed's status as a banking regulator, they were able to conduct the first study to take into account virtually all of the factors used in mortgage lending decisions. They asked the 131 banks in the Boston area that had received 25 or more mortgage applications in 1990 to review their loan files and gather 38 additional pieces of information for each application from a black or Hispanic (about 1,200 applications) and for a randomly selected set of 3,300 applications by whites. Once again, the banks' attacks on the alleged insufficiency of existing data had led to the gathering of more and better information.

Using a special variant of the standard statistical technique known as multiple regression analysis, the Boston Fed's analysts then sought to explain why minorities in the Boston area were denied mortgages 2.7 times as often as whites. To what extent, the researchers asked, did legitimate factors account for the disparity?

Banks, hoping to be exonerated by the Boston Fed's study, were dismayed at the results. The additional information showed that, as the banks claimed, blacks and Hispanics were on average poorer, had worse credit histories, and requested mortgage loans that were larger relative to their incomes. But it also showed that these and similar factors only told part of the story. Even if black and Hispanic borrowers had been just as creditworthy as the average white applicant with respect to all 38 of the factors considered, they still would have been 56% more likely to be denied a mortgage. Only the applicants' minority status could account for the difference. As Alicia Munnell, who was then the Boston Fed's Research Director, put it, "The study eliminates all the other possible factors that could be influencing decisions." The long-sought "smoking gun" had been found.

After the Smokescreen Clears

Pushed beyond the stage of denial—in spite of the inevitable, and quickly discredited, objections published by *Forbes*, *Business Week*, and the *Wall Street Journal*—bankers and federal regulators have begun to recognize the value of measures that had been urged on them for years by community advocates. Bank responses have included taking a systematic "second look" at minority loan applications recommended for denial; training bank employees to increase understanding of fair lending issues and sensitivity to cultural differences; hiring more minority loan officers; revising certain traditional credit standards that are biased toward white cultural practices; forging working relationships with realtors and appraisal firms that have positive records in minority communities; developing new mortgage lending products adapted to the special circumstances and needs of minority borrowers; and using internal "testing" programs to identify whether or not bank employees are in fact offering equal treatment to minority applicants.

At the same time, the four federal bank regulatory agencies began taking steps to ensure that banks are complying with fair lending laws. But they acted only after Congressional hearings had brought to light what Deepak Bhargava of the Association of Community Organizations for Reform Now (ACORN) characterized as "a long and sorry record" of regulatory failure. Even New York's Republican Senator Alphonse D'Amato was moved to ask whether the "regulatory agencies [were] asleep at the switch, or worse, turning a blind eye?"

In fact, between 1978 and 1990 three successive directors of the OCC's fair lending office resigned in frustration at the attitude of the agency's leadership, which not only refused to allow them to take the steps they regarded as necessary to enforce the law, but even refused to release reports documenting possible discrimination. A single community organization in one medium-sized Ohio city, the Toledo Fair Housing Center, was able to identify and successfully pursue numerous cases of lending discrimination annually, while all four of the federal bank regulators—taken together—only referred one case of racial discrimination in lending to the Department of Justice in 18 years. And until its September 1992 settlement requiring Georgia's Decatur Federal Savings & Loan to pay $1 million to 48 black applicants denied mortgage loans, the Justice Department had never charged a single bank with racial discrimination in mortgage lending.

The Power of Disclosure

It remains to be seen whether, and to what extent, this story will have a happy ending. It will be years before we know whether the hard-won gains by community-based groups and their advocates will bring about an actual reduction in lending discrimination.

The Boston Fed study established the fact of discrimination in mortgage lending. But with its narrow focus on data from completed loan applications, the study did not attempt to measure the full extent of discrimination. For example, many potential minority borrowers encounter responses to their initial contacts with banks that discourage them from ever applying, and the property values recorded in loan files may have been furnished by appraisers who systematically undervalue homes in minority neighborhoods.

The community reinvestment movement is right to insist that banks are obliged by the CRA to do more than simply deal fairly with the loan applicants who come through their doors. A whole range of aggressive, affirmative initiatives will be necessary to extend credit and financial services to currently underserved communities. Moreover, without constant pressure from community groups, regulators will likely bow to pressure from banks and fail to enforce community-oriented laws and regulations.

If properly enforced, disclosure laws should continue to be useful. Many aspects of the normal operation of our economic system cannot stand the light of day. With that in mind, the community reinvestment movement has recently been emphasizing its long-standing call for the extension of disclosure requirements to the realm of business lending.

Activists believe that businesses based in low-income communities and those owned by minorities have had an even harder time obtaining credit than minority homebuyers. But until there is something comparable to HMDA for small business lending, it will be impossible to persuasively document the existence and extent of the problem. And as the ongoing struggle for fair mortgage lending has demonstrated, exposing the nature of a problem can go a long way toward forcing its solution. ❏

Resources: Alicia Munnell and others, "Mortgage Lending in Boston: Interpreting HMDA Data," Federal Reserve Bank of Boston, October 1992. "Discrimination in the Housing and Mortgage Markets," a special issue of *Housing Policy Debate*, Vol. 3, No. 2, 1992. "Mortgage Lending Discrimination: A Review of Existing Evidence," Urban Institute, 1999; John Yinger, "Closed Doors, Opportunities Lost: The Continuing Costs of Housing Discrimination," Russell Sage Foundation, 1995; Helen Ladd, "Evidence of Discrimination in Mortgage Lending," *Journal of Economic Perspectives, Spring 1998.*

Article 3.7

UPDATE ON MORTGAGE LENDING DISCRIMINATION

After a disastrous detour, we're back where we started.

BY JIM CAMPEN
October 2010

In the 1980s and early 1990s, racial discrimination in mortgage lending resulted in less access to home loans for predominantly black and Latino borrowers and neighborhoods. Home mortgages were a fairly standardized product, and the problem was that banks avoided lending in minority neighborhoods (redlining) and denied applications from blacks and Latinos at disproportionately high rates compared to equally creditworthy white applicants (lending discrimination). The preceding article tells this story in some detail, from the vantage point of the mid-1990s.

Soon afterwards, however, a different form of lending discrimination rose to prominence as high-cost subprime loans became increasingly common. Precisely because borrowers and neighborhoods of color had limited access to the traditional prime loans, they were vulnerable for exploitation by predatory lenders pushing the new product.

Redlining was soon over-shadowed by "reverse redlining." Instead of being ignored, borrowers and neighborhoods of color were now aggressively targeted for high-cost subprime loans. Community groups documented and aggressively publicized the problem, and the U.S. Department of Housing and Urban Development (HUD) reported in 2000 that "subprime loans are five times more likely in black neighborhoods than in white neighborhoods." By the final year of the Clinton administration, government regulators were mobilizing to take action against this plague. But once the Bush administration took over in 2001, predatory lenders had nothing to fear from the federal government.

In the early 2000s, predatory lending began to take on a new and more explosive form. Mortgage brokers earned high fees for persuading borrowers to take on high-cost loans from lenders, who then sold the loans to big Wall Street firms, who in turn packaged them into "mortgage-backed securities" that were sold to investors. Everybody earned big fees along the way—in fact, the worse the deal was for borrowers, the bigger the fees for everyone else—and so the system gathered incredible momentum. Wall Street's demand for loan volume led ultimately to a complete lack of lending standards and millions upon millions of loans were made to borrowers who had no realistic prospect of repaying them.

For present purposes, the most important aspect of this appalling story is that these exploitative high-cost loans were strongly targeted to borrowers and neighborhoods of color. My own research on lending in Greater Boston during 2006, the peak year of the subprime lending boom, found that 49% of all home-purchase loans to blacks, and 48% of all home-purchase loans to Latinos, were high-cost loans, compared to just 11% of all loans to whites—and that the share of high-cost loans in predominantly minority neighborhoods was 4.4 times greater than it was in predominantly white neighborhoods. Similar racial and ethnic disparities were documented in numerous studies all across the country. Echoing what researchers at the

Boston Fed did fifteen years earlier (see previous article), the Center for Responsible Lending made use of industry data to demonstrate that these disparities could be only partially accounted for by differences in credit scores and other legitimate measures of borrower risk. In other words, they proved that racial discrimination was at least partly responsible for the observed racial disparities.

Nevertheless, federal regulators again did virtually nothing in response to the abundant evidence of violations of fair housing laws. Their most vigorous action was when the Comptroller of the Currency, the principal regulator of the nation's largest banks, actually went to court to stop New York's attorney general from enforcing that state's anti-discrimination laws against big national banks.

Finally, in 2007, the housing bubble popped and subprime lenders collapsed. Millions of homeowners who had received high-cost subprime loans either lost their homes to foreclosure or are in danger of being foreclosed upon soon. Because they were targeted by the predatory lenders, blacks and Latinos have been hit the hardest by this foreclosure tsunami. For example, researchers at the Center for Responsible Lending estimated that among recent mortgage borrowers, "nearly 8% of both African Americans and Latinos have lost their homes to foreclosures, compared to just 4.5% of whites."

By 2008, borrowers and neighborhoods of color were no longer being targeted by predatory lenders, as that industry had all but disappeared in the aftermath of the subprime meltdown. Instead, the more traditional form of discrimination again rose to the foreground. A recent report by a group of community-based organizations from seven cities across the country found that between 2006 and 2008 prime mortgage lending decreased 60.3% in predominantly minority neighborhoods while falling less than half that much (28.4%) in predominantly white neighborhoods. Home Mortgage Disclosure Act data for 2009, as tabulated by the Federal Reserve, showed that the denial rate for black applicants for conventional mortgage loans was 2.48 times greater than the denial rate for their white counterparts (45.7% vs. 18.4%; the denial rate for Latinos was 35.9%). This denial rate ratio is even higher than those which created such outrage when denial rate data first became public in the early 1990s, as described at the beginning of the preceding article ("Lending Insights").

Geoff Smith, senior vice president of Chicago's Woodstock Institute, summed up the new situation this way: "After inflicting harm on neighborhoods of color through years of problematic subprime loans, banks are now pulling back at a time when these communities are most in need of responsible loans and investment. We are concerned that we have gone from a period of reverse redlining to a period of re-redlining." ❑

Sources: U.S. Dept. of Housing and Urban Development, "Unequal Burden: Income & Racial Disparities in Subprime Lending in America," 2000 (archives.hud.gov/reports/subprime/subprime.cfm); Jim Campen, "Changing Patterns XIV: Mortgage Lending to Traditionally Underserved Borrowers & Neighborhoods in Boston, Greater Boston, and Massachusetts, 2006," Massachusetts Community and Banking Council (www.mcbc.info/files/ChangingPatternsXIV_0.pdf); Center for Responsible Lending, "Unfair Lending: the Effect of Race and Ethnicity on the Price of Subprime Mortgages," 2006, and "Foreclosures by Race and Ethnicity: The Demographics of a Crisis," 2010 (both available at www.responsiblelending.org); California Reinvestment Coalition and six other groups, "Paying More for the American Dream IV: The Decline of Prime Mortgage Lending in Communities of Color," 2010 (available at: www.woodstockinst.org).

Article 3.8

A MATTER OF LIFE AND DEBT: THE IMPACT OF PREDATORY LENDING ON THE BLACK COMMUNITY

BY JABULANI LEFFALL
March/April 2003

Think of it as a word problem. Problem is the operative word: If "company A" lends $50,000 to "consumer F" at an interest rate 7 points above the prime rate, charging finance fees equal to 10% of the loan and a prepayment penalty, how long would it take for consumer F to pay back the interest, let alone the principal?

Sound complicated? Well it is and that's how the lenders want it to be. The answer to the problem: too long. (As long as possible is also acceptable.) This complex equation is what is known as predatory lending—loans made with abusive terms like hidden or excessive fees and foreclosure defaults. Predatory lending banks use deceptive solicitation and often target borrowers who should qualify for credit on better terms.

While poor people in general are the main quarry in this multi-billion dollar business, it's African Americans who are the biggest losers. "We are targeted more than any other group through aggressive marketing and mail-out campaigns," says Yolanda Clark, a Los Angeles-based black mortgage broker who deals with home-buyers every day.

Although not all subprime (high interest) loans are predatory, almost all predatory loans are subprime. And, according to a November 2002 report by the Association of Community Organizers for Reform Now (ACORN), subprime lenders account for more than half of all housing refinance loans made in predominately black neighborhoods. From 1995 to 2001 the number of subprime purchase loans to African Americans rose 686%.

Large financial concerns and the subprime lending lobby deny that blacks are being targeted. They point out the true fact that whites procure subprime loans in greater number than blacks and that the loans some black consumers get reflect their poor credit.

But even though more whites get subprime loans, the likelihood that these same loans are predatory is higher for blacks, according to another report, "Risk or Race?" issued last year by the Center for Community Change. Its findings dispel the claim that bad credit or poverty explains predatory lending patterns. In fact, the study found that racial inequities increased as homeowners' salaries and creditworthiness went up.

The report, which ranks all 331 metropolitan areas in the nation, finds that:

- African Americans are three times more likely than whites to receive a subprime loan.

- Upper-income African Americans are more likely to receive subprime loans than are lower-income whites.

- Subprime lending and racial disparities are found in all regions and in urban areas of all sizes.

Allen J. Fishbein, general counsel of the Center for Community Change, says the overall racial disparities are due to a lack of mainstream prime lenders in the black community.

Predatory lenders contribute to neighborhood deterioration by stripping homeowners of their equity and overcharging those who can least afford it, adds David Swanson, ACORN's spokesman.

"The circle of debt is killing our community," says Earl Ofari Hutchinson, an author and talk show host for KPFK, a Pacifica affiliate in Los Angeles. "It's peonage and indentured servitude to the loans. Black people in greater and greater numbers are subjected to piracy by legalized thieves."

Lena J

Lena J, a community resource adviser for United Way and a resident of Inglewood, Calif.—a predominately black city on the outskirts of Los Angeles—knows the perils of predatory lending all too well.

Ms. J requested that her last name not be used out of fear of reprisal from her lender. She bought her home three years ago for $149,000, with two loans through a neighborhood bank. She pays interest rates of 7.2% and 7.3%. (The prime rate currently hovers slightly above 4%.)

When Ms. J decided she needed a second mortgage, she went to Household International, Inc. subsidiary Beneficial to apply for a personal line of credit to pay off her car loans and provide some extra cash for home improvement.

Beneficial first told her that the loan was denied. Then, out of the blue, she got a call saying it had been approved and was being processed. The total amount of the loan was $52,904 including $3,903 in points and fees at an interest rate of 11.5%. Money is money, she surmised. So she rushed back over to Beneficial and signed up.

Beneficial neglected to mention that there was a prepayment penalty on her loan for five years costing six months interest minus 20% of the loan amount.

Even worse, Beneficial set up her loan as a home equity loan instead of the regular line of credit that she requested.

Beneficial indicated in fine print that it would pay off her second mortgage. But when Ms. J got the checks from Beneficial, they were for the wrong amounts. Even though the loan went through and $21,000 for her second mortgage is listed on page two of her Truth in Lending Disclosure form, Beneficial never paid that amount.

It has to be true if it's on the "Truth in Lending Disclosure" form right? Wrong. While Beneficial did send her a check, the company paid off far less of her mortgage balance than it led her to believe it would. Meanwhile Ms. J thought her second mortgage had been paid in full by Beneficial and so did not submit her second mortgage payments. Late charges hit her like a ton of bricks falling from a "fixer upper."

Ms. J now makes three payments per month when she should only have two. Her monthly payments (on the original housing loans and the Beneficial loans combined) total $1,150. Her monthly net income is less than $2,000.

She joins a host of others forced to pay 60% or more of their net income toward high-interest mortgages. A domino effect ensues, as there is less money for other essentials such as groceries, phone and utilities and car payments. If Ms. J does not make her payments, she pays in a different way—foreclosure.

False and misleading Beneficial information (in both its written and person-to-person communication with Ms. J) were factors in her victimization. Because Ms. J trusted Beneficial and did not suspect a shady deal was brewing, when she found out the loan was approved, she signed on the dotted line. Ms. J cannot take her fight in earnest to the courts—because a signature, even on a confusing loan form, is binding in most cases.

Definitions

The line between "legal" subprime lending and "predatory lending" is a contested one. Many deny that a clear definition of predatory lending exists. Without a widely understood definition of the term, the enemy remains faceless. People cannot fight what they do not understand.

Although several states and localities have recently passed laws clarifying the scope of illegal lending practices, and recent court settlements may have begun to curb some of the worst fraudulent practices of a few large corporations, a wide scope of deceptive activity remains legal in most of the country.

Further, although predatory lending is a discriminatory practice, most of the media has not defined it as such. It is not treated as a matter of overt racial discrimination the way racial profiling, police brutality, and voter disenfranchisement sometimes are. Instead, too often the Ms. J's of the world are simply labeled "irresponsible" and left to fend for themselves.

Federal Reserve Board Governor Edward M. Gramlich, who has called for additional research to explore the "significance" of predatory lending, gave a vague and unmistakably political take on the definition question.

The Federal Reserve is charged with supervising and regulating banking institutions and protecting the credit rights of consumers. Addressing the Consumer Federation of America, Gramlich said: "Just as with safety and soundness and unfair and deceptive trade practices," there should be no final definition of the term "predatory lending."

Gramlich's remarks are about as clear as what happened to Ms. J. It is evident that he wants to tread lightly until the debate reaches Capitol Hill. When in doubt, commission a study.

The truth of the matter is that a list of predatory lending practices can be named, and the effects of predatory lending can be measured. An independent study on the economic cost of predatory lending in the housing arena by the Durham, N.C.-based Coalition for Responsible Lending identified three clusters of predatory lending practices and analyzed their costs:

1. *Equity Stripping*: Charging borrowers exorbitant processing fees, resulting in substantially higher payments that are subtracted from the equity of the home when a borrower refinances or sells his or her house.

2. *Rate-Risk Disparities*: Charging borrowers a higher rate of interest than their credit histories would justify.

3. *Excessive Foreclosures*: Homeowners struggling to make payments under the combined weight of excessive fees and high interest rates often pay the ultimate price—the loss of their home and all the equity they have accumulated.

The Coalition for Responsible Lending's report goes on to say that the equity of the neighbors of the foreclosed is also reduced as foreclosures start to permeate the neighborhood. "Finally," the study states, "there are significant social costs to the pending wholesale loss of neighborhoods of homeowners, particularly in African-American communities."

And the housing finance arena represents just one branch of the predatory lending industry. Housing finance predatory lenders target consumers of a particular stratum; those with incomes high enough to permit homeownership. More pervasive still are smaller-scale predatory-lending operations geared to personal finance. (See the sidebar for discussion of one such type: the payday loan.)

High Finance Connections

Predatory lenders have been called "pirates" and "scavengers" by their victims, but while this banking niche is on its face morally reprehensible, these "pirates" are not from some underworld of organized crime. They are among the most respected institutions in the world, companies whose leaders mix with powerful dignitaries as stewards of high finance. Their billboards celebrate the American dream.

But for two groups in particular: Citigroup Inc. and Household International Inc.—better known by their opponents as "Citigrope" and "Chokehold"—the term "high finance" takes on a whole new meaning. Both are mainstream institutions with ties to predatory lending practices.

"Citigrope"

New York-based Citigroup is the world's second largest financial services concern and is America's largest consumer finance firm. Its 2001 revenue was $112 billion with profits of $14 billion.

Citigroup's chief executive, Sanford Weill, is revered on Wall Street as a banking legend and the "best deal-maker on the planet." Weill presided over the historic 1998 merger between Traveler's Group and Citibank (hence Citigroup) and parlayed his company into the top ten of the Fortune 500.

In 2001's Fortune 500 edition, Fortune magazine said of Weill: "Weill is a star: His shareholders earned an average annual total return of 40.8% (in 2001) a stunning result that only 15 other companies in the list—all of them smaller—beat."

In the years since the article appeared, both Citigroup and Weill have drawn fire for analyst improprieties at Salomon Smith Barney—its investment banking arm—and more recently for the actions of CitiFinancial, its subprime consumer-lending arm.

CitiFinancial sells bill consolidation, debt refinancing and subprime home equity home improvement and personal loans through more than 2,000 offices in North America. It was CitiFinancial's $31 billion acquisition of notorious predatory lender Associates First Capital in 2000 that tarnished Citigroup's reputation. In 2001, The Federal Trade Commission (FTC) alleged that Associates violated the Federal Trade Commission Act through what it called "deceptive marketing practices that induced consumers to refinance existing debts into home loans with high interest rates, costs, and fees, and to purchase high-cost credit insurance."

The FTC also said the company violated the Truth in Lending Act, the Fair Credit Reporting Act, and Equal Credit Opportunity Act, and used unfair tactics in collecting consumers' payments on its loans.

Jodie Bernstein, then the Director of the FTC's Bureau of Consumer Protection, stated in a press release:

(Associates) hid essential information from consumers, misrepresented loan terms, flipped loans, and packed optional fees to raise the costs of the loans. What had made the alleged practices more egregious is that they primarily victimized consumers who were the most vulnerable—hard working homeowners who had to borrow to meet emergency needs and often had no other access to capital.

To protect the merger and shield itself from liability and attacks from the press, Citigroup launched a website called "Tell Citibank." The homepage says: "Associates Customer: Are you a customer of Associates First Capital? If so, you already may be a victim of predatory lending."

Despite Citigroup's newly deployed campaign for the little guy, it once again found itself the object of protest late last year. A San Francisco-based advocacy group, The California Reinvestment Committee (CRC), attacked the parent company for discrimination and openly fought the bank's expansion in the western United States.

Said CRC executive director Alan Fisher, "We fear a growing Citigroup presence in California and believe it will be harmful to California communities."

According to the CRC, Citigroup hides behind its subsidiary CitiFinancial, which CRC contends still charges high points and fees on subprime loans, imposes prepayment penalties that trap borrowers into high cost loans, and sets arbitration provisions denying borrowers access to legal recourse.

The CRC further contends that CitiFinancial lends subprime monies to African-American and Latino borrowers, while low-cost lenders are three to four times as likely to deny African Americans as they are white applicants.

"It's the bait and switch," says Donnette Heard, treasurer for the Los Angeles-based Multicultural Real Estate Alliance For Urban Change. "If the big bank denies you, they send you to their subprime lenders who will then contact you. They keep your business and deal with you on their terms."

"Chokehold"

Such is the case with Chicago-based Household International, Inc. whose Beneficial subsidiary played the bait and switch with Ms. J from Inglewood.

According to Internet business portal Hoovers, Household has "made lending to the little people profitable." With a company slogan that says: "Helping everyday people everyday," it is the second largest consumer finance company behind Citigroup.

Yet for the past several years, consumer advocacy groups and Attorneys General from scores of states have dragged Household through the courts for duping the Ms. J's of America into high-interest hell.

"Ghetto" Banking

Pick an inner-city, any inner-city, and take a drive. If you keep your eyes open you'll see large neon signs: "Instant Cash Advance," "Currency Exchange," and "Pay Day Loans." The signs are pervasive in places where poor people live. They call to mind the lyrics from the theme song of a popular black sit-com, "Good Times." Residents of these neighborhoods are "Keeping their heads above water" and subjected to "easy credit rip-offs."

Predatory lending is not limited to the home financing and refinancing lending markets. It's even more prevalent in the realm of personal finance. With small storefronts that residents dub "Ghetto Banks," profit- seeking financial institutions catch desperate and impoverished people in their crosshairs.

Over ten million American families lack formal bank accounts. They are an easy mark for the check cashing stores, collateral loan companies, and pay day lenders that siphon almost as much from their wages—up to 20 cents on the dollar—as F.I.C.A. These entities are able to take advantage of consumers because there are often no other financial service providers present in low-income areas.

These "ghetto," or what consumer advocates call "shadow" banks are in effect the siblings of the mainstream banks that fund them. The kicker is that the large banks that deny loans and accounts to low-income people are the same ones that end up doing business with poor folks, albeit indirectly.

For example, Wells Fargo, the seventh largest bank in the country, has arranged more than $700 million in loans since 1998 to three of the nation's largest check cashing companies: Ace Cash Express, EZ Corp., and Cash America. Moreover, many check cashers and payday lenders have sought to lease national bank charters to avoid legislative interference and circumvent state usury laws.

In Chicago, the country's ninth most segregated metropolitan area, small loan and check cashing outlets saturate the streets. One of them is Illinois Title Lenders Inc., where applicants put their cars up for collateral in exchange for loans. The lender holds the vehicle title and keeps the car in the event of default. In some cases, the lender reposseses the vehicle even if the loan is less than the car's value.

Far from the "fringe" of the banking industry, Illinois Title Lenders Inc. has partnered with the American Chartered Bank (one of the twenty-five largest banks in the state of Illinois). Other mainstream lenders have also profited from the "alternative" loan arena. Bank of America, PNC Bank, LaSalle National Bank, Finova

In 2001 Household still managed to post $13 billion in revenues with a profit of $1.9 billion. Moreover, Household caught a break in November of 2002 when powerful British Bank HSBC, led by chairman Sir John Bond, snapped it up in a $14 billion dollar deal. At the time of the deal, Bond assured investors that Household's "aggressive" lending practices were a thing of the past. Bond laughed his way to the bank because Household's legal troubles and bad press helped him acquire the company at a bargain-basement price. It was nevertheless one of the largest acquisitions of 2002.

With assets of more than $100 billion and about 50 million customers at 1,400 retail branches, Household will lift the earnings before taxes of HSBC's North American operation to more than 30% of the conglomerate's total profits.

Capital Corp., and Providian have all been involved at one time or another in Illinois' "alternative" loan sector. Banks like these issue payday loans that bind consumers to unreasonable terms and require them to waive their rights to legal recourse.

To see how exploitative payday loans can be, one need not look further than the loan application at a franchise called "Instant Cash Advance: Chicago's answer for fast cash." Applicants are asked to sign a pledge in fine print at the bottom of the page, effectively signing away their consumer rights in three ways:

- The applicant is pegged for direct mail and other marketing schemes including possible mail fraud and identity theft: I fully release all parties, companies their subsidiaries & employees, past or present, from any and all liability for any damage that may result. My signature below indicates that for purposes of verification and qualification, I have voluntarily waived the protection of all rights to privacy laws.
- The applicant forfeits the ability to fight back if ripped off: Furthermore, I also voluntarily waive my right to pursue or take any legal action against Instant Cash Advance, employees past or present, subsidiaries or agents thereof.
- The applicant, not likely to fully understand what he or she is getting into, hammers a nail into his or her financial coffin: I fully understand that any information I provide found to be false or fabricated will be grounds for denial of credit with Instant Cash Advance. I agree that I have fully read this statement.

If an applicant borrows $100 from a payday lender by writing a check for $115 or $120 that the lender will hold until payday, the applicant is paying interest equivalent to taking out a loan at a 400% annual percentage rate (APR). When payday comes, a clerk asks the applicant if he or she would like to roll the loan over to the next pay period. Often the applicant agrees, perpetuating the cycle of revolving debt.

Recent legislation aims to curtail payday loan groups. In October 2002, The Office of the Comptroller of the Currency, the regulatory body that oversees federally chartered banks, ordered banks in Texas, Pennsylvania, California, and Virginia to stop subsidizing check cashers in certain localities.

Many more such efforts will be required to end the reign of the "ghetto banks." In the meantime, consumer advocates and lawmakers are urging low-income consumers to avoid payday loans. But for potential victims who are cash-strapped, have no cushion of wealth, and no access to low-interest credit, abstinence is easier said than done.

It will also boost HSBC's credit card business, adding about 2 million new Household customers.

This deal, much like Citigroup's acquisition of Associates, is not without controversy. The Bronx, N.Y.-based Inner City Press (ICP), which in the past attacked big banks such as Citigroup, opposes the HSBC-Household deal. ICP revealed data showing that HSBC, even before the acquisition was announced, denied African-American loan applications 2.7 times more frequently than whites' applications. Groups like the ICP believe HSBC will willingly participate in the bait and switch, using Household and its units to trap consumers.

What Citigroup and Household have in common, other than being lenders under fire, is that they both were involved in multi-billion dollar mergers in which subprime lenders sought refuge. The danger of the absorption of subprime lending groups into publicly traded mainstream banks is that the holding companies do not have to submit transparent financial records for private subsidiaries to the Securities and Exchange Commission (SEC) or any other regulatory body. The figures can hide in long, tedious financial statements and be signed off on by accounting firms and lawyers retained by these large companies.

For instance, Associates was absorbed into CitiFinancial, a private arm of Citigroup, which is traded on the New York Stock Exchange. Moreover, now that it has acquired Household and is facing public scrutiny, publicly traded HSBC may clean up the house by burying Household financials deep into the number soup that comprises an SEC filing.

Both Citigroup and Household declined to comment for this article. Company spokespeople did, however, point to the large settlements made to predatory lending plaintiffs.

In the fall of 2002, Citigroup put up almost $250 million and Household about $484 million. The combined settlement money represents the largest sum in American history paid to settle a consumer lending complaint.

But considering that since 1995 predatory lending institutions have raked in almost $100 billion, the $734 million is, in layman's terms, chump change.

Citigroup settled with the FTC to shake the shame off its merger with Associates. In the case of Household, regulators and attorneys general from 20 states had accused it of violating state laws by misrepresenting loan terms and failing to disclose material information. "We could have litigated, but the headline and litigation risk over an extended period would have been worse for the company," said Household's Chief Executive William Aldinger in a conference call with analysts last October. "We made a call to get it over with quickly." Household said it would record a $330 million charge in the third quarter as a result of the settlement and that its earnings for 2003 would miss Wall Street expectations.

Since the settlement, Citigroup and Household have issued "best practices guidelines" that they say can further prevent future exploitation of borrowers with low-incomes or weak credit histories.

One promise they have made is to reform up-front points and fees. In the opinion of ACORN's David Swanson, Household should lower its cap on up-front points and fees from 5% of the loan amount to 3%. Citigroup already caps them at 3%.

Yet a cap on points and fees does not help if there is no limit to how high a basic interest rate can go. If a lender still really wants to bilk a borrower, it can lower the points and raise the interest rate. For example, if maximum points are 3% of the loan instead of 5 or 6%, a lender can raise a rate to 12 or 13% and be satisfied with a 3% cap on points.

There are also stipulations in both Household's and Citigroup's guidelines that ban the selling of single-premium credit insurance and establish customer hotlines for complaints (e.g., "Tell Citibank").

Despite Citigroup's and Household's mea culpa, the companies still differ in where they draw the line on abusive practice. And neither will concede that a good number of their predatory loans were issued based on race.

The Fight for Predatory Lending Reform

"The fight needs to be taken to the seats of local, state and national governments," says ACORN spokesman David Swanson. And it has been. In the past year alone nearly a dozen state and local city government bodies have debated and passed anti-predatory lending legislation. By November of 2002 the New York, Los Angeles, and Oakland city councils had each passed such ordinances.

In New York, the ordinance bans the city from doing business with predatory lenders or companies that purchase predatory loans. ACORN members in Manhattan packed City Hall at each stage in this process and successfully promoted this bill over the fervent opposition of major lenders, including Citigroup. ACORN's New York branch estimates that the ordinance will save homeowners between $75 million and $100 million. The legislation is expected to take effect sometime this year. Los Angeles' proposed ordinance was even more comprehensive.

According to ACORN, there are several state-level bills on the table in New Jersey, Massachusetts, and New Mexico —where in November the group protested at a local branch of Wells Fargo, with victims talking about the damage caused by the predatory loans they received from the lender. Most of the bills would ban prepayment penalties, put caps on points, and establish Annual Percentage Rate (APR) thresholds.

Georgia and North Carolina already have strict predatory lending regulations. In North Carolina it is a violation to make a high-cost home loan if a lender believes the consumer will be unable to make the scheduled payments. North Carolina also makes it a violation to issue any loan that "does not have reasonable tangible net benefit to the borrower." Both states require all homeowners to seek loan counseling, a measure which consumer advocates support.

In the wake of the state bills, Sen. Paul Sarbanes (D-Maryland), the chair of the Senate Banking Committee in the 107th U.S. Congress, proposed a bill with provisions to ban certain practices characteristic in subprime lending, such as prepayment penalties, credit insurance bundling, financing of fees, and balloon payments (large, lump-sum payments scheduled at the end of a series of smaller payments).

But while ACORN's David Swanson praises these recent small victories, as well as the apparent move toward curbing or eradicating most forms of predatory lending, he is concerned about what might happen if a Republican-controlled Congress and White House decide to reverse the progress that has been made.

"I'd hate think that this will all go for naught. That's why we're urging people to get involved in whatever way they can. We can't let the work be in vain," Swanson adds.

Groups such as the Coalition for Responsible Lending, ACORN, and the Center for Community Change say predatory lenders are likely to push laws banning state and local restrictions on abusive lending.

Late last year, Rep. Bob Ney (R-Ohio) passed around a draft for a bill that ACORN claims bans states from passing laws to protect borrowers. ACORN also alleges that the bill was co-written by Wright Andrews of Butera and Andrews, the firm that represents a coalition of subprime lenders.

Time and filibusters will tell. There is uncertainty about which bills will or will not be passed by session's end. There is also uncertainty as to whether the financial settlements from Citigroup and Household will be enough to placate opponents of predatory lending. So, as the days go by, the lawmakers legislate, corporate mergers and acquisitions commence, and the seats of power shift, the interest accrues and the bills pile up—particularly in the black community.

And one thing does remain certain: Ms. J of Inglewood and those like her have bills to pay next month and the month after that. ❏

This story was produced under the George Washington Williams Fellowship for Journalists of Color, a project sponsored by the Independent Press Association.

Article 3.9

FLAME BROILED SHARK

BY DAVID SWANSON
July/August 2004

The Association for Community Organizations for Reform Now (ACORN) gained notoriety and widespread media coverage in 2006-2009 in the wake of a series of right-wing attacks alleging, among other things, that its affiliates had engaged in voter-registration fraud. Even though the most serious allegations have been discredited, ACORN is now largely dissolved. At the time this article was written, however, ACORN was best known as the leading group organizing on behalf of poor people in the United States. —Eds.

If someone told you that a number of low-income people, most of them African-American or Latino, most of them women, most of them elderly, had been robbed of much of their equity or of their entire homes by a predatory mortgage lender, you might not be surprised. But if you heard that these women and men had brought the nation's largest high-cost lender to its knees, forced it to sell out to a foreign company, and won back a half a billion dollars that had been taken from them, you'd probably ask what country this had happened in. Surely it couldn't have been in the United States, land of unbridled corporate power.

And yet it was. In 2001, these families, all members of the Association of Community Organizations for Reform Now (ACORN), launched a campaign against the nation's largest and most notorious predatory lender, Household International (also known as Household Finance or Beneficial). The 2003 settlement included a ban on talking about the damage Household had inflicted on borrowers and neighborhoods. That's one reason many people haven't heard this story—the families who defeated Household are in effect barred from publicly criticizing the corporation and teaching others the lessons they learned. (I was ACORN's communications coordinator during much of the Household campaign but left before it ended. No one asked me not to tell this story.)

In low-income minority neighborhoods in the United States, the little wealth that exists lies in home equity (see "Home Equity as a Percent of Net Worth"). People of color have made gains in home ownership during the past few decades, thanks in part to efforts by community groups like ACORN and National People's Action to force banks to make loans in communities of color (see "Minority Homeownership Is Growing"). Overall, these gains have been good for the new homeowners and good for their neighborhoods.

But low-income home ownership is fragile. Half of all extremely low-income homeowners pay more than half of their income for housing, according to the National Low Income Housing Coalition. Because low-income homeownership is not protected by additional savings, a temporary loss of income or a sudden large expense, such as a medical bill, can mean the loss of the home.

High-cost lenders—including large national operations like Household, Wells Fargo, and Citigroup, as well as small-time local sharks—strip away, rather than build up, equity in poor neighborhoods. Predatory high-cost lenders turn the usual logic of lending upside down. They make their money by intentionally issuing loans that borrowers will be unable to repay. Their loans invariably leave borrowers worse off, not better off.

Most high-cost (also called "subprime") loans are home-mortgage refinance loans. They carry excessive, and sometimes variable, interest rates and exorbitant fees. The more abusive lenders bundle bogus products like credit insurance into their loans, which accrue more interest and fees. Some lenders quietly omit taxes and insurance costs from monthly mortgage statements, causing crises when the yearly tax and insurance bills arrive. Others encourage borrowers to consolidate credit card and other debt within the mortgage, which further decreases home equity and places the home at greater risk. Loans may even exceed the value of the home, trapping people in debt they cannot refinance with a responsible lender. Hidden balloon payments force repeated refinancing (with fees each time). When borrowers find themselves unable to meet payments, the predatory lender refinances them repeatedly and ultimately seizes the house. Borrowers often have little recourse, as mandatory arbitration clauses written into their loan contracts prevent them from taking lenders to court.

High-cost loans are not made only to people with poor credit. Fannie Mae estimates that as many as half of all subprime borrowers could have qualified for a lower-cost mortgage. After British financial corporation HSBC bought Household International in March 2003, it announced that 46% of Household's real estate-backed loans had been made to borrowers with 'A' credit. But Household had made no 'A' (standard low-cost) loans. In fact, Household was a leading cause of the rows of vacant houses appearing in ACORN neighborhoods in the 1990s.

Fighting Back

ACORN members didn't take this abuse lying down. Their grassroots effort against Household relied on numerous strategies, including shareholder activism, political advocacy, and the old stand-by of direct action. It offers a model for low-income communities seeking to challenge exploitative corporations.

Minority Homeownership Is Growing

Over the past decade [1994-2004], homeownership rates among minority households have risen more quickly than among other groups. In 1993, 42.6% of African-American and 40.0% of Latino households owned homes. In 2002, 48.9% and 47.4% of those groups owned homes, respectively. This reflects a more rapid rate of increase than for whites, whose homeownership grew from an already high 70.4% to 74.7%. Minorities, as a share of all first-time homebuyers, rose from 19.1% in 1993 to 30% in 1999. Indeed, minorities accounted for 41% of net growth in homeowners during that same period, according to Harvard University's Joint Center for Housing Studies.

In 2001, ACORN members launched the campaign with simultaneous protests inside Household offices in cities around the country, and then began work to pass anti-predatory lending legislation at local, state, and federal levels.

Later that year, ACORN, together with the advocacy group Coalition for Responsible Wealth, introduced a shareholder resolution that proposed to tie Household executives' compensation to the termination of the company's predatory lending practices. When Household held its annual meeting in a suburb of Tampa, Fla., a crowd of ACORN members arrived at the event wearing shark suits and holding shark balloons. The resolution won 5% of the shareholders' vote. In 2002, Household held its meeting an hour and a half from the nearest airport in rural Kentucky. ACORN members weren't deterred by the remote location—they came from all over the country by car. The protest may have been the biggest thing the town of London, Ky., had ever seen. This time, 30% of the shareholders supported the resolution.

ACORN also helped borrowers file a number of class-action suits against Household for practices that were clearly illegal under existing law, and it let Wall Street analysts know what Household stood to lose from these lawsuits. ACORN urged state attorneys general and federal regulators to investigate the firm, and simultaneously put pressure on stores, including Best Buy, that issued Household credit cards. As a result of ACORN agitation, various local and state governments passed resolutions urging their pension funds to divest from the firm.

In the summer of 2002, ACORN members did something that really got the attention of Household executives and board members. On a beautiful day, thousands of Household borrowers poured out of buses onto the lawns of the company CEO and board members in the wealthy suburbs north of Chicago. They knocked on the officials' doors, speaking directly to the people whose policies had hurt them from a distance. When forced to leave, ACORN members plastered "Wanted" posters all over the neighborhood.

Through all of this, ACORN worked the media. It kept a database of borrowers' stories, and put reporters in touch with them, generating several hundred national print articles and television and radio spots. It also maintained an enormous website about Household (which has since been removed as part of the gag-order agreement).

HOME EQUITY AS A PERCENT OF NET WORTH, BY INCOME QUINTILE, 2000

	Lowest	Next-Lowest	Middle	Next-to-Highest	Highest
Non-Hispanic Whites	85.6	77.7	70.8	62.9	44.4
Hispanics	90.0	73.5	76.3	70.9	64.9
African Americans	NA	78.7	70.9	73.5	67.8

Source: **U.S. Census Bureau, May 2003.**

Meanwhile, ACORN Housing Corporation, a nonprofit loan-counseling agency created by ACORN, helped many borrowers cancel rip-off services, such as credit insurance, that were built into their loans, and, when possible, refinance out of their Household loans altogether.

Household's Concessions

For more than two years, a small handful of ACORN staff organized thousands of members in an unrelenting effort, until Household International could no longer sustain the negative attention, shareholder discontent, and legal and regulatory pressures. In early 2003, the lender agreed to pay $489 million in restitution to borrowers through the 50 state attorneys general. The company later agreed to pay millions more to ACORN to fund new financial literacy programs. This was one of the largest consumer settlements in history, but it amounted to only a fraction of what Household had taken from people, and it could not undo all the damage done to families who had lost their homes. In addition to the payments, the company will:

- Ensure that new loans actually provide a benefit to consumers prior to issuing the loans.

- Reform and improve disclosures to consumers.

- Reimburse states to cover the costs of the investigations into Household's practices.

- Limit prepayment penalties to the first two years of a loan.

- Limit points and origination fees, upfront charges built into the loan, to 5%. (A "point" is one percentage point of the loan amount.)

- Eliminate "piggyback" second mortgages. (When Household issued home loans, it would simultaneously issue a second, smaller, loan at an even higher rate. It often labeled these second loans "lines of credit" in order to avoid federal regulations that limit the rate that can be charged.)

- Implement a "Foreclosure Avoidance Program" to provide relief to borrowers who are at risk of losing their homes due to delinquent payments (for example, reducing interest rates, waiving unpaid late charges, deferring interest, and reducing the principal).

ACORN-led efforts won legislative and corporate reforms as well. Several cities and states (including Arkansas, California, New Mexico, New Jersey, and New York) have banned abusive practices that were once routine. One practice ACORN targeted aggressively was "single-premium credit insurance," a nearly useless and overpriced insurance policy that predatory lenders added to many loans (often falsely describing it as a requirement or failing to tell borrowers it had been included). In 2002, Household and other major lenders announced they would drop the product. This was one of several corporate reforms ACORN won during the course of the campaign.

This campaign demonstrates that a well-organized grassroots effort can combat corporate exploitation and extract significant concessions. By pursuing different strategies at once, ACORN repeatedly hit Household with the unexpected, and put it on the defensive. The outcome is good news for low-income neighborhoods, and bad news for Wells Fargo, the predatory lender who is next on ACORN's list. ❑

Chapter 4

THE FINANCIAL CRISIS

Article 4.1

THE GREED FALLACY
You can't explain a change with a constant.

BY ARTHUR MacEWAN
November/December 2008

Various people explain the current financial crisis as a result of "greed." There is, however, no indication of a change in the degree or extent of greed on Wall Street (or anywhere else) in the last several years. Greed is a constant. If greed were the cause of the financial crisis, we would be in financial crisis pretty much all the time.

But the financial markets have not been in perpetual crisis. Nothing close to the current crisis has taken place since 1929. Yes, there was 1987 and the savings-and-loan debacle of that era. But, the current crisis is already more dramatic—and threatens to get a good deal worse. This crisis emerged over the last decade and appeared full-blown only at the beginning of 2008 (though, if you were looking, it was moving up on the horizon a year or two earlier). The current mess, therefore, is a change, a departure from the normal course of financial markets. So something has to have changed to have brought it about. The constant of greed cannot be the explanation.

So what changed? The answer is relatively simple: the extent of regulation changed.

As a formal matter, the change in regulation is most clearly marked by the Gramm-Leach-Bliley Act of 1999, passed by the Republican-dominated Congress and signed into law by Bill Clinton. This act in large part repealed the Glass-Steagall Act of 1933, which had imposed various regulations on the financial industry after the debacle of 1929. Among other things, Glass-Steagall prohibited a firm from being engaged in different sorts of financial services. One firm could not be both an investment bank (organizing the funding of firms' investment activities) and a commercial bank (handling the checking and savings accounts of individuals and firms and making loans); nor could it be one of these types of banks and an insurance firm.

However, the replacement of Glass-Steagall by Gramm-Leach-Bliley was only the formal part of the change that took place in recent decades. Informally, the relation between the government and the financial sector has increasingly become one of reduced regulation. In particular, as the financial sector evolved new forms of operation—hedge funds and private equity funds, for example—there was no attempt on the part of Washington to develop regulations for these activities. Also, even where regulations existed, the regulators became increasingly lax in enforcement.

The movement away from regulation might be seen as a consequence of "free market" ideology, the belief as propounded by its advocates that government should leave the private sector alone. But to see the problem simply as ideology run amok is to ignore the question of where the ideology comes from. Put simply, the ideology is generated by firms themselves because they want to be as free as possible to pursue profit-making activity. So they push the idea of the "free market" and deregulation any way they can. But let me leave aside for now the ways in which ideas come to dominate Washington and the society in general; enough to recognize that deregulation became increasingly the dominant idea from the early 1980s onward. (But, given the current presidential campaign, one cannot refrain from noting that one way the firms get their ideas to dominate is through the money they lavish on candidates.)

When financial firms are not regulated, they tend to take on more and more risky activities. When markets are rising, risk does not seem to be very much of a problem; all—or virtually all—investments seem to be making money. So why not take some chances? Furthermore, if one firm doesn't take a particular risk—put money into a chancy operation—then one of its competitors will. So competition pushes them into more and more risky operations.

The danger of risk is not simply that one investment—one loan, for example—made by a financial firm will turn out bad-ly, or even that a group of loans will turn out badly. The danger arises in the relation between its loans (obligations to the firm), the money it borrows from others (the firm's obligations to its creditors) and its capital (the funds put in by investors, the stockholders). If some of the loans it has made go bad (i.e., if the debtors default), it can still meet its obligations to its creditors with its capital. But if the firm is unregulated, it will tend to make more and more loans and take on more and more debt. The ratio of debt to capital can become very high, and, then, if trouble with the loans develops, the bank cannot meet its obligations with its capital.

In the current crisis, the deflation of the housing bubble was the catalyst to the general crumbling of financial structures. The housing bubble was in large part a product of the Federal Reserve Bank's policies under the guidance of the much-heralded Alan Greenspan, but let's leave that issue aside for now.

When the housing bubble burst, many financial institutions found themselves in trouble. They had taken on too much risk in relation to their capital. The lack of regulation had allowed them to get in this trouble.

But the trouble is much worse than it might have been because of the repeal of the provisions of Glass-Steagall that prevented the merging of investment banks, commercial banks, and insurance companies. Under the current circumstances, when trouble develops in one part of a firm's operations, it is immediately transmitted throughout the other segments of that firm. And from there, the trouble spreads to all the other entities to which it is connected—through credits, insurance deals, deposits, and a myriad set of complicated (unregulated) financial arrangements.

AIG is the example *par excellence*. Ostensibly an insurance company, AIG has morphed into a multi-faceted financial institution, doing everything from selling life insurance in rural India to speculating in various esoteric types of investments on Wall Street. Its huge size, combined with the extent of its intertwining with other financial firms, meant that its failure would have had very large impacts around the world.

The efforts of the U.S. government may or may not be able to contain the current financial crisis. Success would not breathe life back into the Lehman Brothers, Bear Stearns, and who knows how many other major operators that are on their deathbeds. But it would prevent the financial crisis from precipitating a severe general depression; it would prevent a movement from 1929 to 1932.

The real issue, however, is what is learned from the current financial mess. One thing should be evident, namely that greed did not cause the crisis. The cause was a change in the way markets have been allowed to operate, a change brought on by the rise of deregulation. Markets, especially financial markets, are never very stable when left to themselves. It turns out that the "invisible hand" does some very nasty, messy things when there is no visible hand of regulation affecting the process.

The problem is that maintaining some form of regulation is a very difficult business. As I have said, the firms themselves do not want to be regulated. The current moment may allow some re-imposition of financial regulation. But as soon as we turn our backs, the pressure will be on again to let the firms operate according to the "free market." Let's not forget where that leads. ❑

Article 4.2

CRISIS AND NEOLIBERAL CAPITALISM

BY DAVID KOTZ
November/December 2008

The Financial Crisis and the Real Economy

It is impossible to predict the course of the financial crisis. The effects of the crisis on the real economy could be very large, especially if it engulfs more and more of the financial sector. But even if the financial crisis is contained, the bursting of the housing bubble—which began in 2007 and is bound to continue for some time—will have a powerful downward impact on the economy.

A speculative "bubble" arose in the housing sector of the U.S. economy starting around 2002. By the summer of 2007, housing prices had risen by 70% since 1995 corrected for inflation. Yet since 2002 the real value of home rents had been flat. By 2006 the ratio of the Housing Price Index to the Homeowners Equivalent Rent had risen sharply to an all-time high of 168.3, compared to 110.0 in 1995. This is clear evidence of a huge asset bubble in the U.S. housing market. This bubble created an estimated $8 trillion in inflated new wealth, which was about 38% of the peak total housing wealth of $21 trillion. When this bubble started to collapse in 2007, it set the stage for both a financial crisis and a recession in the "real" economy.

There are two ways in which the collapsing housing bubble affects the real economy. First, there is a downward wealth effect on housing investment and consumer spending. The collapse of the bubble in the housing sector has led to a sharp drop in residential investment. Since the second quarter of 2007, it has been falling at 21.6% annual rate. Second, falling home values are causing a reduction in consumer spending. Since 2002 households had been borrowing against their homes to get funds for consumer spending. One study estimated that during 2004-06 Americans took $840 billion per year from their home equity through borrowing and capital gains from the sale of housing. This was almost 10% of disposable personal income in the United States.

Suddenly, in 2007, people could no longer supplement their income with funds borrowed against their home, which has now led to a large drop in consumer spending, at a 3.1% per year rate in the third quarter of 2008. This happened *before* the financial crisis had begun to affect consumer spending. If all of the estimated $8 trillion of inflated home value disappears, the estimated effect on aggregate consumption would be a reduction of about $320 billion to $480 billion per year, or about 5% of total consumption. Dean Baker, co-director of the Center for Economic and Policy Research and a respected analyst of the financial crisis, estimated the total effect of the collapsing housing bubble to be a decline of between 3.1% and 7.0% of GDP.

The collapse of the bubble also affects investment in new plant and equipment by business. After several quarters of little growth, business investment fell at a 1%

annual rate in the first quarter of 2008. The bubble-propelled and debt-financed expansions of 1991-2000 and 2001-2007 produced a growing amount of productive capacity, relative to ordinary income. As the current crash develops, industry will find it has substantial excess productive capacity. As a result, the incentive for business investment may be depressed for some time. In the last recession in the United States, in 2001, business fixed investment fell for two consecutive years, at an accelerating rate, for this reason.

A severe recession was averted in 2001–2002 by the start of the housing bubble. It does not seem possible for a new bubble to arise and avert a serious recession this time. Also, the financial crisis is likely to make the coming recession more severe. One way this happens is that banks' reluctance to lend to business due to the financial crisis will worsen the recession. Secondly, the stock market collapse precipitated by the financial crisis will have effects similar to the effects of the housing price collapse—it will tend to reduce consumer and investment demand. The only bright spot for the U.S. economy has been exports, but they are not likely to continue to do well in the face of a spreading global recession.

The Restructuring is Just Beginning

Every form of capitalism has contradictions that eventually bring about a structural crisis of that form of capitalism. In the 1970s the system of state-regulated capitalism, having produced rapid growth and high profits for a few decades, stopped working effectively and went into structural crisis. The predominant form of capitalism changed to the "neoliberal" form, which means a type of capitalism in which the state plays a limited role in the economy, particularly withdrawing from activities that benefit ordinary people. It now appears that neoliberal capitalism can no longer overcome two key problems and is entering a structural crisis of its own. First, the high and rising inequality it generates means that the majority has insufficient income to buy the growing output of the economy without relying on an unsustainable buildup of household debt. Second, the deregulated financial system of neoliberal capitalism is inherently unstable, as we have so clearly seen in recent months.

From 1945 to 1973, a regulated form of capitalism predominated in the world, including in the United States. Regulated capitalism here included extensive government regulation of business and finance, regulation of the macroeconomy (aimed partly at achieving a relatively low unemployment rate), social programs that amounted to a modest welfare state, relatively cooperative relations between big business and trade unions, restrained competition between big corporations, and trade and capital flows regulated by governments and international institutions.

The shift to neoliberal capitalism in the United States involved the deregulation of business and finance, the reduction of active government macroeconomic policy (and a shift of aim to assuring low inflation, not low unemployment), sharply reduced social programs, a big business and government attack against labor unions, unrestrained ("cutthroat") competition among large corporations, and relatively free movement of goods, services, and capital across national boundaries. This neoliberal transformation of capitalism was relatively thorough in the United

States, the United Kingdom, and in international financial institutions such as the International Monetary Fund and World Bank.

As neoliberal capitalism enters a period of crisis, we can see the rapid loss of legitimacy of the previously reigning dominant "free market" ideology. This is similar to the sudden demise of the previously dominant Keynesian ideology of regulated capitalism in the 1970s. Capitalism is going to be restructured, in the United States and globally, during the coming years. The outcome of this restructuring process, however, is not pre-determined.

So far the bankers have led the initial stage of restructuring. Treasury Secretary Henry Paulson, the former CEO of Wall Street giant Goldman Sachs, has been succeeding so far in getting the government to rescue the banks in ways that mainly benefit the bankers. This process has encouraged rapidly growing concentration of the financial sector, as the largest banks merge with one another and get big cash infusions and new federal backing.

However, the restructuring is just beginning. We can fight for changes that would benefit the majority rather than the bankers. First, the underlying reason for the financial crisis is all those people unable to make the payments on their mortgages. The government should pass an emergency measure to ease mortgage terms to reflect the declining values of homes and the declining economy. This would impose a one-time loss on the financial institutions that invested in the risky new mortgage-based securities, but it would also make it easier to know the value of the mortgage-backed securities, eliminating a source of great uncertainty in the financial system.

Second, millions of people have learned the important lesson that banks and other financial institutions are not ordinary private companies. If General Mills loses money, or even goes bankrupt, it harms its shareholders and workers—but its competitors gain. But if a few major banks lose money and are in danger of going under, this threatens the entire financial system, and with it the economy as a whole.

The obvious conclusion is that the financial sector cannot be operated on a profit and loss basis. Instead, it should become part of the public sector, operated to serve the public interest. If banks, which are granted the power to create our money supply, and whose credit is essential to the welfare of the entire public, were made public institutions, then public policy aims could guide their actions. They could be directed to stay away from speculative activities and instead make loans for socially valuable purposes. This would include steering credit into renewable energy technologies, fuel-efficient vehicles, low cost housing, and other good purposes. An advantage of public ownership of the banks over another cycle of government regulation of private banks is that reregulated private banks would simply press for the elimination of the regulations—as they did suc-cessfully starting in the early 1980s.

The developing financial and economic crises have exposed the high-flying financial operators for what they always were—thieves who got rich without doing anything productive. This has also exposed their fallacious free-market ideology. This is a promising time to build popular movements that can fight for progressive changes in our economy. ❏

Article 4.3

FROM TULIPS TO MORTGAGE-BACKED SECURITIES

BY GERALD FRIEDMAN
January/February 2008

Thirty years ago, economist Charles Kindleberger published a little book, *Manias, Panics, and Crashes*, describing the normal tendency of capitalist financial markets to fluctuate between speculative excess (or "irrational exuberance" in the words of a recent central banker) and panic. Kindleberger describes about 40 of these panics over the nearly 260 years from 1720–1975, or one every seven years. Following Kindleberger's arithmetic, we were due for a panic because it had been seven years since the high-tech bubble burst and the stock market panic of 2000–1. And the panic came, bringing in its wake a tsunami of economic woe, liquidity shortages, cancelled investments, rising unemployment, and economic distress.

Of course, more than mechanics and arithmetic are involved in the current financial panic. But there is a sense of inevitability about the manias and panics of capitalist financial markets, a sense described by writers from Karl Marx to John Maynard Keynes, Hyman Minsky, John Kenneth Galbraith, and Robert Shiller. The problem is that financial markets trade in unknown and unknowable future returns. Lacking real information, they are inevitably driven by the madness of crowds.

Unlike tangible commodities whose price should reflect its real value and real cost of production, financial assets are not priced according to any real returns, nor even according to some expected return, but rather according to expectations of what others will pay in the future, or, even worse, expectations of future expectations that others will have of assets' future return. Whether it is Dutch tulips in 1637, the South Sea Bubble of 1720, Florida real estate in the 1920s, or mortgage-backed securities today, it is always the same story of financial markets floating like a manic-depressive from euphoria to panic to bust. When unregulated, this process is made still worse by market manipulation, and simple fraud. Speculative markets like these can make some rich, and can even be exciting to watch, like a good game of poker; but this is a dangerous and irresponsible way to manage an economy.

There was a time when governments understood. Learning from past financial disasters, the United States established rules to limit the scope of financial euphoria and panic by strictly segregating different types of banks, by limiting financial speculation, and by requiring clear accounting of financial transactions. While they were regulated, financial markets contributed to the best period of growth in American history, the "glorious thirty" after World War II. To be sure, restrictions on speculative behavior and strict regulations made this a boring time to be a banker, and they limited earnings in the financial services sector. But, limited to a secondary role, finance served a greater good by providing liquidity for a long period of steady and relatively egalitarian economic growth.

Of course, over time we forgot why we had regulated financial markets, memory loss helped along by the combined efforts of free-market economists and self-interested bankers and others on Wall Street. To promote "competition," we lowered the barriers between different types of financial institutions, widening the scope of financial markets. We moved activities such as home mortgage lending onto national markets and allowed a rash of bank mergers to create huge financial institutions too large to be allowed to fail, but never too large to operate irresponsibly. Despite the growing scope and centralization of financial activity, the government accepted arguments that we could trust financial firms to self-regulate because it was in their interest to maintain credible accounting.

So we reap the whirlwind with a market collapse building to Great Depression levels. Once again, we learn history's lesson from direct experience: capitalist financial markets cannot be trusted. It is time to either re-regulate or move beyond. ❑

Article 4.4

DERIVATIVES AND DEREGULATION

BY MARTY WOLFSON
November/December 2008

It has become commonplace to describe the current financial crisis as the most serious since the Great Depression. Although we have more tools now to avoid a depression, the current crisis presents in some ways more significant challenges than did the banking crises of the 1930s.

And it's not over.

The form of the current crisis is similar to others we have seen in the past: a speculative increase in asset prices, overly optimistic expectations, and an expansion of debt sustainable only if the speculative bubble continues. Then the bubble pops, debt can't be repaid, and losses mount at financial institutions. The risk of bank failures rises and lenders get scared. They panic, refuse to lend to anyone that seems at all risky, and seek safety in cash or super-safe assets.

In the early 1930s, there was no federal deposit insurance and little federal government intervention. Depositor runs took down the banking system.

In more recent crises, though, the Federal Reserve successfully developed and used its powers as a lender of last resort. Deposit insurance helped to reassure small depositors and, if needed, the Federal Deposit Insurance Corporation stepped in and bailed out threatened banks. It could guarantee all liabilities of a failing bank and arrange mergers with healthier banks. These tools generally worked to reduce panicked reactions and prevent the freezing up of credit.

But this time, after the collapse of the speculative bubble in housing prices, the course of events has been different. The Federal Reserve was forced to expand the concept of a lender of last resort in unprecedented ways. It has lent to investment banks and insurance companies, not just regulated depository institutions. It has taken all kinds of assets as collateral for its loans, not just the high-grade securities it traditionally accepted. It has even lent to nonfinancial corporations (by buying their commercial paper).

What is surprising is that these dramatic actions and expensive bailouts of financial institutions, such as American International Group (AIG) and even Fannie Mae and Freddie Mac, were insufficient to reassure lenders about the ability of financial institutions to honor their repayment commitments. Treasury Secretary Paulson's plan to use $700 billion to buy "toxic assets" from financial institutions, signed into law by President Bush on October 3rd [2008], failed to stop what had become by then a generalized panic and freeze-up of credit. It took a coordinated global initiative to inject capital directly into financial institutions, plus a federal guarantee on bank debt and unlimited FDIC insurance on non-interest-bearing (mostly business) accounts at banks, announced on October 12th [2008], to begin to have an effect on unfreezing credit markets.

The "TED spread," a widely watched measure of credit risk that had spiked sharply during the panic, began to reverse its path following the October 12 [2008] announcement. The TED spread measures the difference between an interest rate that banks charge when lending to each other (the London Interbank Offered Rate, or LIBOR) and the interest rate on U.S. Treasury bills. Because the Treasury is assumed to be "risk-free," the difference between it and LIBOR measures the perceived relative risk of lending to banks.

Why has this panic been so much more difficult to control? The answer has to do with the widespread use of complicated and opaque securities, known as derivatives, in a deregulated, interconnected, and global financial system.

A derivative is a financial contract that derives its value from something else, such as an asset or an index. At the root of the current crisis are derivatives known as mortgage-backed securities (MBSs). MBSs are claims to payments from an underlying pool of mortgages. The ability of MBS issuers to repay their debt, and thus the value of the MBS, is derived from the ability of homeowners to meet their mortgage payments.

In the process leading up to the crisis, a mortgage broker typically extended a mortgage to a borrower, and then turned to a commercial bank to fund the loan. The bank might sell the loan to Fannie Mae, which would pool a group of mortgages together and sell the resulting MBS to an investment bank like Lehman Brothers. Lehman, in turn, repackaged the MBS in various ways, and issued even more complicated derivatives called collateralized debt obligations (CDOs). Buyers of the CDOs might be other banks, hedge funds, or other lenders.

At the base of this complicated pyramid of derivatives might be a subprime borrower whose lender did not explain an adjustable-rate loan, or another borrower whose ability to meet mortgage payments depended on a continued escalation of home prices. As subprime borrowers' rates reset, and especially as housing price speculation collapsed, the whole house of cards came crashing down.

Why were mortgage loans made that could not be repaid? And why did supposedly sophisticated investors buy MBSs and CDOs based on these loans? First of all, the mortgage brokers and commercial banks that made and funded these loans quickly sold them off and no longer had any responsibility for them. Second, rating agencies like Moody's and Standard & Poor's gave these derivatives stellar AAA ratings, signifying a credit risk of almost zero. Recent Congressional hearings have highlighted the conflict of interest that these rating agencies had: they were being paid by the issuers of the derivatives they were rating. Third, financial institutions up and down the line were making money and nobody was limiting what they could do. In the deregulated financial environment, federal regulators stood aside as housing speculation spun out of control and did little to regulate, or even document, the growth of complicated derivatives.

Finally, financial institutions' concerns about the creditworthiness of the derivatives they held were eased because they thought they could protect themselves against possible loss. For example, by using another type of derivative known as a credit default swap, holders of MBSs and CDOs could make periodic premium payments to another financial institution, like American International Group (AIG), to insure themselves against default by the issuers of the MBSs and CDOs. (This insurance contract was technically classified as a derivative rather than insurance in order to escape regulation.) However, if an insurer like AIG is unable to honor all its insurance contracts, then the protection against loss is illusory.

The total value of all the securities insured by credit default swaps at the end of 2007 was estimated by the Bank of International Settlements to be $58 trillion, and by the International Swaps and Derivatives Association to be $62 trillion. (The estimates could vary by as much as $4 trillion because unregulated credit default swaps do not have to be officially reported to regulatory agencies. Moreover, even greater ambiguity surrounds these contracts because insurers can transfer their liability to other parties, and the insured party may be unaware of the creditworthiness or even the identity of the new insurer.)

Surprisingly, though, the value of the actual securities that form the basis of these credit default swaps was only about $6 trillion. How could $6 trillion worth of assets be insured at ten times that amount? The discrepancy is due to the fact that it is possible to speculate on the likelihood of default of a security without actually owning the security: all the speculator has to do is enter into a credit default swap contract with an insurer. The total volume of "insured securities" can thus escalate dramatically.

Because derivatives are so complex, because so much speculation and debt are involved, and because it is so hard to know how much is at risk (and exactly who is at risk), regulators are unsure of the implications of the failure of a particular financial institution. That is why they have been so fearful of the consequences of letting a troubled institution fail.

The exception that did indeed prove the rule was Lehman Brothers. The Federal Reserve and Treasury did not bail it out, and its failure led to an intensification of the problems in credit markets. A money market fund, the Reserve Primary Fund, announced that it would only pay 97 cents on the dollar to its investors, because its investments in Lehman Brothers could not be redeemed. The Treasury moved quickly to announce that it would insure money market funds, in order to prevent a run on the funds. However, the Lehman failure raised further concerns that lenders had about the derivatives portfolios of other banks, and about the possibility that the banks would not have enough capital to cover potential losses.

Secretary Paulson's initial plan to buy "toxic" assets (including MBSs and CDOs) from financial institutions was designed to address these concerns about bank capital. However, his plan was probably also negatively affected by uncertainty. Because these "toxic" assets are complex and nobody wants to buy them, there is no market for them and their value is uncertain. And because the Paulson plan's unstated objective was to boost bank capital by overpaying for these assets, the difficulties in pricing the assets raised the prospects of long delays and questions about whether the plan to increase bank capital would be successful. Lenders continued to hold back. They may also have hesitated because of concern about a political backlash against a taxpayer subsidy for the very banks that many people blamed for the crisis.

By injecting capital directly into the banks, the global initiative announced on October 12th [2008] raised the prospect of returns on the capital investment for taxpayers. It also avoided the uncertainties of buying individual assets and helped to reduce the panic.

But the crisis isn't over. Reducing the panic is only the first step. There is now likely to be a longer-term credit crunch that will continue to threaten the broader economy. Banks and other lenders will be wary for quite some time. Losses on mortgage-related assets will continue as years of housing speculation—financed with heaps of borrowed money—continues to unwind. Bank lending will lag as banks rebuild their capital and overcome their pessimistic expectations.

It will be up to the federal government to pick up the slack that the banks will leave. We will need programs to enable people to stay in their homes and stabilize their communities. We will need to create jobs by investing in infrastructure, renewable energy, and education. We will need a "trickle-up" approach that puts people first and raises living standards and opportunities.

At the same time, we need a regulatory structure for the financial system that puts limits on risk and manipulation. It is clear that deregulation, and the entire neoliberal model that has dominated economic policy for the past 30 years, has run aground. It has sown the seeds of financial crisis, and this crisis has led us to the edge of an abyss. Only by dramatically reorienting our economic and financial structure can we avoid the abyss and create the kind of society that meets our needs. The nature of that new structure should be the subject of intensive democratic discussion and debate in the days to come. ❑

Article 4.5

DEALING WITH A ROTTEN TOOTH

BY ARTHUR MacEWAN
November/December 2008

> Dear Dr. Dollar:
> *Isn't the "bailout" of Wall Street like having a rotten tooth extracted? The extraction is very unpleasant, but it beats the alternative. Even if the dentist charges an unreasonably high fee, I am still going to pay and have the job done. Later I will worry about taking better care of my teeth. So shouldn't people quit complaining about the bailout, suck it up, and get the job done?*
> —Peter Wagner, Weston, Mass.

I do like thinking about the mess in the financial markets as a "rotten tooth," for something is certainly "rotten" in the current situation. And there is a way in which the analogy is useful: just as we are heavily dependent on the dentist to deal with our teeth, we are heavily dependent on the banks and other financial institutions for the operation of our economy. But if we are going to use the dentist-finance analogy, we need to take it a bit further.

In particular, if the dentist who tells me I need my tooth yanked out in an emergency extraction is the same dentist who for years has been telling me that my teeth are fine, then I get suspicious. This dentist has been making money from me all along, and now, when the crisis of a rotten tooth emerges, the dentist stands to make more money while I incur the pain. The situation is similar to the bailout of the financial system: the banks keep their profits in good times, but the losses are imposed on the rest of us in bad times. At the very least, when the people responsible for a problem—dentists or bankers—tell me to solve the problem in a way that benefits them, I want to get a second opinion, figure out the options, and proceed with caution.

As we have been learning in recent weeks, there is more than one option for dealing with the "rotten tooth." In part because of public pressure (i.e., complaining), the Treasury shifted away from its initial plan to buy up the bad assets in the financial system and is now taking partial ownership of the banks by providing them with capital. Not only is the second plan more likely to work (in the sense of preventing a breakdown of the financial system), but it is also more likely to cost the rest of us less over the long run (because as the banks recover and start to earn profits, the government will share in those profits).

There are other options that the U.S. government might follow as well. For example, the main reason we care about what happens to the banks is that their failures could spread to the rest of us, causing a severe depression. But instead of working simply from the top down, the U.S. government would do well to work from the bottom up—by focusing on the problems of people losing their homes due to foreclosures and by providing a large economic stimulus program through spending on schools, infrastructure, health care, and other real economic needs.

And, just as with my tooth, if the problem really did arise because of the bad practices of those who were supposed to take care of the situation (wasn't this the dentist who had been telling me all was well?), then we should give some immediate attention to proper regulation. The current financial crisis could have been avoided but for the deregulation craze of recent decades. Fixing the deregulation disaster should not be put off to the distant future.

Regulation is not a panacea. There can certainly be bad regulations, sometimes brought about by the firms themselves in an effort to use regulation to secure their power and profits. Establishing good regulations is a constant battle, as the large firms devote huge amounts of their resources to get deregulation or to shape regulation in their favor. Yet without regulation, markets—especially financial markets—are prone to instability, and at times that instability can have severe impacts on the rest of us.

While the dentist analogy may be incomplete, it does bring out a very important point. Because we are excessively dependent on the operations of a relatively small number of very large firms, when they get in trouble, we can be forced to bail them out. Not a good situation. Indeed, the situation is made worse as the current crisis is leading to more consolidation of the banking industry; with the encouragement of the Federal Reserve and the Treasury, big banks are being taken over by even bigger banks. At the very least, if we are going to allow some firms to become "too big to fail," then we would do well to watch them pretty carefully—that is, to regulate them and thus do all we can to prevent them from operating in ways that put us all at risk.

[Full disclosure: Last month I had a tooth extracted and it wasn't all that bad—certainly not as painful as the current Wall Street bailout! —A.M.] ❑

Article 4.6

PONZI SCHEMES AND SPECULATIVE BUBBLES

BY ARTHUR MacEWAN
July/August 2009

> Dear Dr. Dollar:
> *What is the difference between a Ponzi scheme and the way the banks and other investors operated during the housing bubble?*
> —Leela Choiniere, Austin, Texas

As badly as our banking system operated in recent years, the housing bubble was not a Ponzi scheme. In some respects, however, it was even worse than a Ponzi scheme!

A Ponzi scheme is based on fraud. The operators of the scheme deceive the participants, telling them that their money is being used to make real or financial investments that have a high return. In fact, no such investments are made, and the operators of the scheme are simply paying high returns to the early participants with the funds put in by the later participants. A Ponzi scheme has to grow—and grow rapidly—in order to stay viable. When its growth slows, the early participants can no longer be paid the returns they expect. At this point, the operators disappear with what's left of the participants' funds—unless the authorities step in and arrest them, which is what happened with Charles Ponzi in 1920 and Bernard Madoff this year.

Fraud certainly was very important in the housing bubble of recent years. But the housing bubble—like bubbles generally—did not depend on fraud, and most of its development was there for everyone to see. With the principal problems out in the open and with the authorities not only ignoring those problems but contributing to their development, one might say that the situation with the housing bubble was worse than a Ponzi scheme. And Madoff bilked his marks out of only $50 billion, while trillions were lost in the housing bubble.

Bubbles involve actual investments in real or financial assets—housing in the years since 2000, high-tech stocks in the 1990s, and Dutch tulips in the 17th century. People invest believing that the price of the assets will continue to rise; as long as people keep investing, the price does rise. While some early speculators can make out very well, this speculation will not last indefinitely. Once prices start to fall, panic sets in and the later investors lose.

A bubble is similar to a Ponzi scheme: early participants can do well while later ones incur losses; it is based on false expectations; and it ultimately falls apart. But there need be no fraudulent operator at the center of a bubble. Also, while a Ponzi scheme depends on people giving their money to someone else to invest (e.g., Madoff), people made their own housing investments—though mortgage companies and banks made large fees for handling these investments.

Often, government plays a role in bubbles. The housing bubble was in part generated by the Federal Reserve maintaining low interest rates. Easy money meant readily obtainable loans and, at least in the short run, low monthly payments. Also,

Fed Chairman Alan Greenspan denied the housing bubble's existence—not fraud exactly, but deception that kept the bubble going. (Greenspan, whose view was ideologically driven, got support in his bubble denial from the academic work of the man who was to be his successor, Ben Bernanke.)

In addition, government regulatory agencies turned a blind eye to the highly risky practices of financial firms, practices that both encouraged the development of the bubble and made the impact all the worse when it burst. Moreover, the private rating agencies (e.g., Moody's and Standard and Poor's) were complicit. Dependent on the financial institutions for their fees, they gave excessively good ratings to these risky investments. Perhaps not fraud in the legal sense, but certainly misleading.

During the 1990s, the government made tax law changes that contributed to the emergence of the housing bubble. With the Taxpayer Relief Act of 1997, a couple could gain up to $500,000 selling their home without any capital gains tax liability (half that for a single person). Previously, capital gains taxes could be avoided only if the proceeds were used to buy another home or if the seller was over 55 (and a couple could then avoid taxes only on the first $250,000). So buying and then selling houses became a more profitable operation.

And, yes, substantial fraud was involved. For example, mortgage companies and banks used deceit to get people to take on mortgages when there was no possibility that the borrowers would be able to meet the payments. Not only was this fraud, but this fraud depended on government authorities ignoring their regulatory responsibilities.

So, no, a bubble and a Ponzi scheme are not the same. But they have elements in common. Usually, however, the losers in a Ponzi scheme are simply the direct investors, the schemer's marks. A bubble like the housing bubble can wreak havoc on all of us. ❑

Article 4.7

THE BAILOUT OF FANNIE MAE AND FREDDIE MAC

BY FRED MOSELEY
September/October 2008

On Sunday, September 7 [2008], Treasury Secretary Henry Paulson announced that the U.S. government was taking control of Fannie Mae and Freddie Mac, the two giant home mortgage companies, which together either own or guarantee almost half of the mortgages in the United States. This takeover stands in striking contrast to the generally laissez-faire philosophy of the U.S. government, especially the Republican Party. Why did Paulson take this highly unusual action? And what will be the future of Fannie and Freddie? To delve into these questions is to underscore the critical fault line between private profits and public aims—in this case, the aim of making homeownership affordable—a fault line that ran right through the hybrid structure of Fannie and Freddie.

A Brief History

Fannie Mae (short for the Federal National Mortgage Association) was created as an agency of the federal government in 1938 in an attempt to provide additional funds to the home mortgage market and to help the housing industry recover from the Great Depression. Fannie Mae purchased approved mortgages from commercial banks, which could then use the funds to originate additional mortgages. It continued to fulfill this function on a modest scale in the early postwar years.

Fannie Mae was privatized in 1968, in part to help reduce the budget deficit caused by the Vietnam War (a short-sighted goal, if ever there was one). In 1970, Freddie Mac (Federal Home Loan Mortgage Corporation) was created as a private company in order to provide competition for Fannie Mae. Chartered by the federal government, both are (or were, until the takeover) so-called government-sponsored enterprises: private enterprises whose main goal is to maximize profit for the shareholders who own them, but also quasi-public enterprises with a mandated goal of increasing the availability of affordable mortgages to families in the United States. In the end, this dual mandate proved to be untenable.

In order to obtain funds to purchase mortgages, Fannie and Freddie sell short-term bonds. In other words, their business plan involves borrowing short-term and lending long-term, because interest rates are higher on long-term loans than on short-term loans. However, such "speculative finance" is risky because it depends on the willingness of short-term creditors to continue to loan to Fannie and Freddie by rolling over or refinancing their short-term loans. If creditors were to lose confidence in Fannie and Freddie and refuse to do so, then they would be in danger of bankruptcy. This is what almost happened in the recent crisis.

Beginning in the 1970s, Fannie and Freddie began to develop and sell "mortgage-backed securities"—hundreds of mortgages bundled together and sold to investors as a security, similar to a bond. They also guaranteed these securities (so that if a mortgage defaulted, they would repurchase it from the investors) and made money by charging a fee for this guarantee (like an insurance premium). This major financial innovation enabled the two companies to buy more mortgages from commercial banks, thereby increasing the supply of credit in the home mortgage market, which in turn was supposed to push mortgage interest rates lower, making houses more affordable. These early mortgage-backed securities consisted entirely of "prime" mortgages—that is, loans at favorable interest rates, typically made to creditworthy borrowers with full documentation and a substantial down payment.

The securities that Fannie and Freddie sold were widely perceived by investors to carry an implicit government guarantee: if Fannie or Freddie were ever in danger of bankruptcy, then the federal government would pay off their debts (even though this government guarantee was explicitly denied in legislation and in the loan agreements them-selves). This perceived guarantee enabled Fannie and Freddie to borrow money at lower interest rates because loans to them were viewed as less risky.

In the 1980s, Wall Street investment banks also began to package and sell mortgage-backed securities. In the 1990s and 2000s, these "private label" mortgage-backed securities expanded rapidly in volume and also in reach, coming to include "subprime" mortgages—loans at higher interest rates with less favorable terms, geared toward less credit-worthy borrowers and typically requiring little or no documentation and little or no down payment.

The subprime innovation was entirely the work of the investment banks; as of 2000, Fannie and Freddie owned or guaranteed almost no subprime mortgages. This innovation greatly increased the supply of credit for home mortgages and led to the extraordinary housing boom of the last decade, and also eventually to the crisis. As a result of these changes, the share of mortgage-backed securities sold by Fannie and Freddie fell to around 40% by 2005.

In the recent housing boom, the companies—especially Freddie—began to take greater risks. While continuing to bundle prime mortgages into securities and sell them to investors, Fannie and Freddie began to buymortgage-backed securities issued by investment banks, including some based on subprime and Alt-A (between prime and subprime) mortgages. Why did they begin buying as well as selling mortgage-backed securities? Buying these private-label securities gave Fannie and Freddie a way to get in on the subprime action—while still avoiding direct purchases of subprime mortgages from the banks and mortgage companies that originated them. It was a way both to increase their profits at the behest of their shareholders, and, in response to pressure from the government, to make more mortgages available to low- and middle-income families. Of course, it also opened them up to the risks of the subprime arena. Moreover, the prime mortgages they continued to buy and guarantee were increasingly at inflated, bubble prices, making them vulnerable to the eventual bust and the decline of housing prices.

Anatomy of a Crisis

When the subprime crisis began in the summer of 2007, Fannie and Freddie at first appeared to be relatively unaffected, and were even counted on to increase their purchases of mortgages in order to support the mortgage market and help overcome the

crisis. Congress facilitated this by relaxing some of its regulations on the two companies: the maximum value of mortgages that they could purchase was increased substantially; their reserve capital requirements, already much lower than for commercial banks, were reduced further; and restrictions on their growth were lifted. As a
result of these changes and the drying up of private label mortgage-backed securities, the share of all mortgage-backed securities sold by Fannie and Freddie doubled
to approximately 80%. Without Fannie and Freddie, the mortgage and housing crises of the last year would have been much worse.

As the overall crisis unfolded, however, the financial situation of Fannie and
Freddie deteriorated. Delinquency and foreclosure rates for the mortgages they own
or guarantee, while lower than for the industry as a whole, increased rapidly and
beyond expectations. The two companies together reported losses of $14 billion in
the last year. Their actual losses have been much worse. As of mid-2008, the two
had lost about $45 billion due to the decline in the value of their mortgage-backed
securities, mostly those backed by subprime and Alt-A mortgages. But by labeling
that decline "temporary," they could leave the losses off their balance sheets. If these
losses were counted, as they should be, then Freddie's capital would be completely
wiped out (a value of -$5.6 billion), and Fannie's would be reduced to a razor-thin
margin of $12.2 billion (less than 2% of its assets), likely becoming negative in the
coming quarters. In addition, both Fannie and Freddie count as assets "tax deferred
losses" that can be used in future years to offset tax bills—if they make a profit.
Without this dubious (but legal) accounting trick, the net assets of both Fannie and
Freddie would be below zero, -$20 billion and -$32 billion respectively.

The financial crisis of Fannie and Freddie worsened in early July. The price of
their stock, which had already fallen by more than half since last summer, declined
another 50% in a few weeks, for a total decline of over 80%. Fear spread that Fannie
and Freddie's creditors would refuse to roll over their short-term loans to the two.
If that were to happen, then the U.S. home mortgage market and the housing construction industry probably would have collapsed completely, and the U.S. economy
would have fallen into an even deeper recession. Furthermore, approximately 20% of
the mortgage-backed securities and debt of Fannie and Freddie are owned by foreign
investors. Mainly these are foreign governments, most significantly China. If these foreign investors became unwilling to continue to lend Fannie and Freddie money, this
would have precipitated a steep fall in the value of the dollar which, on top of recent
significant declines, would have dealt another blow to the U.S. economy. Clearly, the
potential crisis here was serious enough to spur government action.

In late July, Congress passed a law authorizing the Treasury to provide unlimited
amounts of money to Fannie and Freddie, either by buying new issues of stock or by
making loans, and also to take over the companies in a conservator arrangement
if necessary.

Government Takeover

Through August [2008] the financial condition of Fannie and Freddie continued
to deteriorate (especially Freddie), and confidence in their ability to survive waned.
Foreign investors in particular reduced their purchases of the companies' debt, and

mortgage rates increased. The Treasury concluded that it had to implement a takeover in order to reassure creditors and restore stability to the home mortgage market.

The Treasury plan has three main components:

- It commits up to $200 billion over the next 15 months for purchases of preferred shares of Fannie and Freddie as necessary to keep the companies solvent;

- It establishes a special lending facility that will provide emergency loans in case of a liquidity crisis;

- It commits to purchase unspecified amounts of Fannie and Freddie's mortgage-backed securities "as deemed appropriate."

The day after Paulson's announcement, William Poole, ex-president of the Federal Reserve Bank of St. Louis, estimated that the total cost to taxpayers would be in the neighborhood of $300 billion.

The top managers and the boards of directors of both companies will be dismissed and replaced by new, government-appointed managers. Other than that, the Treasury hopes that day-to-day operations at Fannie and Freddie will be "business as usual." They will continue to borrow money from creditors, now reassured by the government's intervention and more willing to lend to them, and they will continue to purchase and guarantee prime mortgages. In fact, Treasury Department plans call for the volume of mortgages purchased by the two companies to increase over the next year in order to push the supply of mortgage loans up and mortgage interest rates down.

The Treasury plan is a complete bailout of the creditors of Fannie and Freddie, who will be repaid in full, with taxpayer money if necessary. In contrast, owners of Fannie or Freddie stock will lose to some degree: dividends will be suspended for the foreseeable future, and their stock is now worth very little. But their stock was not expropriated. Nor was it wiped out entirely; it could regain value in the future as the home mortgage market recovers. Without the intervention, both companies would have gone bankrupt and the stockowners would have lost everything. So the intervention does represent at least a modest bailout for shareholders.

The most controversial issue in the months ahead will be the future of Fannie and Freddie. Should they become public enterprises permanently? Should they be re-privatized? Should they be sold off in pieces and cease to exist? Secretary Paulson made it clear that the government's current conservatorship is a holding action, and that decisions about the companies' ultimate status will only be made once the next administration and the next Congress are in office. Paulson said that Fannie and Freddie's current structure is unworkable because of its dual and conflicting goals of making housing affordable and maximizing profit—a radical statement, if you think about it! And he suggested that the two should either be fully public enterprises, or else they should be fully private enterprises without any government backing.

In the upcoming debate, the left should advocate forcefully for a public home mortgage agency, one whose sole purpose is to provide affordable housing without the conflicting purpose of maximizing profit. This would stabilize the home mortgage market and help it avoid the boom/bust cycle of private mortgage markets that has brought on the current crisis.

More fundamentally, because decent affordable housing is a basic economic right, providing credit for home purchases should be a function of the government rather than of private businesses whose primary goal is maximum profit. The provision of credit for housing should not be an arena where enormous profits are made, as has been the case in recent years. Without these huge profits, mortgages would be cheaper and houses more affordable. Plus, the kinds of fraudulent lending practices that played a significant role in the recent housing boom would be minimized.

With the presidential election just weeks away, the crisis of Fannie, Freddie, and the whole home lending market is poised to become a major campaign issue. McCain has said that he wants Fannie and Freddie to "go away"—i.e., to be broken up and disappear, leaving the mortgage market entirely to private enterprises. Obama has emphasized the conflict between the public aim of making housing widely affordable and the private aim of making a profit, but so far he has not come down on one side or the other. Now he will have to decide. I hope that he will be a strong advocate of a public home mortgage agency, and I think this would help him to get elected. ❑

Update on the Future of Fannie Mae and Freddie Mac, October 2010

As it turned out, the future of Fannie Mae and Freddie Mac was not an issue in the 2008 presidential campaign. Neither candidate (or party) knew what to do about Fannie and Freddie, especially in the midst of the worst housing crisis since the Great Depression, so they avoided the subject. And the Obama administration continued to avoid the subject, at least in public, as a lower priority than health-care reform and financial reform—until August 17, when Treasury Secretary Geithner convened a one-day conference on "The Future of Housing Finance." The Obama administration has promised their proposal by next January. So the moment of decision on the future of Fannie and Freddie is approaching.

Indications are that Obama will propose that Fannie and Freddie be restructured into a public mortgage insurance agency, which would provide insurance for mortgages owned by private banks, and would not buy and hold any mortgages in their own portfolio. The private banks would pay a premium for the insurance in order to limit taxpayer risk, similar to the insurance premiums for FDIC. Stricter regulation and eligibility requirements for mortgages will probably also be included.

Geithner argues that the main advantage of a government insurance agency over a strictly private mortgage market (without government guarantees) is that it would increase the availability of credit for mortgages at a lower rate of interest, especially in times of economic downturns, like the current crisis. Without the government guarantee, investors would generally charge a higher rate of interest to finance 30-year fixed rate mortgages for households, and may not be willing to lend at all in economic downturns. The interest rate spread in normal times between a purely private mortgage system (e.g., jumbo loans which exceed the maximum for Fannie-Freddie mortgages) and a mortgage system with government insurance in recent decades has been between .25% and .5%. However, in the current recession, this spread increased sharply to 1.5% and is still today almost 1%. The current recession has clearly demonstrated that private banks and other investors will flee the mortgage market in a serious recession unless there are government guarantees. Only about 10% of new mortgages since the recession began have been without government guarantees. Where would the mortgage market and the economy be today without Fannie and Freddie? The mortgage market would be about one-tenth of its present size, and the economy would be in correspondingly much worse shape.

In spite of these obvious risks, Republicans want to do away with the government role in the mortgage market altogether. They argue that private banks would increase competition, which would lower costs and lower mortgage rates. But this argument is disingenuous, to say the least; everyone but free-market true-believers recognizes that, without explicit government backing, mortgage rates would be higher and in a crisis would be much higher. In such a Republican world, houses would be less affordable and home ownership would decline. And in a crisis, new home ownership would become almost impossible. Because of their blind allegiance to the "free market," Republicans are willing to be reckless with our economy and our lives. Obviously, we should not allow them to do this.

Although a government insurance agency would be much better than a purely private mortgage market, there is an even better way to reduce interest rates on mortgages to levels even lower than the Obama insurance plan would: transform Fannie and Freddie into a public mortgage bank (rather than an insurance company) that would buy eligible mortgages from originators and hold them in their own portfolio. Actually, this would be a "return to the past" and to the original structure of Fannie Mae from its beginning in the Great Depression (to provide more affordable mortgages) until its privatization in 1968 (to help pay for the Vietnam War). This public bank option was not discussed at the August conference, but should be part of the discussion.

Such a public bank could charge lower interest rates than private banks (even with government insurance) because the main goal of private banks is to maximize profit and maximize shareholder value, and also to allow for multimillion-dollar salaries of bank executives. A public mortgage bank would have a different objective: not to maximize profit, shareholder value, and executive salaries, but to increase the availability of affordable housing. This goal would not be pursued to the point of losing money, but the profit margin could be less. And the executive salaries would be more in line with high civil servant salaries. Public bank mortgages would also have an upper limit, perhaps $500,000. The public bank provision of low-interest mortgages would not apply to more expensive houses or to second homes.

A relevant comparison is with student loans. The explicit argument of the Obama administration for their "direct lender" model is that they can provide student loans more cheaply than the private companies they have been subsidizing, and can also use the savings to fund more Pell grants for low-income students. What a great idea! The same logic could be applied to housing.

Another related advantage of a public bank over private banks is that its profit would not have to go to private shareholders (there would be none), but would instead become public income that could be used to pursue public policy goals, such as building more affordable housing.

Another advantage of a public bank over the Obama insurance plan is that it would eliminate the risk (which is probably significant) that the insurance premium charged to banks would be too low, and that in the next serious crisis, taxpayers would once again suffer the losses, rather than the private banks that profited from the mortgages during the good times.

A public bank would raise funds to buy mortgages by borrowing money in the capital market (i.e., by selling bonds), the same way that private banks raise funds to finance their mortgages. But this borrowed money would not add to the government deficit, because the money would be invested in mortgages, which would eventually be recovered, together with a modest profit.

The future of Fannie and Freddie will be one of the most important economic policy issues in 2011. The Left should attempt to put the public bank option on the table for discussion, and should advocate its adoption, as the best way to achieve the objective of more affordable housing for all Americans and a more stable economy. ❏

Article 4.8

TIME FOR *PERMANENT* NATIONALIZATION!
If the big banks are "too big to fail," they should be public.

BY FRED MOSELEY
March/April 2009

The Treasury Department's recent bailouts of major U.S. banks will result in a massive transfer of income from taxpayers to those banks' bondholders.

Under the government's current bailout plan, the total sum of money transferred from taxpayers to bondholders will probably be at least several hundred billion dollars and could be as much as $1 trillion, which is about $3,300 for each man, woman, and child in the United States. These bondholders took risks and made lots of money during the recent boom, but now taxpayers are being forced to bail them out and pay for their losses.

This trillion-dollar transfer of income from taxpayers to bondholders is an economic injustice that should be stopped immediately, and it can be stopped—if the government fully and permanently nationalizes the banks that are "too big to fail."

The TARP program ("Troubled Asset Relief Program") has gone through several incarnations. It was originally intended to purchase high-risk mortgage-backed securities from banks. But this plan floundered because it is very difficult in the current circumstances to determine the value of these risky assets and thus the price the government should pay for them. The main policy for the first $350 billion spent so far has been to invest government capital into banks by buying preferred stock (which is the equivalent of a loan), which receives a 5% rate of return (Warren Buffet gets a 10% rate of return when he buys preferred stocks these days) and has no voting rights. Managers of the banks are not being replaced, and there are usually cosmetic limits on executive pay, unlikely to be enforced. So these bank managers, who are largely responsible for the banking crisis, will continue to be rewarded with salaries of millions of dollars per year, paid for in part with taxpayer money. Existing bank stock loses value as the bank issues stock secured by TARP funds.

But the main beneficiaries of the government bailout money are the bondholders of the banks (see box, "Bank Bonds"). In the event of future losses, which are likely to be enormous, the government bailout money will be used directly or indirectly to pay off the bondholders. This could eventually take all of the available TARP money, and perhaps even more. So the government bailout of the banks is ultimately a bailout of the banks' bondholders, paid for by taxpayers.

The Bush administration's rationale for this approach to the bailout was that if the government did not bail out the banks and their bondholders, then the whole financial system in the United States would collapse. Nobody would lend money to anybody, and the economy would seize up (in the memorable words of George W. Bush: "this sucker would go down"). Bush Treasury Secretary Paulson presented us with an unavoidable dilemma—either bail out the bondholders with taxpayers' money or suffer a severe recession or depression.

If Paulson's assertion were correct, it would be a stinging indictment of our current financial system. It would imply that the capitalist financial system, left on its own, is inherently unstable, and can only avoid sparking major economic crises by being bailed out by the government, at the taxpayers' expense. There is a double indictment here: the capitalist financial system is inherently unstable and the necessary bailouts are economically unjust.

But there is a better alternative, a more equitable, "taxpayer friendly" option: Permanently nationalize banks that are "too big to fail" and run these banks according to public policy objectives (affordable housing, green energy, etc.), rather than with the objective of private profit maximization. The nationalization of banks, if it's done right, would clearly be superior to current bailout policies because it would not involve a massive transfer of wealth from taxpayers to bondholders.

Besides providing a more equitable response to the current banking crisis, nationalizing the biggest banks will help ensure that a crisis like this never happens again, and we never again have to bail out the banks and their bondholders to "save the economy." Once some banks have become "too big to fail" and everyone understands that the government will always bail out these large banks to avoid a systematic collapse, it follows that these banks should be nationalized. Otherwise, the implicit promise of a bailout gives megabanks a license to take lots of risks and make lots of money in good times, and then let the taxpayers pay for their losses in the bad times. Economists call this dilemma the "moral hazard" problem. In this case, we might instead call it the "economic injustice" problem.

The best way to avoid this legal robbery of taxpayers is to nationalize the banks. If taxpayers are going to pay for banks' losses, then they should also receive their profits. The main justification for private profit is to encourage capitalists to invest and to invest wisely because they would suffer the losses if their investment fails. But if the losses fall not on capitalists, but instead on the taxpayers, then this justification for private profit disappears.

Freed from the need to maximize short-term profit, nationalized banks would also make the economy more stable in the future. They would take fewer risks during an expansion to avoid debt-induced bubbles, which inevitably burst and cause so much hardship. For example, there would be fewer housing bubbles; instead, the deposits of these megabanks would be invested in decent affordable housing

---

Bank Bonds

Bank bonds are loans to banks by the bondholders, in contrast to common stocks, which are capital invested in banks by their owners. Bank bonds are a relatively new phenomenon in the U.S. economy (and the rest of the world). Until the 1980s, almost all loans by banks were financed from money deposited in the banks by depositors. Then in the 1980s, banks began to borrow more and more money by selling bonds to bondholders; this became a primary way that banks financed their loans. This debt strategy of banks enabled them to invest ever larger sums and make more profits. However, this debt strategy left the banking system more unstable and vulnerable to collapse because banks would have to repay their bondholders. And when major banks were unable to do so, the banking system fell into crisis.

available to all. With housing more affordable, mortgages would be more affordable and less risky.

The newly nationalized banks could also increase their lending to credit-worthy businesses and households, and thereby help stabilize the economy and lessen the severity of the current recession. As things stand, banks do not want to increase their lending, since the creditworthiness of any borrower is difficult to determine, especially that of other banks that may also hold toxic assets. They have suffered enormous losses over the last year, and they fear that more enormous losses are still to come. Banks prefer instead to hoard capital as a cushion against these expected future losses.

What the government is doing now is giving money to banks in one way or another, and then begging them to please lend this money to businesses and households. Nationalization is clearly the better solution. Instead of giving money to the banks and begging them to lend, the government should nationalize the banks in trouble and lend directly to credit-worthy businesses and households.

How would the nationalization of banks work? I suggest the following general principles and guidelines:

(1) The federal government would become the owner of any "systemically significant" bank that asks for a government rescue or goes into bankruptcy proceedings. The value of existing stock would be wiped out, as it would be in a normal bankruptcy.

(2) The government would itself operate the banks. Top management would be replaced by government banking officials, and the managers would not receive "golden parachutes" of any kind.

(3) Most importantly, the banks' long-term bonds would be converted into common stock in the banks. This would restore the banks to solvency, so they could start lending again. The private common stock would be subordinate to the government preferred stock in the capital structure, which would mean that any future losses would be taken out of the private stock before the government stock. Bondholders could also be given the option of converting their stocks back to bonds at a later date, with a significant write-down or discount, determined by bankruptcy judges.

These "bonds-to-stocks" swaps (often called "debt-to-equity" swaps), or partial write-downs if the bondholders so choose, are a crucial aspect of an equitable nationalization of banks. The bondholders lent their money and signed contracts that stipulated that if the banks went bankrupt, they might suffer losses. Now the banks are bankrupt and the bondholders should take the losses.

This process of accelerated bankruptcy and nationalization should be applied in the future to any banks that are in danger of bankruptcy and are deemed to be "systemically significant." This would include the next crises at Citigroup and Bank of America. Other banks in danger of bankruptcy that are not systemically significant should be allowed to fail. There should be no more bailouts of the bondholders at the expense of taxpayers. In addition, the banks who received some of the first $350 billion should be subject to stricter conditions along the lines that Congress attached to the second $350 billion—that banks should be required to increase their lending to businesses and consumers, to fully account for how they have spent the government capital, and to follow strict limitations on executive compensation. The government should withdraw its capital from any banks that fail to meet these standards.

There is one other acceptable option: the government could create entirely new banks that would purchase good assets from banks and increase lending to creditworthy borrowers. These government banks are sometimes called "good banks," in contrast to the "bad bank" proposals that have been floated recently, according to which the government would set up a bank to purchase bad ("toxic") assets from banks. The term "good bank" is no doubt more politically acceptable than "government bank," but the meaning is the same. The only difference between the "good bank" proposal and the nationalization proposal I've outlined here is that my proposal would start with existing banks and turn them into government banks.

In recent weeks, there has been more and more talk about and even acceptance of the "nationalization" of banks. the *Washington Post* recently ran an op-ed by NYU economists Nouriel Roubini and Matthew Richardson entitled "Nationalize the Banks! We Are All Swedes Now," and *New York Times* business columnist Joe Nocera has written about how more and more economists and analysts are beginning to call for nationalization: "Nationalization. I just said it. The roof didn't cave in."

Even former Fed chair Alan Greenspan, whom many regard as one of the main architects of the current crisis, recently told the *Financial Times* that (temporary) nationalization may be the "least bad option." He added, "I understand that once in a hundred years this is what you do."

But there are three crucial differences between such pseudo-nationalizations and full-fledged, genuine nationalization:

(1) The pseudo-nationalizations are intended to be temporary. In this, they follow the model of the Swedish government, which temporarily nationalized some major banks in the early 1990s, and has subsequently almost entirely re-privatized them. Real nationalization would be permanent; if banks are "too big to fail," then they have to be public, to avoid more crises and unjust bailouts in the future.

(2) In pseudo-nationalizations, the government has little or no decision-making power in running the banks. In real nationalization, the government would have complete control over the banks, and would run the banks according to public policy objectives democratically decided.

(3) In pseudo-nationalizations, bondholders don't lose anything, and the loans owed by the banks to the bondholders are paid in full, in large part by taxpayers' money. In real nationalization, the bondholders would suffer their own losses, just as they reaped the profits by themselves in the good times, and the taxpayers would not pay for the losses.

In mid-February, Treasury Secretary Timothy Geithner announced the Obama administration's plans for the bank bailout—renamed the "Financial Stability Plan." This plan is very similar to Paulson's two versions of TARP: it includes both purchases of high-risk mortgage-backed securities from banks and also investing capital in banks. The main new feature is that government capital is supposed to be invested together with private capital. But in order to attract private capital, the government will have to provide sufficient guarantees, so most of the risks will still fall on taxpayers. So Geithner's Financial Stability Plan has the same fundamental flaw as Paulson's TARP: it bails out the banks and their bondholders at the expense of taxpayers.

The public should demand that the Obama administration cancel these plans for further bank bailouts and consider other options, including genuine, permanent nationalization. Permanent nationalization with bonds-to-stocks swaps for bondholders is the most equitable solution to the current banking crisis, and would provide a better basis for a more stable and public-oriented banking system in the future. ❏

Sources: Dean Baker, "Time for Bank Rationalization," cepr.net; Willem Buiter, "Good Bank/ New Bank vs. Bad Bank: a Rare Example of a No-Brainer," blogs.ft.com/maverecon; Krishna Guha and Edward Luce, "Greenspan Backs Bank Nationalization," Financial Times, February 18, 2008; Joe Nocera, "A Stress Test for the Latest Bailout Plan," New York Times, February 13, 2009; James Petras, "No Bailout for Wall Street Billionaires," countercurrents.org; Matthew Richardson and Nouriel Roubini, "Nationalize the Banks! We're All Swedes Now," Washington Post, February 15, 2009; Joseph Stiglitz, "Is the Entire Bailout Strategy Flawed? Let's Rethink This Before It's Too Late," alternet.org.

Article 4.9

THE BAILOUTS REVISITED
Who gets bailed out and why? Is there any alternative to "Too Big to Fail"?

BY MARTY WOLFSON
September/October 2009

Bank of America got bailed out, but Lehman Brothers was allowed to fail. The insurance company American International Group (AIG) was rescued, but in July federal authorities refused to bail out a significant lender to small and medium-sized businesses, the CIT Group (not to be confused with Citigroup, which did get bailed out).

What is the logic behind these decisions? Who is being bailed out—and who should be? The AIG story offers an instructive case study, one that sheds light on these and other questions.

Last September, the Federal Reserve Board announced that it was lending AIG up to $85 billion to prevent the firm's collapse. Unless it bailed out AIG, the Fed warned, financial markets could panic, loans could become more difficult to get, and many more businesses, jobs, and homes could be lost. To counter public anger over the bailout, the Fed argued that the ultimate beneficiaries would be the American people.

Citing proprietary information, AIG initially released few details about how it paid out the money it received. But this March, AIG's plan to pay $165 million in bonuses to employees at its Financial Products unit hit the headlines. An angry firestorm erupted: why should public bailout money be used to pay excessive bonuses to the very people who had caused the problem? U.S. officials and AIG CEO Edward Liddy denounced the payments as outrageous, but claimed they could not rescind the bonuses because they were bound by legal contracts. As it turned out, many AIG employees returned the bonuses voluntarily. And in a rare display of bipartisanship, the House of Representatives voted 328 to 93 to enact a 90% tax on bonuses paid to executives at companies that had received at least $5 billion in bailout money.

But the AIG bailout involved billions of dollars. The Financial Products employees only got millions. Who got the rest of the money? Under mounting public pressure, and after consulting with the Federal Reserve, AIG finally revealed who the beneficiaries were.

It's the Banks!

Yes, the money went primarily to large banks, those same banks that took their own large risks in the mortgage and derivatives markets and that are already receiving billions of dollars in federal bailout money. The banks are using AIG's bailout money to avoid taking losses on their contracts with the company.

Why did AIG, an insurance company, have such extensive dealings with the large banks, and why did those transactions cause so much trouble for AIG?

The story begins with AIG's London-based Financial Products unit, which issued a large volume of derivatives contracts known as credit default swaps (CDSs).

These were essentially insurance contracts that provided for payments to their purchasers (known as "counterparties") in the event of losses on collateralized debt obligations (CDOs), another kind of derivative. Many of the CDOs were based in complicated ways on payments on home mortgages. When the speculative housing bubble popped, mortgages could not be repaid, the CDOs lost value, and AIG was liable for payment on its CDSs.

By September 2008, AIG's situation had deteriorated to the point where its credit ratings were downgraded; this meant the company was required to post collateral on its CDS contracts, i.e., to make billions of dollars in cash payments to its counterparties to provide some protection for them against possible future losses. Despite its more than $1 trillion in assets, AIG did not have the cash. Without assistance it would have had to declare bankruptcy. After attempts to get the funding from private parties, including Goldman Sachs and JPMorgan Chase, failed, the Federal Reserve stepped in. The initial $85 billion credit line was followed by an additional $52.5 billion in credit two months later. By March 2009 the Treasury had invested $70 billion directly in the company, after which the Fed cut back its initial credit line to $25 billion.

AIG paid out those billions in several categories. Between September and December of 2008, $22.4 billion went to holders of CDSs as cash collateral. This cash was paid not only to those who sought insurance for CDOs they actually held, but also to speculators who purchased CDSs without owning the underlying securities. (Data to evaluate the extent of speculation involved had not been published by the time this article went to press.)

The largest beneficiaries of these payments were Société Générale, Deutsche Bank, Goldman Sachs, and Merrill Lynch.

Second, in an effort to stop the collateral calls on these CDSs, AIG spent $27.1 billion to purchase insured CDOs from its counterparties in return for their agreement to terminate the CDSs. Again, the largest beneficiaries of this program were Société Générale, Goldman Sachs, Merrill Lynch, and Deutsche Bank.

Third, it turned out that a significant cash drain on AIG was its securities lending program. Counterparties borrowed securities from AIG and in turn posted cash collateral with AIG. When AIG got into trouble, though, the counterparties decided that they wanted their cash back and sought to return the securities they had borrowed. However, AIG had used the cash to buy mortgage-backed securities, the same securities that were falling in value as the housing market crashed. So $43.7 billion of AIG's bailout money went to those counterparties—chiefly Barclays, Deutsche Bank, BNP Paribas, Goldman Sachs, and Bank of America, with Citigroup and Merrill Lynch not too far behind.

Necessary Bailouts?

Without all that bailout money going to the banks via AIG, wouldn't the financial system have crashed, the banks have stopped lending, and the recession have gotten worse? Well, no.

At least, the banks did not need to receive all the money they did. If a regulatory agency such as the Federal Reserve or the Federal Deposit Insurance Corporation had taken over AIG, it could have used the appropriate tools to, as Fed chair Ben

Bernanke told a House committee this March, "put AIG into conservatorship or receivership, unwind it slowly, protect policyholders, and impose haircuts on creditors and counterparties as appropriate. That outcome would have been far preferable to the situation we find ourselves in now." (A haircut in this context is a reduction in the amount a claimant will receive.)

A sudden and disruptive bankruptcy of AIG could indeed have caused a crash of the financial system, especially as it would have come just one day after the sudden fall of Lehman Brothers on September 15. It is the element of surprise and uncertainty that leads to panic in financial markets. On the other hand, an orderly takeover of AIG such as Bernanke described, with clear information on how much counterparties would be paid, likely could have avoided such a panic.

So why didn't the Federal Reserve take over AIG? It said it did not have the legal authority to take over a nonbank financial institution like AIG. Indeed, to his credit, Bernanke frequently asks for such authority when he testifies to Congress. So why didn't the Fed demand it last September? Wasn't such authority important enough to make it a condition of the bailout? And couldn't Congress have passed the necessary legislation as quickly as it passed the bank bailout bill last fall and the tax on AIG bonuses? Even if that took a few weeks, the Fed could have lent money to AIG to keep it from failing until it had the authority to take the company over.

Of course, the Fed already has the authority to take over large troubled banks—but refuses to use it. Now, Fed and Treasury officials claim that since all the major banks passed the recently administered "stress test," such takeovers are unnecessary. However, even some of the banks that passed the test were judged to be in need of more capital. If they can't get it from private markets then, according to Treasury Secretary Timothy Geithner, the government is prepared to supply them with the capital they need.

In other words, the federal government's strategy of transferring extraordinary amounts of public money to large banks that lose money on risky deals will continue. In fact, the same strategy is evident in the Treasury's proposed Public Private Investment Program, which uses public money to subsidize hedge funds and other private investors to buy toxic assets from the banks. The subsidy allows the private investors to pay a higher price to the banks for their toxic assets than the banks could have received otherwise.

Bail Out the People

The consistent principle behind this strategy is that no large bank can fail. This is why the relatively small CIT Group wasn't rescued from potential bankruptcy but Bank of America was. The decision not to bail out Lehman Brothers, which led to panic in financial markets, is now considered a mistake. However, policymakers drew the wrong lesson from the Lehman episode: that all large bank failures must be prevented. They failed to recognize the important distinction between disruptive and controlled failures.

Yes, there are banks that are too big to fail suddenly and disruptively. However, any insolvent bank, no matter what its size, should be taken over in a careful and deliberative way. If this means nationalization, then so be it. Continental Illinois

National Bank, at the time the 11th largest bank in the United States, was essentially nationalized in 1984, ending the turmoil in financial markets that Continental's difficulties had created.

This "too big to fail" strategy equates stabilizing the financial system and promoting the people's welfare with saving the corporate existence of individual large banks. Likewise the auto companies: while GM and Chrysler have been treated much more harshly than the banks, the auto bailout was similarly designed to keep these two corporate entities alive above all else, even at the expense of thousands of autoworker jobs.

The federal government's current bank-bailout strategy may be well-meaning, but there are four problems with it. It uses public money unnecessarily and is unfair to taxpayers. It may not work: it risks keeping alive "zombie banks" that are really insolvent and unwilling to lend, a recipe for repeating Japan's "lost decade" experience. It makes financial reform going forward much more difficult. Protecting the markets for derivative products like CDOs and CDSs allows for a repeat of the risky practices that got us into the current crisis. And finally, by guaranteeing the corporate existence of large banks, we are maintaining their power and priorities and thus are not likely to see gains on predatory lending, foreclosure abuse, and other areas where reform is sorely needed.

If we want to help the people who are suffering in this crisis and recession, then we should make financial policies with them directly in mind. Just throwing money at the banks will not get the job done. ❑

Chapter 5

THE STOCK MARKET

Article 5.1

THE GREAT STOCK ILLUSION

BY ELLEN FRANK
November/December 2002

During the 1980s and 1990s, the Dow Jones and Standard & Poor's indices of stock prices soared ten-fold. The NASDAQ index had, by the year 2000, sky-rocketed to 25 times its 1980 level. Before the bubble burst, bullish expectations reached a feverish crescendo. Three separate books—Dow 36,000, Dow 40,000 and Dow 100,000—appeared in 1999 forecasting further boundless growth in stock prices. Bullish Wall Street gurus like Goldman's Abby Cohen and Salomon's Jack Grubman were quoted everywhere, insisting that prices could go nowhere but up.

But as early as 1996, skeptics were warning that it couldn't last. Fed chair Alan Greenspan fretted aloud about "irrational exuberance." Yale finance profes-sor Robert Shiller, in his 2001 book titled Irrational Exuberance, insisted that U.S. equities prices were being driven up by wishful thinking and self-fulfilling market sentiment, nourished by a culture that championed wealth and lionized the wealthy. Dean Baker and Marc Weisbrot of the Washington-based Center for Economic and Policy Research contended in 1999 that the U.S. stock market looked like a classic speculative bubble—as evidence they cited the rapidly diverg-ing relationship between stock prices and corporate earnings and reckoned that, to justify the prices at which stocks were selling, profits would have to grow at rates that were frankly impossible.

In 1999 alone, the market value of U.S. equities swelled by an astounding $4 trillion. During that same year, U.S. output, on which stocks represent a claim, rose by a mere $500 billion. What would have happened if stockholders in 1999 had all tried to sell their stock and convert their $4 trillion into actual goods and ser-vices? The answer is that most would have failed. In a scramble to turn $4 trillion of paper gains into $500 billion worth of real goods and services, the paper wealth was bound to dissolve, because it never existed, save as a kind of mass delusion.

The Illusion of Wealth Creation

Throughout the 1990s, each new record set by the Dow or NASDAQ elicited grateful cheers for CEOs who were hailed for "creating wealth." American workers, whose retirement savings were largely invested in stocks, were encouraged to buy more stock—even to bet their Social Security funds in the market—and assured that stocks always paid off "in the long run," that a "buy-and-hold" strategy couldn't lose. Neither the financial media nor America's politicians bothered to warn the public about the gaping disparity between the inflated claims on economic output that stocks represented and the actual production of the economy. But by the end of the decade, insiders saw the writing on the wall. They rushed to the exits, trying to realize stock gains before the contradictions inherent in the market overwhelmed them. Prices tumbled, wiping out trillions in illusory money.

The case of Enron Corp. is the most notorious, but it is unfortunately not unique. When Enron filed for bankruptcy protection in November of 2001 its stock, which had traded as high as $90 per share a year before, plummeted to less than $1. *New York Times* reporter Jeffrey Seglin writes that the elevators in Enron's Houston headquarters sported TV sets tuned to CNBC, constantly tracking the firm's stock price and acclaiming the bull market generally. As Enron stock climbed in the late 1990s, these daily market updates made employees— whose retirement accounts were largely invested in company shares—feel quite wealthy, though most Enron workers were not in fact free to sell these shares. Enron's contributions of company stock to employee retirement accounts didn't vest until workers reached age 50. For years, Enron had hawked its stock to employees, to pension fund managers, and to the world as a surefire investment. Many employees used their own 401(k) funds, over and above the firm's matching contributions, to purchase additional shares. But as the firm disintegrated amid accusations of accounting fraud, plan managers froze employee accounts, so that workers were unable to unload even the stock they owned outright. With employee accounts frozen, Enron executives and board members are estimated to have dumped their own stock and options, netting $1.2 billion cash—almost exactly the amount employees lost from retirement accounts.

Soon after Enron's collapse, telecommunications giant Global Crossing imploded amid accusations of accounting irregularities. Global Crossing's stock, which had traded at nearly $100 per share, became virtually worthless, but not before CEO Gary Winnick exercised his own options and walked away with $734 million. Qwest Communications director Phil Anschutz cashed in $1.6 billion in the two years before the firm stumbled under a crushing debt load; the stock subsequently lost 96% of its value. The three top officers of telecom equipment maker JDS Uniphase collectively raked in $1.1 billion between 1999 and 2001. The stock is now trading at $2 per share. An investigation by the *Wall Street Journal* and Thompson Financial analysts estimates that top telecommunications executives captured a staggering $14.2 billion in stock gains between 1997 and 2001. The industry is now reeling, with 60 firms bankrupt and 500,000 jobs lost. The Journal reports that, as of August 2002, insiders at 38 telecom companies had walked away with gains greater than the current market value of their firms. "All told, it is one of the greatest transfers of wealth from investors—big and small—in American history," reporter Dennis Berman writes. "Telecom executives ... made hundreds of millions of dollars, while many investors took huge, unprecedented losses."

Executives in the energy and telecom sectors were not the only ones to rake in impressive gains. Michael Eisner of Disney Corp. set an early record for CEO pay in 1998, netting $575 million, most in option sales. Disney stock has since fallen by two-thirds. Lawrence Ellison, CEO of Oracle Corp., made $706 million when he sold 29 million shares of Oracle stock in January 2001. Ellison's sales flooded the market for Oracle shares and contributed, along with reports of declining profits, to the stock's losing two-thirds of its value over the next few months. Between 1999 and 2001, Dennis Kozlowski of Tyco International sold $258 million of Tyco stock back to the company, on top of a salary and other compensation valued near $30 million. Kozlowski defended this windfall with the claim that his leadership had "created $37 billion in shareholder wealth." By the time Kozlowski quit Tyco under indictment for sales tax fraud in 2002, $80 billion of Tyco's shareholder wealth had evaporated.

Analyzing companies whose stock had fallen by at least 75%, Fortune magazine discovered that "executives and directors of the 1035 companies that met our criteria took out, by our estimate, roughly $66 billion."

The Illusion of Retirement Security

During the bull market, hundreds of U.S. corporations were also stuffing employee savings accounts with corporate equity, creating a class of captive and friendly shareholders who were in many cases enjoined from selling the stock. Studies by the Employee Benefit Research Council found that, while federal law restricts holdings of company stock to 10% of assets in regulated, defined-benefit pension plans, 401(k)-type plans hold an average 19% of assets in company stock. This fraction rises to 32% when companies match employee contributions with stock and to 53% where companies have influence over plan investments. Pfizer Corporation, by all accounts the worst offender, ties up 81% of employee 401(k) s in company stock, but Coca-Cola runs a close second with 76% of plan assets in stock. Before the firm went bankrupt, WorldCom employees had 40% of their 401(k)s in the firm's shares. Such stock contributions cost firms virtually nothing in the short run and, since employees usually aren't permitted to sell the stock for years, companies needn't worry about diluting the value of equity held by important shareholders—or by their executive option-holders. Commenting on recent business lobbying efforts to gut legislation that would restrict stock contributions to retirement plans, Marc Machiz, formerly of the Labor Department's retirement division, told the *Wall Street Journal*, "business loves having people in employer stock and lobbied very hard to kill this stuff."

Until recently, most employees were untroubled by these trends. The market after all was setting new records daily. Quarterly 401(k) statements recorded fantastic returns year after year. Financial advisers assured the public that stocks were and always would be good investments. But corporate insiders proved far less willing to bank on illusory stock wealth when securing their own retirements.

Pearl Meyer and Partners, an executive compensation research firm, estimates that corporate executives eschew 401(k) plans for themselves and instead negotiate sizable cash pensions—the average senior executive is covered by a defined-benefit plan promising 60% of salary after 30 years of service. Under pressure from the board, CEO Richard McGinn quit Lucent at age 52 with $12 million in severance and a cash pension paying $870,000 annually. Lucent's employees, on the other hand, receive a 401(k) plan with 17% of its assets invested in Lucent stock. The stock plunged from $77 to $10 after McGinn's departure. Today it trades at around $1.00. Forty-two thousand Lucent workers lost their jobs as the firm sank.

When Louis Gerstner left IBM in 2002, after receiving $14 million in pay and an estimated $400 million in stock options, he negotiated a retirement package that promises "to cover car, office and club membership expenses for 10 years." IBM's employees, in contrast, have been agitating since 1999 over the firm's decision to replace its defined benefit pension with a 401(k)-type pension plan that, employee representatives estimate, will reduce pensions by one-third to one-half and save the firm $200 million annually. Economist Paul Krugman reports in the *New York Times* that Halliburton Corp. eliminated its employee pensions; first, though, the company "took an $8.5 million charge against earnings to reflect the cost of its parting gift" to CEO Dick Cheney. *Business Week*, surveying the impact of 401(k)s on employee retirement security, concludes that "CEOs deftly phased out rich defined-benefit plans and moved workers into you're-on-your-own 401(k)s, shredding a major safety net even as they locked in lifetime benefits for themselves."

Since 401(k)s were introduced in the early 1980s their use has grown explosively, and they have largely supplanted traditional defined-benefit pensions. In 2002, three of every four dollars contributed to retirement accounts went into 401(k)s. It is thanks to 401(k)s and other retirement savings plans that middle-income Americans became stock-owners in the 1980s and 1990s. It is probably also thanks to 401(k)s, and the huge demand for stocks they generated, that stock prices rose continuously in the 1990s. And it will almost certainly be thanks to 401(k)s that the problems inherent in using the stock market as a vehicle to distribute income will become glaringly apparent once the baby-boom generation begins to retire and liquidate its stock.

If stocks begin again to rise at historical averages—something financial advisors routinely project and prospective retirees are counting on—the discrepancy between what the stock market promises and what the economy delivers will widen dramatically. Something will have to give. Stocks cannot rise faster than the economy grows, not if people are actually to live off the proceeds.

Or rather, stock prices can't rise that fast unless corporate profits—on which stocks represent a legal claim—also surpass GDP gains. But if corporate earnings outpace economic growth, wages will have to stagnate or decline.

Pension economist Douglas Orr believes it is no accident that 401(k)s proliferated in a period of declining earnings and intense economic insecurity for most U.S. wage-earners. From 1980 until the latter half of the 1990s, the position of the typical American employee deteriorated noticeably. Wages fell, unemployment rose, benefits were slashed, stress levels and work hours climbed as U.S. firms "downsized" and "restructured" to cut costs and satiate investor hunger for higher profits. Firms like General Electric cut tens of thousands of jobs and made remaining jobs far less secure in order to generate earnings growth averaging 15% each year. Welch's ruthless union-busting and cost-cutting earned him the nickname "Neutron Jack" among rank-and-file employees. GE's attitude towards its employees was summed up by union negotiator Steve Tormey: "No matter how many records are broken in productivity or profits, it's always 'what have you done for me lately?' The workers are considered lemons and they are squeezed dry." Welch was championed as a hero on Wall Street, his management techniques widely emulated by firms across the nation. During his tenure, GE's stock price soared as the firm slashed employment by nearly 50%.

The Institute for Policy Studies, in a recent study, found that rising stock prices and soaring CEO pay packages are commonly associated with layoffs. CEOs of firms that "announced layoffs of 1000 or more workers in 2000 earned about 80 percent more, on average, than the executives of the 365 firms surveyed by *Business Week*."

Throughout the 1980s and 1990s, workers whose jobs were disappearing and wages collapsing consoled themselves by watching the paper value of their 401(k) s swell. With labor weak and labor incomes falling, wage and salary earners chose to cast their lot with capital. In betting on the stock market, though, workers are in reality betting that wage incomes will stagnate and trying to offset this by grabbing a slice from the profit pie. This has already proved a losing strategy for most.

Even at the peak of the 1990s bull market, the net wealth—assets minus debts— of the typical household fell from $55,000 to $50,000, as families borrowed heavily to protect their living standards in the face of stagnant wages. Until or unless the nation's capital stock is equitably distributed, there will always be a clash of interests between owners of capital and their employees. If stocks and profits are routinely besting the economy, then either wage-earners are lagging behind or somebody is cooking the books.

Yet surveys show that Americans like 401(k)s. In part, this is because savings accounts are portable, an important consideration in a world where workers can expect to change jobs several times over their working lives. But partly it is because savings plans provide the illusion of self-sufficiency and independence. When retirees spend down their savings, it feels as if they are "paying their own way." They do not feel like dependents, consuming the fruits of other people's labor. Yet they are. It is the nature of retirement that retirees opt out of production and rely on the young to keep the economy rolling. Pensions are always a claim on the real economy—they represent a transfer of goods and services from working adults to non-working retirees, who no longer contribute to economic output. The shift from defined-benefit pensions to 401(k)s and other savings plans in no way changes the fact that pensions transfer resources, but it does change the rules that will govern how those transfers take place—who pays and who benefits.

Private defined-benefit pensions impose a direct claim on corporate profits. In promising a fixed payment over a number of years, corporations commit to transfer a portion of future earnings to retirees. Under these plans, employers promise an annual lifetime benefit at retirement, the amount determined by an employee's prior earnings and years of service in the company. How the benefit will be paid, where the funds will come from, whether there are enough funds to last through a worker's life—this is the company's concern. Longevity risk—the risk that a worker will outlive the money put aside for her retirement—falls on the employer. Retirees benefit, but at a cost to shareholders. Similarly, public pension programs, whether through Social Security or through the civil service, entail a promise to retirees at the expense of the taxpaying public.

Today, the vast majority of workers, if they have pension coverage at all, participate in "defined-contribution" plans, in which they and their employer contribute a fixed monthly sum and invest the proceeds with a money management firm. At retirement, the employee owns whatever funds have accrued in the account and must make the money last until she dies. Defined-contribution plans are a claim on nothing. Workers are given a shot at capturing some of the cash floating around Wall Street, but no promise that they will succeed. 401(k)s will add a huge element of chance to the American retirement experience. Some will sell high, some will not. Some will realize gains. Some will not.

Pearl Meyer and Partners estimate that outstanding, unexercised executive stock options and employee stock incentives today amount to some $2 trillion. Any effort to cash in this amount, in addition to the stock held in retirement accounts, would have a dramatic impact on stock prices. American workers and retirees, in assessing their chances for coming out ahead in the competition to liquidate stock, might ponder this question: If, as employees in private negotiations with their corporate employers, they have been unable to protect their incomes or jobs or health or retirement benefits, how likely is it that they will instead be able to wrest gains from Wall Street where corporate insiders are firmly in control of information and access to deals? ❑

Article 5.2

STOCK VOLATILITY

BY ELLEN FRANK
May/June 2002

> Dear Dr. Dollar:
>
> *During the course of a single day, a stock can go up and down frequently. These changes supposedly reflect the changing demand for that stock (and its potential resale value) or changing expectations of a company's profitability. But this seems too vague to me. How can these factors be so volatile? Who actually decides, or what is the mechanism for deciding, when a stock price should go up or down and by how much?*
>
> —Joseph Balszak, Muskegon, Mich.

Let's start with your last question first—how are stock prices determined? Shares in most large established corporations are listed on organized exchanges like the New York or American Stock Exchanges. Shares in most smaller or newer firms are listed on the NASDAQ—an electronic system that tracks stock prices.

Every time a stock is sold, the exchange records the price at which it changes hands. If, a few seconds or minutes later, another trade takes place, the price at which that trade is made becomes the new market price, and so on. Organized exchanges like the New York Stock Exchange will occasionally suspend trading in a stock if the price is excessively volatile, if there is a severe mismatch between supply and demand (many people wanting to sell, no one wanting to buy) or if they suspect that insiders are deliberately manipulating a stock's price. But in normal circumstances, there is no official arbiter of stock prices, no person or institution that "decides" a price. The market price of a stock is simply the price at which a willing buyer and seller agree to trade.

Why then do prices fluctuate so much? The vast bulk of stock trades are made by professional traders who buy and sell shares all day long, hoping to profit from small changes in share prices. Since these traders do not hold stocks over the long haul, they are not terribly interested in such long-term considerations as a company's profitability or the value of its assets. Or rather, they are interested in such factors mostly insofar as news that would affect a company's long-term prospects might cause *other traders* to buy the stock, causing its price to rise. If a trader believes that others will buy shares (in the expectation that prices will rise), then she will buy as well, hoping to sell when the price rises. If others believe the same thing, then the wave of buying pressure will, in fact, *cause* the price to rise.

Back in the 1930s, economist John Maynard Keynes compared the stock market to a contest then popular in British tabloids, in which contestants had to look at photos and choose the faces that *other contestants* would pick as the prettiest. Each contestant had to look for photos "likeliest to catch the fancy of the other competitors, all of whom are looking at the problem from the same point of view." Similarly, stock traders try to guess which stocks other traders will buy. The successful trader is the one who anticipates and outfoxes the market, buying before a stock's price rises and selling before it falls.

Financial firms employ thousands of market strategists and technical analysts who spend hours poring over historical stock data, trying to divine the logic behind these price changes. If they could unlock the secret of stock prices, they could arm their traders with the ability to always buy low and sell high. So far, no one has found this particular holy grail. And so traders continue to guess and gamble and, in doing so, send prices gyrating.

For small investors, who do hold stock for the long term and will need to cash in their stocks at some point to finance their retirements, the volatility of the market can be a source of constant anxiety. Every time a share in, say, General Electric is traded, the new price is used to revalue all outstanding shares—just as the value of your home appreciates when the house down the block sells for more than a similar house sold last week. But the value of your home wouldn't be so high if every house on your block were suddenly put up for sale. Similarly, if all ten billion outstanding shares of General Electric—or even a small fraction of them—were put up for sale, they wouldn't fetch anywhere near the current market price. Small investors need to keep in mind that the gains and losses on their 401(k) statements are just hypothetical paper gains and losses. You won't know the true value of your stocks until you actually try to sell them. ❑

Article 5.3

TEACHING ABOUT STOCKS FOR FUN AND PROPAGANDA

BY MARK MAIER
March/April 2001

Every year, more than a million U.S. primary, middle, and high school students play the stock market at school. They use pretend money and imaginary trades, but students experience the feel of real-world finance, tallying their gains as they buy and sell stock at prices relayed electronically from the real-life stock exchanges. These stock market simulations come with complete lesson plans, worksheets, professional advice from real stockbrokers, and even cash prizes. No wonder they are so popular. Melissa, a secondary school student, raves, "We are all having a blast and no one has even skipped class." Teachers, too, are pleased. A middle school computer teacher in West Bend, Wisconsin, notes, "The very first thing in the morning, before the pledge of allegiance, they want to check their stocks."

But stock market games and their accompanying curriculum guides present a rosy, one-sided picture of Wall Street, in which everyone starts out rich and all that matters is short-term profits. Omitting the less attractive side of the stock market fits conveniently with the corporate underwriters' viewpoint, but it is poor training for future citizens and investors.

$100,000 is a Nice Start

The most popular stock market games are played on the web using a variety of internet sources. The oldest and still most commonly adopted is The Stock Market Game, a program trademarked by an affiliate of the Securities Industry Association. Teachers often use it in conjunction with a curriculum distributed by the National Council on Economic Education (NCEE), a nonprofit organization of education, business and labor leaders. Increasingly, teachers are turning to commercially produced stock market games that are free of charge. Commercial games sometimes offer complex stock trades, as well as research assistance that is unavailable at nonprofit sites. Commercial games are designed to attract students and other individuals to the web site's advertisements, usually for the company's real-life, paid stock transactions.

Nearly all games follow a common script. Students begin with a tidy sum, usually $100,000, with no reference to the source of this initial endowment – although one curriculum offers the unlikely scenario that students have inherited money from "Uncle Mort," who helped Brazilian Indians profit from rain forest products. Since everyone starts out with the same amount of money, the games perpetuate the idea that individual effort is the reason that some people get rich and others do not.

Of course, in real life the starting line isn't even. Fewer than one out of ten households owns $100,000 in *total* financial assets, including not only stocks but also bonds, bank accounts, and retirement accounts. And stocks themselves are distributed in a very lopsided manner, with 10% of shareholders owning 90% of all

---

Stock Market Lingo

Financial assets– Items of wealth, such as stocks and bonds, that represent a paper claim to a future flow of income (differentiated from other assets such as real estate, factories, or patents).

Risk– The probabilities of various outcomes for a financial asset: How likely is it that the asset will lose a lot? A little? Nothing?

Portfolio– A collection of assets owned by an individual, business, or fund. The main purpose of owning a portfolio – instead of one asset – is to diversify and therefore reduce risk.

Diversification– Experts recommend that investors reduce a portfolio's risk by including assets that tend to move up and down at different times. For example, an investor may want to own stock in oil producers that do well when fuel prices rise, in order to counterbalance utilities that may be in trouble if fuel prices go up.

Mutual funds– The pooling of investor assets in order to benefit from less expensive diversification and professional management than a single investor could afford. The largest mutual funds include Fidelity Investments and the Vanguard Group.

Stocks and bonds– Technically, stocks are units of ownership in a corporation, but most shareholders do not influence corporate policy; instead, they hold stock simply for its potential dividends and increases in price. Bonds are long-term loans to businesses or government that do not involve ownership. Usually bonds provide a set interest payment for a set number of years.

Random stock market– Economists use this term to explain why it is so difficult to make above-average profits in the stock market. In this view, stock prices appear to move randomly because information about a corporation's prospects is already reflected in its current price.

Bubble– Sometimes the price of a single stock, the entire stock market, or a national currency will spiral upwards simply because many investors buy into the expectation of even higher prices. When these expectations collapse, the bubble bursts, and the price falls calamitously for those still holding the asset.

---

stock, while the top 1% owns more than half of all shares. Unequal distribution of stocks goes unmentioned in teaching guides such as the New York Stock Exchange's *The Stock Market Wants You,* or the NCEE's *Learning from the Market.* Instead, these manuals emphasize the recent broadening of stock ownership, so that 50% of households now own stock. A true-to-life stock market simulation would show that, while it is true that more U.S. households own some stock than in the past, owner-ship has become even more unequal: The rich now own an even larger percentage of all stock than they did 20 years ago.

Shortsighted and Risky

Even for the small number of students who one day will own a substantial amount of stock, the games are poor practice for real-world investing. The short time period during which students buy and sell stocks—typically eight to 12 weeks to fit comfortably in a school term—means that students focus on short-term gains. Professional advisors recommend a much longer-term perspective, holding stock for a decade or more in order to avoid periodic downturns in stock prices.

> ### *"Play" the Market on the Web*
>
> Stock market simulations are so sophisticated that they look just like actual trading. Participants can choose from nearly all available stocks, mutual funds, margin purchases, short selling—all at prices delayed usually only a few minutes from actual stock market prices. Many schools use *The Stock Market Game*, sponsored by the Securities Industry Association but commercial-free. However, in recent years non-profit simulation games have been displaced by explicitly commercial sites such as CNBC's *Student Stock Tournament* (now used in more than 10,000 schools), *Final Bell* from Sandbox, *MarketPlayer.com*, and *Virtual Stock Exchange*. Because of advertising, these stock competitions are free. Also, they offer cash prizes, as well as links to research that is unavailable in the traditional, non-profit world. Some web sites have extended the simulations to the "buying" and "selling" of predictions about events other than the stock market, including athletes' performances at *Wall Street Sports* and film earnings at the *Hollywood Stock Exchange*.

In addition, stock market games reward students who take excessive risks. Analysis of game winners shows that the best strategy is for students to ignore diversification—owning stock in a variety of corporations, which is the starting point for all prudent investment. By focusing on a few stocks known to swing wildly in price, some students, either through blind luck or an ill-advised risky portfolio, will end the game with big winnings, beating students who took the safer, diversified route. When it became apparent that students with such careless investments consistently won stock market competitions, some games forced students to invest in at least four stocks and to make a minimum number of trades. But the winning strategy remains to gamble as much as possible.

Most students take a naïve approach, choosing portfolios based on brand names they know—McDonalds, Colgate-Palmolive, and Disney in one typical Boston seventh-grade classroom. The training manuals accompanying the best-selling games tell students that they will win if they carefully study these corporations. Several games use McDonalds as an example, suggesting that if students saw the burger chain introduce a popular new menu item, then this would be a good time to buy McDonalds stock.

No expert would agree. If McDonalds' profitability improves because of a new menu item, then other stock investors would have already purchased McDonalds stock, pushing up the price to a point where further gains are unlikely. Economists debate the full impact of this effect. It may be possible for a few experts, or those with privileged access to new information, to buy and sell stock with above-average success. Alternatively, the stock market may behave irrationally, not following the wisdom of any investor. But it is well proved that the strategy recommended for students – buying and selling stocks based on readily available information – is no better than a random choice of stocks and, on average, will cause students to lose because profits are reduced by broker's fees.

In a typical classroom, the stock market's random fluctuations will ensure that a handful of students will do well, tallying high profits and winning prizes put up at commercial web sites. Pride in such gains is misplaced. Students with losing stocks may feel an undeserved sense of personal failure, wrongly perceiving themselves as less clever than the game winners. When they are adults, students may expect the same returns earned by the lucky few, a lesson no more valid than if students practiced betting on horses.

The stock market game's easy profits also might make students more receptive to recommendations to privatize Social Security. After all, if investing is simple and fun, wouldn't we be better off making individual decisions about our retirement funds? In the real world, privatization would be inequitable, risky, and more costly than a simulation game in which everyone starts off with the same $100,000 and there are no penalties for a losing investment strategy.

It is easy to see why teachers want to take advantage of student interest in stocks. Algebra teacher Tony Smith explains: "I have never seen kids so excited to come to class." Stock market simulations grab students' attention with real-world applications of math and research skills. The games can also be used to teach economics. However, rather than asking students to pick a winning portfolio, teachers should use the stock market to show students the actual workings of corporate America. For example, reading the stock pages could help students to see corporate ownership behind popular name brands. Beginning with Oscar Meyer wieners, a student will learn that they are produced by Philip Morris, the same corporation that owns Marlboro, Miller beer, and Velveeta cheese. These examples would show students the power over food marketing held by corporations such as the Philip Morris-Kraft conglomerate, and the problems of its recent merger with Nabisco foods.

Up with Stocks

The instructor's manuals that accompany stock market games puff up the importance of stock markets in the U.S. economy, implying incorrectly that stocks are the source of most new corporate investment. Instead, retained profits or bank loans, not new stock issues, are the preferred source of funding for new plant and equipment. In fact, U.S. corporations have been buying back their own stock in order to keep stock prices high. As a result, the stock market is an overall *drain* on corporations' ability to build for the future.

Stock market games also teach that buying stock gives one "ownership" of a corporation, that is, voting rights in decision-making. As one student put it, "I thought it was so cool I owned a part of McDonalds." The reality is that corporate governance is a complex process, with decision-making split between management and those with large numbers of shares. Sometimes a major shareholder will intervene in corporate decision-making. For example, in January, when the Gateway computer company was doing poorly, Ted Waitt—who owned nearly a third of the stock— took over as chief executive. But small shareholders, even when they act collectively, rarely influence company policy. Instead of perpetuating the myth of shareholder democracy, a better curriculum would ask students to find out how a local corporation decides to introduce a new product or move its production facilities.

The Casino Economy

Finally, stock market games almost never explore the problems caused by speculation. A 15-year-old Mamaroneck, New York, high school student explained: "It was so cool… my money could make money without me doing anything!" This attitude, held by real-world investors as well, worries many economists who predict that the current bubble will burst, bringing down stock prices and likely causing a recession. Remarkably, such possibilities are not mentioned in any of the leading teacher manuals. Instead, the stock market is portrayed as a wise judge, rewarding those who make the right choices. An accurate curriculum would point out that speculation is not only risky for individual investors but also potentially harmful for the entire economy, since it might divert funds from socially useful purposes.

One can easily imagine an exciting simulation game that includes the real-world possibility of prices first rising irrationally, only to fall when investors lose confidence. Students might buy and sell stocks as quickly as they can, passing the hot stock to someone else—until the bubble bursts and the stocks are worthless.

For some purposes like teaching math, stock market games provide a dose of reality. Brad, a sixth grader in Pasadena, California, points proudly to the stock chart he keeps at home: "It *wasn't* math; we used percentages and multiplication to figure out how much we made." It might be too much to expect schoolteachers to pass up such an easy way to spice up a humdrum class. Certainly, the lure of a compelling game, along with glitzy corporate-sponsored lesson plans, is attractive to overworked teachers. But if students are to learn how the economy actually works, then teachers need to use stock market games with great caution, supplementing them with alternative activities to show the real world of unequal resources, impotent small shareholders, and reckless speculative bubbles. ❑

Resources: *The Stock Market Game* <www.smgww.org>.

Article 5.4

WHO GETS THOSE TRILLIONS?

BY ARTHUR MacEWAN
January/February 2009

> Dear Dr. Dollar:
> *As housing prices have fallen, it seems that people have lost a huge amount in terms of the value of their homes. We are told that, over the whole country, trillions of dollars in home equity have been lost. Who gets those trillions? And, likewise, what about the trillions lost in the stock market?*
> —Carlos Rafael Alicea Negrón, Bronx, N.Y.

The simple answer to your question is that no one gets the lost trillions; they are simply gone. But, like all simple answers, this one doesn't explain very much.

Suppose that seven years ago, you bought your house for $200,000. Housing prices continued to rise, and at the beginning of 2007 you saw that other people in your neighborhood were selling houses similar to yours for $400,000. So you, quite reasonably, figured that your house was worth $400,000.

But now the housing bubble has burst. Similar houses in your neighborhood are selling for "only" $300,000 and thus it is now quite reasonable to figure that the value of your house has dropped by $100,000 as compared to the beginning of 2007. (Multiply this $100,000 by roughly 75 million homes across the country, and you have losses of $7.5 trillion.)

Your house, however, was not involved in any actual transaction at this lower value. So no one has gained the value you lost. If, for example, last year one of your neighbors had sold an equivalent house for $400,000 and now buys your house for $300,000 this neighbor would have gained what you lost. But most houses are not bought and sold in any given year. Their value is determined by those equivalent (or similar) houses that are actually bought and sold.

Moreover, even if someone bought your house at $300,000, that person would gain the value you lost only in the special case of the example above, where the person was lucky enough to have sold an equivalent house at $400,000. If instead that person was a new entrant to the housing market or a person who had just sold a similar house elsewhere for $300,000, then no one would be gaining what you lost.

Thus in the great majority of cases, the $100,000 value would simply be gone, and no one would have gotten it.

The situation on the stock market is similar. The values of stocks are determined by the sales that actually take place. When we hear that today the value of Mega Corporation's stock fell from $100 a share to $75 dollars a share, this means that the price of shares that were traded today were selling at $75 while those that were traded yesterday were selling for $100. But most shares of Mega Corporation were not actually traded either day. Their value fell—just like the value of your house fell when neighbors sold their houses—but no one gained this lost value. As in the housing market, the values of stocks have declined by trillions, but the trillions are simply gone.

Of course as with the situation in the housing market, some actual gains of value can take place when stock prices fall. If someone sold a share of Mega Corporation yesterday for $100 and bought it today for $75, this person obtained a gain. But with most of the declines in stock values, no one gets a gain.

To understand what has happened recently, it is useful to keep in mind that the high housing values of recent years were the result of a speculative bubble. The values increased not because there was some real change in the houses themselves. The houses were not providing more living services to the degree that their prices rose. The prices of housing rose because people expected them to rise more. The situation was a speculative bubble, and housing prices rose far above their historical trend.

And just as, in general, the loss of value when prices fell was not balanced by a gain, the gains that people saw when the bubbles expanded were not balanced by losses. As the bubble grew and the value of your house rose from $200,000 to $400,000, no one experienced an equivalent loss. Virtually all home buyers and owners were winners.

But speculative bubbles do not last. ❑

Article 5.5

LABOR'S CAPITAL
Putting Pension Wealth to Work for Workers

BY ADRIA SCHARF
September/October 2005

Pension fund assets are the largest single source of investment capital in the country. Of the roughly $17 trillion in private equity in the U.S. economy, $6 to 7 trillion is held in employee pensions. About $1.3 trillion is in union pension plans (jointly trusteed labor-management plans or collectively bargained company-sponsored plans) and $2.1 trillion is in public employee pension plans. Several trillion more are in defined contribution plans and company-sponsored defined benefit plans with no union representation. These vast sums were generated by—and belong to—workers; they're really workers' deferred wages.

Workers' retirement dollars course through Wall Street, but most of the capital owned *by* working people is invested with no regard *for* working people or their communities. Pension dollars finance sweatshops overseas, hold shares of public companies that conduct mass layoffs, and underwrite myriad anti-union low-road corporate practices. In one emblematic example, the Florida public pension system bought out the Edison Corporation, the for-profit school operator, in November 2003, with the deferred wages of Florida government employees—including public school teachers. (With just three appointed trustees, one of whom is Governor Jeb Bush, Florida is one of the few states with no worker representation on the board of its state-employee retirement fund.)

The custodians of workers' pensions—plan trustees and investment managers—argue that they are bound by their "fiduciary responsibility" to consider only narrow financial factors when making investment decisions. They maintain they have a singular obligation to maximize financial returns and minimize financial risk for beneficiaries—with no regard for broader concerns. But from the perspective of the teachers whose dollars funded an enterprise that aims to privatize their jobs, investing in Edison, however promising the expected return (and given Edison's track record, it wasn't very promising!), makes no sense.

A legal concept enshrined in the 1974 Employee Retirement Income Security Act (ERISA) and other statutes, "fiduciary responsibility" does constrain the decision-making of those charged with taking care of other people's money. It obligates fiduciaries (e.g., trustees and fund managers) to invest retirement assets for the exclusive benefit of the pension beneficiaries. According to ERISA, fiduciaries must act with the care, skill, prudence, and diligence that a "prudent man" would use. Exactly what that means, though, is contested.

The law does *not* say that plan trustees must maximize short-term return. It does, in fact, give fiduciaries some leeway to direct pension assets to worker- and community-friendly projects. In 1994, the U.S. Department of Labor issued rule clarifications that expressly permit fiduciaries to make "economically targeted investments" (ETIs), or investments that take into account collateral benefits like good jobs, housing, improved social service facilities, alternative energy, strengthened infrastructure, and economic development. Trustees and fund managers are free to consider a double bottom line, prioritizing investments that have a social pay-off so long as their expected risk-adjusted financial returns are equal to other, similar, investments. Despite a backlash against ETIs from Newt Gingrich conservatives in the 1990s, Clinton's Labor Department rules still hold.

Nevertheless, the dominant mentality among the asset management professionals who make a living off what United Steelworkers president Leo Gerard calls "the deferred-wage food table" staunchly resists considering any factors apart from financial risk and return.

This is beginning to change in some corners of the pension fund world, principally (no surprise) where workers and beneficiaries have some control over their pension capital. In jointly managed union defined-benefit (known as "Taft-Hartley") plans and public-employee pension plans, the ETI movement is gaining ground. "Taft-Hartley pension trustees have grown more comfortable with economically targeted investments as a result of a variety of influences, one being the Labor Department itself," says Robert Pleasure of the Center for Working Capital, an independent capital stewardship-educational institute started by the AFL-CIO. Concurrently, more public pension fund trustees have begun adopting ETIs that promote housing and economic development within state borders. Most union and public pension trustees now understand that, as long as they follow a careful process and protect returns, ETIs do not breach their fiduciary duty, and may in certain cases actually be sounder investments than over-inflated Wall Street stocks.

Saving Jobs: Heartland Labor Capital Network

During the run-up of Wall Street share prices in the 1990s, investment funds virtually redlined basic industries, preferring to direct dollars into hot public technology stocks and emerging foreign markets, which despite the rhetoric of fiduciary responsibility were often speculative, unsound, investments. Even most collectively bargained funds put their assets exclusively in Wall Street stocks, in part because some pension trustees feared that if they didn't, they could be held liable. (During an earlier period, the Labor Department aggressively pursued union pension trustees for breaches of fiduciary duty. In rare cases where trustees were found liable, their personal finances and possessions were at risk.) But in the past five years, more union pension funds and labor-friendly fund managers have begun directing assets into investments that bolster the "heartland" economy: worker-friendly private equity, and, wherever possible, unionized industries and companies that offer "card-check" and "neutrality." ("Card-check" requires automatic union recognition if a majority of employees present signed authorization cards; "neutrality" means employers agree to remain neutral during organizing campaigns.)

The Heartland Labor Capital Network is at the center of this movement. The network's Tom Croft says he and his allies want to "make sure there's an economy still around in the future to which working people will be able to contribute." Croft estimates that about $3 to $4 billion in new dollars have been directed to worker-friendly private equity since 1999—including venture capital, buyout funds, and "special situations" funds that invest in financially distressed companies, saving jobs and preventing closures. Several work closely with unions to direct capital into labor-friendly investments.

One such fund, New York-based KPS Special Situations, has saved over 10,000 unionized manufacturing jobs through its two funds, KPS Special Situations I and II, according to a company representative. In 2003, St. Louis-based Wire Rope Corporation, the nation's leading producer of high carbon wire and wire rope products, was in bankruptcy with nearly 1,000 unionized steelworker jobs in jeopardy. KPS bought the company and restructured it in collaboration with the United Steelworkers International. Approximately 20% of KPS's committed capital is from Taft-Hartley pension dollars; as a result, the Wire Rope transaction included some union pension assets.

The Heartland Labor Capital Network and its union partners want to expand this sort of strategic deployment of capital by building a national capital pool of "Heartland Funds" financed by union pension assets and other sources. These funds have already begun to make direct investments in smaller worker-friendly manufacturing and related enterprises; labor representatives participate alongside investment experts on their advisory boards.

"It's simple. Workers' assets should be invested in enterprises and construction projects that will help to build their cities, rebuild their schools, and rebuild America's infrastructure," says Croft.

"Capital Stewardship": The AFL-CIO

For the AFL-CIO, ETIs are nothing new. Its Housing Investment Trust (HIT), formed in 1964, is the largest labor-sponsored investment vehicle in the country that produces collateral benefits for workers and their neighborhoods. Hundreds of union pension funds invest in the $2 billion trust, which leverages public financing to build housing, including low-income and affordable units, using union labor. HIT, together with its sister fund the Building Investment Trust (BIT), recently announced a new investment program that is expected to generate up to $1 billion in investment in apartment development and rehabilitation by 2005 in targeted cities including New York, Chicago, and Philadelphia. The initiative will finance thousands of units of housing and millions of hours of union construction work. HIT and BIT require owners of many of the projects they help finance to agree to card-check recognition and neutrality for their employees.

HIT and BIT are two examples of union-owned investment vehicles. There are many others—including the LongView ULTRA Construction Loan Fund, which finances projects that use 100% union labor; the Boilermakers' Co-Generation and Infrastructure Fund; and the United Food and Commercial Workers' Shopping Center Mortgage Loan Program—and their ranks are growing.

Since 1997, the AFL-CIO and its member unions have redoubled their efforts to increase labor's control over its capital through a variety of means. The AFL-CIO's Capital Stewardship Program promotes corporate governance reform, investment manager accountability, pro-worker investment strategies, international pension fund cooperation, and trustee education. It also evaluates worker-friendly pension funds on how well they actually advance workers' rights, among other criteria. The Center for Working Capital provides education and training to hundreds of union and public pension fund trustees each year, organizes conferences, and sponsors research on capital stewardship issues including ETIs.

Public Pension Plans Join In

At least 29 states have ETI policies directing a portion of their funds, usually less than 5%, to economic development within state borders. The combined public pension assets in ETI programs amount to about $55 billion, according to a recent report commissioned by the Vermont state treasurer. The vast majority of these ETIs are in residential housing and other real estate.

The California Public Employees' Retirement System (CalPERS) is an ETI pioneer among state pension funds. The single largest pension fund in the country, it has $153.8 billion in assets and provides retirement benefits to over 1.4 million members. In the mid-1990s, when financing for housing construction dried up in California, CalPERS invested hundreds of millions of dollars to finance about 4% of the state's single-family housing market. Its ETI policy is expansive. While it requires economically targeted investments earn maximum returns for their level of risk and fall within geographic and asset-diversification guidelines, CalPERS also considers the investments' benefits to its members and to state residents, their job creation potential, and the economic and social needs of different groups in the state's population. CalPERS directs about 2% of its assets—about $20 billion as of May 2001—to investments that provide collateral social benefits. It also requires construction and maintenance contractors to provide decent wages and benefits.

Other state pension funds have followed CalPERs' lead. In 2003, the Massachusetts treasury expanded its ETI program, which is funded by the state's $32 billion pension. Treasurer Timothy Cahill expects to do "two dozen or more" ETI investments in 2004, up from the single investment made in 2003, according to the *Boston Business Journal*. "It doesn't hurt our bottom line, and it helps locally," Cahill explained. The immediate priority will be job creation. Washington, Wisconsin, and New York also have strong ETI programs.

In their current form and at their current scale, economically targeted investments in the United States are not a panacea. Pension law does impose constraints. Many consultants and lawyers admonish trustees to limit ETIs to a small portion of an overall pension investment portfolio. And union trustees must pursue ETIs carefully, following a checklist of "prudence" procedures, to protect themselves from liability. The most significant constraint is simply that these investments must generate risk-adjusted returns equal to alternative investments—this means that many deserving not-for-profit efforts and experiments in economic democracy are automatically ruled out. Still, there's more wiggle room in the law than has been broadly recognized. And when deployed strategically to bolster the labor movement, support employee buyouts, generate good jobs, or build affordable housing, economically targeted investments are a form of worker direction over capital whose potential has only begun to be realized. And (until the day that capital is abolished altogether) that represents an important foothold.

As early as the mid-1970s, business expert Peter Drucker warned in *Unseen Revolution* of a coming era of "pension-fund socialism" in which the ownership of massive amounts of capital by pension funds would bring about profound changes to the social and economic power structure. Today, workers' pensions prop up the U.S. economy. They're a point of leverage like no other. Union and public pension funds are the most promising means for working people to shape the deployment of capital on a large scale, while directing assets to investments with collateral benefits. If workers and the trustees of their pension wealth recognize the power they hold, they could alter the contours of capitalism. ❑

Article 5.6

DOW'S REBOUND AFTER THE GREAT RECESSION INCONSEQUENTIAL FOR MOST AMERICANS

BY SYLVIA A. ALLEGRETTO
October 2010

The Dow has rebounded nicely following the bursting of the housing bubble in 2008 and the Great Recession that followed. As of October 2010, the Dow was just above 11,000—a significant improvement over its recent low of 6,630 in March 2009. The Dow has surpassed the 10,000 mark for the greater part of 2010 even as there has not been much improvement in the overall economy. It is clear that there is a disconnect between the stock market and the broader economy, as measured in terms of job growth or the unemployment rate. Thus, it is important to put stock market gains into perspective for average working families. Fostered by the constant focus and widespread attention given to the performance of the stock market, conventional wisdom has it that everyone in the United States is heavily invested in the stock market. However, the data tell a different story.

The most recent triennial data from the Survey of Consumer Finances show that the historically increasing trend in the shares of all households owning any stock was reversed after 2001, when just over half (51.9%) were in the stock market in some form. In 2004 the share fell to just under half (48.6%), which was the first such decline on record (Figure 1), and there was little improvement in 2007when the share was about the same (49.1%).

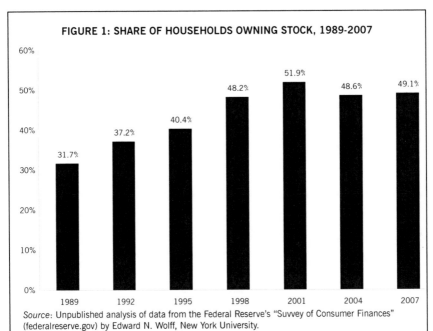

FIGURE 1: SHARE OF HOUSEHOLDS OWNING STOCK, 1989-2007

Source: Unpublished analysis of data from the Federal Reserve's "Suvvey of Consumer Finances" (federalreserve.gov) by Edward N. Wolff, New York University.

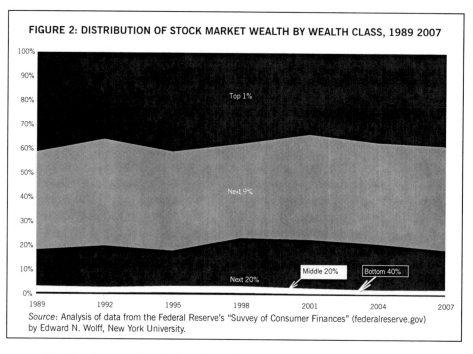

FIGURE 2: DISTRIBUTION OF STOCK MARKET WEALTH BY WEALTH CLASS, 1989 2007

Source: Analysis of data from the Federal Reserve's "Suvvey of Consumer Finances" (federalreserve.gov) by Edward N. Wolff, New York University.

The distribution of stocks by value is highly tilted to the wealthiest Americans, as shown in Figure 2. In 2007, the wealthiest one percent owned 38.2% of all stocks, while the next 9% owned 43.0%. Hence, the wealthiest 10% controlled about 80% of all stocks while the bottom 90% owned just over 20%. Given the starkness and persistence of inequality in stock holdings, there is no reason to think those in the bottom 90% are doing any better in 2010.

For the most part, lower-, middle-, and even upper-middle-income working-age households depend on their paychecks, not stock portfolios, to meet their everyday needs. Typical working families that own stock do so in retirement plans that are costly to turn into cash. Therefore, increasing stock value does little to help them make ends meet at a time when wages for most workers have been stagnant for decades. ❑

Sources: The figures are unpublished updates of Figure 5F and Table 5.7 from *The State of Working America 2006/2007* by Lawrence Mishel, Jared Bernstein, and Sylvia Allegretto, an Economic Policy Institute Book (Ithaca, N.Y.: ILR Press, an imprint of Cornell University Press, 2007).

Article 5.7

SOCIALLY RESPONSIBLE INVESTING COMES OF AGE

BY STEVE FAHRER
July/August 1998

Tracy and Tom Hamilton needed a loan to enlarge their organic chicken farm in New Mexico. But though they logged years of success with their crops, the local banks, unfamiliar with organic farming methods, turned them down flat. Today their farm is flourishing because their local community development corporation came through with a much needed loan.

When the owners of a Chicago restaurant decided to sell because Latinos were moving into the neighborhood, waitress Lucia Montealvo saw her chance to go into business for herself. But though she, her husband, and their extended family pooled all their money, it still was not enough to buy the eatery. As immigrants, with no collateral, where could they go for a loan? Montealvo bought the restaurant with the help of a microenterprise loan from Acción International.

These entrepreneurs reaped the benefits of community investing, a growing movement that provides low-cost capital to businesses that serve social needs, such as neighborhood development and affordable housing. Along with shareholder activism and "screened" mutual funds, community investing is one of the growing methods of "socially responsible investing" (SRI)—activities that try to challenge irresponsible corporate behavior and channel investment where the market does not want to go.

According to the Social Investment Forum, a non-profit membership organization of more than 400 investment practitioners and institutions, over $1.2 trillion, or 10% of all investment, was engaged in SRI in some form in 1997. SRI has become more acceptable and leaders in the field are increasing their efforts to expand its reach.

SRI operates within a framework that accepts great inequalities of power and wealth in the financial markets. Even with the best of intentions, SRI alone will not stop companies from polluting the environment or discriminating at the workplace. But as an educational tool, used in conjunction with other forms of social activism, SRI can have an impact.

Screening

SRI grew out of opposition to the Vietnam War. Dow Chemical, the maker of Napalm (used for firebombs) became a vilified corporate symbol for many and the target of corporate actions. The South Africa divestment movement followed, in which activists challenged universities and pension funds to get rid of their stock in companies with investments in South Africa. Nelson Mandela credits the pressure created by worldwide divestment campaigns with helping to rid South Africa of apartheid.

The divestment campaigns taught investors a valuable lesson. If you can divest from South Africa, why not divest from environmental polluters, companies that discriminate, and producers of weapons, nuclear power, tobacco, and alcohol? When possible, why not invest in companies that have useful products, treat their workers fairly, place women and minorities on their boards, or make charitable contributions to the communities where they are located?

Screening investment portfolios was not a new idea. For decades many religious investors avoided investing in the sin stocks—tobacco, alcohol, and gambling. But interest rose in the 1980s because of the drastic shift toward self-funded retirement plans in the United States. Fewer working people rely on union pensions or pensions controlled by their employer, and many more now have 401(k)'s or other retirement plans where they manage their own investments.

This new management responsibility can be intimidating, but it also provides an opportunity for self-education, organizing, and action. Fifteen years ago there were few avenues for those who did not want to invest in tobacco, weapons, or nuclear power, but in the past few years the number of socially screened mutual funds has tripled to more than 140. Socially responsible investing has become acceptable, and even the large brokerage firms and mutual fund companies have entered the field. Currently $529 billion, or 5% of all the money invested in the United States, is screened in some fashion.

Screening is a way to make retirement savings more consistent with one's values, such as investing in a mutual fund that will avoid owning shares of Shell Oil. There have been numerous consumer and labor campaigns against Shell Oil since the 1980s because of the company's investments in South Africa, its environmental practices, and most recently its collusion in the Nigerian government's repression of the Ogoni people. If you have participated in a boycott of Shell, it is inconsistent to own Shell stock in your 401(k) plan.

The campaign to force institutional and government portfolios to divest their tobacco stocks is probably the most active one right now. Just last April, San Francisco's Pension Fund became the first major municipal pension fund to vote to divest from tobacco stock. Earlier in the year, Oakland, Calif., voted to remove its short-term investments from money market funds which own tobacco stocks. "If we're heading a campaign against tobacco billboards, it doesn't make any sense to invest money in the same industry we are trying to discourage," said City Councilwoman June Bruner. And the city of Arcata, Calif., voted to withdraw $6.2 million from the state government's $10 billion Local Agency Investment Fund, because the fund does not exclude companies that pollute the environment, produce tobacco products, or violate worker rights.

Community Investments Expand

Community investments make social benefits, not profit maximization, their main concern. Today investors have put about $4 billion into financing local development initiatives, affordable housing, and small business lending in poor urban and rural areas. The need for such investment continues to grow as the government cuts its support of community development.

Most of this financing is done through community development financial intermediaries (CDFIs), such as community development loan funds and credit unions.

For these loans to be effective they often carry a below-market rate, which is made possible by lenders who are willing to provide capital at even lower rates.

Because community investing has traditionally had low returns and high minimum investments, it has been the domain of wealthy investors and charitable institutions. Despite the success of CDFIs in meeting credit gaps, the pool of community capital available remains small. CDFIs are not well known and have had a hard time attracting capital, particularly outside of major metropolitan areas.

But this may be changing. Efforts are underway to attract a wider range of investors to community investing by reducing the risks and the minimum amount of money needed. For example, Calvert Group, the largest family of socially responsible mutual funds, has been placing 1% of its money into community investments since 1990, one of the only mutual funds to do so.

In order to expand the pool of available capital, Calvert has recently begun offering "Community Investment Notes," which are similar to bank certificates of deposit (CDs), but without a government guarantee of repayment. Both the Hamiltons and Lucia Montealvo got loans from CDFIs that Calvert's Notes had helped to fund.

Calvert has used the combined $16 million pool of social capital from the mutual funds and the Notes to make 140 below-market rate investments in 75 nonprofit community groups. These investments support low-income housing and small business development in the United States and abroad, such as as the Environmental Enterprises Assistance Fund, Institute for Community Economics, and the Self Help Ventures Fund/Credit Union.

The Community Investment Notes are offered for as little as $1,000, for terms of one to five years, and investors can choose interest rates of 0% to 4%. The low minimum, large pool of projects receiving loans, and existence of a reserve fund to cushion losses from project failures are designed to make the Notes attractive to small investors as well as wealthy individuals and institutions.

Community funding intermediaries are also financing efforts around the world. The Environmental Enterprises Assistance Fund (EEAF), for example, is a non-profit that provides long-term risk capital to environmental businesses in developing countries. It makes investments of $100,000 to $750,000, primarily in Central America, including projects in agriculture, nature tourism, renewable energy, and recycling. EEAF has managed investments for a waste water treatment facility in Costa Rica, an aluminum recycling company in Honduras, and supported the expansion of a solar leasing business based in the Dominican Republic.

These innovations are positive developments, but it is important not to overstate their impact. Community development strategies cannot provide enough jobs and services to substitute for welfare and the social safety net. Nor can investment funds make up the great disparity of wealth between the developed world and countries in Asia, Africa and Latin America.

Shareholder Activism

Shareholder activism, the form of socially responsible investing with perhaps the most visible impact, is growing fast. Last year, institutional investors leveraged $736 billion worth of stocks in shareholder resolutions, and the leading campaigner, the Interfaith Center for Corporate Responsibility (ICCR), sponsored 159 shareholder resolutions involving 116 companies.

ICCR is a coalition of 275 religious institutional investors who "expect companies to pursue the social and environmental bottom line as vigorously as they pursue profits," says Tim Smith, its executive director. Forty of the resolutions spurred companies either to agree to the shareholder requests or enter a dialogue with them. Smith listed some of this year's successes: Sara Lee's divestiture of its tobacco business; Coca Cola and Baxter International's endorsements of the Coalition of Environmentally Responsible Economic Principles (CERES) designed to regulate corporate environmental behavior; and Allstate's breaking ranks with the insurance industry and acknowledging that global climate change is a real threat to people and property.

The groups of shareholders who initiate resolutions at corporate annual meetings rarely win the votes. That's because most shares of major corporations are held by institutions and mutual funds that want to maximize profits without regard to social concerns. But even when the votes go against them, the pressure of resolution campaigns, including adverse publicity, still can change corporate behavior.

Working with the ICCR, my own firm, Progressive Asset Management (PAM), has initiated resolutions on behalf of its clients which addressed: Pacific Telesis stop the use of clearcut rainforest timber for paper in phonebooks; International Paper and Union Camp, to eliminate the chlorine and dioxins in paper production; and Unocal, to prevent the San Francisco Bay from becoming more polluted.

PAM and its allies scored an impressive victory at the Walt Disney Company shareholder meeting in 1997. Disturbed by scenes of Haitian sweatshop workers making Disney pajamas, our resolution asked the company to take responsibility for monitoring the labor practices of the 4,000 suppliers it contracts with. The resolution won the support of 39 million shares (8.5% of the total). After first issuing denials, Disney eventually acknowledged the problem and agreed to issue a code of conduct governing child and forced labor, discrimination, compensation, and environmental protection. Disney also agreed to post the code in factories in the language of the country where the plant was situated, to monitor compliance with the code, and to pay the prevailing wage.

The resolution succeeded because it was part of a grassroots protest campaign against the publicity-shy company. The National Labor Committee, along with many other groups, organized protests at Disney stores nationwide, raising awareness of Disney's sweatshops. The shareholder resolution provided another avenue for action because consumer-oriented corporations do not want negative publicity.

Any success is bound to be noticed, and the SEC, which oversees corporate governance and security laws, recently tried to hamper activists by issuing rules giving corporations the right to disallow some shareholder resolutions, and making it harder to resubmit resolutions. A coalition of pension funds, endowments, and social issue groups challenged the SEC's proposed rules and for the moment have thwarted efforts to raise the threshold required to resubmit shareholder resolutions. Republicans in Congress have also proposed legislation to restrict labor unions from filing shareholder resolutions.

Community investing, shareholder activism, and screened investments are all part of a greater struggle to control how capital is used. And with millions more people investing their retirement money, SRI is a growing arena for action. While it is beginning to open new avenues for challenging corporate behavior, it cannot substitute for other forms of social change activism we might employ as workers, citizens, or community residents.

To become a truly political force the practitioners of socially responsible investing will have to take on the big questions like saving social security, reinstituting progressive taxation, and challenging trade and investment policies that allow corporations to privatize profits and socialize costs. This is new ground, and it starts with each individual educating themselves as to what is being done with their capital—however large or small. ❑

Resources: Interfaith Center for Corporate Responsibility (iccr.org), Progressive Asset Management (progressive-asset.com), Social Investment Forum (socialinvest.org)

Chapter 6

RETIREMENT FINANCE

EMPIRE AND ENTITLEMENTS

BY ARTHUR MacEWAN
January/February 2010

Dear Dr. Dollar:

In his book Colossus *(2004), Niall Ferguson argues that a major problem with Social Security and Medicare is their underfunded liabilities—to the tune of $45 trillion. Ferguson uses a 2003 report by Jagadeesh Gokhale and Kent Smetters to substantiate the seriousness of the issue. Can you comment on the report and Ferguson's claim?*

—Charles M. LeCrone, Shelbyville, IL

In *Colossus*, Niall Ferguson, perhaps the most prolific apologist for the global military adventures of the U.S. government, worries that the United States may not be able to continue to play its role of maintaining order in the world. "Order," he maintains, "is the necessary precondition for liberty." (One wonders about the liberty of those peoples whose societies are rent asunder by U.S. occupying forces, to say nothing of those who have died in the process. But leave that aside.)

Ferguson's argument is a variation of the idea of "imperial overreach," by which imperial nations have tried to extend their power too far, placed too great a burden on their ability to finance the operations, thus weakened the economic basis of their power, and gone into decline. But for Ferguson, it is not the cost of foreign operations that "threatens the American with overreach. It is expenditure that is much closer to home." Here he turns to the Gokhale-Smetters report, "Fiscal and Generational Imbalances" (2003), which, he tells us, shows that it is Social Security and Medicare expenditures that threaten the foundation of U.S. global operations.

The report purports to show that, given current levels of taxation and obligations, the present value of the future Social Security and Medicare expenditures will exceed revenues by $44.2 trillion dollars (not Ferguson's $45 trillion, but let's not quibble over $800 billion). Ferguson claims that this "unfunded liability" will have to be covered by increased taxes or reduced benefits, and he presents it as a very large amount of money. It is, he notes, four times the value of the country's 2003 annual output. (Present value is the value now of future income or expenditures, discounted to reflect the fact that something in the future is worth less than something now. For example, with a discount rate of 5%, the present value of $1.05 next year is $1.00.)

As with so much of the misleading arguments about Social Security and Medicare, the Center for Economic and Policy Research has responded effectively to the Gokhale-Smetters report. In a paper titled "The Forty-Four Trillion Dollar Deficit Scare," Dean Baker and David Rosnick point out that instead of comparing the present value of the future accumulated liability with current output, we should compare it with the present value of future accumulated output, which Gokhale and Smetters estimate at $682 trillion. So the future "unfunded liability" is equal to 6.5% of future output—not trivial but not nearly as scary as "four times the value of the country's annual output."

The gap could therefore be covered were taxes to increase by 6.5% of national output. Ferguson tells us that at present "Americans are scarcely undertaxed." So it is "fanciful," he claims, to expect tax increases of sufficient magnitude to handle the problem. Yet, most other high-income countries have much higher overall tax rates than does the United States, without apparent damage to their economic growth and prosperity. While a tax increase this large would certainly be politically problematic, there is no reason to dismiss it as economically outlandish. In any case, with his dismissal of tax increases, Ferguson leads his readers to the only possible solution: cut the benefits.

As Baker and Rosnick demonstrate, however, the problem does not lie with the programs but with the excessively high and absurdly increasing cost of medical services. It turns out that $36.6 trillion of Gokhale and Smitters' $44.2 trillion comes form rising Medicare costs, which are driven by the rising cost of medical services. So the problem is the nature of our health care system—can you say "private insurance companies"?—not "excessive" entitlement programs. If the United States established a reasonable health care system, there would be no need for a large tax increase or a Social Security or Medicare cut.

Finally, whether or not any category of government spending is "excessive" depends on one's judgment of the worth of the object of that spending. For Ferguson, apparently, social services for the elderly are not worth the money, but there is no limit to the value of the "order" imposed by the U.S. empire. ❏

Article 6.2

SOCIAL SECURITY Q&A: SEPARATING FACT FROM FICTION

BY DOUG ORR
May/June 2005; revised October 2010

The opponents of Social Security will stop at nothing in their long crusade to destroy the most efficient retirement system in the world. Opponents have taken two tracks to attack Social Security. The first is to claim the system as it is will fail, and the second is to claim that privatization is a better way to provide for retirement security. The first claim was the favorite from 1935 to about 2001. Then the privatization claim became the vogue. Now the first is back on the table.

With corporations routinely defaulting on their pension promises, more and more workers must rely on their individual wealth to make up the difference. The stock market collapse at the turn of the millennium wiped out much of the financial wealth of middle class Americans, and the collapse of the housing bubble has wiped out much of their remaining wealth. Making any cuts to Social Security now, either by raising the retirement age or cutting benefits, would have a huge impact on their remaining retirement income and are not necessary to "save the system." In fact, to make the most of the modifications currently being proposed by Obama's commission would be the height of folly.

With all the fear-mongering falsehoods flying around, it can be difficult to separate fact from fiction. Below, Doug Orr helps D&S readers do just this, with clear, and sometimes surprising, answers to many common Social Security-related questions.

—Eds.

Have opponents actually lied to the public about Social Security?
Yes. Former President George W. Bush repeatedly claimed that those who put their money in private accounts would be "guaranteed" a better return than they would receive from the current Social Security system. But every sale of stock on the stock market includes the disclaimer: "the return on this investment is not guaranteed and may be negative" for good reason. During the 20th century, there were several periods lasting more than ten years when the return on stocks was negative. After the Dow Jones stock index went down by over 75% between 1929 and 1933, the Dow did not return to its 1929 level until 1953. In claiming that the rate of return on a stock investment is guaranteed to be greater than the return on any other asset, Bush was lying. If an investment-firm broker made this claim to his clients, he would be arrested and charged with stock fraud. Michael Milken went to jail for several years for making just this type of promise about financial investments.

In fact, under the former President Bush's privatization proposal, a 20-year-old worker joining the labor force today would have seen her guaranteed Social Security benefits reduced by 46%. Bush's own Social Security commission admitted that private accounts were unlikely to make up for this drop in guaranteed benefits. The brokerage firm Goldman Sachs estimated that even with private accounts, retirement income of younger workers would have been reduced by 42% compared to what they would have received if no changes were made to Social Security.

Former President Bush also misrepresented the truth when he claimed that Social Security trustees say the system will be "bankrupt" in 2042. Bankruptcy is defined as "the inability to pay ones debts" or, when applied to a business, "shutting down as a result of insolvency." Nothing the trustees have said or published indicates that Social Security will fold as a result of insolvency.

Until 1984, the trust fund was "pay-as-you-go," meaning current benefits were paid using current tax revenues. In 1984, Congress raised payroll taxes to prepare for the retirement of the baby boom generation. As a result, the Social Security trust fund, which holds government bonds as assets, has been growing. When the baby boomers retire, these bonds will be sold to help pay their retirement benefits.

If the trust fund went to zero, Social Security would simply revert to pay-as-you-go. It would continue to pay benefits using (then-current) tax revenues, and in doing so, it would be able to cover about 70% of promised benefit levels. According to analysis by the Center for Economic and Policy Research, a 70% benefit level then would actually be higher than 2005 benefit levels in constant dollars (because of wage adjustments). In other words, retirees would be taking home more in real terms than today's retirees do. The system won't be bankrupt in any sense. On this point, President Bush was "consciously misrepresenting the truth with the intent to deceive." That is what the dictionary defines as lying.

I used to hear about having too few workers to support all the retirees in Social Security. Now I am hearing that argument again. It is true?

Opponents of Social Security have hated it since its creation in 1935. The first prediction of a Social Security crisis was published in 1936! The Heritage Foundation and Cato Institute are home to many of the program's opponents today, and they fixate on the concept of a "demographic imperative." In 1960, the United States had 5.1 workers per retiree, in 1998 we had 3.4, and by 2030 we will have only 2.1. Opponents claim that with these demographic changes, revenues will eventually be insufficient to pay Social Security retirement benefits.

The logic is appealingly simple, but wrong for two reasons. First, this "old-age dependency" ratio in itself is irrelevant. No amount of financial manipulation can change this fact: all current consumption must come from current physical output. The consumption of all dependents (non-workers) must come from the output produced by current workers. It's the "overall dependency ratio"—the number of workers relative to all non-workers, including the aged, the young, the disabled, and those choosing not to work—that determines whether society can "afford" the baby boomers' retirement years. In the 1960s we had only 0.62 workers for each dependent, and we were building new schools and the interstate highway system and getting ready to put a man on the moon. No one bemoaned a demographic crisis or looked for ways to cut the resources allocated to children; in fact, the living standards of most families rose rapidly. In 2030, we will have 0.98 workers per dependent. We'll have more workers per dependent in the future than we did in the past. While it is true a larger share of total output will be allocated to the aged, just as a larger share was allocated to children in the 1960s, society will easily produce adequate output to support all workers and dependents, and at a higher standard of living.

Second, the "demographic imperative" ignores productivity growth. Average worker productivity has grown by about 2% per year, adjusted for inflation, for the past half-century. That means real output per worker doubles every 36 years. This productivity growth is projected to continue, so by 2040, each worker will produce twice as much as today. Suppose each of three workers today produces $1,000 of real output per week and one retiree is allocated $500 (half of his final salary)—then each worker gets $833. In 2040, two such workers will produce $2,000 real output per week each (real output adjusts for inflation). If each retiree gets $1,000, each worker still gets $1,500. The consumption levels of both workers and retirees go up. Thus, paying for the baby boomers' retirement need not decrease their children's standard of living. A larger share of output going to retirees does not imply that the standard of living of those still working will be lower. Those still working will have a slightly smaller share of a much larger pie.

So that means that there is not funding problem for Social Security?

Not exactly. When the Greenspan Commission (yes, the same Alan Greenspan who helped created the current financial crisis) raised Social Security tax rates in 1984, it claimed that this would solve the funding problem far into the future. Based on past experience that would have been true. Social Security tax revenues are based on the level of wages paid, and historically, real wages (wages adjusted for the effects of inflation) had been growing along with productivity. This is what mainstream economic theory tells us is supposed to happen. But starting in the early 1980s, real wages actually started falling, even as productivity continued to increase. By 2009, the average real wage was just $16.40 (in 2005 dollars), exactly the same as it had been in 1966. So while labor productivity is now more than twice as high, wages have stagnated. If the wage had continued to grow with productivity, the real wage in 2009 would have been $38.50, more than twice as much. If wages paid in 2010 were twice as high as they currently are, the revenues flowing into the Social Security system would also be twice as high. But stagnating wages have put a strain on the system.

How can we address the funding gap that some people claim is going to occur?

One change would be to remove the cap on the Social Security payroll tax. John Miller discusses this option in "Go Ahead and Lift the Cap," in this chapter. A second option is to follow the lead of other industrialized countries. Social Security funding currently relies on taxing only wage and salary incomes. Over the past three decades, as corporations have driven down the real wages of the vast majority (80%) of employees, the share of total national income going to wages and salaries has declined, and the share going to capital income (from financial assets) has gone up. This erosion of the wage share of total income has reduced the share of total income flowing into the Social Security system. The retirement systems of the rest of the industrialized world are funded out of general tax revenues. The logic is that everyone in society benefits from the efforts of workers, so all should contribute to the support of retired workers. In the two years after the end of the recession in 2001, real wages had gone up by only 2.8%, but corporate profits had gone up by 62.8%. If we expand the Social Security tax to cover all forms of income, the revenue from this vastly increased profit income would allow the tax rate on wages to be significantly lower. This would provide an enormous benefit to small businesses and the self-employed as well as to everyone who works for wages and salaries.

Are there other more creative funding ideas?

Yes, but Congress is not even discussing one key idea—a "speculation reduction tax." When we buy a jacket, we pay a sales tax, but when a speculator buys a share of stock, or a collateralized debt obligation (CDO), or a credit default swap, they pay no tax at all. The current economic crisis in the United States was precipitated by massive increases in speculation in the financial sector of the economy in ever more exotic financial instruments. One goal of the ongoing re-regulation of that sector is to reduce this speculation. A speculation reduction tax could solve two problems at once. Many economists, both conservative and liberal, support the idea of a tax on speculation in the financial markets. This is often called a "Tobin tax" after one of its proponents. The tax rate would not have to be very high to have a big impact. The tax rate could go down if as the length of time the asset is held goes up. If a speculator buys a stock or CDO and holds it less than a day, the tax could be 5% of the selling price. If they hold it a week, it could be 2%. If they hold it a month it could be one percent, and so on. One recent estimate indicates that a flat rate of just 0.5% on all financial transactions would raise more than $145 billion per year, which is twice the size of the projected Social Security shortfall. If all of this revenue were dedicated to Social Security, the system would be solvent indefinitely. In fact the surplus in the system would be so large we would need to lower the tax rate on wages and raise the level of retirement benefits paid.

Former President Bush claimed the trust fund is just a bunch of government IOUs and therefore worthless. Is this true?

The trust fund does just contain IOUs, but they're not worthless. If they are, someone should tell that to the very smart and very rich people, and the central banks of Japan, China, and many other countries that hold a large share of their assets in U.S. government bonds.

When the trust fund was created in 1935, the law stipulated that any excess revenues coming into the Social Security system must be used to purchase federal government bonds. (At the time, the stock market had just lost over 75% of its value and was understood to be unsafe.) Federal bonds are absolutely safe; the government of the United States has never defaulted on any bond obligation. Former President Bush appeared to be ready to break this tradition. He appeared to want the Treasury to "selectively default" on the bonds in the Social Security trust fund. He obviously felt the United States doesn't have to meet its obligation to the working people of America the way it meets its obligations to ultra-wealthy bondholders. His suggestion that the U.S. government might not be willing to repay its debt obligations was remarkable and for a time completely disrupted global financial markets.

What will happen when the assets held in the trust fund are needed to help pay for benefits?

The trust will start selling the bonds. Currently it has to sell them back to the Treasury, although the law could easily be changed to allow sales to the same people, institutions, and governments who were buying U.S. bonds this past year. But let's assume the government has to buy them back.

If the government were running a surplus, as it did for the last four years of the Clinton administration, it would use that surplus to pay for them. If, on the other hand, the government were running a balanced budget but not a surplus, it would need to issue new Treasury bonds to pay for the bonds it would buy from the trust fund. In finance, this is called "rolling over" debt, and every major corporation in the world does it every day. At no point would the government need to roll over more than $300 billion in any given year to pay for the trust fund bonds. We already know the federal government can easily sell $475 billion per year in bonds, because it did that in 2005 and interest rates did not even go up—in fact, they remained relatively low.

So there's no problem, right?

Actually, there is one thing that could cause a problem: the government running a massive deficit, as it started doing during the Reagan and George H.W. Bush administrations, and again in a much larger way under George W. Bush. In that case, selling more bonds could put a very real strain the financial system's ability to absorb the creation of this new debt. If the government is borrowing massive amounts at the same time that private pension plans are selling assets to fund their pension promises and Social Security is selling assets from the trust fund, there is the potential for a very large increase in interest rates.

High interest rates slow economic growth by making it more expensive for consumers to buy homes or for businesses to invest in new infrastructure. But high interest rates also depress financial asset prices. A five-percentage-point rise in interest rates reduces the selling price of a bond that matures in ten years by 50%. In a 1994 paper, Sylvester Schieber, an advisor to former President Bush on pension and Social Security reform, predicted this potential drop in asset prices.

While this drop in financial asset prices would have little effect on the majority of Americans, it would have a huge impact on the wealthiest 0.5%. This is the issue that Federal Reserve chairman Alan Greenspan tried to raise in his last three years at the Fed. Greenspan said, "You don't have the resources to do it all." So he wanted to cut Social Security benefits to protect the asset values of the ultra-rich.

Even if the Social Security system isn't going to go bankrupt by 2029, 2042, or 2058, won't the Social Security trust fund begin cashing in the IOUs from the federal government as early as 2018?

The contributions to Social Security will become less than the benefits paid out in 2018, based on the trustees' overly pessimistic assumptions. (See "The SSA's Cracked Crystal Ball," in this chapter.) But that doesn't mean that the Social Security Administration will need to start selling bonds. The interest income from the existing bonds will be sufficient to make up the difference until 2028. *If* the trustees' pessimistic assumptions are true, they will need to start selling bonds in 2028 and the trust fund will be reduced to zero in 2042. At that point, as I mentioned above, the Social Security system would simply revert back to pure pay-as-you-go, operating just as it did successfully from 1936 to 1983.

Shouldn't we consider benefit cuts today to help prevent a potential shortfall in the future?

Congress, correctly, has not been willing to cut benefits. They don't need to, and they shouldn't. Telling your kids today that they only get to eat one plate of rice each day and have to get their clothes at Goodwill because there is a *chance* that you might lose your job 40 years from now would be irrational. It would be equally irrational to implement benefit cuts immediately on the *chance* that the trust fund might go to zero in 2042—especially when future recipients would still be getting more in real terms than recipients do today.

Other economics writers, such as Newsweek's Robert Samuelson suggest lowering benefits to wealthy people. Is this a good idea?

Lowering benefits just for the wealthy is also a bad idea. That's like proposing that, after an accident, someone who drives a Lexus should only get half of the replacement value of their car, while someone who drives a Ford Focus should get the full replacement value. Social Security is a universal insurance system. This change would make the system less universal and pit one group of workers against another.

What would it mean to index Social Security benefits to prices rather than to wages as is done now? David Brooks of the New York Times and others say this would prevent the system from going broke.

Right now, the formula for Social Security benefits in the first year of retirement is based on an average of the worker's wages over a 35-year period, accounting for productivity increases and for inflation. Productivity is figured in by adjusting the worker's earnings by the change in average annual wages. In effect, the worker's own 35-year average wage is recalculated as if it had been earned in the three years before retirement. The reason for this adjustment is simple: With more education and more and better machines, labor productivity (what each worker can produce in an hour's time) rises. Thus, each worker produces more real output and, assuming that wages rise with productivity (which was true up until 1980), workers' standards of living improve. If workers contribute more to society's output, they deserve more in return. This is how market economies are supposed to work.

If productivity rises by 3% a year, the standard of living should go up by 3% a year. But what if inflation is also 3%? In that case, if wages rise by just 3%, workers would not be able to purchase any more real output than the year before. That's why the wage increase must also be adjusted for inflation. To correct for this, wages would need to rise by 6% (3% for productivity and 3% for inflation).

When the opponents of Social Security proposed indexing initial Social Security benefits only to price increases, they were really suggesting stripping out the part of wage increases that result from rising productivity and only allowing for inflation. It's the equivalent of linking your retirement benefits to the very first job you take, rather than the job you hold at retirement. It freezes your retirement standard of living at whatever the standard of living was when you entered the workforce. According to former President Bush's Social Security commission, if this "price indexing" approach were implemented, future retirees would see their retirement income drastically reduced—if you retire in 2022, benefits would be 10% lower, in 2042, 26% lower, and in 2075, 54% lower.

Currently, once you retire, your benefit is adjusted annually for inflation but not for the change in wages. This cost of living adjustment (COLA), based on the inflation rate, helps maintain retirees' standard of living at the level they had when they retired, although their standard of living slowly falls behind that of the rest of society as the overall standard of living rises with productivity. Without the COLA, the individual's standard of living would fall even below what it was when he or she retired.

So what do opponents mean by "progressive" indexing?

This is just applying price indexing to only some workers. It would change the current indexation of benefits for "high" income and "middle" income individuals, leaving the current formula in place for the bottom 30% of wage earners. The highest wage earners' benefits would be adjusted for inflation, but not for productivity growth. Middle-wage earners (those between 30% and 70%) would have their benefits only partially adjusted for productivity growth.

When former President Bush talked about his tax cuts, he defined "middle income" as $200,000, which is actually in the top 2% of income. But when he talked about Social Security he defined middle income as $36,500 in 2005, and high income as $58,400. Under "progressive indexing," the retirement benefits of all workers would ultimately be reduced to match those of low-income workers regardless of how much they contributed to the system. This would result in a massive increase in poverty among the elderly, undermine political support for the system, and destroy Social Security. This does not fit the definition of a "progressive" policy.

What impact would the conversion to private accounts have on the national debt?

The government would have to borrow an additional $4 trillion over the next 20 years to make up the money that would be drained out of the system by private accounts. Former President Bush and Congress racked up an average $793 billion deficit each year Bush was in office. Social Security privatization would raise the size of the government's deficit by another $300 billion per year for the next 20 years. This does not seem to bother Republicans, as long as they are in power. In fact, by the time the second Bush left office, the national debt had grown to $12.1 trillion. Over half of that amount had been created by Bush's tax cuts for the very wealthy. Another 30% of the national debt had been created by the tax cuts for the wealthy under Presidents Reagan and George H.W. Bush. Fully 81% of the national debt was created by just these three Republican presidents.

How would the rest of the U.S. economy be affected if the private accounts replaced the current system?

Put simply, moving to a system of private accounts would not only put retirement income at risk—it would likely put the entire economy at risk.

The current Social Security system generates powerful, economy-stimulating multiplier effects. This was part of its original intent. In the early 1930s, the vast majority of the elderly were poor. While they were working, they could not afford to both save for retirement and put food on the table, and most had no employer pension. When Social Security began, elders spent every penny of that income. In turn, each dollar they spent was spent again by the people and businesses from whom they had bought things. In much the same way, every dollar that goes out in pensions today creates about 2.5 times as much total income. If the move to private accounts reduces elders' spending levels, as almost all analysts predict, that reduction in spending will have an even larger impact on slowing economic growth.

The current Social Security system also reduces the income disparity between the rich and the poor. Private accounts would increase inequality—and increased inequality hinders economic growth. For example, a 1994 World Bank study of 25 countries demonstrated that as income inequality rises, productivity growth is reduced. Market economies can fall apart completely if the level of inequality becomes too extreme. The rapid increase in income inequality that occurred in the 1920s was one of the causes of the Great Depression. And the rapid increase in inequality under the Reagan and two Bush administrations was one of the causes of the current "Great Recession."

Won't having people invest in stocks strengthen the business sector?

There is a commonly accepted myth that buying stock in the stock market provides funds directly to businesses that they can use for new investment. This is completely incorrect. Only when someone buys stock that is part of an initial public offering (IPO) does the money go directly to the firm. If you were to buy a share of Microsoft stock tomorrow, the money you pay would go to the owner of that stock and not to Microsoft. If a large number of people were to suddenly enter the stock market, it would drive up the selling price of stock and create a windfall for those who currently own stock, but it would not provide a penny to the firms whose stock is traded. Economists Dean Baker and Bob Pollin did a study a decade ago during the IPO boom that illustrates this distinction. They found that for every $113 in stocks traded, less than one dollar actually went to businesses to finance real investment.

England initiated private accounts in 1984 that failed miserably. Is it likely that private accounts would fail in the United States?

The British experiment with private accounts has indeed failed to provide an adequate and stable retirement income for the majority of citizens. The United Kingdom is now trying to figure out how to switch back to a defined-benefit system of retirement insurance. The problem is that the trillions of pounds that were diverted into the stock market can't be brought back into the defined-benefit system.

Chile's system is one that former President Bush often mentioned to justify his push for private accounts. One of Bush's advisors on Social Security was José Piñera, who designed the system in Chile for the Pinochet military dictatorship. Under that government, workers were encouraged to opt out of the system of pension insurance and into private accounts. Over the past 25 years, the return on stocks in Chile has averaged over 10%—a higher return than we can expect in the U.S. stock market over the next 25 years. Yet, even with that extremely high rate of return, the average Chilean retiree relying on private savings will receive a benefit less than half as large as someone who had remained in the old system, and those benefits, unlike those of the old system, last only 20 years. If a retiree is "unlucky" enough to live longer than that, he will simply run out of retirement income. Those in the old system not only receive a higher benefit, but the benefit lasts as long as they live and continues to provide benefits to their surviving spouse.

A recent survey shows that 90% of Chileans who opted for the private accounts wish they had remained in the old system. The only people who have benefited by the new system are the wealthiest top 2% of the population.

The United States' Social Security system is the most efficiently run insurance program in the world, with overhead of only 0.7% of annual benefits. For every $100 paid into the system, $99.30 is paid out in benefits to retirees. In the British and Chilean systems, at retirement, workers convert their private accounts to annuities provided by private insurance companies. In the United States, overhead for annuities provided by private firms average about 20%; for every $100 paid in, $20 gets siphoned off. And almost no annuities are indexed for inflation.

There is a third important experiment with "private accounts" to consider: the United States' own experiment with defined-contribution retirement plans. Since 1975, corporations have been phasing out their old defined-benefit pensions and replacing them with private savings accounts such as 401(k)s. In 1975, 39% of private-sector workers were covered by defined-benefit pensions, and only 6% by defined-contribution savings plans. By 1998 the share covered by real pensions had plummeted to just 18% and the percent relying on private accounts had risen to 38%.

·What has this rapid reversal done to retirement income security? A 2002 study by New York University economist Edward Wolff defines retirement income insecurity as having less than half of your final working income in your first year of retirement. In 1989, less than 30% of workers aged 47 to 64 faced retirement income insecurity. Yet by 1999, after the shift to greater reliance on private accounts, even after the most rapid run-up in stock values in U.S. history, almost 43% of workers in this age group faced retirement income insecurity.

We don't have to look to other countries to see the results of a shift to private accounts. That experiment has already been tried in the United States, and it failed.

How large is the employer's contribution for every dollar put into the system by the wage earner? What happens to the employer's contribution to Social Security under the private accounts proposal?
The employee pays a payroll tax of 6.2% on every dollar earned, up to an income level of $106,000. The maximum amount of tax paid annually is $6,572. The employer pays a tax that is exactly equal to that paid by the employee.

It's difficult to answer the second part of the question precisely, since the proponents of private accounts do not provide details of their actual proposal. While the plan developed by former President Bush's first-term Social Security advisory commission did not speak to this issue directly, in his first term he suggested that employer contributions should be reduced by the same amount as employee contributions. If that occurred, employers would see their portion of payroll taxes drop from 6.2% to 2.2% (a reduction of 64.5%). This would be a huge windfall for corporations.

Former President Bush's top five campaign donations in 2004 were from large brokerages. For instance, Morgan Stanley gave $600,480 and was the largest contributor to the Bush campaign. Do these brokerages stand to benefit financially from the privatization of Social Security?

This industry was the biggest contributor to former President Bush in both the 2000 and 2004 campaigns. How much it stands to gain depends on how many people decide to opt for the private accounts; estimates range from $40 billion to $80 billion per year.

It's likely that only the 16 brokerage firms that are allowed to interact with the Federal Reserve Bank would be permitted to manage private accounts. Divide $40 billion by 16 and you get $2.5 billion for each firm. A $2.5 billion annual return on a $600,000 "investment" in the Bush campaign is pretty amazing!

The reason so many Enron employees lost so much is that they forgot the first step of investing—diversify! Isn't diversification the key?

You are correct that history shows that diversified investing provides the best opportunity for success. But it does not guarantee success.

My research, and that of others, addresses this issue directly. If the amount contributed to Social Security by a median-income worker had been put into a diversified portfolio, and if that individual were to live 20 years into retirement, and if the economic outcomes (real wage and stock market growth rates) of any 10-year period during the 20th century were applied to that portfolio, only the period of the 1990s would result in higher retirement income from the portfolio than the existing Social Security system.

If that person were to live longer than 20 years, even the decade of the 1990s would not have outperformed Social Security. The only reason that anyone is willing to look seriously at private accounts is because of the aberrant behavior of the stock market during the 1990s.

Today, most retirees relying on 401(k) plans have significantly lower retirement income than those who were able to hold on to their old defined-benefit pension plans. It is not only workers at bankrupt companies like Enron who have been hurt; Enron highlights the level of risk imposed upon all workers by private accounts. We've been told repeatedly that if we diversify our holdings in private accounts sufficiently, we don't face much risk. But when the stock market goes down significantly (e.g., 45% in 2001-2002), diversification does not provide much protection.

Former Bush Social Security advisor Sylvester Scheiber, who works for the corporate benefits consulting firm the Wyatt Group, wrote an article in 1994 predicting that the financial markets are likely to lose as much as half of their value as the baby boom generation retires and starts to sell its financial assets to pay for food and rent. This is why he has been advising his corporate clients for decades to replace their real defined-benefit pension plans with 401(k) plans. It shifts the cost of a financial collapse from the corporation to the employees.

How important are the assumptions being made about economic growth and stock market returns to the privatization proposals?

The growth numbers underlying the talk of a shortfall in the trust fund are extremely pessimistic, while the stock market projections behind the privatization proposals are extremely optimistic. Privatization supporters assume that long-term GDP growth will be only 1.8%, yet they claim the return on stocks will be 7% per year. Other than the Great Depression, the slowest decade of growth in U.S. history was the 1980s, with a growth rate of 2.4%. If the economy grows at 2.4%, the Social Security trust fund never goes to zero.

But what if we use these assumptions? In 2004, the GDP was almost $12 trillion, and the value of publicly traded stock was about $40 trillion, a ratio of 3.3 to one. If, as in the past, half of the return on stocks takes the form of an increase in stock prices, in 60 years the value of the stock market will be a lopsided nine times the size of the economy. If the other half of the return came from dividends, fully one-third of GDP would need to be paid out in dividends at that time. This scenario is impossible. The assumptions don't make sense.

Young people say they want more control over their Social Security investments. How do you explain the purpose of Social Security to today's young workers?

The best way to explain Social Security is to say what it is. It's an insurance system that protects your income when you retire or face disability, and provides income to your children if you die. Former President Bush wanted you to look at Social Security as an investment, but it is not. It is a form of insurance that guarantees you a constant stream of income in retirement or in case of disability, adjusted to protect against inflation, for as long as you live.

Social Security can be compared to other types of insurance such as home insurance. You insure your home because if it should burn down, you would not be able to afford to rebuild it with your personal income alone. If your house never burns down, you will pay into the insurance fund and never get a penny back. But fire insurance isn't a "bad investment" because it *isn't* an investment *at all*. You are purchasing security.

Unlike fire insurance, Social Security inevitably gives most of us our money back. But the fact that we get money back does not change the fact that Social Security is a form of insurance, not an investment. Only the richest of the rich can afford not to have insurance and to rely solely on their own savings and investments to fund their retirement or risk of disability.

Young people must also understand that financial investments are inherently risky. Many investments fail, and when they do, you lose all of the money you invested. Today's 25-year-olds have only seen the stock market go up, except for two (very large) drops. But you don't have to go back to the 1930s to see a different picture: If you put money into the stock market in 1970 and waited until 1980 to take it out, you would have lost money. There is absolutely no guarantee that stock speculators will see the high returns those who support private accounts are falsely promising. ❑

Article 6.3

AFRICAN AMERICANS AND SOCIAL SECURITY
Why the Privatization Advocates Are Wrong

BY WILLIAM E. SPRIGGS
November/December 2004

Proponents of Social Security privatization are trying to claim that the current program is unfair to African Americans and that a privatized program would serve African Americans better. This argument lends support to the privatization agenda while at the same time giving its advocates a compassionate gloss. But the claims about African Americans and Social Security are wrong.

The Old Age Survivors and Disability Insurance Program (OASDI), popularly known as Social Security, was put in place by Franklin Roosevelt to establish a solid bulwark of economic rights for the public—specifically, as he put it, "the right to adequate protection from the economic fears of old age, sickness, accident, and unemployment." Most Americans associate Social Security only with the retirement—or old age—benefit. Yet it was created to do much more, and it does.

As its original name suggests, Social Security is an insurance program that protects workers and their families against the income loss that occurs when a worker retires, becomes disabled, or dies. All workers will eventually either grow too old to compete in the labor market, become disabled, or die. OASDI insures all workers and their families against these universal risks, while spreading the costs and benefits of that insurance protection among the entire workforce. Currently, 70% of Social Security funds go to retirees, 15% to disabled workers, and 15% to survivors.

Social Security is a "pay as you go" system, which means the taxes paid by today's workers are not set aside to pay their own benefits down the road, but rather go to pay the benefits of current Social Security recipients. It's financed using the Federal Insurance Contribution Act (or FICA) payroll tax, paid by all working Americans on earnings of less than about $90,000 a year. While the payroll tax is not progressive, Social Security benefits are—that is, low-wage workers receive a greater percentage of pre-retirement earnings from the program than higher-wage workers.

In the 1980s, recognizing that the baby boom generation would strain this system, Congress passed reforms to raise extra tax revenues above and beyond the current need and set up a trust fund to hold the reserve. Trustees were appointed and charged with keeping Social Security solvent. Today's trustees warn that their projections, which are based on modest assumptions about the long-term growth of the U.S. economy, show the system could face a shortfall around 2042, when either benefits would have to be cut or the FICA tax raised.

Those who oppose the social nature of the program have pounced on its projected shortfall in revenues to argue that the program cannot—or ought not—be fixed, but should instead be fundamentally changed (see box, "Privatization Advocates"). Privatization proponents are seeking to frame the issue as a matter of social

Privatization Advocates

Powerful advocates for privatization include libertarian and conservative think tanks and advocacy groups such as the Cato Institute, the Heritage Foundation, Americans for Tax Reform, and Citizens for a Sound Economy, all driven by an ideological commitment to the abolition of federal social programs.

Wall Street too is thirsty for the $1.4 trillion that privatization would funnel into equities if the taxes collected to support the Social Security system were invested privately rather than reinvested in federal government bonds. That's not to mention the windfall of fees privatization would deliver for banks, brokerage houses, and investment firms.

Just after he took office, President Bush appointed a commission to examine privatizing the Social Security system. The commission could not figure out how to maintain payments to current recipients while diverting tax dollars to the savings of current workers, nor could it resolve how to cover the benefits of the disabled or resolve issues surrounding survivors' benefits. Although the president did not succeed in carrying out Social Security privatization in his first term, he has made the partial privatization of Social Security retirement accounts the top priority of his second-term domestic agenda.

justice, as if Social Security "reform" would primarily benefit low-income workers, blue-collar workers, people of color, and women. Prompted by disparities in life expectancy between whites and African Americans and the racial wealth gap, a growing chorus within the privatization movement is claiming that privatizing Social Security would be beneficial to African Americans.

Opponents attack the program on the basis of an analogy to private retirement accounts. Early generations of Social Security beneficiaries received much more in benefits than they had paid into the system in taxes. Privatization proponents argue those early recipients received a "higher rate of return" on their "investment" while current and future generations are being "robbed" because they will see "lower rates of return." They argue the current system of social insurance—particularly the retirement program—should be privatized, switching from the current "pay-as-you-go" system to one in which individual workers claim their own contribution and decide where and how to invest it.

But this logic inverts the premise of social insurance. Rather than sharing risk across the entire workforce to ensure that all workers and their families are protected from the three inevitabilities of old age, disability, and death, privatizing Social Security retirement benefits would enable high-wage workers to reap gains from private retirement investment without having to help protect lower-wage workers from their (disproportionate) risks of disability and death. High-wage workers, who are more likely to live long enough to retire, could in fact do better on average if they opt out of the general risk pool and devote all their money to retirement without having to cover the risk of those who may become disabled or die, although they would of course be subjecting their retirement dollars to greater risk. But low-wage workers, who are far more likely to need disability or survivors' benefits to help their families and are less likely to live long enough to retire, would then be left with lower disability and survivors' benefits, and possibly no guaranteed benefits. This is what the

Social Security privatization movement envisions. But you wouldn't know it from reading their literature.

And when the myths about Social Security's financial straits meet another American myth—race—even more confusion follows. Here is a look at three misleading claims by privatization proponents about African Americans and Social Security.

Myth #1

Several conservative research groups argue that Social Security is a bad deal for African Americans because of their lower life expectancies. "Lifetime Social Security benefits depend, in large part, on longevity," writes the Cato Institute's Michael Tanner in his briefing paper "Disparate Impact: Social Security and African Americans." "At every age, African-American men and women both have shorter life expectancies than do their white counterparts. ... As a result, a black man or woman earning exactly the same lifetime wages, and paying exactly the same lifetime Social Security taxes, as his or her white counter-part will likely receive a far lower rate of return." Or as the Americans for Tax Reform web site puts it: "A black male born today has a life expectancy of 64.8 years. But the Social Security retirement age for that worker in the future will be 67 years. That means probably the majority of black males will never even receive Social Security retirement benefits."

The longevity myth is the foundation of all the race-based arguments for Social Security privatization. There are several problems with it.

First, the shorter life expectancy of African Americans compared to whites is the result of higher morbidity in mid-life, and is most acute for African-American men. The life expectancies of African-American women and white men are virtually equal. So the life expectancy argument can really only be made about African-American men.

Second, the claim that OASDI is unfair to African Americans because their expected benefits are less than their expected payments is usually raised and then answered from the perspective of the retirement (or "old age") benefit alone. That is an inaccurate way to look at the problem. Because OASDI also serves families of workers who become disabled or die, a correct measure would take into account the probability of all three risk factors—old age, disability, and death. Both survivor benefits and disability benefits, in fact, go disproportionately to African Americans.

While African Americans make up 12% of the U.S. population, 23% of children receiving Social Security survivor benefits are African American, as are about 17% of disability beneficiaries. On average, a worker who receives disability benefits or a family that receives survivor benefits gets far more in return than the worker paid in FICA taxes, notwithstanding privatizers' attempts to argue that Social Security is a bad deal.

Survivors' benefits also provide an important boost to poor families more generally. A recent study by the National Urban League Institute for Opportunity and Equality showed that the benefit lifted 1 million children out of poverty and helped another 1 million avoid extreme poverty (living below half the poverty line).

Federal Policy for Defined-Benefit Plans

For almost a century, the U.S. government has promoted defined-benefit pension plans because they increase productivity and reinforce the employment relationship while stabilizing retirement income. In 1919, the federal government was faced with a meltdown of the defined-benefit plans of legacy railroads that struggled in competition with small, low-cost start-ups that didn't provide pensions to their young workers. This is analogous to regional air carriers like Jet Blue decimating United Airlines and other legacy airlines today. In response, the mandatory, industry-wide Railroad Retirement system was established in 1935, a decade before Social Security, requiring all railroads to pay into a multi-employer pension fund.

During World War II and in the post-war period, court cases and tax laws favored rapid growth in defined-benefit plans. An unusually large pension default at the Studebaker automobile corporation in South Bend, Ind., in 1964, led Congress to pass comprehensive pension regulatory legislation, the Employee Retirement Income Security Act (ERISA), in 1974. ERISA established the PBGC to insure firms' defined-benefit pensions in the event of bankruptcy (which, even before 1974, happened infrequently; one out of 1,000 defined-benefit sponsors had defaulted in 10 years). Since its creation in 1974, the PBGC has operated without ever missing a payment it owes, despite having an overall balance-sheet deficit in most years, using the premium income that every plan sponsor (single employers, multiple employers, or unions) pays to carry the agency through normal cyclical downturns.

In creating an insurance structure, the legislation required companies to fund their defined-benefit promises over time, anticipating "moral hazard" problems (when an insured entity becomes lax, relying on another body to bail it out). ERISA intended companies to have flexibility, contributing more in good times and less in bad. Originally, companies had 40 years to reach 100% funding, using wage, investment returns, and interest-rate projections. In the late 1980s and 1990s, faster funding was required of plans that were less than 70% funded. (A pension's funded status refers to its ratio of assets to liabilities. If a plan is more than 90% funded, that is, if its current assets amount to 90% of the present value of promises, including expected future promises, made to its participants, it is considered fully funded.)

Finally, among workers who do live long enough to get the retirement benefit, life expectancies don't differ much by racial group. For example, at age 65, the life expectancies of African-American and white men are virtually the same.

President Bush's Social Security commission proposed the partial privatization of Social Security retirement accounts, but cautioned that it could not figure out how to maintain equal benefits for the other risk pools. The commission suggested that disability and survivor's benefits would have to be reduced if the privatization plan proceeds.

This vision is of a retirement program designed for the benefit of the worker who retires—only. A program with that focus would work against, not for, African Americans because of the higher morbidity rates in middle age and the smaller share of African Americans who live to retirement.

Myth #2

African Americans have less education, and so are in the work force longer, than whites, and yet Social Security only credits 35 years of work experience in figuring benefits. Tanner says, "benefits are calculated on the basis of the highest 35 years of earnings over a worker's lifetime. Workers must still pay Social Security taxes during years outside those 35, but those taxes do not count toward or earn additional benefits. Generally, those low-earnings years occur early in an individual's life. That is particularly important to African Americans because they are likely to enter the workforce at an earlier age than whites...."

This claim misinterprets the benefit formula for Social Security. Yes, African Americans on average are slightly less educated than whites. The gap is mostly because of a higher college completion rate for white men compared to African-American men. But the education argument fails to acknowledge that white teenagers have a significantly higher labor force participation rate (at 46%) than do African-American teens (29%). The higher labor force participation of white teenagers helps to explain why young white adults do better in the labor market than young African-American adults. (The racial gaps in unemployment are considerably greater for teenagers and young adults than for those over 25.)

These differences in early labor market experiences mean that African-American men have more years of zero earnings than do whites. So while the statement about education is true, the inference from education differences to work histories is false. By taking only 35 years of work history into account in the benefit formula, the Social Security formula is progressive. It in effect ignores years of zero or very low earnings. This levels the playing field among long-time workers, putting African Americans with more years of zero earnings on par with whites. By contrast, a private system based on total years of earnings would exacerbate racial labor market disparities.

Myth #3

A third claim put forward by critics of Social Security is that African-American retirees are more dependent on Social Security than whites. Tanner writes: "Elderly African Americans are much more likely than their white counterparts to be dependent on Social Security benefits for most or all of their retirement income." Therefore, he concludes, "African Americans would be among those with the most to gain from the privatization of Social Security—transforming the program into a system of individually owned, privately invested accounts." Law professor and senior policy advisor to Americans for Tax Reform Peter Ferrara adds, "the personal accounts would produce far higher returns and benefits for lower-income workers, African Americans, Hispanics, women and other minorities."

It's true that African-American retirees are more likely than whites to rely on Social Security as their only income in old age. It's the sole source of retirement income for 40% of elderly African Americans. This is a result of discrimination in the labor market that limits the share of African Americans with jobs that offer pension benefits. Privatizing Social Security would not change labor market discrimination or its effects.

Privatizing Social Security would, however, exacerbate the earnings differences between African Americans and whites, since benefits would be based solely on individual savings. What would help African-American retirees is not privatization, but rather changing the redistributive aspects of Social Security to make it even more progressive.

The current formula for Social Security benefits is progressive in two ways: low earners get a higher share of their earnings than do higher wage earners and the lowest years of earning are ignored. Changes in the formula to raise the benefits floor enough to lift all retired Social Security recipients out of poverty would make it still more progressive. Increasing and updating the Supplemental Security Income payment, which helps low earners, could accomplish the same goal for SSI recipients. (SSI is a program administered by Social Security for very low earners and the poor who are disabled, blind, or at least 65 years old.)

The proponents of privatization argue that the heavy reliance of African-American seniors on Social Security requires higher rates of return—returns that are only possible by putting money into the stock market. Yet given the lack of access to private pensions for African-American seniors and their low savings from lifetimes of low earnings, such a notion is perverse. It would have African Americans gamble with their only leg of retirement's supposed three-legged stool—pension, savings, and Social Security. And, given the much higher risk that African Americans face of both death before retirement and of disability, it would be a risky gamble indeed to lower those benefits while jeopardizing their only retirement leg.

Privatizing the retirement program, and separating the integrated elements of Social Security, would split America. The divisions would be many: between those more likely to be disabled and those who are not; between those more likely to die before retirement and those more likely to retire; between children who get survivors' benefits and the elderly who get retirement benefits; between those who retire with high-yield investments and those who fare poorly in retirement. The "horizontal equity" of the program (treating similar people in a similar way) would be lost, as volatile stock fluctuations and the timing of retirement could greatly affect individuals' rates of return. The "vertical equity" of the program (its progressive nature, insuring a floor for benefits) would be placed in greater jeopardy with the shift from social to private benefits.

Social Security works because it is "social." It is America's only universal federal program. The proposed changes would place Social Security in the same political space as the rest of America's federal programs—and African Americans have seen time and again how those politics work. ❑

Article 6.4

THE SOCIAL SECURITY ADMINISTRATION'S CRACKED CRYSTAL BALL

BY JOHN MILLER
November/December 2004

2042. That's the year the Social Security Trust Fund will run out of money, according to the Social Security Administration (SSA). But its doomsday prophesy is based on overly pessimistic assumptions about our economic future: The SSA expects the U.S. economy to expand at an average annual rate of just 1.8% from 2015 to 2080—far slower than the 3.0% average growth rate the economy posted over the last 75 years.

What's behind the gloomy growth projections? Is there anything to them—or has the SSA's economic crystal ball malfunctioned?

Flawed Forecast

The Social Security Administration foresees a future of sluggish economic growth in which labor productivity, or output per worker, improves slowly; total employment barely grows; and workers put in no additional hours on the job. (It reasons that economic growth, or growth of national output, must equal the sum of labor productivity increases, increases in total employment, and increases in the average hours worked.)

In its widely cited "intermediate" 1.8% growth scenario, labor productivity improves by just 1.6% a year and workforce growth slows almost to a standstill at 0.2% a year—rates well below their historical averages. (See Table 1.) Under these assumptions, and if average work time holds steady, Social Security exhausts its trust fund in the year 2042, at which point it faces an initial shortfall of 27% of its obligations. After that, Social Security would be able to pay out just 70% of the benefits it owes to retirees.

The problem is not with the logic of the method the Social Security Administration uses to make its projections, but rather with its demographic and economic assumptions. Its forecast of 1.6% annual labor productivity growth is especially suspect. When the nonpartisan Congressional Budget Office (CBO) assessed the financial health of Social Security earlier this year, it assumed that productivity would improve at a rate of 1.9% per year. In the CBO forecast, faster productivity growth, along with a lower unemployment rate, boosts wages—the tax base of the system—allowing Social Security to remain solvent until 2052, 10 years longer than the SSA had projected just a few months earlier.

One doesn't have to buy into the hype about the magic of the new economy to conclude that the CBO came closer to getting the projected productivity growth rates right than the SSA did. The federal government's own Bureau of Labor Statistics estimates that productivity rates in the nonfarm sector improved at a 2.3% average pace from 1947 through 2003. Adjusting for the gap of 0.2 percentage points between the productivity growth of the nonfarm business sector and the economy as a whole still leaves productivity across the economy growing by a healthy 2.1% over

TABLE 1
SOCIAL SECURITY ADMINISTRATION'S PRINCIPAL ECONOMIC ASSUMPTIONS[a]
Annual Percentage Increase

Year	Real Gross Domestic Product[b]	Productivity (Total U.S. Economy)	Total Employment[c]	Average Hours Worked
2004	4.4%	2.7%	1.7%	0.0%
2005	3.6%	1.8%	1.7%	0.0%
2006	3.2%	1.9%	1.3%	0.0%
2007	3.0%	1.9%	1.1%	0.0%
2008	1.0%	1.8%	2.8%	0.0%
2009	2.7%	1.8%	0.9%	0.0%
2010	2.6%	1.7%	0.8%	0.0%
2011	2.4%	1.7%	0.8%	0.0%
2012	2.3%	1.6%	0.6%	0.0%
2013	2.2%	1.6%	0.6%	0.0%

Average Annual Percentage Increase

2010 to 2015	2.2%	1.6%	0.6%	0.0%
2015 to 2080	1.8%	1.6%	0.2%	0.0%

[a] These are the "intermediate economic assumptions" that the Social Security Administration regards as most plausible. The SSA also reports a "low cost" forecast that projects a 2.6% real growth rate from 2015 to 2080 and a "high cost" forecast that projects a 1.1% real growth rate from 2015 to 2080.

[b] Real Gross Domestic Product is calculated in constant 1996 dollars.

[c] Total employment is the total of civilian and military employment in the U.S. economy.

Source: Social Security Administration, 2004 *Annual Report of the Board of Trustees* (March 23, 2004), Table V.B.1 and Table V.B.2, pp. 89 and 94.

the postwar period. That historical record convinces economist Dean Baker, from the Washington-based Center for Economic and Policy Research, that a productivity growth rate of 2.0% a year is a "very reasonable" assumption.

The drastic deceleration of employment growth, from its historic (1960 to 2000) average of 1.78% to 0.2% per year, is also overstated. As the trustees see it, employment will grow far more slowly as the baby-boomers leave the labor force. That is true as far as it goes. But if their projections are correct, the country will soon face a chronic labor shortage. And in that context, the immigration rate is unlikely to slow, as they assume, to 900,000 a year. Rather, future immigration rates would likely be at least as high as they were in the 1990s, when 1.3 million people entered the United States annually, and possibly even higher if immigration laws are relaxed in response to a labor shortage. Faster immigration would boost employment growth and add workers, who would pay into Social Security, helping to relieve the financial strain on the system created by the retirement of the baby-boom generation.

In its own optimistic or "low cost" scenario, the SSA erases the shortfall in the trust fund by assuming a faster productivity growth rate (of 1.9%), a lower unemployment rate (of 4.5% per year), and higher net immigration (of 1.3 million people per year). The still rather sluggish 2.6% average growth rate that results would wipe out the rest of the imbalance in the system and leave a sizeable surplus in the trust fund—0.15% of GDP over the next 75 years.

Making Short Work of the Shortfall

Even in the unlikely event that the pessimistic predictions the SSA has conjured up actually do come to pass, the Social Security imbalance could be easily remedied.

The Social Security Trust Fund needs $3.7 trillion to meet its unfunded obligations over the next 75 years. That is a lot of money—about 1.89% of taxable payroll and about 0.7% of GDP over that period. But it's far less than the 2.0% of GDP the 2001 to 2003 tax cuts will cost over the next 75 years if they are made permanent. (Many of the tax cuts are currently scheduled to sunset in 2010.) The portion of the Bush tax cuts going to the richest 1% of taxpayers alone will cost 0.6% of GDP— more than the CBO projected shortfall of 0.4% of GDP.

Here are a few ways to make short work of any remaining shortfall without cutting retirement benefits or raising taxes for low- or middle-income workers. First, newly hired state and local government workers could be brought into the system. (About 3.5 million state and local government workers are not now covered by Social Security.) That move alone would eliminate about 30% of the projected deficit.

In addition, we could raise the cap on wages subject to payroll taxes. Under current law, Social Security is funded by a payroll tax on the first $87,900 of a person's income. As a result of this cap on covered income, the tax applies to just 84.5% of all wages today—but historically it applied to 90%. Increasing the cap for the next decade so that the payroll tax covers 87.3% of all wages, or halfway back to the 90% standard, would eliminate nearly one-third of the SSA's projected deficit.

Finally, stopping the repeal of the estate tax, a tax giveaway that benefits only the richest taxpayers, would go a long way toward closing the gap. Economists Peter Diamond and Peter Orszag, writing for The Century Fund, advocate dedicating the revenues generated by renewing the estate tax to the Social Security Trust Fund. They suggest an estate tax set at its planned 2009 level, which would exempt $3.5 million of an individual's estate. The tax would fall exclusively on the wealthiest 0.3% of taxpayers. That alone would close another one-quarter of the SSA's projected shortfall. Returning the estate tax to its 2001 (pre-tax cut) level (with a $675,000 exemption for individuals) would do yet more to relieve any financial strain on Social Security.

Any way you look at it, Social Security can remain on sound financial footing even in the dreariest of economic futures, so long as alarmist reports like those of its trustees don't become an excuse to corrupt the system. ❏

Resources: Congressional Budget Office, *The Outlook for Social Security* (June 2004); Social Security Administration, *2004 Annual Report of the Board of Trustees* (March 23, 2004); "What the Trustees' Report Indicates About the Financial Status of Social Security," Robert Greenstein, Center on Budget and Policy Priorities (March 31, 2004); "The Implications of the Social Security Projections Issued By the Congressional Budget Office" Robert Greenstein, Peter Orszag, and Richard Kogan, Center on Budget and Policy Priorities (June 24, 2004); "Letter to Rudolph G. Penner" from Dean Baker, co-director of the Center For Economic and Policy Research (January 26, 2004); *Countdown to Reform: The Great Social Security Debate*, Henry Aaron and Robert Reischauer, The Century Foundation Press, 1998.

Article 6.5

THE MYTH OF THE SOCIAL SECURITY TRUST FUND

BY ELLEN FRANK
May/June 1999

Since the 1980s, American workers have been paying more into the Social Security system than retirees are taking out. These excess payroll taxes, now running at about $100 billion per year, go to the Social Security Trust Fund, "saved" for the coming baby-boom retirement, when there will be as few as two workers for every retiree. The Trust Fund now contains some $900 billion; by 2021, it will be worth nearly $4 trillion dollars.

The Social Security Administration (SSA)—using, it should be noted, very grim forecasts of future economic growth—predicts that sometime early in the 21st century, workers' payroll taxes will equal only three-quarters of the benefits currently legislated for retirees. To cover this potential shortfall, the SSA plans gradually to spend down the Trust Fund, until 10 or 20 or 30 years later, depending on whose numbers you believe, the $4 trillion runs out. This, in a nutshell, is the Social Security "crisis."

Supposedly to make the surplus funds grow faster and last longer, Congressional Republicans propose placing Social Security funds in the stock market. Clinton has put forth a complicated plan (see box) also intended to enlarge the Trust Fund so that it lasts through 2050. Both sides have acceded to gradual cuts in Social Security benefits—achieved by raising the retirement age to 67 and reducing annual cost-of-living adjustments—so that a larger share of today's payroll tax dollars can be saved for the baby-boom Trust Fund.

All of these recommendations, indeed the Trust Fund itself, rest on a deceptive premise. Today's workers are being taxed both to support current retirees and, via Trust Fund surpluses, to partially pre-fund their own retirement. Yet pre-funding a universal public pension plan is neither attainable nor desirable.

Many people, when discussing the Trust Fund, apparently have in mind a great heap of money stacked high in some underground vault. As more boomers retire, the SSA opens the vault, dusts off the cobwebs and doles out the cash. But there is no such pile of money. When excess payroll taxes come into the SSA, the cash is turned over to the Treasury which, in turn, issues interest-bearing bonds to the SSA. The Treasury then spends the cash on welfare, roads, weapons, tax cuts.

When, in 2020 or thereabouts, payroll taxes fall short of retirees' needs, officials at SSA will begin taking their bonds back to the Treasury to redeem them for the cash with which to pay benefits. Where, in 2020, will the Treasury obtain the cash to repay the SSA? They will either have to print it, borrow it, levy additional taxes on the public of 2020 or they will have to cut benefits. There is no getting around this. Treasury, after all, spends the funds as they come in; they are not languishing in a vault. If Social Security benefits remain intact, the government will be liable to raise funds for retirement benefits in 2020. The bonds issued by the Treasury represent nothing more than a promise to do this; the public of the future will either raise the funds and keep this promise or they will renege on the obligation.

The "saving" we are doing today through Social Security does not in any way reduce the need to tax, borrow or cut benefits in the future. If the Trust Fund were to disappear tomorrow nothing would change; the baby boom retirement burden would be made neither heavier nor lighter.

Which raises an obvious question. If the excess payroll taxes being "saved" today can't ease the burden of caring for retirees in the future, why are we paying them? The idea of "saving up," through higher payroll taxes, for the baby-boomer retirement originated with the Reagan Administration—ostensibly proposed to "save" Social Security when the system faced its last "crisis," in the 1980s. The Trust Fund surpluses were small at first, barely noticeable in the deluge of fiscal red ink of the Reagan/Bush era. Sold to the public as a method for pre-funding the impending baby-boom retirement, the Trust Fund's real function was to disguise the shift of federal tax burdens from the wealthy to those with moderate and low incomes. Today, nearly one-third of federal revenues derive from the payroll tax, perhaps the most regressive of all federal taxes. Of this money, about one-fifth is not needed to pay current Social Security benefits. It is credited to the Trust Fund, but is destined, in fact, for general government spending.

Democratic Party defenders of this charade argue that the Trust Fund, though devoid of economic merit, is politically necessary. The Trust Fund may be an empty gesture, but it is not made in bad faith. While admittedly regressive, the funds represent an implicit assurance to current workers that benefits will be there for them tomorrow. The illusion of pre-funding instills confidence among voters that their benefits are "paid up" and thus secure. Further, the surpluses provide a veneer of financial planning which defuses right-wing attacks on Social Security. Excessive payroll taxes, in this view, are a small price to pay for political insurance against Republican attacks.

But this argument is wrong. In fact, as the Social Security surplus has grown in size and significance, public confidence in the system has been shaken and the right-wing assault has taken on new ferocity. Currently, projected federal budget surpluses for the next three years can be attributed entirely to excess Social Security taxes. For anti-government Republicans, these surpluses are a provocation, not a deterrent. They evoke greed and fear: greed for the tax cuts, corporate giveaways, and Wall Street management fees, that Social Security surpluses could pay for without exposing Republican budget politics for the fraud it is. That greed was on display this past winter, but has now been replaced by fear.

The right wing deeply abhors the Trust Fund and fears precisely the implicit contract with the future that it represents. Conservative economists understand all too clearly that the Trust Fund bonds are nothing more than a promise that society will one day be asked to keep. When the bonds come due, they worry, who will pay? Currently, Social Security benefits are financed through a tax on low-and middle-income wage earners, but this group cannot be expected alone to carry the entire burden of the baby-boom retirement.

Who else will be asked to give up income in the future so that retirees can eat? The National Association of Manufacturers, no doubt concerned that its members' profits might be targeted, has endorsed the full and immediate privatization of Social Security, to foreclose the establishment of an uncontrolled "baby boomer entitlement." *Wall Street Journal* columnist Alan Murray writes ominously of the "aging baby-boomer assault on the federal budget" and the threat that "general revenues" (perhaps corporate taxes!) rather than payroll taxes, may one day be used to cover Social Security's "accrued liabilities." Economist Milton Friedman, always a shill for corporate interests, recently proposed in The *New York Times* that the Trust Fund be liquidated and the Social Security system disbanded.

Recently, conservative Republicans have come to fear as well that the excess payroll taxes flowing to Social Security will be exposed for the sham they are and that workers will demand an accounting of funds purportedly saved on their behalf. In recent weeks, Congressional Republicans have been scrambling to "wall off" the Trust Fund from "raids" by the Treasury. Draping themselves in the language of financial prudence, they insist that "every penny" of the surpluses be used "to save Social Security."

In practice, this amounts to using the surpluses to repay federal debt, a ruse which effectively transfers tax dollars from wage-earners to bond-holders. The Cato Institute, alarmed that the public might actually decide to spend its own money, advocates placing Trust Fund revenues in a privately managed money market fund. Above all, Republicans in Congress are terrified that the surplus funds pouring into Social Security might actually be used on the public's behalf.

And this, indeed, is precisely what those who believe in Social Security should be promoting. The mythical image of piles of money squirreled away on behalf of future retirees has become a serious impediment to responsible, even intelligible, discussion of Social Security. As recent Republican proposals should make abundantly clear, the language of saving and financial planning threatens to sink Social Security's supporters into the muck of right-wing economics. It is long past time to shift the terms of the debate. The Social Security debate is not about saving or interest rates or compound 30-year rates of return. It is about who pays taxes in this country, on whose behalf that money is spent and what the obligations of government are to its citizens.

All funds being paid into Social Security will be spent, either on tax cuts, Wall Street investment accounts, debt reduction or something socially useful. The left's task in this debate is to make this point clear and to ask, explicitly, what the money will be spent on, who will spend it and how, exactly, that spending will ease the burden of caring for an aging population.

All the Trust Funds and IRA's in the world cannot change the fact that, in 20 years or so, the task of caring for the growing ranks of the aged will fall, inevitably, to the younger generation and will require their labor, energy and commitment. If the workers of the 21st century are ill-fed and uneducated, if the environment is ravaged, the air unbreathable, the climate hostile to health, the aged will languish, regardless of the money put aside today. As a society, the United States is not well set up to care for an aging population and there is no reason to believe that throwing money at Wall Street will improve this situation. We lack affordable and accessible housing and transportation; pollution and climate change are taking a harsh toll on the elderly; Medicare is riddled with fraud and our nursing homes are a national disgrace.

Imagine what could be done with the $100 billion plus currently flowing into Social Security each year. Imagine how secure our retirees could be made if these funds were used to construct housing, train scientists, cleanup the environment, build public health facilities, and educate future workers. The Social Security surpluses are paid by low- and middle-income workers and should be spent on programs that will benefit them and help their children to care for them as they age. Money earmarked for their future should be spent in securing that future: on schools, parks, infrastructure, the environment, our children.

Unless the funds are spent on their behalf, the bonds piling up in the Social Security Trust Fund today do nothing to help future retirees. They can, however, positively hurt today's workers. If these regressive and excessive tax dollars are squandered, as Democrats and Republicans now propose, to pay down the national debt or reduce (progressive) income taxes, this will amount to a federally sanctioned redistribution of income from wage-earners to the wealthy (see box). Furthermore, by aggravating income inequality, these proposals will worsen, not improve, the long-term accounting imbalances of the Social Security system, since the projected cost of caring for retirees will fall on a workforce whose share of national income is shrinking. How long then before the next "crisis" is announced and further cuts proposed to "save" Social Security?

Many sincere supporters of Social Security are wary of exposing the Trust Fund charade. They fear that without the Trust Fund, the Democratic party's political commitment to Social Security's future will falter and the entire system will gradually collapse under continued right-wing assault. But this may happen with or without the Trust Fund. Early in the 21st century, payroll taxes may fall short of legislated benefits and, at that time, resources will be raised to support retirees or they will not be. Either Americans then will agree to care for the aged collectively or those without children to support them will be forced to work until they die. The battle over the baby-boomer retirement is of vital consequence. It will test the very meaning of our society and democracy, but it cannot, in fact, be won today.

Only today's battles can be won today, and they must focus on who is paying taxes and how the government today can best serve the people. There is no political advantage to be gained from expediency in this debate. Those who wish to inherit a just and humane future must fight for a just and humane present. ❏

Resources: Annual Report of the Board of Trustees of the Federal Old-Age and Survivors Insurance and Disability Insurance Trust Funds, 1998; Cato Policy Report, September 1998; "Defusing the Baby-Boomer Time-Bomb," Dean Baker, Economic Policy Institute, 1998; "Clinton Plays to Aging Baby Boomers," Alan Murray, *Wall Street Journal*, March 29, 1999.

Article 6.6

GO AHEAD AND LIFT THE CAP
Assessing a Campaign Flyer on Social Security

BY JOHN MILLER
March/April 2008

> **Barack Obama.** A plan with a trillion dollar tax increase on America's hard-working families. Lifting the cap on Social Security taxes to send more of Nevada families' hard-earned dollars to Washington. Senator Obama said, "I think that lifting the cap [on Social Security taxes] is probably going to be the best option."

> **Hillary Clinton.** A blueprint to rebuild the road to middle-class prosperity. Provide tax relief for the middle class and address Social Security without putting burdens on hard-working families or seniors. Strengthen Social Security and the economy by returning to balanced budgets.

> *—Official campaign flyer distributed by Nevadans*
> *for Hillary, January 2008*

Back in January, even before things got really nasty in the Democratic primary, Barack Obama and Hillary Clinton were already going after each other about taxes and Social Security.

The Clinton campaign sent a flyer to Nevada voters before that state's January 19 [2008] Democratic caucuses, accusing Obama of planning to impose "a trillion dollar tax increase on America's hard-working families" by lifting the cap on income subject to Social Security taxes. Clinton, the flyer claimed, does "not want to fix the problems of Social Security on the backs of middle-class families and seniors."

The truth was something different. First, Obama did not exactly propose removing the cap, which was $97,500 in 2007. (In other words, employers and employees each pay a flat percentage of the first $97,500 of each employee's salary, but no tax on the income above that.) He did discuss adjusting it as "the best way to approach this [reforming Social Security]," preferable to either cutting benefits or increasing the retirement age, later adding that he would consider keeping the exemption from $97,500 to around $200,000, lifting it only for any income above $200,000.

More important, lifting the cap would in no way increase the tax burden on middle-income families. Just under 6% of U.S. wage earners make more than $97,500 in wages, so even removing the cap altogether would raise taxes only for that small group.

Now, there is a legitimate progressive objection to Obama's discussion of fixing Social Security by adjusting the cap: any talk of reforming Social Security inevitably plays into the hands of those out to privatize it by trumping up a phony crisis. But that hardly seems to be the point of the Clinton campaign flyer.

Too bad it wasn't. Clinton gets it: in the past she herself has warned that acting as if Social Security is in crisis is "a Republican trap." Yet last October, an Associated Press reporter overhead her telling an Iowa voter that she would consider lifting the cap on payroll taxes as long as wages between $97,500 and $200,000 remained exempt—precisely the proposal she derides in the Nevada flyer.

Inside Social Security

Let's remind ourselves that Social Security, which cut poverty rates among the elderly from 35% in 1960 to 9.4% in 2006, is no Robin Hood plan that robs the rich to pay for the retirement of the working class. Rather, it is a mildly redistributive public retirement program financed by contributions from the wages of working people. In fact, Social Security taxes fall far more heavily on the poor and working class than on the well-to-do. Payroll taxes are a fixed 12.4% (actually 6.2% on employees and 6.2% on employers); they are levied only on wage income, not on property income; and the cap on wages subject to the tax (the subject of the debate between Clinton and Obama) means that while most workers pay the tax on every dollar of their income, the highest earners pay it only on a part.

Even FDR acknowledged that relying on payroll contributions to finance Social Security was regressive, although he famously argued that with those contributions in place, "no damn politician can ever scrap my Social Security program."

George W. Bush's 2005 push to privatize Social Security only underscored FDR's point. Bush made more than 40 trips around the United States to stump for his plan, but fewer people supported Social Security privatization afterwards than before he started. Ironically enough, the only aspect of Social Security reform that has generated widespread support is lifting the cap: in a February 2005 Washington Post poll, 81% of respondents agreed that Americans should pay Social Security taxes on wages over the cap.

This is no radical or hare-brained idea. It has the endorsement of the AARP, the largest seniors' lobby. And there is a clear precedent. A similar cap used to apply to the payroll tax that funds Medicare, but a 1993 law removed that cap and now every dollar of wage income is taxed to pay for Medicare. It certainly does not warrant the derision heaped on it by the Clinton campaign or the unwillingness of the Obama campaign to embrace it. In fact, lifting the cap would rewrite this one rule to favor working people more—just what the Obama campaign claims to support.

Lifting the cap on Social Security taxes would raise a significant amount of revenue: $1.3 trillion dollars over ten years according to the libertarian Cato Institute, and $124 billon a year according to the left-of-center Citizens for Tax Justice. Long term, lifting the payroll tax cap would just about cover the shortfall Social Security will face if economic growth slows to a snail's pace in the decades ahead, as forecast by the Social Security Administration (SSA). (See "The Social Security Administration's Cracked Crystal Ball" and "Social Security Isn't Broken," in this volume, for critiques of the SSA's forecasts.) According to Stephen Goss, the SSA's chief actuary, lifting the cap while giving commensurate benefit hikes to high-income taxpayers once they retire would cover 93% of the SSA's projected shortfall in Social Security revenues over the next 75 years. Removing the cap without raising

EFFECT OF REMOVING THE EARNINGS CAP ON SOCIAL SECURITY TAXES BY INCOME CATEGORY

RESULTING SOCIAL SECURITY TAX INCREASE AND TOTAL SOCIAL SECURITY TAX AS SHARES OF TOTAL INCOME IN 2007

Income Group	Increase in Social Social Security Tax	Revised total Security Tax Paid
$0 – 10K	—	6.8%
$10 – 20K	—	6.2%
$20 – 30K	—	7.8%
$30 – 40K	—	8.7%
$40 – 50K	—	9.0%
$50 – 75K	—	9.4%
$75 – 100K	+0.0%	9.7%
$100 – 150K	+0.5%	9.6%
$150 – 200K	+1.5%	9.1%
$200 – 300K	+2.7%	8.3%
$300 – 400K	+4.1%	7.7%
$400 – 500K	+4.5%	7.4%
$500 – 750K	+4.7%	6.9%
$750K – 1M	+4.7%	6.4%
$1 – 2M	+4.4%	5.5%
$2 – 5M	+4.0%	4.5%
$5 – 10M	+3.8%	4.0%
$10 – 20M	+3.2%	3.3%
over $20M	+2.7%	2.7%

Source: "An Analysis of Eliminating the Cap on Earnings Subject to the Social Security Tax & Related Issues," (Citizens for Tax Justice, November 30, 2006).

those benefits would actually produce a surplus in the system over the same period— even if the economy creeps along as the SSA predicts it will.

Finally, the combination of the cap and the unprecedented inequality of the last two decades has shrunk the Social Security tax base. Some 90% of wages fell below the cap in 1983. Today, with the increased concentration of income among the highest-paid, that figure is down to 84%—even as the number of workers with earnings above the cap has dropped. The cap would have to rise to $140,000 just to once again cover 90% of all wages; the additional revenues resulting from just this change would close about one-third of the long-term Social Security deficit projected by the SSA.

Hardly Soaking the Rich

Making high earners pay the Social Security tax on all of their wage income, as low- and middle-income earners already have to, might not strike you as class warfare—but the high flyers sure think it is. Just listen to the financial establishment squeal. Investment Management chairman Robert Pozen, architect of the benefit-cutting proposal endorsed by the Bush administration (and deceptively labeled "progressive indexing"), warns that lifting the cap would represent "one of the greatest tax increases of all time" and "is so crazy it's beyond belief." The editors of the Wall Street Journal agreed. And the conservative Heritage Foundation ginned up numbers purporting to show that lifting the cap would impose a "massive 12.4 percentage point tax hike" that would return federal tax rates to levels not seen since the 1970s.

Just how wet would the rich get if the cap on Social Security taxes was lifted? The data suggest they would get damp, but hardly soaked.

For starters, lifting the cap affects just 5.9% of wage-earners. This group benefited massively from three rounds of Bush tax cuts, as evidenced by the fact that the effective federal tax rate (i.e., the share of income actually paid in federal taxes, once all deductions and exemptions have been taken) on the richest 5% of taxpayers fell from 31.1% in 2000 to 28.9% in 2005, according to the Congressional Budget Office.

So, lifting the wage cap on Social Secu-rity taxes would not do much more than reverse those tax giveaways to the wealthy. And the wealthiest taxpayers, those with incomes over $1 million, would still be paying a smaller portion of their income in payroll taxes than all other taxpayers. (See table.) For the top 5% of taxpayers, lifting the cap would push their effective federal tax rate up to 31.5%, a bit above where it was when Bush took office but still below the 31.8% level they paid back in 1979, before nearly three decades of pro-rich tax cutting. The top 1% would pay an effective federal tax rate of 33.8% —again, higher than it was in 2000 but still well below its 1979 level of 37.0%.

That is hardly soaking the rich. In any case they can afford it. The best-off 5% of households had an average income of $520,200 in 2005, some 81% higher than in 1979 after correcting for inflation. The richest 1%, with an average income of $1,558,500 in 2005, saw their after-tax income rise a whopping 176% over the same period.

Lifting the cap on payroll taxes would not only resolve any alleged crisis in Social Security, but also help to right the economic wrongs of the last few decades. And it is popular to boot. Isn't that an idea any progressive politician should seriously consider? ❑

Sources: M. Sullivan, "Budget Magic and the Social Security Tax Cap," *Tax Notes*, 3/14/05; "Social Security: Raising or Eliminating the Taxable Earnings Base," Congressional Rsch Svc, 5/2/05; R. Dederman et al., "Keep the Social Security Wage Cap; Nearly a Million Jobs Hang in the Balance," Center for Data Analysis Report #05-04 (Heritage Foundation, 4/22/05); Robert C. Pozen, "A 'Progressive' Solution to Social Security," *Wall Street Journal*, 3/15/05; "Social Security Progressives," *WSJ*, 3/15/05; Greg Ip, "Wage Gap Figures in Social Security's Ills," *WSJ*, 4/11/05; "Social Security Memorandum to Stephen C. Goss," 2/7/05; "An Analysis of Eliminating the Cap on Earnings Subject to the Social Security Tax & Related Issues," (Citizens for Tax Justice, 11/30/06); "Obama: Clinton Also Considering $1 Trillion Social Security Tax Hike on Wealth," (Associated Press, 1/16/08); "Barack Obama on Social Security," *On the Issues*; "Effective Federal Tax Rates, 1979 to 2005," Congressional Budget Office, 12/07.

Article 6.7

HARD WORK AT AN ADVANCED AGE

BY AMY GLUCKMAN
September/October 2010

Among the many proposals that the Social-Security-is-in-crisis crowd is touting is an increase in the retirement age. The Social Security "full retirement age" was 65 from the program's inception until 1983, when Congress legislated a gradual increase, based on year of birth, to 67. The 1983 amendments did not change the age of earliest eligibility for Social Security retirement benefits, which remains 62. However, those who opt to start receiving benefits before they reach the full retirement age for their cohort face a lifetime cut in their monthly payment.

At first glance, it seems reasonable to push the retirement age upward in line with average life expectancy, which rose rapidly in the United States during the 20th century. But that rise in life expectancy owes a great deal to sharp drops in infant and child mortality. For those who survive to adulthood and especially to old age,

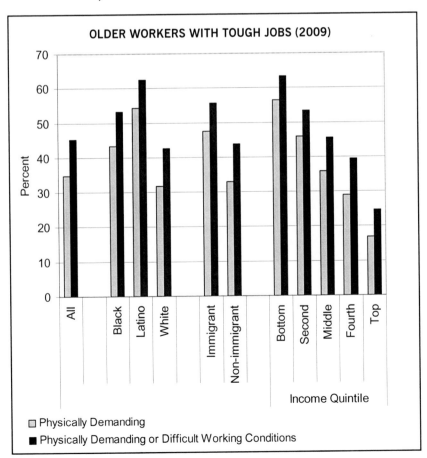

the change is far less dramatic. People who turned 65 in 1940, the first year monthly Social Security retirement benefits were paid out, could expect to live to nearly 79; those who turned 65 in 1990 had a life expectancy only about four years longer.

What would it mean to ratchet up the full retirement age further? The answer is: it depends. Some 60- and 70-somethings can readily continue working and postpone receiving Social Security benefits; a few have sufficient personal savings and/or private pensions that they will never need to rely on Social Security at all. But for the millions of older custodians, cooks, cashiers, construction workers, and others who do physically demanding work, having to put in even a few more years on the job before they can receive their full Social Security benefits is a different story.

A surprising number of older workers have these kinds of jobs, as a study by Hye Jin Rho of the Center for Economic and Policy Research shows. Following the classifications used in the U.S. Labor Department's Occupational Information Network database, the study defines "physically demanding" jobs as those that require significant time standing or walking, repetitive motions, or handling and moving objects. "Difficult working conditions" include outdoor work, use of hazardous equipment, and exposure to contaminants. Of the 18.8 million U.S. workers who are 58 or older, over 45% have physically demanding jobs and/or difficult working conditions. The rate is even higher for the 5.2 million workers 66 and up (48.2%).

Certain groups of older workers perform these tough jobs at disproportionate rates (see figure). Not surprisingly, the workers who can least afford to take an early-retirement penalty in their monthly Social Security check are often those who are most likely to reach their mid-60s saying, "Time to quit!" ❑

Sources: Hye Jin Rho, "Hard Work? Patterns in Physically Demanding Labor Among Older Workers," Center for Economic and Policy Research, August 2010; U.S. Social Security Administration, "Life Expectancy for Social Security"; Laura Shrestha, "Life Expectancy in the United States," Congressional Research Service, August 2006.

Article 6.8

WHEN BAD THINGS HAPPEN TO GOOD PENSIONS

BY TERESA GHILARDUCCI
May/June 2005

February [2005] was a momentous month for American workers' retirement security. Just days after President Bush called for the partial privatization of Social
Security, his administration proposed major modifications to the system that guarantees employer-sponsored defined-benefit pensions. Both initiatives break with
longstanding "insurance" models of old-age income security and accelerate the use
of individual accounts.

Defined-benefit pensions, like Social Security, provide a modest but steady
stream of income for the duration of a retiree's life. Both systems are based on collective risk sharing: they gather premium contributions from populations facing
similar risks—such as old age or disability—and provide a guaranteed stream of
income to individuals when those risks befall them.

Much as the administration is using a financing problem in the Social Security
system as an excuse to demand big changes that would endanger Social Security
itself, it's using a deficit in the agency that insures defined-benefit pensions to call
for "reforms" that would imperil those very pensions.

Both of Bush's proposals would undermine the retirement security of working people and their families. But the two proposals also deeply contradict each
other. By making the puzzling claim that the Social Security trust fund, which
holds only U.S. Treasury bonds, owns no "real money," the Social Security proposal urges younger workers to divert Social Security contributions into individual
accounts. On the other hand, most independent analysts believe the administration's proposed pension reform would lead corporations to load up on bonds
in order to stabilize their asset portfolios—and their credit ratings—and over
time drive them out of the defined-benefit system altogether. The Social Security
proposal is based on the premise that individuals don't own enough stock; the
pension proposal is based on the premise that pension funds fall short because
they own too much.

The administration's proposals place us at a crossroads. We can either hasten
the end of group and social insurance and move toward individual accounts—
personal savings accounts and 401(k)s—or we can save Social Security and expand
incentives for employers to provide defined-benefit pensions to workers.

Why Defined-Benefit Plans Should Be Strengthened—Not Undermined

Unlike defined-contribution plans like 401(k)s, which yield benefits—or losses—
based on the contributions and investment prowess of the individual worker,
defined benefits are predictable; they're usually based on a worker's pay rate and
length of employment. For the median worker, defined-benefit wealth is higher than
defined-contribution account wealth, and because the former is paid as an annuity,

TABLE 1
COMPARISON BETWEEN DEFINED BENEFIT AND DEFINED CONTRIBUTION PLANS: THE RISKS FOR THE EMPLOYEE

	Defined Benefit plans	*Defined Contribution plans*
Chance that pension benefit will be larger than expected (Investment Benefit)	No (unless union and/or employer increases benefits)	Yes (if investments exceed expectations)
Risk that pension fund investments will fall short (Investment Risk)	No	Yes (if individuals make investment mistakes or investments unpredictably fail)
Risk that retiree will outlive their benefits. (Longevity Risk)	No	Yes
Risk that inflation will diminish the pension's buying power (Inflation risk)	Yes	Yes
Risk that a plan sponsor's bankruptcy will diminish the pension (Employer Bankruptcy Risk)	Some (only very high paid DB participants aren't fully insured by the PBGC)	Yes (almost half of all 401(k) assets are in employer stock)
Risk that administration costs can increase and diminish returns)	Borne by employer	Borne by employee
Ease of pension portability between jobs	No	Yes

workers collect for as long as they live. (See Table 1 on next page for the risks associated with defined-benefit versus defined-contribution plans.)

Defined-benefit plans offer another, frequently overlooked, benefit to society: they serve as an equalizing force. For over 40 years, American retirement policies have reduced income inequality between the top tier and the rest, narrowing consumption gaps as people age. Social Security and defined-benefit plans set an income floor underneath the working class that does not fluctuate with the financial markets. Among current retirees (Americans born between 1926 and 1935), the ratio of the income that goes to the top 20% versus the middle 20% of the income distribution is 234%. For retired boomers (workers born between 1946 and 1956), the gap will be 285%, and it will continue to rise for subsequent generations. This growth in inequality is tied to the decline of defined-benefit pensions and the rise of defined-contribution plans as shares of the income of elderly households. Current retirees have 20% of their income coming from defined-benefit plans while future retirees are projected to have only 11%.

Under the current system, companies with defined-benefit pensions pay insurance premiums to the Pension Benefit Guaranty Corporation (PBGC), a government corporation created in 1974 to insure pension assets. If a pension plan fails, the PBGC takes control of it and continues to pay covered workers' retirement benefits up to a cap. The PBGC receives no federal tax dollars, relying instead

TABLE 2
THE EFFECT THE BUSH PROPOSALS WILL HAVE ON PREMIUMS
OF UNHEALTHY AND HEALTHY COMPANIES SPONSORING DB PLANS

Category of firm	Total PBGC premiums paid by firms as a percent of the expected losses imposed on the PBGC		
	Actual in 2004	*Proposed under Bush plan*	*Percent increase in premiums*
Below Investment Grade Firms	8%	16%	113%
Above Investment Grade Firms	66%	340%	240%

Source: Coronado and Schieber, 2005

primarily on insurance premiums paid by employers and unions who sponsor defined-benefit pensions.

Bush's Pension Proposal

On February 7 [2005], the Bush administration unveiled a sweeping rewrite of federal pension law in the form of a proposal it calls "Strengthen Funding for Single-Employer Pension Plans." The administration claims to want to strengthen pensions by fixing the problem of "underfunded plan terminations"—which, it argues, "are placing an increasing strain on the pension insurance system."

The proposal is tailored to an imagined reality where most companies grossly underfund their plans, and it ignores fundamental problems caused by the rise of risky defined-contribution plans and the one-time contraction of the steel and airline industries. If enacted, it would destroy the very system the administration claims it wants to save.

The plan dramatically increases PBGC premiums for single-employer defined-benefit sponsors, doubling premiums for "at risk" firms (those with unfunded liabilities that are likely to default) and tripling premiums for healthy firms (see Table 2). Whereas today, healthy firms pay premiums equal to 66% of their "expected losses" (meaning the amount they would owe to current and future retirees if they defaulted), the Bush plan would raise healthy firms' premiums to 340% of their expected losses. It thus penalizes healthy companies for sponsoring defined-benefit pensions.

For the first time, a company's ability to provide such pensions to its workers would be linked to the company's own creditworthiness. The plan divides companies into two groups: those above and those below "investment grade." Companies that fall below investment grade face large premium rate hikes and have just five years to reach a 90% pension-funding level. (See "Federal Policy for Defined-Benefit Plans" for more on pension funding requirements.) An estimated one-fourth of the nation's largest firms, including Delta Air Lines, Goodyear Tire and Rubber, United States Steel, and Lucent Technologies, are currently below investment grade. In this way, the plan intensifies the funding obligations of companies already experiencing financial difficulties. At the same time, it prohibits firms from building up a cushion

TABLE 3
STEEL AND AIRLINES CONSTITUTE MOST OF THE PBGC'S CLAIMS

	Percentage of PBGC-insured Plan Participants and Claims on the PBGC from its Inception to 2004	
	Steel	*Airlines*
Participants (all workers covered by a defined benefit pension)	3%	2%
Claims	56%	17%

Source: PBGC Annual Report, 2004

of credit during flush periods. For decades, companies have contributed more during boom years so as to lighten their funding obligations during slow periods. The Bush plan takes away that flexibility.

What's more, firms would be required to value their plan assets according to their market value, rather than using an average or smoothed valuation of assets, as they do now. This change will produce greater year-to-year volatility in asset prices and funding obligations. Measures of liability (the amount a plan owes to current and future beneficiaries) would also become more volatile: The plan requires firms to use a complex method to calculate the present value of future liabilities. Firms now use a single interest rate in the calculations; under the Bush plan their interest rates would be pegged to when their workers are expected to retire. Firms with younger employees would use a higher interest rate tied to a long-term bond, while firms with older employees would use a low rate, which would make their liabilities soar. These accounting changes will hurt older plans in blue-collar manufacturing and make contributions more uncertain.

Bush claims the changes would result in "increased accuracy." But he fails to mention that they will make defined-benefit plans more expensive for companies to offer, required contributions less predictable, and valuations much more complicated to compute—something companies, especially small and medium sized ones, complain about.

The volatility produced by the new accounting framework would force firms to shift their pension investments from stocks to bonds. In fact, bonds, with their predictable rates of return, would become the only reasonable investment to include in a corporate pension fund. But bonds' low yields would drive up the cost of providing a plan—and hasten the elimination of the defined-benefit pension.

The Bush proposal starts from the wrong premise. It assumes that many firms purposefully underfund their plans because they know that the PBGC will pick up the shortfall if they go bankrupt. (Economists call this the "moral hazard" problem.) Similarly, it reduces employer flexibility in the belief that firms will use the flexible rules to "game the system." It anticipates bad faith behavior rather than mixing protections against bad behavior with positive incentives for promoting and strengthening the system, which, in reality, most companies deal with in good faith and want to keep strong.

Why the Shortfall?

There's no question that the PBGC is facing a serious shortfall. In 2004, its budget plummeted into a $23 billion hole from a 2000 (stock-swollen) surplus of $10 billion. The dramatic fall was caused by crippling mass bankruptcies and defaults in the steel and airline industries. The agency was designed to cope with isolated cases of default, not sector-wide crises. Since 2002, about 70% of the $8 billion the PBGC has absorbed in pension losses was related to steel and airline defaults. It is expected to absorb another $6.6 billion from United Airlines. The independent monitoring organization Center for Federal Financial Institutions (COFFI) projects a program deficit of $16.2 billion in 2013. According to its founder, former Treasury staffer Douglas Elliot, the PBGC might require a program bailout of $56 to $100 billion by 2020 under certain scenarios.

The Bush proposal may have been prompted by the PBGC's deficit, but it does not address the two most fundamental causes of the agency's financing troubles: First, its premium base is shrinking thanks to the financial industry and to government regulations that privilege defined-contribution plans over defined-benefit plans; second, two industries recently caused unusual PBGC outlays. (In 2004 less than 5% of all defined-benefit participants constituted over two-thirds of the claims—see Table 3.) Underfunding of plans, the problem the Bush plan targets, is rare; a minority of companies underfund, and most are not at risk of defaulting.

Fewer DB Plans— The number of private defined-benefit plans peaked in the mid-1980s at 112,000, when they covered 40% of the U.S. work force. By 2004, just 31,000 remained, covering only 20% of workers. New economy companies like Microsoft and Wal-Mart never adopted the plans and old economy companies such as GE and IBM (along with 18% to 20% of other long-time sponsors) are freezing and terminating their plans.

When I served on the PBGC advisory board during the Clinton administration, we used to say "pension plans aren't created—they're sold." Vendors, brokers, money management firms, and mutual funds charge more for individual account management than defined-benefit management, so they actively market 401(k)-type programs to employers. Employers find these plans attractive because they can subcontract record keeping and paperwork to vendors while passing administration costs on to their workers. Under employer-sponsored defined-benefit plans, employers bear the administrative costs—and the long-term liability. Moreover, the decline of unions, the shrinking of the manufacturing sector, and the erosion of durable employment relationships more generally have all combined to cut the number of defined-benefit pensions.

As more companies replace their guaranteed defined-benefit pensions with defined-contribution plans, the PBGC's financial position erodes because defined-contribution sponsors don't pay premiums to the PBGC. For a while, the effects of these long-term problems were masked by the stock market bubble, but no longer.

A glimmer of evidence suggests the decline is slowing. Four major companies, SBC, UMC, UK Barclays, and TransCanada, adopted defined-benefit plans in 2004. And public-sector employees are fending off muscular attempts, the latest one by California Governor Arnold Schwarzenegger, to convert their defined-benefit plans to defined-contribution plans.

External Industry Factors— The second threat to the defined-benefit pension has nothing to do with the pension system's internal flaws, but with outside economic and political events and trends, namely the dramatic acceleration in the off-shoring of U.S. manufacturing; strong dollar policies that boosted cheap imports; the 9/11 attacks; and fuel price hikes. These combined factors have pummeled the airline and steel sectors. Bethlehem Steel, Delta Airways, US Airways, and the giant United Airlines, plus one large company in another sector, Polaroid, have all offloaded some of their pension liabilities onto the PBGC within the past few years. In doing so, the steel and airline sectors brought down some of America's largest pension plans. The pension losses in these two industries have overwhelmed the PBGC. Given the exceptional confluence of factors at work here, Congress should not expect the PBGC to absorb the impacts of two major industry collapses with its own premium revenues.

The Bush administration is simply wrong in assuming that corporate moral hazard and poor funding lie behind the PBGC's woes. Most firms actually behave as though they are committed to their plans. My survey of over 700 firms over a 19-year period (1981–1998) shows that when rates of return of defined-benefit pension funds were high—in good times—firms contributed more to both their defined-benefit and defined-contribution plans, just as the 1974 pension law known as ERISA intended. The airline and steel industries alone stopped contributing recently when both industries, facing crises, altered course and cut back their contributions when the defined-benefit plans were earning high rates of return. (There are two explanations, not mutually exclusive, for this reversal. One is that these industries decided to offload their liabilities onto the PBGC and workers; the other is that when the rest of the economy was doing all right, these industries were experiencing their own sector-specific recessions.) This is an unusual behavior pattern—the exception, not the rule. Beyond these sectors, far fewer firms withhold contributions to the PBGC during flush periods than the Bush administration contends.

Toward Secure Retirement Income

Raising pension funding standards as aggressively as the Bush administration proposes tightens the rules to the point where plan sponsors could no longer afford or want to afford most of the defined-benefit pensions they now offer. According to Pensions and Investments, Ron Gebhardtsbauer, senior pension fellow at the American Academy of Actuaries, predicts, "Instead of investing their pension assets in stocks, companies will simply shut down their pension plans, set up defined-contribution plans and let the employees invest in stocks." Surveys show that when asked what poses a threat to defined-benefit plans, firms point to market downturns and volatility caused by eliminating actuarial smoothing in favor of "mark to market" funding schemes (exactly what Bush plans to implement). Standard & Poor's Ratings Services agrees. Credit ratings would likely fall for defined-benefit sponsors because of increased pension costs and volatility. Given the specter of lowered credit ratings, companies will use bonds to stabilize their fund pension contributions, and their reputation in the finance community, at the same time that the new regulations push them to drop their defined-benefit plans altogether.

There are three chief ways to truly advance defined-benefit pensions. They all involve strengthening the PBGC. The first is to promote cash balance plans, a form of defined-benefit pension typically distributed in some form of annuity for the life of a retiree and spouse. Employers appreciate cash balance plans because, like in a 401(k), the employer contribution is predictable: the employer contributes a defined amount of money to an account every year. But unlike in a 401(k), individuals don't have to manage their own money and they bear no risk—the employer guarantees the rate of return. Because they are a form of defined-benefit pension, cash balance plans are insured by the PBGC. More defined-benefit plans of any type would bring fresh revenues to the PBGC, yet the Bush administration has dragged its feet in forming regulatory rules to make firms feel comfortable with providing them.

Second, Congress should infuse the PBGC with revenue, perhaps from taxes on goods and services tied to the airline and steel industries that have most strained the system. The PBGC's recent losses coincided with windfalls of low prices for steel-made products and air travel. Consumers could help pay some portion of the price of industry dislocation and workers' retirements if Congress imposed a modest tax on airline tickets and tons of steel (domestically produced or imported), and dedicated the revenue to the PBGC. More broadly, reforms to strengthen rather than destroy the defined-benefit system and the PBGC will have to deal with the health of the airline industry and steel industry—like we did almost a 100 years ago with railroads. (See "Federal Policy for Defined-Benefit Plans.")

Third, the PBGC is modeled as insurance; strengthening it requires applying insurance principles. Any proper insurance system distinguishes between catastrophic events and normal ones. Other insurance companies have "reinsurance" to cover catastrophes, recognizing that larger-than-usual claims, if absorbed only by premium payers, can severely damage an entire insurance system. But the PBGC itself currently has no insurance. The need for a bailout should be avoided by correcting this mistake.

Government policy makers recognized long ago that in a competitive capitalist economy, some employers might be driven out of business before they had fully funded the pension benefits they had promised their workers. Congress knew that mandating plan sponsors to back up their benefit promises by requiring them to fund their pension trusts according to a prescribed payment schedule was not enough. It recognized that business failure is a possibility and wisely added the PBGC as a backstop for retirees, should their company fail. It also knew that the defined-benefit system had to renew itself by attracting new sponsors to adopt such plans, and mandated, by statute, that the PBCG encourage and maintain the defined-benefit system and keep premiums as low as possible.

Even as it's lobbying to dismantle the nation's only form of social insurance, Social Security, and drive workers into individual accounts, the Bush administration is taking aim at the only other source of guaranteed retirement income available to millions of working people, the defined-benefit pension. The defined-benefit pension system needs to be strengthened and expanded—not undermined. The president, and officials at the PBGC who are now supporting the president's proposals, are in an awkward position: they are purportedly saving an agency by eliminating its reason to exist. ❏

Resources: American Academy of Actuaries, "Analysis of the president's proposals to strengthen the single employer pension funding," 2005, <www.actuary.org/pdf/pension/funding–single. pdf>; Vineeta Anand, "Pension Reform: White House might be in the mood to deal," Pensions and Investments, January 2005; Julia L. Coronado and Sylvester J. Schieber, "Saving Private Pension Insurance: An Evaluation of Current Proposal to Shore up the PBGC," Watson – Wyatt Worldwide, 2005; Center on Federal Financial Institutions, "PBGC Updated Cash Flow Model from COFFI, November 18, 2004; T. Ghilarducci and Weis Sun, "Pension Regulation and Destabilization: Are firms forced to decrease pension funding in an upturn and to contribute in a recession?" University of Notre Dame, Faculty of Economics, 2005; Scott Sprinzen, "Pension Plans and Credit Ratings," *Business Week*, March 31, 2005; Fay Hansen, "Rethinking Employee Benefits," Business Finance, 2005; Department of Labor, "The administration's single employer defined benefit pension reform proposal," <www.dol.gov/ebsa/pensionreform.html>; James Wooten, The Employee Retirement Income Security Act of 1974: A Political History, California/Milbank Books on Health and the Public Policy.

Article 6.9

NO MORE SAVINGS!
The Case for Social Wealth

BY ELLEN FRANK
May/June 2004

Pundits from the political left and right don't agree about war in Iraq, gay marriage, national energy policy, tax breaks, free trade, or much else. But they do agree on one thing: Americans don't save enough. The reasons are hotly disputed. Right-wingers contend that the tax code rewards spenders and punishes savers. Liberals argue that working families earn too little to save. Environmentalists complain of a work-spend rat race fueled by relentless advertising. But the bottom line seems beyond dispute.

Data on wealth-holding reveal that few Americans possess adequate wealth to finance a comfortable retirement. Virtually none have cash sufficient to survive an extended bout of unemployment. Only a handful of very affluent households could pay for health care if their insurance lapsed, cover nursing costs if they became disabled, or see their children through college without piling up student loans. Wealth is so heavily concentrated at the very top of the income distribution that even upper-middle class households are dangerously exposed to the vagaries of life and the economy.

With low savings and inadequate personal wealth identified as the problem, the solutions seem so clear as to rally wide bipartisan support: Provide tax credits for savings. Encourage employers to establish workplace savings plans. Educate people about family budgeting and financial investing. Promote home ownership so people can build home equity. Develop tax-favored plans to pay for college, retirement, and medical needs. More leftish proposals urge the government to redistribute wealth through federally sponsored "children's development accounts" or "American stakeholder accounts," so that Americans at all income levels can, as the Demos-USA website puts it, "enjoy the security and benefits that come with owning assets."

But such policies fail to address the paradoxical role savings play in market economies. Furthermore, looking at economic security solely through the lens of personal finance deflects focus away from a better, more direct, and far more reliable way to ensure Americans' well-being: promoting social wealth.

The Paradox of Thrift

Savings is most usefully envisaged as a physical concept. Each year businesses turn out automobiles, computers, lumber, and steel. Households (or consumers) buy much, but not all, of this output. The goods and services they leave behind represent the economy's savings.

Economics students are encouraged to visualize the economy as a metaphorical plumbing system through which goods and money flow. Firms produce goods, which flow through the marketplace and are sold for money. The money flows into peoples' pockets as income, which flows back into the marketplace as demand for goods.

Savings represent a leak in the economic plumbing. If other purchasers don't step up and buy the output that thrifty consumers shun, firms lay off workers and curb production, for there is no profit in making goods that people don't want to buy.

On the other hand, whatever consumers don't buy is available for businesses to purchase in order to expand their capacity. When banks buy computers or developers buy lumber and steel, then the excess goods find a market and production continues apace. Economists refer to business purchases of new plant and equipment as "investment."

In the plumbing metaphor, investment is an injection—an additional flow of spending into the economy to offset the leaks caused by household saving.

During the industrial revolution, intense competition meant that whatever goods households did not buy or could not afford would be snatched up by emerging businesses, at least much of the time. By the turn of the 20th century, however, low-paid consumers had become a drag on economic growth. Small entrepreneurial businesses gave way to immense monopolistic firms like U.S. Steel and Standard Oil whose profits vastly exceeded what they could spend on expansion. Indeed expansion often looked pointless since, given the low level of household spending, the only buyers for their output were other businesses, who themselves faced the same dilemma.

As market economies matured, savings became a source of economic stagnation. Even the conspicuous consumption of Gilded Age business owners couldn't provide enough demand for the goods churned out of large industrial factories. Henry Ford was the first American corporate leader to deliberately pay his workers above-market wages, reasoning correctly that a better-paid work force would provide the only reliable market for his automobiles.

Today, thanks to democratic suffrage, labor unions, social welfare programs, and a generally more egalitarian culture, wages are far higher in industrialized economies than they were a century ago; wage and salary earners now secure nearly four-fifths of national income. And thrift seems a quaint virtue of our benighted grandparents. In the United States, the personal savings rate—the percentage of income flowing to households that they did not spend—fell to 1% in the late 1990s. Today, with a stagnant economy making consumers more cautious, the personal savings rate has risen—but only to around 4%.

Because working households consume virtually every penny they earn, goods and services produced are very likely to find buyers and continue to be produced. This is an important reason why the United States and Europe no longer experience the devastating depressions that beset industrialized countries prior to World War II.

Yet there is a surprisingly broad consensus that these low savings are a bad thing. Americans are often chastised for their lack of thrift, their failure to provide for themselves financially, their rash and excessive borrowing. Politicians and economists constantly exhort Americans to save more and devise endless schemes to induce them to do so.

At the same time, Americans also face relentless pressure to spend. After September 11, President Bush told the public they could best serve their country by continuing to shop. In the media, economic experts bemoan declines in "consumer confidence" and applaud reports of buoyant retail or auto sales. The U.S. economy, we are told, is a consumer economy—our spendthrift ways and shop-til-you-drop culture the motor that propels it. Free-spending consumers armed with multiple credit cards keep the stores hopping, the restaurants full, and the factories humming.

Our schizophrenic outlook on saving and spending has two roots. First, the idea of saving meshes seamlessly with a conservative ideological outlook. In what author George Lakoff calls the "strict-father morality" that informs conservative Republican politics, abstinence, thrift, self-reliance, and competitive individualism are moral virtues. Institutions that discourage saving—like Social Security, unemployment insurance, government health programs, state-funded student aid—are by definition socialistic and result in an immoral reliance on others. Former Treasury Secretary Paul O'Neill bluntly expressed this idea to a reporter for the *Financial Times* in 2001. "Able-bodied adults," O'Neill opined, "should save enough on a regular basis so that they can provide for their own retirement and for that matter for their health and medical needs." Otherwise, he continued, elderly people are just "dumping their problems on the broader society."

This ideological position, which is widely but not deeply shared among U.S. voters, receives financial and political support from the finance industry. Financial firms have funded most of the research, lobbying, and public relations for the campaign to "privatize" Social Security, replacing the current system of guaranteed, publicly-funded pensions with individual investment accounts. The finance industry and its wealthy clients also advocate "consumption taxes"—levying taxes on income spent, but not on income saved—so as to "encourage saving" and "reward thrift." Not coincidentally, the finance industry specializes in committing accumulated pools of money to the purchase of stocks, bonds and other paper assets, for which it receives generous fees and commissions.

Our entire economic system requires that people spend freely. Yet political rhetoric combined with pressure from the financial services industry urges individuals to save, or at least to try to save. This rhetoric finds a receptive audience in ordinary households anxious over their own finances and among many progressive public-interest groups alarmed by the threadbare balance sheets of so many American households.

So here is the paradox. People need protection against adversity, and an ample savings account provides such protection. But if ordinary households try to save and protect themselves against hard times, the unused factories, barren malls, and empty restaurants would bring those hard times upon them.

Social Wealth

The only way to address the paradox is to reconcile individuals' need for economic security with the public need for a stable economy. The solution therefore lies not in personal thrift or individual wealth, but in social insurance and public wealth.

When a country promotes economic security with dependable public investments and insurance programs, individuals have less need to amass private savings. Social Security, for example, provides the elderly with a direct claim on the nation's economic output after they retire. This guarantees that retirees keep spending and reduces the incentive for working adults to save. By restraining personal savings, Social Security improves the chances that income earned will translate into income spent, making the overall economy more stable.

Of course, Americans still need to save up for old-age; Social Security benefits replace, on average, only one-third of prior earnings. This argues not for more saving, however, but for more generous Social Security benefits. In Europe, public pensions replace from 50% to 70% of prior earnings.

Programs like Social Security and unemployment insurance align private motivation with the public interest in a high level of economic activity. Moreover, social insurance programs reduce people's exposure to volatile financial markets. Proponents of private asset building seem to overlook the lesson of the late 1990s stock market boom: that the personal wealth of small-scale savers is perilously vulnerable to stock market downswings, price manipulation, and fraud by corporate insiders.

It is commonplace to disparage social insurance programs as "big government" intrusions that burden the public with onerous taxes. But the case for a robust public sector is at least as much an economic as a moral one. Ordinary individuals and households fare better when they are assured some secure political claim on the economy's output, not only because of the payouts they receive as individuals, but because social claims on the economy render the economy itself more stable.

Well-funded public programs, for one thing, create reliable income streams and employment. Universal public schooling, for example, means that a sizable portion of our nation's income is devoted to building, equipping, staffing, and maintaining schools. This spending is less susceptible than private-sector spending to business cycles, price fluctuations, and job losses.

Programs that build social wealth also substantially ameliorate the sting of joblessness and minimize the broader economic fallout of unemployment when downturns do occur. Public schools, colleges, parks, libraries, hospitals, and transportation systems, as well as social insurance programs like unemployment compensation and disability coverage, all ensure that the unemployed continue to consume at least a minimal level of goods and services. Their children can still attend school and visit the playground. If there were no social supports, the unemployed would be forced to withdraw altogether from the economy, dragging wages down and setting off destabilizing depressions.

In a series of articles on the first Bush tax cut in 2001, the *New York Times* profiled Dr. Robert Cline, an Austin, Texas, surgeon whose $300,000 annual income still left him worried about financing college educations for his six children. Dr. Cline himself attended the University of Texas, at a cost of $250 per semester ($650 for medical school), but figured that "his own children's education will likely cost tens of thousands of dollars each." Dr. Cline supported the 2001 tax cut, the *Times* reported. Ironically, though, that cut contributed to an environment in which institutions like the University of Texas raise tuitions, restrict enrollments, and drive Dr. Cline and others to attempt to amass enough personal wealth to pay for their children's education.

Unlike Dr. Cline, most people will never accumulate sufficient hoards of wealth to afford expensive high-quality services like education or to indemnify themselves against the myriad risks of old age, poor health, and unemployment. Even when middle-income households do manage to stockpile savings, they have little control over the rate at which their assets can be converted to cash.

Virtually all people—certainly the 93% of U.S. households earning less than $150,000—would fare better collectively than they could individually. Programs that provide direct access to important goods and services—publicly financed education, recreation, health care, and pensions—reduce the inequities that follow inevitably from an entirely individualized economy. The vast majority of people are better off with the high probability of a secure income and guaranteed access to key services such as health care than with the low-probability prospect of becoming rich.

The next time a political candidate recommends some tax-exempt individual asset-building scheme, progressively minded people should ask her these questions. If consumers indeed save more and the government thus collects less tax revenue, who will buy the goods these thrifty consumers now forgo? Who will employ the workers who used to manufacture those goods? Who will build the public assets that lower tax revenues render unaffordable? And how exactly does creating millions of little pots of gold substitute for a collective commitment to social welfare? ❑

Chapter 7

THE INTERNATIONAL FINANCIAL SYSTEM

Article 7.1

THE GIANT POOL OF MONEY

BY ARTHUR MacEWAN
September/October 2009

> Dear Dr. Dollar:
> *On May 9, the public radio program* This American Life *broadcast an explanation of the housing crisis with the title: "The Giant Pool of Money." With too much money looking for investment opportunities, lots of bad investments were made—including the bad loans to home buyers. But where did this "giant pool of money" come from? Was this really a source of the home mortgage crisis?*
> —Gail Radford, Buffalo, N.Y.

The show was both entertaining and interesting. A good show, but maybe a bit more explanation will be useful.

There was indeed a "giant pool of money" that was an important part of the story of the home mortgage crisis—well, not "money" as we usually think of it, but financial assets, which I'll get to in a moment. And that pool of money is an important link in the larger economic crisis story.

The giant pool of money was the build-up of financial assets—U.S. Treasury bonds, for example, and other assets that pay a fixed income. According to the program, the amount of these assets had grown from roughly $36 trillion in 2000 to $70 trillion in 2008. That's $70 *trillion*, with a T, which is a lot of money, roughly the same as total world output in 2008.

These financial assets built up for a number of reasons. One was the doubling of oil prices (after adjusting for inflation) between 2000 and 2007, largely due to the U.S. invasion of Iraq. This put a lot of money in the hands of governments in oil-producing countries and private individuals connected to the oil industry.

A second factor was the large build-up of reserves (i.e., the excess of receipts from exports over payments for imports) by several low-income countries, most notably China. One reason some countries operated in this manner was simply to keep the cost of their currency low in terms of U.S. dollars, thus maintaining demand for their exports. (Using their own currencies to buy dollars, they were increasing both the supply of their currencies and the demand for dollars; this pushed the price of their currencies down and of dollars up.) But another reason was to protect themselves from the sort of problems they had faced in the early 1980s, when world recession cut their export earnings and left them unable to meet their import costs and pay their debts—thus the debt crisis of that era.

This build-up of dollar reserves by governments (actually, central banks) of other countries was also a result of the budgetary deficits of the Bush administration. Spending more than it was taking in as taxes (after the big tax cuts for the wealthy and with the heavy war spending), the Bush administration needed to borrow. Foreign governments, by buying the U.S. securities, were providing the loans.

Still a third factor explaining the giant pool of financial assets was the high level of inequality within the United States and elsewhere in the global economy. Since 1993, half of all income gains in the United States have gone to the highest-income 1% of households. While the very rich spend a good share of their money on mansions, fancy cars, and other luxuries, there was plenty more money for them to put into investments—the stock market but also fixed-income securities (i.e., bonds).

So there is the giant pool of money or, again, of financial assets.

The financial assets became a problem for two connected reasons. First, in the recovery following the 2001 recession, economic growth was very slow; there were thus very limited real investment opportunities. Between 2001 and 2007, private fixed investment (adjusted for inflation) grew by only 11%, whereas in the same number of years following the recession of the early 1990s, investment grew by 59%.

Second, in an effort to stimulate more growth, the Federal Reserve kept interest rates very low. But the low interest rates meant low returns on financial assets— U.S. government bonds in particular, but financial assets in general. So the holders of financial assets went searching for new investment opportunities, which, as the radio program explained, meant pushing money into high-risk mortgages. The rest, as they say, is history.

So the giant pool of money was the link that tied high inequality, the war, and rising financial imbalances in the world economy (caused in large part by the U.S. government's budgetary policies) to the housing crisis and thus to the more general financial crisis. ❏

Article 7.2

W(H)ITHER THE DOLLAR?

The U.S. trade deficit, the global economic crisis, and the dollar's status as the world's reserve currency.

BY KATHERINE SCIACCHITANO
May/June 2010

For more than half a century, the dollar was both a symbol and an instrument of U.S. economic and military power. At the height of the financial crisis in the fall of 2008, the dollar served as a safe haven for investors, and demand for U.S. Treasury bonds ("Treasuries") spiked. More recently, the United States has faced a vacillating dollar, calls to replace the greenback as the global reserve currency, and an international consensus that it should save more and spend less.

At first glance, circumstances seem to give reason for concern. The U.S. budget deficit is over 10% of GDP. China has begun a long-anticipated move away from Treasuries, threatening to make U.S. government borrowing more expensive. And the adoption of austerity measures in Greece—with a budget deficit barely 3% higher than the United States—hovers as a reminder that the bond market can enforce wage cuts and pension freezes on developed as well as developing countries.

These pressures on the dollar and for fiscal cut-backs and austerity come at an awkward time given the level of public outlays required to deal with the crisis and the need to attract international capital to pay for them. But the pressures also highlight the central role of the dollar in the crisis. Understanding that role is critical to grasping the link between the financial recklessness we've been told is to blame for the crisis and the deeper causes of the crisis in the real economy: that link is the outsize U.S. trade deficit.

Trade deficits are a form of debt. For mainstream economists, the cure for the U.S. deficit is thus increased "savings": spend less and the bottom line will improve. But the U.S. trade deficit didn't balloon because U.S. households or the government went on a spending spree. It ballooned because, from the 1980s on, successive U.S. administrations pursued a high-dollar policy that sacrificed U.S. manufacturing for finance, and that combined low-wage, export-led growth in the global South with low-wage, debt-driven consumption at home. From the late nineties, U.S. dollars that went out to pay for imports increasingly came back not as demand for U.S. goods, but as demand for investments that fueled U.S. housing and stock market bubbles. Understanding the history of how the dollar helped create these imbalances, and how these imbalances in turn led to the housing bubble and subprime crash, sheds important light on how labor and the left should respond to pressures for austerity and "saving" as the solution to the crisis.

Gold, Deficits, and Austerity

A good place to start is with the charge that the Federal Reserve triggered the housing bubble by lowering interest rates after the dot-com bubble burst and plunged the country into recession in 2001.

In 2001, manufacturing was too weak to lead a recovery, and the Bush administration was ideologically opposed to fiscal stimulus other than tax cuts for the wealthy. So the real question isn't why the Fed lowered rates; it's why it was able to. In 2000, the U.S. trade deficit stood at 3.7% of GDP. Any other country with this size deficit would have had to tighten its belt and jump-start exports, not embark on stimulating domestic demand that could deepen the deficit even more.

The Fed's ability to lower interest rates despite the U.S. trade deficit stemmed from the dollar's role as the world's currency, which was established during the Bretton Woods negotiations for a new international monetary system at the end of World War II.

A key purpose of an international monetary system—Bretton Woods or any other—is to keep international trade and debt in balance. Trade has to be mutual. One country can't do all the selling while other does all the buying; both must be able to buy and sell. If one or more countries develop trade deficits that persist, they won't be able to continue to import without borrowing and going into debt. At the same time, some other country or countries will have corresponding trade surpluses. The result is a global trade imbalance. To get back "in balance," the deficit country has to import less, export more, or both. The surplus country has to do the reverse.

In practice, economic pressure is stronger on deficit countries to adjust their trade balances by importing less, since it's deficit countries that could run out of money to pay for imports. Importing less can be accomplished with import quotas (which block imports over a set level) or tariffs (which decrease demand for imports by imposing a tax on them). It can also be accomplished with "austerity"—squeezing demand by lowering wages.

Under the gold standard, this squeezing took place automatically. Gold was shipped out of a country to pay for a trade deficit. Since money had to be backed by gold, having less gold meant less money in domestic circulation. So prices and wages fell. Falling wages in turn lowered demand for imports and boosted exports. The deficit was corrected, but at the cost of recession, austerity, and hardship for workers. In other words, the gold standard was deflationary.

Bretton Woods

The gold standard lasted until the Great Depression, and in fact helped to cause it. Beyond the high levels of unemployment, one of the most vivid lessons from the global catastrophe that ensued was the collapse of world trade, as country after country tried to deal with falling exports by limiting imports. After World War II, the industrialized countries wanted an international monetary system that could correct trade imbalances without imposing austerity and risking another depression. This was particularly important given the post-war levels of global debt and deficits, which could have suppressed demand and blocked trade again. Countries pursued these aims at the Bretton Woods negotiations in 1944, in Bretton Woods, New Hampshire.

John Maynard Keynes headed the British delegation. Keynes was already famous for his advocacy of government spending to bolster demand and maintain employment during recessions and depressions. England also owed large war debts to the United States and had suffered from high unemployment for over two decades. Keynes therefore had a keen interest in creating a system that prevented the build-up of global debt and avoided placing the full pressure of correcting trade imbalances on debtor countries.

His proposed solution was an international clearing union—a system of accounts kept in a fictitious unit called the "bancor." Accounts would be tallied each year to see which countries were in deficit and which were in surplus. Countries with trade deficits would have to work to import less and export more. In the meantime, they would have the unconditional right—for a period—to an "overdraft" of bancors, the size of the overdraft to be based on the size of previous surpluses. These overdrafts would both support continued imports of necessities and guarantee uninterrupted global trade. At the same time, countries running trade surpluses would be expected to get back in balance too by importing more, and would be fined if their surpluses persisted.

Keynes was also adamant that capital controls be part of the new system. Capital controls are restrictions on the movement of capital across borders. Keynes wanted countries to be able to resort to macroeconomic tools such as deficit spending, lowering interest rates, and expanding money supplies to bolster employment and wages when needed. He worried that without capital controls, capital flight—investors taking their money and running—could veto economic policies and force countries to raise interest rates, cut spending, and lower wages instead, putting downward pressure on global demand as the gold standard had.

Keynes's system wouldn't have solved the problems of capitalism—in his terms, the problem of insufficient demand, and in Marx's terms the problems of overproduction and under-consumption. But by creating incentives for surplus countries to import more, it would have supported global demand and job growth and made the kind of trade imbalances that exist today—including the U.S. trade deficit—much less likely. It would also have taken the pressure off deficit countries to adopt austerity measures. And it would have prevented surplus countries from using the power of debt to dictate economic policy to deficit countries.

At the end of World War II, the United States was, however, the largest surplus country in the world, and it intended to remain so for the foreseeable future. The New Deal had lowered unemployment during the Depression. But political opposition to deficit spending had prevented full recovery until arms production for the war restored manufacturing. Many feared that without continued large U.S. trade surpluses and expanded export markets, unemployment would return to Depression-era levels.

The United States therefore blocked Keynes' proposal. Capital controls were permitted for the time being, largely because of the danger that capital would flee war-torn Europe. But penalties for surplus countries were abandoned; pressures remained primarily on deficit countries to correct. Instead of an international clearing union with automatic rights to overdrafts, the International Monetary Fund (IMF) was established to make short-term loans to deficit countries. And instead of the neutral bancor, the dollar—backed by the U.S. pledge to redeem dollars with gold at $35 an ounce—would be the world currency.

Limits of the System

The system worked for just over twenty-five years, not because trade was balanced, but because the United States was able and willing to recycle its huge trade surpluses. U.S. military spending stayed high because of the U.S. cold-war role as "global cop." And massive aid was given to Europe to rebuild. Dollars went out as foreign aid and military spending (both closely coordinated). They came back as demand for U.S. goods.

At the same time, memory of the Depression created a kind of Keynesian consensus in the advanced industrial democracies to use fiscal and monetary policy to maintain full employment. Labor movements, strengthened by both the war and the post-war boom, pushed wage settlements and welfare spending higher. Global demand was high.

Two problems doomed the system. First, the IMF retained the power to impose conditions on debtor countries, and the United States retained the power to control the IMF.

Second, the United States stood outside the rules of the game: The larger the world economy grew, the more dollars would be needed in circulation; U.S. trade deficits would eventually have to provide them. Other countries would have to correct their trade deficits by tightening their belts to import less, exporting more by devaluing their currencies to push down prices, or relying on savings from trade surpluses denominated in dollars (known as "reserves") to pay for their excess of imports over exports. But precisely because countries needed dollar reserves to pay for international transactions and to provide cushions against periods of deficits, other countries would need to hold the U.S. dollars they earned by investing them in U.S. assets. This meant that U.S. dollars that went out for imports would come back and be reinvested in the United States. Once there, these dollars could be used to finance continued spending on imports—and a larger U.S. trade deficit. At that point, sustaining world trade would depend not on recycling U.S. surpluses, but on recycling U.S. deficits. The ultimate result would be large, destabilizing global capital flows.

The Crisis of the Seventies

The turning point came in the early seventies. Europe and Japan had rebuilt from the war and were now export powers in their own right. The U.S. trade surplus was turning into a deficit. And the global rate of profit in manufacturing was falling. The United States had also embarked on its "War on Poverty" just as it increased spending on its real war in Vietnam, and this "guns and butter" strategy—an attempt to quell domestic opposition from the civil right and anti-war movements while maintaining global military dominance—led to high inflation.

The result was global economic crisis: the purchasing power of the dollar fell, just as more and more dollars were flowing out of the United States and being held by foreigners.

What had kept the United States from overspending up to this point was its Bretton Woods commitment to exchange dollars for gold at the rate of $35 an ounce. Now countries and investors that didn't want to stand by and watch as the purchasing power of their dollar holdings fell—as well as countries that objected to the Vietnam War—held the United States to its pledge.

There wasn't enough gold in Ft. Knox. The United States would have to retrench its global military role, reign in domestic spending, or change the rules of the game. It changed the rules of the game. In August 1971, Nixon closed the gold window; the United States would no longer redeem dollars for gold. Countries and individuals would have to hold dollars, or dump them and find another currency that was more certain to hold its value. There was none.

The result was that the dollar remained the global reserve currency. But the world moved from a system where the United States could spend only if could back its spending by gold, to a system where its spending was limited only by the quantity of dollars the rest of the world was willing to hold. The value of the dollar would fluctuate with the level of global demand for U.S. products and investment. The value of other currencies would fluctuate with the dollar.

Trading Manufacturing for Finance

The result of this newfound freedom to spend was a decade of global inflation and crises of the dollar. As inflation grew, each dollar purchased less. As each dollar purchased less, the global demand to hold dollars dropped—and with it the dollar's exchange rate. As the exchange rate fell, imports became even more expensive, and inflation ratcheted up again. The cycle intensified when OPEC—which priced its oil in dollars—raised its prices to compensate for the falling dollar.

Owners of finance capital were unhappy because inflation was eroding the value of dollar assets. Owners of manufacturing capital were unhappy because the global rate of profit in manufacturing was dropping. And both U.S. politicians and elites were unhappy because the falling dollar was eroding U.S. military power by making it more expensive.

The response of the Reagan administration was to unleash neoliberalism on both the national and global levels—the so-called Reagan revolution. On the domestic front, inflation was quelled, and the labor movement was put in its place, with high interest rates and the worst recession since the Depression. Corporate profits were boosted directly through deregulation, privatization, and tax cuts, and indirectly by attacks on unions, unemployment insurance, and social spending.

When it was over, profits were up, inflation and wages were down, and the dollar had changed direction. High interest rates attracted a stream of investment capital into the United States, pushing up demand for the currency, and with it the exchange rate. The inflows paid for the growing trade and budget deficits—Reagan had cut domestic spending, but increased military spending. And they provided abundant capital for finance and overseas investment. But the high dollar also made U.S. exports more expensive for the rest of the world. The United States had effectively traded manufacturing for finance and debt.

Simultaneously, debt was used as a hammer to impose neoliberalism on the Third World. As the price of oil rose in the seventies, OPEC countries deposited their growing trade surpluses—so-called petro-dollars—in U.S. banks, which in turn loaned them to poor countries to pay for the soaring price of oil. Initially set at very low interest rates, loan payments skyrocketed when the United States jacked up its rates to deal with inflation. Third World countries began defaulting, starting with Mexico in 1981. In response, and in exchange for more loans, the U.S.-controlled IMF imposed austerity programs, also known as "structural adjustment programs."

The programs were similar to the policies in the United States, but much more severe, and they operated in reverse. Instead of pushing up exchange rates to attract finance capital as the United States had done, Third World countries were told to devalue their currencies to attract foreign direct investment and export their way out of debt. Capital controls were dismantled to enable transnational corporations to enter and exit at will. Governments were forced to slash spending on social programs and infrastructure to push down wages and demand for imports. Services were privatized to create opportunities for private capital, and finance was deregulated.

Policies dovetailed perfectly. As the high dollar hollowed out U.S. manufacturing, countries in the Global South were turned into low-wage export platforms. As U.S. wages stagnated or fell, imports became cheaper, masking the pain. Meanwhile, the high dollar lowered the cost of overseas production. Interest payments on third world debt—which continued to grow—swelled the already large capital flows into the United States and provided even more funds for overseas investment.

The view from the heights of finance looked promising. But Latin America was entering what became known as "the lost decade." And the United State was shifting from exporting goods to exporting demand, and from recycling its trade surplus to recycling its deficit. The world was becoming dependent on the United States as the "consumer of last resort." The United States was becoming dependent on finance and debt.

Consolidating Neoliberalism

The growth of finance in the eighties magnified its political clout in the nineties. With the bond market threatening to charge higher rates for government debt, Clinton abandoned campaign pledges to invest in U.S. infrastructure, education, and industry. Instead, he balanced the budget; he adopted his own high-dollar policy, based on the theory that global competition would keep imports cheap, inflation low, and the living standard high—regardless of sluggish wage growth; and he continued deregulation of the finance industry—repealing Glass-Steagall and refusing to regulate derivatives. By the end of Clinton's second term, the U.S. trade deficit had hit a record 3.7% of GDP; household debt had soared to nearly 69% of GDP and financial profits had risen to 30% of GDP, almost twice as high as they had been at any time up to the mid 1980s.

Internationally, Clinton consolidated IMF-style structural adjustment policies under the rubric of "the Washington Consensus," initiated a new era of trade agreements modeled on the North American Free Trade Agreement, and led the charge to consolidate the elimination of capital controls.

The elimination of capital controls deepened global economic instability in several ways.

First, eliminating restrictions on capital mobility made it easier for capital to go in search of the lowest wages. This expanded the globalization of production, intensifying downward pressure on wages and global demand.

Second, removing capital controls increased the political power of capital by enabling it to "vote with its feet." This accelerated the deregulation of global finance and—as Keynes predicted—limited countries' abilities to run full-employment policies. Regulation of business was punished, as was deficit spending, regardless of its purpose. Low inflation and deregulation of labor markets—weakening unions and making wages more "flexible"—were rewarded.

Finally, capital mobility fed asset bubbles and increased financial speculation and exchange rate volatility. As speculative capital rushed into countries, exchange rates rose; as it fled, they fell. Speculators began betting more and more on currencies themselves, further magnifying rate swings. Rising exchange rates made exports uncompetitive, hurting employment and wages. Falling exchange rates increased the competitiveness of exports, but made imports and foreign borrowing more expensive, except for the United States, which borrows in its own currency. Countries could try to prevent capital flight by raising interest rates, but only at the cost of dampening growth and lost of jobs. Lacking capital controls, there was little countries could do to prevent excessive inflows and bubbles.

Prelude to a Crash

This increased capital mobility, deregulation, and speculation weakened the real economy, further depressed global demand, and greatly magnified economic instability. From the eighties onward, international financial crises broke out approximately every five years, in countries ranging from Mexico to the former Soviet Union.

By far the largest crisis prior to the sub-prime meltdown took place in East Asia in the mid-nineties. Speculative capital began flowing into East Asia in the mid nineties. In 1997, the bubble burst. By the summer of 1998, stock markets around the world were crashing from the ripple effects. The IMF stepped in with $40 billion in loans, bailing out investors but imposing harsh conditions on workers and governments. Millions were left unemployed as Asia plunged into depression.

When the dust settled, Asian countries said "never again." Their solution was to build up large dollar reserves—savings cushions—so they would never have to turn to the IMF for another loan. To build up reserves, countries had to run large trade surpluses. This meant selling even more to the United States, the only market in the world able and willing to run ever-larger trade deficits to absorb their exports.

In addition to further weakening U.S. manufacturing, the Asia crisis set the stage for the sub-prime crisis in several ways.

First, as capital initially fled Asia, it sought out the United States as a "safe haven," igniting the U.S. stock market and nascent housing bubbles.

Second, the longer-term recycling of burgeoning Asian surpluses ensured an abundant and ongoing source of capital to finance not only the mounting trade deficit, but also the billowing U.S. consumer debt more generally.

Third, preventing their exchange rates from rising with their trade surpluses and making their exports uncompetitive required Asian central banks to print money, swelling global capital flows even more.

Between 1998 and 2007, when the U.S. housing bubble burst, many policy makers and mainstream economists came to believe this inflow of dollars and debt would never stop. It simply seemed too mutually beneficial to end. By financing the U.S. trade deficit, Asian countries guaranteed U.S. consumers would continue to purchase their goods. The United States in turn got cheap imports, cheap money for consumer finance, and inflated stock and real estate markets that appeared to be self-financing and to compensate for stagnating wages. At the same time, foreign holders of dollars bought increasing quantities of U.S. Treasuries, saving the U.S. government from having to raise interest rates to attract purchasers, and giving the United States cheap financing for its budget deficit as well.

It was this ability to keep interest rates low—in particular, the Fed's ability to lower rates after the stock market bubble collapsed in 2000—that set off the last and most destructive stage of the housing bubble. Lower interest rates simultaneously increased the demand for housing (since lower interest rates made mortgages cheaper) and decreased the returns to foreign holders of U.S. Treasuries. These lower returns forced investors to look for other "safe" investments with higher yields. Investors believed they found what they needed in U.S. mortgage securities.

As Wall Street realized what a lucrative international market they had, the big banks purposefully set out to increase the number of mortgages that could be repackaged and sold to investors by lowering lending standards. They also entered into complicated systems of private bets, known as credit default swaps, to insure against the risk of defaults. These credit default swaps created a chain of debt that exponentially magnified risk. When the bubble finally burst, only massive stimulus spending and infusions of capital by the industrialized countries into their banking systems kept the world from falling into another depression.

Deficit Politics

The political establishment—right and center—is now licking its chops, attacking fiscal deficits as if ending them were a solution to the crisis. The underlying theory harks back to the deflationary operation of the gold standard and the conditions imposed by the IMF: Government spending causes trade deficits and inflation by increasing demand. Cutting spending will cut deficits by diminishing demand.

Like Clinton before him, Obama is now caving in to the bond market, fearful that international lenders will raise interest rates on U.S. borrowing. He has created a bipartisan debt commission to focus on long-term fiscal balance—read: cutting Social Security and Medicare—and revived "PAYGO," which requires either cuts or increases in revenue to pay for all new outlays, even as unemployment hovers just under 10%.

By acquiescing, the U.S. public is implicitly blaming itself for the crisis and offering to pay for it twice: first with the millions of jobs lost to the recession, and again by weakening the safety net. But the recent growth of the U.S. budget deficit principally reflects the cost of cleaning up the crisis and of the wars in Iraq and Afghanistan. Assumptions of future deficits are rooted in projected health-care costs in the absence of meaningful reform. And the U.S. trade deficit is driven mainly by the continued high dollar.

The economic crisis won't be resolved by increasing personal savings or enforcing fiscal discipline, because its origins aren't greedy consumers or profligate govern-ments. The real origins of the crisis are the neoliberal response to the crisis of the 1970s—the shift from manufacturing to finance in the United States, and the trans-formation of the Global South into a low-wage export platform for transnational capital to bolster sagging profit rate. The U.S. trade and budget deficits may symbol-ize this transformation. But the systemic problem is a global economic model that separates consumption from production and that has balanced world demand—not just the U.S. economy—on debt and speculation.

Forging an alternative will be the work of generations. As for the present, pre-mature tightening of fiscal policy as countries try to "exit" from the crisis will simply drain global demand and endanger recovery. Demonizing government spending will erode the social wage and undermine democratic debate about the public invest-ment needed for a transition to an environmentally sustainable global economy.

In the United States, where labor market and financial deregulation have gar-nered the most attention in popular critiques of neoliberalism, painting a bulls-eye on government spending also obscures the role of the dollar and U.S. policy in the crisis. For several decades after World War II, U.S. workers benefited materially as the special status of the dollar helped expand export markets for U.S. goods. But as other labor movements throughout the world know from bitter experience, it's the dollar as the world's currency, together with U.S. control of the IMF, that ultimately provided leverage for the United States to create the low-wage export model of growth and financial deregulation that has so unbalanced the global economy and hurt "first" and "third" world workers alike.

Looking Ahead

At the end of World War II, John Maynard Keynes proposed an international mon-etary system with the bancor at its core; the system would have helped balance trade and avoid the debt and deflation in inherent in the gold standard that preceded the Great Depression. Instead, Bretton Woods was negotiated, with the dollar as the world's currency. What's left of that system has now come full circle and created the very problems it was intended to avoid: large trade imbalances and deflationary economic conditions.

For the past two and a half decades, the dollar enabled the United States to run increasing trade deficits while systematically draining capital from some of the poorest countries in the world. This money could have been used for development in the Global South, to replace aging infrastructure in the United States, or to prepare for and prevent climate change. Instead, it paid for U.S. military interventions, out-sourcing, tax cuts for the wealthy, and massive stock market and housing bubbles.

This mismanagement of the dollar hasn't served the long-term interests of workers the United States any more than it has those in of the developing world.

In domestic terms, it has been particularly damaging over the last three decades to U.S. manufacturing, and state budgets and workers are being hit hard by the crisis. Yet even manufacturing workers in the United States cling to the high dollar as if it were a life raft. Many public sector workers advocate cutting back on government spending. And most people in the United States would blame bankers' compensation packages for the sub-prime mess before pointing to the dismantling of capital controls.

After suffering through the worst unemployment since the Depression and paying for the bailout of finance, U.S. unions and the left are right to be angry. On the global scale, there is increased space for activism. Since the summer of 2007, at least 17 countries have imposed or tightened capital controls. Greek workers have been in the streets protesting pension cuts and pay freezes for months now. And a global campaign has been launched for a financial transactions tax that would slow down speculation and provide needed revenue for governments. Together, global labor and the left are actively rethinking and advocating reform of the global financial system, the neoliberal trade agreements, and the role and governance of the International Monetary Fund. And there is increasing discussion of a replacement for the dollar that won't breed deficits, suck capital out of the developing world, impose austerity on deficit countries—or blow bubbles.

All these reforms are critical. All will require more grassroots education. None will come without a struggle. ❏

Sources: C. Fred Bergsten, "The Dollar and the Deficits: How Washington Can Prevent the Next Crisis," Peterson Institute for International Economics, *Foreign Affairs*, Volume 88 No. 6, November 2009; Dean Baker, "The Budget, the Deficit, and the Dollar," Center for Economic Policy and Research, www.cepr.net; Martin Wolf, "Give us fiscal austerity, but not quite yet," *Financial Times* blogs, November 24, 2009; Tom Palley, "Domestic Demand-led Growth: A New Paradigm for Development," paper presented at the Alterantives to Neoliberalism Conference sponsored by the New Rules for Global Finance Coalition, May 21-24, 2002, www.economicswebinstitute.org; Sarah Anderson, "Policy Handcuffs in the Financial Crisis: How U.S. Government And Trade Policy Limit Government Power To Control Capital Flows, " Institute for Policy Studies, February 2009; Susan George, "The World Trade Organisation We Could Have Had," *Le Monde Diplomatique*, January 2007.

Article 7.3

TAX HAVENS AND THE FINANCIAL CRISIS

From offshore havens to financial centers, banking secrecy faces scrutiny.

BY RACHEL KEELER
May/June 2009

When an entire global financial system collapses, it is reasonable to expect some bickering over the ultimate fixing of things. Rumors of dissention and talk of stimulus-paved roads to hell made everyone squeamish going into the April summit of the G20 group of large and industrialized nations in London. French President Nicolas Sarkozy even threatened to walk out on the whole thing if he didn't get his way.

The French were perhaps right to be nervous: they were taking a somewhat socialist stand, declaring that unregulated shadow banking and offshore tax havens were at the heart of the financial crisis and had to be either controlled or eradicated. They were doing it in a city at the center of the shadow system, and at a summit chaired by British Prime Minister Gordon Brown, a man recently described by the *Financial Times* as "one of the principal cheerleaders for the competitive international deregulation of international financial markets."

But Gordon Brown had already announced his intention to lead the global crackdown on tax havens as a first step toward global financial recovery. German Chancellor Angela Merkel had long backed France in calling for regulation of hedge funds, the poster boys of shadow banking charged with fostering the crisis. And, to Sarkozy's delight, everyone kept their promises at the G20.

"Major failures in the financial sector and in financial regulation and supervision were fundamental causes of the crisis," read the summit's reassuringly clear communiqué. World leaders agreed to regulate all systemically important financial institutions, including hedge funds and those located in tax havens, under threat of sanctions for noncompliance. "The era of banking secrecy is over," they concluded, as close to united as anyone could have dreamed.

But unity that looks good on paper is always more difficult to achieve in reality. The lingering questions post-summit are the same ones Sarkozy may have pondered on his way to London: will leaders from countries made rich from offshore banking follow through to shut it down? What is at stake, and what will the globally coordinated regulation everyone agrees is necessary actually look like? Not surprisingly, there are no easy answers.

Nature of the Beast

Over the years, trillions of dollars in both corporate profits and personal wealth have migrated "offshore" in search of rock bottom tax rates and the comfort of no questions asked. Tax havens and other financial centers promoting low tax rates, light regulation, and financial secrecy include a long list of tropical nations like the Cayman Islands as well as whole mainland economies from Switzerland to Singapore.

Tax Justice Network, an international non-profit advocating tax haven reform, estimates one- third of global assets are held offshore. The offshore world harbors $11.5 trillion in individual wealth alone, representing $250 billion in lost annual tax revenue. Treasury figures show tax havens sucking $100 billion a year out of U.S. coffers. And these numbers have all been growing steadily over the past decade. A *Tax Notes* study found that between 1999 and 2002, the amount of profits U.S. companies reported in tax havens grew from $88 billion to $149 billion.

With little patience left for fat-cat tax scams, the public is finally cheering for reform. Tax havens, it seems, have become the perfect embodiment of suddenly unfashionable capitalist greed. Unemployed workers and unhappy investors grow hot with anger as they imagine exotic hideouts where businessmen go to sip poolside martinis and laugh off their national tax burden.

Reformers have tried and failed in the past to shut down these locales. But analysts say 2008, the year the global financial system finally collapsed under its own liberalized weight, made all the difference. Not only are governments now desperate for tax revenue to help fund bailouts, but a recognition of the role offshore financial centers played in the system's implosion is dawning.

Along with the G20 fanfare, economists and policymakers including Treasury Secretary Timothy Geithner have pointed to the shadow banking system as a root cause of the global crisis. They're talking about the raft of highly-leveraged, virtually unregulated investment vehicles developed over the last 20 years: hedge funds, private equity, conduits, structured investment vehicles (SIVs), collateralized debt obligations (CDOs), and other wildly arcane investment banker toys.

While most of these innovations were born of Wall Street imaginations, few found their home in New York. Seventy-five percent of the world's hedge funds are based in four Caribbean tax havens: the Cayman Islands, Bermuda, the British Virgin Islands, and the Bahamas. The two subprime mortgage-backed Bear Stearns funds that collapsed in 2007, precipitating the credit crisis, were incorporated in the Caymans. Jersey and Guernsey, offshore financial centers in the Channel Islands, specialize in private equity. Many SIVs were created offshore, far from regulatory eyes.

We now know that hedge funds made their record profits from offshore bases by taking long-term gambles with short-term loans. The risky funds were often backed by onshore banks but kept off those institutions' books as they were repackaged and sold around the world. Regulators never took much notice: one, because lobbyists told them not to; two, because the funds were so complex that George Soros barely understood them; and three, because many of the deals were happening offshore.

Beneath regulatory radar, shadow bankers were able to scrap capital cushions, conceal illiquidity, and muddle debt accountability while depending on constant refinancing to survive. When the bubble burst and investors made a run for their money, panicked fund managers found it impossible to honor their debts, or even figure out how to price them as the markets crumbled.

William Cohan writes in his new book on the Bear Stearns collapse (*House of Cards: A Tale of Hubris and Wretched Excess on Wall Street*) that it took the brokerage three weeks working day and night to value illiquid securities when two of its Cayman-based hedge funds fell apart in 2007. In the end, the firm realized it was off by $1 billion from its original guesstimate, on just $1.5 billion in funds.

Mortgage-backed securities that once flourished in offshore tax havens are now the toxic assets that U.S. taxpayers are being asked to salvage through the trillion-dollar TARP and TALF programs.

Last Laughs

This convoluted network of offshore escapades is what world leaders have vowed to bring under global regulatory watch in order to restore worldwide financial stability. To their credit, the crackdown on banking secrecy has already begun in a big way.

In February, secret Swiss bank accounts were blown open to permit an unprecedented Internal Revenue Service probe. Europe's UBS bank has admitted to helping wealthy Americans evade what prosecutors believe to be $300 million a year in taxes.

Switzerland, the world's biggest tax haven where at least $2 trillion in offshore money is stashed, has long refused to recognize tax evasion as a crime. Every nation has the sovereign right to set its own tax code, which is why regulators have had such a hard time challenging offshore banking in the past. The dirty secret of tax havens, as President Obama once noted, is that they're mostly legal.

Under U.S. law, tax avoidance (legal) only becomes tax evasion (illegal) in the absence of other, more credible perks. In other words, a company is free to establish foreign subsidiaries in search of financial expertise, global reach, convenience, etc., just so long as tax dodging does not appear to be the sole reason for relocation.

The IRS will tax individual American income wherever it's found, but finding it is often the key. To access account information in Switzerland, authorities had to have proof not merely of tax evasion but of fraud, which is what much white-knuckled investigation finally produced on UBS. In the wake of this success, and under threat of landing on the OECD's new list of "uncooperative" tax havens, all of Europe's secrecy jurisdictions—Liechtenstein, Andorra, Austria, Luxembourg, and Switzerland—have signed information-sharing agreements.

Following the blood trail, congressional investigators descended on the Cayman Islands in March to tour the infamous Ugland House: one building supposedly home to 12,748 U.S. companies. The trip was an attempt to verify some of the implicit accusations made by a Government Accountability Office report in January which found that 83 of the United States' top 100 companies operate subsidiaries in tax havens.

Many of those, including Citigroup (which holds 90 subsidiaries in the Cayman Islands alone), Bank of America, and AIG, have received billions in taxpayer-funded bailouts. But the report failed to establish whether the subsidiaries were set up for the sole purpose of tax evasion.

Offshore Arguments

Politicians are already patting themselves on the back for their success in tackling tax crime. Everyone is making a big deal of the new tax information-exchange standard that all but three nations (Costa Rica, Malaysia, and the Philippines—the OECD's freshly minted blacklist) have agreed to implement in the wake of the G20 meeting. What leaders aren't saying is that before it became a G20 talking point, tax information exchange was actually tax haven *fans'* favored reform measure.

The first thing most offshore officials claim when confronted with criticism is that their countries are not, indeed, tax havens. Since the OECD launched a tax policy campaign in 1996, many of the offshore centers have been working to clean up their acts. A hoard of information-exchange agreements with onshore economies were signed even before Switzerland took the plunge. Geoff Cook, head of Jersey Finance, says Jersey's agreements with the United States, Germany, Sweden, and others have long outpaced what banks in Switzerland and Singapore traditionally maintained. "Our only fear in this is that people wouldn't look into the subject deep enough to draw those distinctions," Cook said.

But analysts say the agreements lack teeth. To request information from offshore, authorities must already have some evidence of misconduct. And the information-exchange standard still only covers illegal tax evasion, not legal tax avoidance. More importantly, what is already evident is that these agreements don't change much about the way offshore financial centers function. Offshore centers that agree to open up their books still have the luxury of setting their own regulatory standards and will continue to attract business based on their shadow banking credentials.

The G20 decided that shadow banking must be subjected to the same regulation as onshore commercial activity, which will also see more diligent oversight. Financial activity everywhere will be required to maintain better capital buffers, they said, monitored by a new Financial Stability Board; and excessive risk-taking will be rebuked. But the push for harmonized regulation across all financial centers revokes a degree of local liberty. Big ideas about state sovereignty and economic growth are at stake, which is probably what made Sarkozy so nervous about taking his regulatory demands global.

"People come here for expertise and knowledge," argues head of Guernsey Finance Peter Niven, and he may have a point. Many in finance think it's wrong to put all the blame on private funds and offshore centers for a crisis of such complex origins. Havens say stripping away their financial freedoms is hypocritical and shortsighted. "It's really not about the Cayman Islands, it's about the U.S. tax gap—and we're the collateral damage," said one frustrated Cayman Island official, adding: "Everybody needs liquidity and everyone needs money. That's what we do."

Predictably, reform critics warn that responding to the global crisis with "too much" regulation will stifle economic growth, something they know world leaders are quite conscious of. "International Financial Centres such as Jersey play an important role as conduits in the flow of international capital around the world by providing liquidity in neighbouring (often onshore) financial centres, the very lubrication which markets now need," wrote Cook in a recent statement.

Overall, attempting to move beyond paltry information exchange to implementing real regulation of shadow banking across national jurisdictions promises to be extremely difficult.

Real Reform

Part of the solution starts at home. Offshore enthusiasts might be the first to point out that the Securities and Exchange Commission never had the remit to regulate *onshore* hedge funds because Congress didn't give it to them. Wall Street deregulation is often cited in Europe as the base rot in the system.

But demanding more regulation onshore won't do any good if you can't regulate in the same way offshore. A serious aspect of the tax haven problem is a kind of global regulatory arbitrage: widespread onshore deregulation over the last 20 years came alongside an affinity for doing business offshore where even less regulation was possible, which in turn encouraged tax haven-style policies in countries like Britain, the United States, Singapore, and Ireland, all fighting to draw finance back into their economies.

President Obama has long been a champion of both domestic and offshore financial reform, and a critic of the deregulation popular during the Bush years. But for global action to happen, Obama needs Europe's help (not to mention cooperation from Asia and the Middle East) and no one knows how deep Gordon Brown's commitment runs. It is only very recently that Brown transformed himself from deregulation cheerleader as chancellor of the exchequer under Tony Blair to global regulatory savior as Britain's new prime minister.

In an interview late last year, Tax Justice Network's John Christensen predicted Britain could become a barrier to reform. "Britain, I think, will become increasingly isolated, particularly in Europe where the City of London is regarded as a tax haven," he said. Even if Gordon Brown is on board, Britain's finance sector hates to see itself sink. Moreover, some say the UK's lax financial regulatory system has saved the wider economy from decay. When British manufacturing declined, the City of London became the nation's new breadwinner. It grew into the powerhouse it is today largely by luring business away from other centers with the promise of adventurous profit-making and mild public oversight.

The City now funnels much of its business through British overseas territories that make up a big faction in the world's offshore banking club. Many offshore officials have accused Britain of making a show of tax haven reform to deflect attention from its own dirty dealings onshore.

Other obstacles to reform could come from Belgium and Luxembourg, which each hold important votes at the Basel Committee on Banking Supervision (a leading international regulatory voice) and the EU. Neither country has shown much enthusiasm for Europe's reform agenda. And no one will soon forget that China nearly neutered the G20 communiqué when it refused to "endorse" an OECD tax haven blacklist that would allow Europe to chastise financial activities in Hong Kong and Macau.

Still, the regulatory tide is strong and rising; even global financial heavyweights may find it unwise or simply impossible to swim against it. For perhaps the first time since the end of World War II, the world appears open to the kind of global cooperation necessary to facilitate global integration in a socially responsible way.

But the tiny nations that have built empires around unfettered financial services will surely continue to fight for their place in the sun. Some may go the way of Darwinian selection. Declining tourism is already crippling economies across the Caribbean. But many more are optimistic about their ability to hang on. Guernsey is pursuing Chinese markets. Jersey claims business in private equity remains strong. Bermuda still has insurance and hopes to dabble in gambling. Many offshore say they welcome the coming reforms.

"We look forward to those challenges," said Michael Dunkley, leader of the United Bermuda Party, noting that Bermuda, a tiny island with a population of just 66,000 people, is not encumbered by big bureaucracy when it comes to getting things done. Whatever new regulations come up, he said: "Bermuda would be at the cutting edge of making sure it worked."

Accusations of capitalist evil aside, one can't help but admire their spirit. ❏

Sources: Willem Buiter, "Making monetary policy in the UK has become simpler, in no small part thanks to Gordon Brown," *Financial Times*, October 26, 2008; G20 Final Communiqué, "The Global Plan for Recovery and Reform," April 2, 2009; Tax Justice Network, taxjustice.net; Martin Sullivan, Data Shows Dramatic Shift of Profits to Tax Havens, *Tax Notes*, September 13, 2004; William Cohan, *House of Cards: A Tale of Hubris and Wretched Excess on Wall Street*, March 2009; U.S. Government Accountability Office, "International Taxation: Large US corporations and federal contractors in jurisdictions listed as tax havens or financial privacy jurisdictions," December 2008; Organisation for Economic Co-operation and Development. "A Progress Report on the Jurisdictions Surveyed by the OECD Global Forum in Implementing the Internationally Agreed Tax Standard," April 2, 2009; Geoff Cook, Response to *Financial Times* Comment, mail. jerseyfinance.je; March 5, 2009; William Brittain-Catlin, "How offshore capitalism ate our economies—and itself," *The Guardian*, Feb. 5, 2009.

Article 7.4

UNFETTERED CAPITAL WREAKS HAVOC

BY ELLEN FRANK
September/October 1998

Once upon a time, and not so very long ago, most countries restricted the flow of money across their borders. National sovereignty in economic affairs depended upon this. In order to manage their economies, in order to prevent mass unemployment and social upheaval, governments needed the ability to invest, borrow, spend, hire people. To pay for their spending, they needed the ability to print money and control interest rates. But the power to print money and control interest rates is meaningless if the wealthy, who own most of the money, can simply trade their money for a foreign currency and abscond with the wealth. Thus, after World War II, virtually every nation (the U.S. being a very rare exception) placed restrictions on how, when, and how much of its currency businesses and speculators could take out of the country. These restrictions were known as short-term capital controls.

As businesses went global in the 1980s, they pressured governments to eliminate capital controls. An American company producing appliances in Italy for the European market didn't want to be stuck holding its earnings forever in the form of lira in Italian banks. The home office wanted dollars in New York. Multinational businesses and banks wanted the freedom to cash in lira for dollars or francs for yen, as they wished. As global companies spread their operations over the world, capital controls dissolved in their wake. And as controls dissolved, first in Europe, then South America, finally in Asia, speculators—bankers, currency traders, mutual fund managers—moved in. In country after country, financial operators poured money in, eagerly trading dollars or yen for pesos, cruzieros, rupiahs, and rubles, then using the proceeds to lend (at high interest rates) to new, fast-growing businesses or to play the local stock market. Fortunes were made in the receiving countries. In Russia, Mexico, Brazil, Indonesia—the list goes on and on—savvy businessmen and corrupt government officials, touting their open markets, sold off parts of the local economy and pocketed the proceeds.

Today, the concerns that drove countries in the past to restrict this sort of money-trading have, as they say, come home to roost. In Mexico, in Russia, in Korea and Thailand, the bankers and fund managers who lent and bought so eagerly proved just as quick to turn heel and flee. When foreign money pulled out of these countries, their stock markets crashed, banks failed, businesses defaulted on loans and closed for lack of credit. The value of the local currencies plummeted, rendering essential imports unaffordable. While the international banks run to the International Monetary Fund (IMF), clamoring for repayment, the victims of these financial hit-and-runs remain in critical condition. Mexico, for example, with its corrosive unemployment, still has not recovered from its encounter with global banks in 1994 (remember the peso crisis?). The countries of East Asia, whose "crisis" began one year ago, are still reeling, the bottom not yet in sight. Russia, virtually comatose since the ruble crisis of 1991, is now devastated by a new round of capital flight.

Boosters of unfettered money—the global finance industry and its mouthpiece, the IMF—predictably, blame the victims. "Crony capitalism!" "Inefficiency!" "Poor fiscal management!" they crow. They, the public is assured, knew it all along. They, we are told, do the world a service, forcing backwards countries to modernize. What the free-market folks fail to explain is this: If these markets were so inefficient, these economies so badly managed, why were the global banks and fund managers so hot to lend them money in the first place?

Market-boosters have another argument. If the public (via the IMF) doesn't pay off the banks' bad loans and restore their shaken confidence, who will provide new loans to these, now desperate and depressed, economies? How will Mexicans buy corn, Indonesians buy rice, Russians buy grain for their hungry? Are they to starve? Furthermore, if the crisis countries can't buy American-made stuff, Americans will lose jobs. The banks appear to have the world economy in a choke-hold. Countries that can't attract money from the global financial markets can't buy goods on world markets. But the global finance companies won't lend countries money—particularly little countries whose currencies aren't of much use internationally—unless the public underwrites the debt. And here's the kicker. If the banks and mutual funds lend lots of money to a country, then get spooked and start pulling out, thereby setting off a financial panic and causing their own losses—they still want to be repaid.

It is by now obvious that the IMF's response to these "crises"—forcing countries to raise interest rates, the better to attract foreign money to pay their debts to foreign money-lenders—while a boon to financial institutions, is disastrous for the world economy. The crisis in Asia has made it abundantly clear that the prospects for world economic cooperation and development can no longer rest on the whims and dictates of the global financial establishment. It is time to reinstate controls on short-term capital movements. Simple restrictions like imposing taxes, waiting periods, or quotas on cross-border money flows are workable, enforceable and demonstrably effective. The power and mobility of global finance must be curbed. ❑

Article 7.5

EXPORT CREDIT AGENCIES: INTERNATIONAL CORPORATE WELFARE

BY DANIELLE KNIGHT
November/December 1999

Dubbed by some of its critics as the "Chernobyl of hydro power," China's Three Gorges dam may prove one of the most destructive dam projects on earth. Experts predict that the dam, to be built on a section of China's Yangtze River underlaid by several seismic faults, will flood thousands of acres of farmland and part of the city of Chongqing. It's also expected to displace as many as 2 million people living in the region, triggering violent social unrest.

Opponents of Three Gorges include scientists and parliamentarians within China, as well as environmental and human rights groups around the world. Even the U.S. Bureau of Reclamation, probably the world's top dam-building agency, pulled out of the project in 1993, announcing that it was "not environmentally or economically feasible."

As plans for Three Gorges go forward, however, little is reported of how this wonder of concrete topography is being funded. In fact, the dam—like other potentially destructive projects worldwide—has been made possible partly by foreign financing, in the form of taxpayer-subsidized loan guarantees and other assistance.

Corporations hoping to cash in on projects like Three Gorges—in this case, by providing turbines and other engineering equipment—are becoming increasingly reliant on public subsidies from their home countries to do so. And many of these subsidies, designed to help a nation's firms compete for business abroad, are coming through government-sponsored organizations known as export lending credit agencies and investment insurance agencies.

Indeed, in recent years much of the funding that used to flow to developing countries in the form of aid has been diverted into subsidizing for-profit investments, through export credit agencies.

Bruce Rich, a senior attorney with the Environmental Defense Fund, says that through such agencies, "leading governments like the U.S. have been pushing the idea of subsidizing the private sector to replace certain forms of aid, rather than continuing with the traditional big loans to governments for things like power infrastructure." But though the switch is being touted as unleashing the "free market," Rich and others point out that corporate investors typically won't get involved in a risky venture like Three Gorges without guarantees from a government-backed agency that if the project loses money, taxpayers will help foot the bill.

"Usually, if multinational corporations are to attract loans by the huge international private banks, they must have some public taxpayer money guaranteeing risk insurance or directly financing the projects," says Rich. He adds, "In the brave new era of the free flow of capital, we're discovering that the private sector isn't as private as it seems. It's really been a privatization of profits and the public assumption of risk, not only financial risk but also environmental and social risk."

Export credit agencies, of which the U.S.-based Export-Import Bank and Overseas Private Investment Corporation (OPIC) are examples, are bilateral finance agencies, whose deals involve two nations or parties. They provide publicly backed loans, guarantees and insurance to corporations from their countries that are seeking to do business in developing countries and emerging markets. The United States, Japan and most Western European countries each sponsor at least one such agency.

At a recent meeting in Washington, D.C., more than 40 non-governmental organizations (NGOs) from about 23 countries kicked off an international campaign to reform these agencies and push them to adopt common human rights and environmental standards. While multilateral international development banks like the World Bank have been successfully pressured to adopt minimal environmental and social guidelines for their projects, most export credit and public insurance agencies still have few or no such standards.

In the case of Three Gorges, Hermes, a German export-credit agency, provided loan guarantees of up to $833 million to the German engineering giant Siemens AG and the turbine manufacturer Voith Hydro. A Swiss lending agency known as Exportrisikogarantie/ERG provided almost $300 million to the Swedish-Swiss company Asea Brown Boveri and the Swiss Sulzer Escher-Wyss, to provide equipment. Canada's Export Development Corporation (EDC) provided a $12.5 million taxpayer-backed loan, enabling the Calgary-based company, Agra Inc. to secure its first contract on the project. Since then, EDC has extended a further $153 million in support of a turbine contract awarded to General Electric Canada.

Between 1988 and 1996, according to a report issued last March, governments around the world pumped enough new money into their export credit and investment insurance agencies to allow them to quadruple their financial commitments, from about $26 billion to $105 billion (this figure includes agencies in the 26 rich nations represented in the Organization for Economic Cooperation and Development, as well as some developing countries). This increase came during a time when lending by other multilateral financial institutions, such as the World Bank, stayed relatively flat.

The report, titled "Race to the Bottom," was put out by the Environmental Defense Fund, the Center for International Environmental Law, an Indonesia-based coalition called Bioforum, India's Narmada Bachao Andolan, and other groups. It warns that even as export credit agencies take an expanding role in financing projects around the globe, they remain the least transparent of all international financial institutions, not even sharing key information on their operations with other agencies and the World Bank.

Because they seldom apply even minimal human rights and environmental standards (though that's changing somewhat for the Export-Import Bank and OPIC), most export credit agencies are able to fund projects like Three Gorges, which institutions like the World Bank avoid. According to the industry publication Canada Business, World Bank officials advised China not to approach them for loans after it became clear that if the bankers funded it, "they would become lightning rods for criticism of the project."

Having succeeded in getting minimal environmental standards adopted at many development banks, activist groups are now turning their attention to the export credit agencies, though many argue that the multilateral institutions have made only token progress in adhering to such guidelines.

"These agencies are often financing projects—many riddled with corruption —that other taxpayer-supported agencies like the World Bank reject as environmentally and economically unsustainable," says Rich.

In this way, taxpayers' funds—which go to both the World Bank and the export credit agencies—are working at cross purposes, he adds. "Of what use is it," Rich wonders, "for the World Bank to implement environmental policies, when projects for which they would require environmental mitigation measures will be financed by publicly supported ECAs without such measures?"

Ex-Im Bank and OPIC

Situated directly across Lafayette Park from the White House stands the Export Import Bank. Known as Ex-Im, this independent government agency was created in the 1930s. Its stated purpose is to promote U.S. jobs through the support of exports, by providing guarantees of working capital loans for U.S. exporters. Ex-Im guarantees the repayment of loans, finances loans to foreign purchasers of U.S. goods and services, and also provides credit insurance against non-payment by foreign buyers for political or commercial risk.

Ex-Im claims that during fiscal year 1998, it supported nearly 13 billion dollars in US exports by 2,060 U.S. exporters, by authorizing some $10.5 billion in loans, guarantees and export credit insurance for US companies. Though the bank had an income of $390 million in 1997, it recorded a net loss on operations of about $1.7 billion last year.

By its own estimates, Ex-Im directly supports and maintains approximately 200,000 jobs annually, while indirectly supporting nearly another million jobs. These numbers are based on Department of Commerce calculations, which add up the claimed financial value of a project, then divide that figure by the amount of money the department believes is needed to create one job. A staff member at the Ex-Im, however, who did not want to be identified, acknowledged that it is "somewhat impossible to calculate the amount of jobs Ex-Im supports."

In fact, many of Ex-Im's clients are actually downsizing their U.S. workforces. General Electric, for example, one of Ex-Im's largest clients, reportedly cut its domestic workforce from 243,000 to 150,000 between 1985 and 1995, while it modestly expanded offshore. In another instance in 1994, Boeing borrowed $1 billion from the bank to export planes to China. Part of the construction was performed in Xian, China; two years later this factory signed a major contract that displaced Boeing workers in Wichita, Kansas.

OPIC, a wholly owned government corporation, has a slightly differently focus. Founded in 1971, its stated mission is "to mobilize and facilitate the participation of United States private capital and skills in the economic and social development of less developed countries and areas, and countries in transition from nonmarket to market economies, thereby complementing the development assistance objectives of the United States."

Specifically, the agency insures investments overseas against a broad range of political risks, such as losing income due to war, insurrection, terrorism or sabotage, or having an investment nationalized by the host country's government. It also finances U.S. corporations overseas through loans and loan guarantees, and finances private investment funds that provide equity to businesses overseas.

OPIC has only been funding this last type of venture since the mid-1980s, when it began setting up private funds to buy part ownership in overseas companies. By 1998, it had set up nearly 30 such funds. OPIC chooses the managers of the funds, and provides loans and loan guarantees to back up their privately raised capital. In 1998, the agency's portfolio was $18.3 billion.

OPIC claims to pay for itself by selling loans and insurance. Actually, in 1998, according to the Interhemispheric Resource Center and Institute for Policy Studies, more than half its revenues came from interest on its U.S. Treasury securities. Also, Congress will on occasion provide funds for particular projects out of the foreign aid budget. On its web page, OPIC claims that during its existence it has made $3 billion in profits. But Doug Norlen, policy director for the Pacific Environment and Resources Center, an environmental group that has been tracking investment in environmentally harmful projects, argues that this supposed "profit" may be largely a result of the way OPIC keeps its books.

"If OPIC is profitable, then somebody needs to tell us why they need to go and ask Congress for money every year," says Norlen. And of course, if any loans or guarantees go bad, the public picks up the tab. As of last year, OPIC estimated that it was carrying $7 million in non-collectable loans, and was exposed via guarantees and insurance claims to the tune of more than $13 billion.

One example of a credit agency-financed project that went south is provided by the Ok Tedi copper and gold Mine in Papua New Guinea, majority-owned and -operated by the Australian company, Broken Hill Proprietary (BHP). Australia's Export Finance and Insurance Corporation provided a $243.8 million line of credit, while the U.S. Ex-Im approved a loan of $81.2 million to an undisclosed U.S. company involved in the project.

The mine devastated 500 square miles of once fertile land when BHP began daily dumping of tens of thousands of tons of mining waste—containing lead, cadmium and other toxic heavy metals—into the nearby Fly and Ok Tedi rivers. In 1996, the company agreed to a $100 million out-of court settlement to compensate about 15,000 parties who claimed fish stocks and crops were destroyed by the pollution. A key component of that agreement is a binding commitment that BHP and their subsidiary, Ok Tedi Mining Ltd., construct tailings containment facilities, expected to cost approximately $300 million.

Global Loan Sharks

As export credit agencies' funding has increased, their share of developing-country debt has also shot up. The IMF estimates that in 1996, loans made or guaranteed by these agencies accounted for 24 percent of developing countries' total indebtedness —more than what's owed to the World Bank and IMF combined.

Often it is national governments, not corporations, that end up in debt to export credit agencies. Pam Foster with the Halifax Initiative, a Canadian organization that works to reform financial institutions, says this occurs because even though the guarantees and loans are granted to companies, in many cases the nation hosting the project is asked to share the risk or loan.

Indonesia offers a prime example of how a country can fall into the clutches of the credit agencies. About 24 percent of its total external debt—approximately $28 billion—is held by such agencies. Titi Soentoro, coordinator of Bioforum, a coalition of 70 Indonesian environmental and human rights organizations, says this funding long helped prop up the family of President Suharto, who was forced from office last year after three decades of autocratic rule.

"ECAs played a key role in assisting many foreign investors in supporting the Suharto regime's system of economic and political monopolies," she says. "Foreign investors, often supported by ECA finance, competed to align themselves with the powerful business interests close to the Suharto Family."

Lack of Common Standards

Some credit agencies notably the two based in the United States, have begun to accept some restrictions on the kind of projects they'll fund. Their analogous agencies in other industrialized countries, however, remain ready and eager to take on deals rejected by OPIC and the Ex-Im Bank.

After years of pressure from U.S. environmental groups, in 1992 the Export-Import Bank did adopt some basic environmental and social standards. Then in February 1998, the Clinton administration updated OPIC's 1985 environmental guidelines.

By law, OPIC is supposed to promote the economic development of the countries in which the investments it insures are located. Therefore, according to Rich of the Environmental Defense Fund, its environmental standards are stricter than Ex-Im's. Since last year, for example, OPIC is not supposed to provide financial backing for large dams or projects that go through primary forests.

Because of its new standards, Ex-Im joined the World Bank in refusing to support Three Gorges, citing a lack of substantive information on mitigating environmental and social impacts. But even while Ex-Im steered clear of the project, German, Swiss and Canadian ECAs stepped into the gap.

"When the Americans pulled back, Canada very smartly stepped in," observed Peter Mayers, vice- president of Agra Inc., one of the Canadian firms involved with the dam.

The Environment Defense Fund and other groups say the lack of common environmental and social standards for export credit and investment insurance agencies allows this kind of ready substitution among funders. Those who monitor the agencies worry that competition among them may actually pressure Ex-Im into weakening the standards it has. Following the Hermes decision to support Three Gorges, U.S. Rep. Donald Manzullo, R-Illinois, the chairman of the House

Sub-Committee on Exports, threatened to strip the Export-Import Bank of its environmental mandate. Manzullo represents a district where Caterpillar, Inc.—which was counting on the support of Ex-Im to secure contracts for Three Gorges—has large factories.

Using the example of Three Gorges and loss of contracts for Caterpillar, Sen. Frank Murkowski, R-Alaska, has proposed legislation that would prohibit the Ex-Im from withholding financing from a project based on its failure to satisfy environmental policies, if any other government is providing funds to its domestic companies.

Campaign for Common Standards

Many of the nations that have approved human rights and social standards for the World Bank, including France and Germany, have repeatedly thwarted efforts to adopt common guidelines for export credit agencies, as urged by the Clinton Administration through the OECD.

Such resistance, says Rich, one of the organizers of the NGO conference in March, shows the "hypocrisy" of the French and German governments "who present themselves as green at international environmental gatherings."

One might expect the new "Red-Green" coalition that has come to power in Germany to be more receptive to reforming Hermes, the German export credit lending agency. The reality, however, is that in Germany, a powerful industial lobby is able to resist such reform. Heffa Shucking of the Urgewald, a coalition of German church, development and environmental groups, says that "Schroder doesn't seem to have a clue" about ECAs, and that the new government "hasn't prioritized the issue."

NGOs that have traditionally worked to reform World Bank policies are just beginning to follow the money and pay attention to export credit and investment insurance agencies, according to Norlen of the Pacific Environment and Resources Center. He and others have been pressing for the OECD to adopt common standards for these agencies, since most member nations have at least one.

Such standards should "at the very least be equal to World Bank guidelines," Norlen maintains. Under pressure from organizations like Urgewald and Environmental Defense Fund, the "Group of Seven" wealthy industrialized nations said earlier this year it hoped to develop common environmental guidelines for export finance agencies by 2001.

"The public wants to know what their agencies are funding," says Norlen. "Once these projects are held up to the light of day, people will demand reforms for these agencies, just as they have for the World Bank. Transparency is key." ❏

Resources: "A Race to the Bottom," the report by Environmental Defense Fund and other NGOs, is available on the Internet at www.eca-watch.org/eca/race_bottom.pdf

Article 7.6

U.S. BANKS AND THE DIRTY MONEY EMPIRES

BY JAMES PETRAS
September/October 2001

Washington and the mass media have portrayed the United States as being in the forefront of the struggle against narcotics trafficking, drug-money laundering, and political corruption. The image is of clean white hands fighting dirty money from the Third World (or the ex-Communist countries). The truth is exactly the opposite. U.S. banks have developed an elaborate set of policies for transferring illicit funds to the U.S. and "laundering" those funds by investing them in legitimate businesses or U.S. government bonds. The U.S. Congress has held numerous hearings, provided detailed exposés of the illicit practices of the banks, passed several anti-laundering laws, and called for stiffer enforcement by public regulators and private bankers. Yet the biggest banks continue their practices and the sums of dirty money grow exponentially. The $500 billion of criminal and dirty money flowing annually into and through the major U.S. banks far exceeds the net revenues of all the information technology companies in the United States. These yearly inflows surpass the net profits repatriated from abroad by the major U.S. oil producers, military industries, and airplane manufacturers combined. Neither the banks nor the government has the will or the interest to put an end to practices that provide such high profits and help maintain U.S. economic supremacy internationally.

Big U.S. Banks and Dirty Money Laundering

"Current estimates are that $500 billion to $1 trillion in illegal funds from organized crime, narcotics trafficking and other criminal misconduct are laundered through banks worldwide each year," writes Senator Carl Levin (D-MI), "with about half going through U.S. banks." The senator's statement, however, only covers proceeds from activities that are crimes under U.S. law. It does not include financial transfers by corrupt political leaders or tax evasion by overseas businesses, since in those cases any criminal activity takes place outside the United States. Raymond Baker, a leading U.S. expert on international finance and guest scholar in economic studies at the Brookings Institution, estimates the total "flow of corrupt money ... into Western coffers" from Third World or ex-Communist economies at $20 to $40 billion a year. He puts the "flow stemming from mis-priced trade" (the difference between the price quoted, for tax purposes, of goods sold abroad, and their real price) at a minimum of $80 billion a year. "My lowest estimate is $100 billion per year by these two means ... a trillion dollars in the decade, at least half to the United States," Baker concludes. "Including other elements of illegal flight capital would produce much higher figures."

The money laundering business, whether "criminal" or "corrupt," is carried out by the United States' most important banks. The bank officials involved in money laundering have backing from the highest levels of the banking institutions. These are not isolated offenses perpetrated by loose cannons. Take the case of Citibank's laundering of Raúl Salinas' $200 million account. The day after Salinas, the brother of Mexico's ex-President Carlos Salinas de Gortari, was arrested and his large-scale theft of government funds was exposed, his private bank manager at Citibank, Amy Elliott, said in a phone conversation with colleagues (the transcript of which was made available to Congressional investigators) that "this goes [on] in the very, very top of the corporation, this was known ... on the very top. We are little pawns in this whole thing."

Citibank is the United States' biggest bank, with 180,000 employees world-wide, operating in 100 countries, with $700 billion in known assets. It operates what are known as "private banking" offices in 30 countries, with over $100 billion in client assets. Private banking is the sector of a bank which caters to extremely wealthy clients, with deposits of $1 million or more. The big banks charge customers for managing their assets and for providing the specialized services of the private banks. These services go beyond routine banking services like check clearing and deposits, to include investment guidance, estate planning, tax assistance, off-shore accounts, and complicated schemes designed to secure the confidentiality of financial transactions. Private banks sell secrecy to their clients, making them ideal for money laundering. They routinely use code names for accounts. Their "concentration accounts" disguise the movement of client funds by co-mingling them with bank funds, cutting off paper trails for billions of dollars in wire transfers. And they locate offshore private investment corporations in countries such as the Cayman Islands and the Bahamas, which have strict banking secrecy laws. These laws allow offshore banks and corporations to hide a depositor's name, nationality, the amount of funds deposited, and when they were deposited. They do not require any declarations from bank officials about sources of funds.

Private investment corporations (PICs) are one particulary tricky way that big banks hold and hide a client's assets. The nominal officers, trustees, and shareholders of these shell corporations are themselves shell corporations controlled by the private bank. The PIC then becomes the official holder of the client's accounts, while the client's identity is buried in so-called "records of jurisdiction" in countries with strict secrecy laws. The big banks keep pre-packaged PICs on the shelf awaiting activation when a private bank client wants one. The system works like Russian matryoshka dolls, shells within shells within shells, which in the end can be impenetrable to legal process.

Hearings held in 1999 by the Senate's Permanent Subcommittee on Investigations (under the Governmental Affairs Committee) revealed that in the Salinas case, private banking personnel at Citibank—which has a larger global private banking operation than any other U.S. bank—helped Salinas transfer $90 to $100 million out of Mexico while disguising the funds' sources and destination. The bank set up a dummy offshore corporation, provided Salinas with a secret code-name, provided an alias for a third party intermediary who deposited the money in a Citibank account in Mexico, transferred the money in a concentration account to New York, and finally moved it to Switzerland and London.

Instead of an account with the name "Raúl Salinas" attached, investigators found a Cayman Islands account held by a PIC called "Trocca, Ltd.," according to

Minority Counsel Robert L. Roach of the Permanent Committee on Investigations. Three Panama shell companies formed Trocca, Ltd.'s board of directors and three Cayman shell companies were its officers and shareholders. "Citibank controls all six of these shell companies and routinely uses them to function as directors and officers of PICs that it makes available to private clients," says Roach. Salinas was only referred to in Citibank documents as "Confidential Client No. 2" or "CC-2."

Historically, big-bank money laundering has been investigated, audited, criticized, and subjected to legislation. The banks have written their own compliance procedures. But the big banks ignore the laws and procedures, and the government ignores their non-compliance. The Permanent Subcommittee on Investigations discovered that Citibank provided "services," moving a total of at least $360 million, for four major political swindlers, all of whom lost their protection when the political winds shifted in their home countries: Raúl Salinas, between $80 and $100 million; Asif Ali Zardari (husband of former Prime Minister of Pakistan), over $40 million; El Hadj Omar Bongo (dictator of Gabon since 1967), over $130 million; Mohammed, Ibrahim, and Abba Sani Abacha (sons of former Nigerian dictator General Sani Abacha), over $110 million. In all cases Citibank violated all of its own procedures and government guidelines: there was no review of the client's background (known as the "client profile"), no determination of the source of the funds, and no inquiry into any violations of the laws of the country where the money originated. On the contrary, the bank facilitated the outflow in its prepackaged format: shell corporations were established, code names were provided, funds were moved through concentration accounts, and the funds were invested in legitimate businesses or in U.S. bonds. In none of these cases did the banks practice "due diligence," taking the steps required by law to ensure that it does not facilitate money laundering. Yet top banking officials have never been brought to court and tried. Even after the arrest of its clients, Citibank continued to provide them with its services, including moving funds to secret accounts.

Another route that the big banks use to launder dirty money is "correspondent banking." Correspondent banking is the provision of banking services by one bank to another. It enables overseas banks to conduct business and provide services for their customers in jurisdictions where the bank has no physical presence. A bank that is licensed in a foreign country and has no office in the United States can use correspondent banking to attract and retain wealthy criminal or corrupt clients interested in laundering money in the United States. Instead of exposing itself to U.S. controls and incurring the high costs of locating in the U.S., the bank will open a correspondent account with an existing U.S. bank. By establishing such a relationship, the foreign bank (called the "respondent") and its customers can receive many or all of the services offered by the U.S. bank (called the "correspondent"). Today, all the big U.S. banks have established multiple correspondent relationships throughout the world so they may engage in international financial transactions for themselves and their clients in places where they do not have a physical presence. The largest U.S. and European banks, located in financial centers like New York or London, serve as correspondents for thousands of other banks. Most of the offshore banks laundering billions for criminal clients have accounts in the United States. Through June 1999, the top five correspondent bank holding companies in the United States held correspondent account balances exceeding $17 billion; the total correspondent balances of the 75 largest U.S. correspondent banks was $34.9 billion. For billionaire criminals an important feature of correspondent relationships is that they provide access to international transfer systems. The biggest banks specializing in international fund transfers (called "money center banks") can process up to $1 trillion in wire transfers a day.

The Damage Done

Hundreds of billions of dollars have been transferred, through the private-banking and correspondent-banking systems, from Africa, Asia, Latin America, and Eastern Europe to the biggest banks in the United States and Europe. In all these regions, liberalization and privatization of the economy have opened up lucrative opportunities for corruption and the easy movement of booty overseas. Authoritarian governments and close ties to Washington, meanwhile, have ensured impunity for most of the guilty parties. Russia alone has seen over $200 billion illegally transferred out of the country in the course of the 1990s. The massive flows of capital out of these regions—really the pillaging of these countries' wealth through the international banking system—is a major factor in their economic instability and mass impoverishment. The resulting economic crises, in turn, have made these countries more vulnerable to the prescriptions of the IMF and World Bank, including liberalized banking and financial systems that lead to further capital flight.

Even by an incomplete accounting (including both "criminal" and "corrupt" funds, but not other illicit capital transfers, such as illegal shifts of real estate or securities titles, wire fraud, etc.), the dirty money coming from abroad into U.S. banks amounted to $3.5 to $6.0 trillion during the 1990s. While this is not the whole picture, it gives us a basis for estimating the significance of the "dirty money factor" in the U.S. economy. The United States currently runs an annual trade deficit of over $400 billion. The gap has to be financed with inflows of funds from abroad—at least a third of which is "dirty money." Without the dirty money the U.S. economy's external accounts would be unsustainable. No wonder the biggest banks in the United States and Europe are actively involved, and the governments of these countries turn a blind eye. That is today's capitalism—built around pillage, criminality, corruption, and complicity. ❑

Resources: "Private Banking and Money Laundering: A Case Study of Opportunities and Vulnerabilities," Permanent Subcommittee on Investigations of the Committee on Governmental Affairs, United States Senate, One Hundred Sixth Congress, November 9-10, 1000; "Report on Correspondent Banking: A Gateway to Money Laundering," Minority Staff of the U.S. Senate Permanent Subcommittee on Investigations, February 2001.

Article 7.7

LEARNING FROM THE SOUTHEAST ASIAN CRISIS

BY JOHN MILLER
November/December 1998

Summer 1997: By August, bullishness on Asia's miracle economies disappears. The Thai economy suffers a financial meltdown. The Thai currency, the baht, loses 40% of its value vis-a-vis the dollar. The Thai stock market crashes, off 70% from its peak in 1994.

The miracle economies of Southeast Asia are in depression. Conditions vary from country to country. Recession prevails in Malaysia, and in Thailand the steep downturn will cost over two million workers their jobs by the end of 1998. In Indonesia, crippling stagflation threatens to double prices at the same time that it pushes nearly one half the population into poverty.

These once high-flying Southeast Asian economies are tending to the wounds from their sudden fall to earth. Thailand and Indonesia are in receivership, undergoing austerity measures administered by the International Monetary Fund (IMF) in return for emergency loans to help repay foreign lenders. Meanwhile Malaysia independently administers similar austerity measures. The $63 billion bailout crafted by the IMF and the U.S. Treasury exceeds the U.S. financed bailout of Mexico in 1995. With South Korea added in, the East Asian bailout package is over $100 billion.

The IMF continues to say that the leading economies in the region—Indonesia, Malaysia, the Philippines, and Thailand—will recover in 1999, if only modestly. But the Thai and Indonesian economies may not have hit bottom yet.

More pessimistic observers fear that the Southeast Asian financial crisis has triggered a deflationary spiral likely to suck all of East Asia, and perhaps the world, into a depression. The threat of economic collapse is real enough, especially if conditions worsen in Japan, the region's most important economy and already suffering a decade-long recession. During most of the 1990s, East Asia accounted for nearly one-half of the expansion of the world economy. In addition, the region's financial crisis has rattled financial markets around the globe in a way the Mexican peso crisis of 1995 never did. Latin American, European, and Russian currencies all have come under attack. Even the booming U.S. economy slowed this summer under the weight of a ballooning trade deficit caused by fewer exports to East Asia.

For those not blinded by free market faith, the Southeast Asian crisis is a shocking reminder of the failures of markets. Capitalism remains much as Marx and Engels described it one hundred and fifty years ago in the Communist Manifesto—dynamic but unstable and destructive. We need to look more closely at what lessons we can learn from the economic sufferings and financial miseries of Southeast Asia.

A Story of Market Failure

The financial crisis in Southeast Asia differs in important ways from previous crises in the developing world. Unlike the Latin American debt crisis of the 1980s, the roots of the current turmoil are in private sector, not public sector, borrowing. Most of the afflicted countries have run budget surpluses or minimal budget deficits in recent years. At the same time, private sector borrowing increased heavily, especially from abroad and especially short-term. For instance, loans to Thai corporations from international banks doubled from 1988 to 1994. By 1997, Thai foreign debt stood at $89 billion—four-fifths of which was owed by private corporations. But most disturbingly, one-half of the debt was short-term, falling due inside a year.

The Southeast Asian miracle economies got into trouble when their export boom came to a halt as these short-term loans were due. For instance, stymied by a decline in First World demand, especially from recession-ridden Japan, Thai exports grew not at all in 1996. Also, opening domestic markets to outside money (under an early round of pressure from the IMF) brought a deluge of short term foreign investment and spurred heavy short-term borrowing from abroad, fueling a building boom. By the mid '90s, a speculative binge in everything from high-rise office towers to condos to golf courses accounted for nearly 40% of growth in Thailand.

Now that the bubble has burst, the region endures a horrendous drying out process. Southeast Asian exports from autos to computer chips to steel to textiles now glut international markets, all made worse by intensifying competition from Chinese exports. Foreign financial capital has fled. Domestic spending is collapsing. Banks fail at unprecedented rates. Unemployment mounts, and as more and more people across the region fall into poverty, the Southeast Asian financial crisis has become a story of tremendous human suffering.

In the language of economists, the crisis is also a story of market failure. Southeast Asian capital markets failed in three critical ways. First, too much capital rushed in. Lured by the prospect of continued double digit growth and searching for new places to invest its overflowing coffers, financial capital continued to flow into the real estate sectors of these economies even when financial instability was widespread and obvious to all. Second, the capital markets and the banking system could not channel these funds into productive uses. Too much money went into real estate and too little went into productive investments likely to sustain the export boom. Third, too much capital rushed out, too quickly. The excessive inflow of capital reversed itself and fled with little regard for the actual strength of a particular economy.

In their more candid moments, leaders of the financial community have owned up to these market failures. For instance, late in 1997, just a few months into the crisis, Stanley Fischer, economic director of the IMF, confessed at a regional meeting in Hong Kong that: "Markets are not always right. Sometimes inflows are excessive and sometimes they may be sustained too long. Markets tend to react late; by then they tend to overreact."

Where the Right Went Wrong

Despite the doubts of their high priests, most financial conservatives continue to believe that international markets are stable, if subject to periodic excesses, and that whatever their excesses in the East Asian crisis might be, they can be traced back to a misguided interference into those markets. The culprit varies—industrial policy, crony capitalism, fixed exchange rates or some other shibboleth. But in each case, these conservatives would have it that the economies of Southeast Asia ran into trouble because nonmarket forces had a hand in allocating credit and economic resources better left entirely up to the financiers.

The conservative solution to the crisis? That is easy, if painful: Put an end to these nonmarket allocations of resources. Alan Greenspan, the chair of the U.S. Federal Reserve, believes that the current crisis will root out "the last vestiges" of this sort of thing and ultimately will be regarded as a milestone in the triumph of market capitalism.

But none of the leading economies of the region relies on government-managed industrial policies to direct economic growth. One World Bank study placed Malaysian and Thai trade policies as among the most open in developing economies. Since the 1970s, another study reports, the Thai government tended to "allow free markets rather than to intervene with them."

Nor was the crony capitalism which the right derides the cause of the current crisis. This widespread practice—of political connections guiding private sector investment decisions—was a constant, not a new element in the Southeast Asian economic mix, just as present in the boom as in the crisis.

"Transparency" refers to the dislosure publicly traded companies are required to make about their operations to their investors. But signs galore of financial instability and overcapacity were there for anyone to see, even first-time visitors to the region. Bangkok alone had over $20 billion of vacant residential and commercial units by 1997. Despite plunging returns, foreign investors pumped more loans into Thailand betting that double-digit growth would continue and make these risks pay off.

In addition, we should remember that this crisis hit first and hardest in Thailand and then Indonesia, the two Asian economies with private domestic banking systems recently deregulated and opened to foreigners. The shortfall of Japanese investment in the early 1990s left Thailand desperate for foreign funds. Under pressure from the IMF and the WTO, Thai authorities moved to further open their economy to foreign investors, allowing foreigners to own stock, real estate and banking operations as well. On top of this, government policies lifted Thai interest rates above those in the West, making Thailand a place where westerners could turn a quick buck.

Tying the value of their currencies to the dollar didn't cause the crisis either. Having stable exchange rates was an important building block for the region's trade relations. It allowed manufacturers to import components from Japan and Korea for assembly in Thailand and elsewhere in Southeast Asia, before being sold in the United States and Europe. And pegging the value of their currency to that of the dollar allowed the Thais, for example, to lure capital into their country, fueling investments. But the Thai authorities did not take the next step of regulating the foreign capital that it attracted into its economy this way.

What seems clear now is that the cause of the economic crisis of Southeast Asia was not misaligned exchange rates, or mistaken domestic policy, or even a lack of transparency in the banking sector, although that surely didn't help. Rather the root cause of the crisis now threatening the world with depression is the abrupt reversal of the excessively rapid rise of capital inflows and the falling global demand for the exports from the region that arose from a global economy increasingly turned over to the rule of markets.

By the end of 1997, the Southeast Asian economies suffered "the equivalent of a massive bank run on the region without any lender of last resort," says economist Jan Kregel. In 1996, a net $78 billion flowed into the region from foreign bank loans and short-term portfolio investments like stocks. In 1997, that turned into a $38 billion outflow from the countries most hit by the crisis—Indonesia, Malaysia, South Korea, Thailand and the Phillippines. The biggest drop came in short-term portfolio investment, such as stocks, and bank lending.

The IMF, the prime candidate to act as lender of last resort, turned down the role—instead putting in place policies that imposed more austerity and yet tighter credit conditions. Steadfastly insisting that the cause of crisis was "home grown" as Stanley Fischer of the IMF put it, the IMF tightened credit for these countries already suffering from the disappearance of capital.

Even by the IMF's standard, these austerity measures were applied in an arbitrary and disproportionate manner. First world economies facing financial crises came in for far different treatment. The leading industrialized economies (and the IMF) are urging Japan to increase government spending, cut taxes, and keep interest rates low to counteract its continued economic stagnation—just the opposite of the IMF prescription for the rest of East Asia.

In the Southeast Asian crisis, some reckless behavior was punished, while other reckless behavior was forgiven. Surely international investors are just as much or more responsible for the instability of the region as its local capitalist, bankers, governments, and workers. Yet foreign investors are being bailed out by the IMF, not punished. That is, foreign lenders will have their loans repaid. The IMF has not deemed the foreign shareholders ravaged by plummeting stock prices and collapsing currencies worthy of a bailout. Go figure.

Lessons for the Left

Left analyses of the crisis need to guard against two excesses: concluding with too much confidence that the Southeast Asian economies have collapsed with rapid growth never to return, and taking the current depression as proof that the growth that preceded the crisis was artificial.

Depressions happen. Or depressions happen again, as Hyman Minsky, the left-leaning economic theorist of financial fragility, would have put it. Financial crises and economic downturns are the flipside of periods of unbridled capitalist growth. For these rapidly expanding, high debt, and now even less regulated Southeast Asian economies to have fallen into crisis is hardly surprising.

But has the current crisis brought the Asian miracle to an end or unleashed the forces that will bring down the world economy? I am not sure. Whether or not the current crisis is the death knell for rapid growth in the region, or the world economy for that matter, I do know that the growth preceding the crisis was dynamic and unstable—much like the capitalist growth that Marx and Engels observed transforming Europe in the middle of the 19th century. That the growth was based on brutal super-exploitation and relied more often on capital from the outside does not make it artificial or "ersatz," ready to disappear for that reason, as some might claim. After all, the region sustained growth over a long time, not just for the last decade when Japanese investment was heaviest.

The enhanced mobility of capital—domestic and foreign—during the 1990s adds to the instability of these economies and reduces the bargaining power of labor. This is a very real concern, especially in economies such as Indonesia and Thailand where a numbing absence of social accountability has left the investors and corporations to operate unchecked. A profoundly flawed economic development has taken hold, both in their earlier period of rapid growth and in the current crisis.

Limited Capital Mobility, Sound Economic Development

The proposal most favored in the region to limit capital mobility is a transaction tax on all cross-border flows of capital, designed by Nobel prize winning economist James Tobin. Although on its own it could not cool out a speculative fever or capital panic, the Tobin tax would discourage speculation. As a bonus, the tax revenues collected would more than adequately fund an IMF-style agency, freed from the dictates of the United States, that would bail out bankers and capital investors only when they invest long term, pay living wages, and respect international labor standards.

In September, Malaysia took the more immediate action of imposing capital controls—banning the trading of the Malaysian Ringgit outside of the country. Malaysia's prime minister Mahathir called the plan, "the only way to isolate the economy from the currency speculators and traders" whom he blames for causing the country's economic crisis. Banning the trading of the ringgit in overseas markets in effect decouples the Malaysian economy from the international currency markets. While Malaysian stock prices plummeted in response, the value of the ringgit remained steady, and Mahathir's move found support from some surprising sources. Maverick mainstream economist, M.I.T.'s Paul Krugman, endorsed the concept of capital controls, for they allowed Malaysian authorities to lower interest rates to counteract Malaysia's recession without causing the ringgit to collapse.

In addition to controlling international capital, whether internationally or domestically, public policy must also compel domestic capital and local elites to accept greater social accountability. Elites seldom pay taxes in these countries. Taxing elites will add to sources of domestic savings and at the same time make more equal the distribution of income. Also giving these governments more money could add to domestic demand —providing a buffer against the shortfall in global demand that had a hand in this crisis. This social accountability must extend to conditions of work as well—notoriously dangerous in Southeast Asia—recognizing the rights of workers to organize, to work in safe conditions, and to earn a living wage.

These forms of social accountability would foster a more sustainable and equitable economic development, and perhaps lay the groundwork for a Southeast Asian economy that does more to relieve human suffering and less to add to it. ❏

Article 7.8

GEORGE BUSH'S FAVORITE VULTURES

BY GREG PALAST
Spring 2007

It's quite a heartwarming story. Rock stars in designer glasses, lefty clergymen, blond-bearded anti-poverty campaigners all joining hands with George Bush and the International Monetary Fund to cut the debts of Africa's poorest nations. The money the African nations save would buy AIDS medicine. Bush did the photo-op thing in the Oval Office with Bono, and the president even popped debt relief into his State of the Union address: "the best hope for lifting lives and eliminating poverty."

However, Bush lies.

And Africans die.

Here's the reality, off camera. Billions of dollars in debt owed by African nations to the U.S. Treasury, the IMF and several European nations were, indeed, written off. But these acts of taxpayer generosity did not buy medicine. Almost all of the savings meant for Africans has been picked off by a crew of speculators known as "vultures."

Zambia, for example, won debt relief last year which was supposed to provide $40 million to improve health care in a nation where 17% of adults suffer from HIV or AIDS.

Forget the medicine. Zambia won't get it. Half the money has been snatched away by a vulture named Donegal International, an affiliate of a Washington, D.C.-based investment group, Debt Advisory International.

"Vulture" is not a name I made up. It's the label used in government circles for investors who, for a small payment, take over the debts owed by one nation to another, then use political muscle, lawsuits, forgery, or bribery to push the debtor nations to cough up payments five, ten, or twenty times the amount of the vultures' original investment.

Consider Zambia. In 1998, Romania offered to let Zambia pay only $4 million to completely write off a $30 million debt. Strangely, the African nation turned down the generous offer. Instead, one Michael Francis Sheehan, using inside information, grabbed the deal for a fund he operates, paying less than $4 million for the right to collect $30 million from Zambia. In January 1999, just weeks after Zambia rejected Romania's offer to pay only $4 million to terminate this debt, its finance ministry agreed, in writing, to pay Sheehan $15 million on that same debt.

Why would Zambia turn down an excellent deal from Romania and, instead, promise a multimillion-dollar windfall to this "vulture"? This mystery was solved when my producer at BBC Television Newsnight obtained the text of an email by Sheehan. The undated note states boldly, "The deal is going to get done for political reasons." Zambia would give Sheehan's firm the higher sum in return for a private $2 million payment to "the [Zambian] President's favorite charity."

A few weeks ago, I greeted Mr. Sheehan as he approached his customized Cadillac. It's quite a car, by the way. Sheehan, who calls himself "Goldfinger" on a Caddy owners' website, has pimped out his ride with magnesium rims and racing tires.

"It was a charitable initiative which did end up building several thousand houses," said Goldfinger. Perhaps.

Goldfinger is a small pecker compared to Paul Singer, the billionaire who controls the biggest vulture fund, Elliott Associates. Singer's group paid just $10 million for Congolese bonds on which he's already won the right to collect $127 million in a U.S. courtroom. He's now suing to parlay that into $400 million, money he may be able to collect only because the sums that Congo owed to U.S. taxpayers have been forgiven.

And Bush could put a halt to it with the stroke of a pen. Under the doctrine of "comity," the president has the constitutional power to halt the speculator's seizure of Congo's cash. U.S. courts won't let concerned citizens overturn the foreign policy established by the president via lawsuit. Instead they are awaiting Bush's note to halt the collection actions. Bush has sent nothing.

Why? Did I mention that since Ken Lay's checkbook was laid to rest, Singer is now the big sugar-daddy for the Republican Party? He put $1.3 million into the Republican campaigns in 2004 (including funding the "Swift Boat" smear of John Kerry). Singer has committed $10 million to Rudy Giuliani's presidential campaign.

Does Bush know that the debt relief for the Congo is getting eaten by Singer the Vulture? Until February 15, Bush could pretend he knew nothing. But on that day, Congressman John Conyers confronted Bush, nose to nose, in the Oval Office, wanting to know why the president had failed use his powers to stop Singer from ripping off the Congo's money—in effect, money donated in the form of debt forgiveness by U.S. taxpayers.

Conyers also wanted the president to explain why the Justice Department stalled an investigation of "Goldfinger" for the $2 million payment to the former president of Zambia. Conyers pointed out, as if the president didn't know, that pay-outs for profit violate anti-bribery laws, including the Foreign Corrupt Practices Act.

Bush promised to "take care of it all in a week." That was three months ago. ❑

Article 7.9

MICROCREDIT AND WOMEN'S POVERTY

BY SUSAN F. FEINER AND DRUCILLA K. BARKER
November/December 2006

The key to understanding why Grameen Bank founder and CEO Muhammad Yunus won the Nobel Peace Prize lies in the current fascination with individualistic myths of wealth and poverty. Many policy-makers believe that poverty is "simply" a problem of individual behavior. By rejecting the notion that poverty has structural causes, they deny the need for collective responses. In fact, according to this tough-love view, broad-based civic commitments to increase employment or provide income supports only make matters worse: helping the poor is pernicious because such aid undermines the incentive for hard work. This ideology is part and parcel of neoliberalism.

For neoliberals the solution to poverty is getting the poor to work harder, get educated, have fewer children, and act more responsibly. Markets reward those who help themselves, and women, who comprise the vast majority of microcredit borrowers, are no exception. Neoliberals champion the Grameen Bank and similar efforts precisely because microcredit programs do not change the structural conditions of globalization—such as loss of land rights, privatization of essential public services, or cutbacks in health and education spending—that reproduce poverty among women in developing nations.

What exactly is microcredit? Yunus, a Bangladeshi banker and economist, pioneered the idea of setting up a bank to make loans to the "poorest of the poor." The term "microcredit" reflects the very small size of the loans, often less than $100. Recognizing that the lack of collateral was often a barrier to borrowing by the poor, Yunus founded the Grameen Bank in the 1970s to make loans in areas of severe rural poverty where there were often no alternatives to what we would call loan sharks.

His solution to these problems was twofold. First, Grameen Bank would hire agents to travel the countryside on a regular schedule, making loans and collecting loan repayments. Second, only women belonging to Grameen's "loan circles" would be eligible for loans. If one woman in a loan circle did not meet her obligations, the others in the circle would either be ineligible for future loans or be held responsible for repayment of her loan. In this way the collective liability of the group served as collateral.

The Grameen Bank toasts its successes: not only do loan repayment rates approach 95%, the poor, empowered by their investments, are not dependent on "handouts." Microcredit advocates see these programs as a solution to poverty because poor women can generate income by using the borrowed funds to start small-scale enterprises, often home-based handicraft production. But these enterprises are almost all in the informal sector, which is fiercely competitive and typically unregulated, in other words, outside the range of any laws that protect workers or ensure their rights. Not surprisingly, women comprise the majority of workers in the informal economy and are heavily represented at the bottom of its already-low income scale.

Women and men have different experiences with work and entrepreneurship because a gender division of labor in most cultures assigns men to paid work outside the home and women to unpaid labor in the home. Consequently, women's paid work is constrained by domestic responsibilities. They either work part time, or they combine paid and unpaid work by working at home. Microcredit encourages women to work at home doing piecework: sewing garments, weaving rugs, assembling toys and electronic components. Home workers—mostly women and children—often work long hours for very poor pay in hazardous conditions, with no legal protections. As progressive journalist Gina Neff has noted, encouraging the growth of the informal sector sounds like advice from one of Dickens' more objectionable characters.

Why then do national governments and international organizations promote microcredit, thereby encouraging women's work in the informal sector? As an anti-poverty program, microcredit fits nicely with the prevailing ideology that defines poverty as an individual problem and that shifts responsibility for addressing it away from government policy-makers and multilateral bank managers onto the backs of poor women.

Microcredit programs do nothing to change the structural conditions that create poverty. But microcredit *has* been a success for the many banks that have adopted it. Of course, lending to the poor has long been a lucrative enterprise. Pawnshops, finance companies, payday loan operations, and loan sharks charge high interest rates precisely because poor people are often desperate for cash and lack access to formal credit networks. According to Sheryl Nance-Nash, a correspondent for Women's eNews, "the interest rates on microfinance vary between 25% to 50%." She notes that these rates "are much lower than informal money lenders, where rates may exceed 10% per month." It is important for the poor to have access to credit on relatively reasonable terms. Still, microcredit lenders are reaping the rewards of extraordinarily high repayment rates on loans that are still at somewhat above-market interest rates.

Anecdotal accounts can easily overstate the concrete gains to borrowers from microcredit. For example, widely cited research by the Canadian International Development Agency (CIDA) reports that "Women in particular face significant barriers to achieving sustained increases in income and improving their status, and require complementary support in other areas, such as training, marketing, literacy, social mobilization, and other financial services (e.g., consumption loans, savings)." The report goes on to conclude that most borrowers realize only very small gains, and that the poorest borrowers benefit the least. CIDA also found little relationship between loan repayment and business success.

However large or small their income gains, poor women are widely believed to find empowerment in access to microcredit loans. According to the World Bank, for instance, microcredit empowers women by giving them more control over household assets and resources, more autonomy and decision-making power, and greater access to participation in public life. This defense of microcredit stands or falls with individual success stories featuring women using their loans to start some sort of small-scale enterprise, perhaps renting a stall in the local market or buying a sewing machine to assemble piece goods. There is no doubt that when they succeed, women and their families are better off than they were before they became micro-debtors.

But the evidence on microcredit and women's empowerment is ambiguous. Access to credit is not the sole determinant of women's power and autonomy. Credit may, for example, increase women's dual burden of market and household labor. It may also increase conflict within the household if men, rather than women, control how loan moneys are used. Moreover, the group pressure over repayment in Grameen's loan circles can just as easily create conflict among women as build solidarity.

Grameen Bank founder Muhammad Yunus won the Nobel Peace Prize because his approach to banking reinforces the neoliberal view that individual behavior is the source of poverty and the neoliberal agenda of restricting state aid to the most vulnerable when and where the need for government assistance is most acute. Progressives working in poor communities around the world disagree. They argue that poverty is structural, so the solutions to poverty must focus not on adjusting the conditions of individuals but on building structures of inclusion. Expanding the state sector to provide the rudiments of a working social infrastructure is, therefore, a far more effective way to help women escape or avoid poverty.

Do the activities of the Grameen Bank and other micro-lenders romanticize individual struggles to escape poverty? Yes. Do these programs help some women "pull themselves up by the bootstraps"? Yes. Will micro-enterprises in the informal sector contribute to ending world poverty? Not a chance. ❏

Resources: Grameen Bank, grameen-info.org; "Informal Economy: Formalizing the Hidden Potential and Raising Standards," ILO Global Employment Forum (Nov. 2001), www-ilo-mirror. cornell.edu/public/english/employment/geforum/informal.htm; Jean L. Pyle, "Sex, Maids, and Export Processing," World Bank, *Engendering Development; Engendering Development Through Gender Equality in Rights, Resources, and Voice* (Oxford University Press, 2001); Naila Kabeer, "Conflicts Over Credit: Re-Evaluating the Empowerment Potential of Loans to Women in Rural Bangladesh," *World Development* 29 (2001); Norman MacIsaac, "The Role of Microcredit in Poverty Reduction and Promoting Gender Equity," South Asia Partnership Canada, Strategic Policy and Planning Division, Asia Branch Canada International Development Agency (June, 1997), www.acdi-cida.gc.ca/index-e.htm.

CONTRIBUTORS

Sylvia A. Allegretto is an economist at the Institute for Research on Labor and Employment at the University of California, Berkeley.

Drucilla K. Barker is professor of economics and women's studies at Hollins University.

William K. Black is executive director of the Institute for Fraud Prevention and teaches economics and law at the University of Missouri at Kansas City.

Jim Campen is professor emeritus of economics at the University of Massachusetts-Boston and is former executive director of Americans for Fairness in Lending. He is also a *Dollars & Sense* Associate.

Steve Fahrer is a partner at Progressive Asset Management, Inc.

Susan F. Feiner is a professor of economics and women's studies at the University of Southern Maine.

Ellen Frank teaches economics at the University of Massachusetts-Boston and is a *Dollars & Sense* Associate.

Gerald Friedman is a professor of economics at the University of Massachusetts Amherst.

Teresa Ghilarducci is a professor of economics at the University of Notre Dame and director of the Higgins Labor Research Center.

Amy Gluckman is co-editor of *Dollars & Sense*.

Dorene Isenberg is a professor of economics at the University of the Redlands.

Howard Karger is professor of social policy at the University of Houston.

Rachel Keeler is a freelance international business journalist. She holds an MSc in Global Politics from the London School of Economics.

Danielle Knight is a reporter for *U.S. News & World Report*, assigned to its investigations team.

David Kotz is professor of economics at the University of Massachusetts-Amherst.

Rob Larson is assistant professor of economics at Ivy Tech Community College in Bloomington, Indiana, and has written for *Z Magazine* and *The Humanist*.

Jabulani Leffall is an award-winning journalist and former editor for both *The London Financial Times* and *Variety*.

Mark Maier teaches economics at Glendale Community College in Glendale, Calif.

Arthur MacEwan, a *Dollars & Sense* Associate, is professor emeritus of economics at the University of Massachusetts-Boston.

John Miller is a member of the *Dollars & Sense* collective and teaches economics at Wheaton College.

Fred Moseley is professor of economics at Mt. Holyoke College.

Doug Orr (co-editor of this volume) teaches economics at City College of San Francisco.

Greg Palast is an investigative reporter for the BBC.

James Petras is an activist-scholar working with socio-political movements in Latin America, Europe, and Asia.

Robert Pollin teaches economics and is co-director of the Political Economy Research Institute at the University of Massachusetts-Amherst. He is also a *Dollars & Sense* Associate.

Steven Pressman is a professor at Monmouth University and a co-editor of the *Review of Political Economy*.

Adria Scharf is executive director of the Richmond Peace Education Center in Richmond, Va., former co-editor of *Dollars & Sense*, and a *Dollars & Sense* Associate.

Katherine Sciacchitano is a former labor lawyer and organizer. She teaches political economy at the National Labor College.

Robert Scott teaches in the Department of Economics and Finance at Monmouth University.

Orlando Segura, Jr. has worked for an Atlanta-based global management consulting company that consults for private equity firms, and for a private equity firm based in Boston.

William E. Spriggs is a senior fellow with the Economic Policy Institute and was the former executive director of the National Urban League Institute for Opportunity and Equality.

Joseph Stiglitz is a professor of economics at Columbia University and former chief economist of the World Bank.

Chris Sturr (co-editor of this volume) is co-editor of *Dollars & Sense*.

David Swanson is a board member of the Progressive Democrats of America and is the Washington director of democrats.com.

Vince Valvano is a principal analyst at Berkeley Policy Associates.

Ramaa Vasudevan is assistant professor of economics at Colorado State University and a member of the *Dollars and Sense* collective.

Marty Wolfson (co-editor of this volume) teaches economics at the University of Notre Dame and is a former economist with the Federal Reserve Board in Washington, D.C.

CPSIA information can be obtained at www.ICGtesting.com
Printed in the USA
BVOW030744140812

297622BV00005B/7/P